iPad® 2

ALL-IN-ONE

FOR
DUMMIES®

3RD EDITION

by Nancy Muir
with Jesse Feiler

WILEY

John Wiley & Sons, Inc.

iPad® 2 All-in-One For Dummies®, 3rd Edition

Published by
John Wiley & Sons, Inc.
111 River Street
Hoboken, NJ 07030-5774

www.wiley.com

Copyright © 2012 by John Wiley & Sons, Inc., Hoboken, New Jersey

Published by John Wiley & Sons, Inc., Hoboken, New Jersey

Published simultaneously in Canada

For general information on our other products and services, please contact our Customer Care Department within the U.S. at 877-762-2974, outside the U.S. at 317-572-3993, or fax 317-572-4002.

For technical support, please visit www.wiley.com/techsupport.

Wiley publishes in a variety of print and electronic formats and by print-on-demand. Some material included with standard print versions of this book may not be included in e-books or in print-on-demand. If this book refers to media such as a CD or DVD that is not included in the version you purchased, you may download this material at http://booksupport.wiley.com. For more information about Wiley products, visit www.wiley.com.

Library of Congress Control Number: 2011945577

ISBN 978-1-118-17677-1 (pbk); ISBN 978-1-118-22712-1 (ebk); ISBN 978-1-118-24019-9 (ebk); ISBN 978-1-118-26482-9 (ebk)

Manufactured in the United States of America

10 9 8 7 6 5 4 3 2 1

WILEY

About the Author

Nancy Muir is the author of over 60 books on technology and business topics. In addition to her writing work, Nancy runs a website on technology for seniors called TechSmartSenior.com and a companion website for her iPad books in the *For Dummies* series, iPadMadeClear.com. She writes a regular column on computers and the Internet on Retirenet.com. Prior to her writing career Nancy was a manager at several publishing companies, and a training manager at Symantec.

Dedication

To Ebb, for everything.

Author's Acknowledgments

I was lucky enough to have Blair Pottenger, the absolute best editor in the world, assigned to lead the team on this book. Blair, I couldn't have gotten through this rush schedule without you. Thanks also to Dennis Cohen for his able work as technical editor, and to Becky Whitney and Heidi Unger, the book's copy editors. Last but never least, thanks to Kyle Looper, Acquisitions Editor, for hiring me to write this book.

Publisher's Acknowledgments

We're proud of this book; please send us your comments at http://dummies.custhelp.com. For other comments, please contact our Customer Care Department within the U.S. at 877-762-2974, outside the U.S. at 317-572-3993, or fax 317-572-4002.

Some of the people who helped bring this book to market include the following:

Acquisitions and Editorial

Project Editor: Blair J. Pottenger

Acquisitions Editor: Kyle Looper

Copy Editors: Becky Whitney, Heidi Unger

Technical Editor: Dennis Cohen

Editorial Manager: Kevin Kirschner

Editorial Assistant: Amanda Graham

Sr. Editorial Assistant: Cherie Case

Cover Photo: © alamy.com/Robert Lehmann

Cartoons: Rich Tennant
(www.the5thwave.com)

Composition Services

Senior Project Coordinator: Kristie Rees

Layout and Graphics: Samantha K. Cherolis, Melanee Habig

Proofreaders: Melissa Cossell, Kathy Simpson

Indexer: BIM Indexing & Proofreading Services

Publishing and Editorial for Technology Dummies

    Richard Swadley, Vice President and Executive Group Publisher

    Andy Cummings, Vice President and Publisher

    Mary Bednarek, Executive Acquisitions Director

    Mary C. Corder, Editorial Director

Publishing for Consumer Dummies

    Kathleen Nebenhaus, Vice President and Executive Publisher

Composition Services

    Debbie Stailey, Director of Composition Services

Contents at a Glance

Table of Contents

Introduction

Slate-style computers have been around for a few years, but it took Apple to make them catch on with the general public in a big way when it introduced the iPad. This small wonder, which weighs less than a pound-and-a-half, has sold millions of units in its first year for good reason: It's well designed and feature rich, and it opens up a world of apps and media viewing in a highly portable format.

About This Book

iPad 2 All-in-One For Dummies, 3rd Edition, has one aim: to be the ultimate reference on the coolest digital device of the day. If you're reasonably computer savvy, you can use this book to get up to speed quickly the day you buy your iPad, and then you can pick up the book again any time you feel like taking your knowledge of the iPad to the next level. Even if you've been puttering with your iPad for a while, you'll still find things between these covers that you didn't know existed.

Though the iPad is relatively simple to use, a lot is packed in there, and you can get even more from it by downloading apps to do seemingly everything under the sun. The book approaches the iPad from every angle: from the basics to powerful road-warrior tools and from productivity apps to ultra-cool games and media.

You can read step-by-step instructions for basic tasks, hot tips for getting the most out of iPad, and reviews of apps, to steer you to the best of the best.

How This Book Is Organized

This book consists of easily read chunks of chapters that are organized into six minibooks. Each minibook covers a different facet of using the iPad, such as having fun or getting work done. Most material is relevant whether you have a first-generation iPad or iPad 2, though I strongly recommend that you update to iOS 5, which is quick and easy to do (see Book I, Chapter 2) because it's the operating system I based this book on.

You don't have to read the chapters in this book in sequence, but if you're new to iPad, consider starting with the basic concepts in Book I. The following sections give you a synopsis of the topics covered in each minibook.

Book I: iPad Basics

This minibook starts with an overview of new features in iPad 2 and iOS 5. It's also where you learn what items come supplied in the iPad box, get an overview of all the preinstalled apps that come with your iPad, and discover how to set up iPad and sync it with your computer, including how to open an iCloud account and back up and share content with other devices. I provide an overview of preinstalled apps and tell you how to acquire more apps. You become acquainted with the iPad touchscreen and cameras, and how to make settings that control how iPad works, including accessibility settings. You also get going with the built-in Safari browser and set up your e-mail account, as well as explore some advice about how to take care of your iPad. Finally, I provide some troubleshooting and maintenance advice to protect your investment.

Book II: Just for Fun

Why wait until later in the book to get to the fun stuff? iPad is a fun device, but the music, videos, photos, and e-books you can view or listen to on it are a big part of its appeal. In fact, iPad is considered by many people to be primarily a content-consuming machine. The addition of front- and back-facing video and still cameras takes advantage of useful apps such as FaceTime for video chatting and Photo Booth for adding way-out effects to snapshots as you take them. You discover how Twitter has been integrated into several apps and all about iMessage for instant messaging. Become expert at using the iBooks and other e-reader apps to read all kinds of books, and explore the Newsstand app to subscribe to and read publications. And don't forget games: Some absolutely awesome games are out there that you may have played on your phone, but they roar to life on the iPad's outstanding screen.

Book III: iPad on the Go

If you travel for business or pleasure, one huge attraction of iPad is its portability and long battery life, and the chapters in this minibook help take you on the road with your iPad. Using a Wi-Fi or 3G connection (or a Personal Hotspot or tethering), you can stay in touch with others and your home office or connect with clients by using video and FaceTime. This minibook also covers the benefits of using iPad when traveling, from finding directions in the Maps app to making travel arrangements or finding that classic hotel or restaurant or the nearest ATM as you roam.

Book IV: Getting Productive with iWork

Some reviewers claim that the iPad isn't useful for getting work done, but they're wrong. Some of the apps that are available help you perform the typical office suite functions, including iWork from Apple. In this minibook, you find out about the iWork for iOS apps, including how to share your work on iWork.com. You also can read how to use Pages for word processing, Numbers to crunch numbers, and Keynote for creating power presentations.

Book V: Using iPad to Get Organized

Several built-in apps in iPad can help you organize your life. You'll find the usual Calendar and Contacts apps to keep your schedule and people in line, as well as a handy Notes app for jotting down quick messages or records for yourself. In this minibook, I advise you on file management on iPad: syncing files to your computer, storing documents online, and printing hard copies. You can also find out about two new features in iOS 5: Reminders and Notification Center.

Book VI: Must-Have iPad Apps

Throughout this edition of *iPad All-in-One For Dummies,* I mention apps that can broaden your iPad horizons, but this minibook is the one that's dedicated to apps. In a variety of categories, such as business, travel, social networking, news, finance, and entertainment, I offer reviews of some of the hottest apps out there. If you want to go beyond the built-in functionality of iPad to a world of possibilities, this is the minibook for you!

Foolish Assumptions

To offer you a book that gives you insight into the powerful ways you can use iPad, I have to assume that you're computer and mobile phone literate. You don't have to be an iPhone user to use this book (though iPhone has a great many similarities to iPad and shares many apps with it). You don't even have to be a Mac-oriented person — PC people do just fine with iPad.

I also assume that you want to take iPad to the next level by getting helpful tips and advice as well as discovering apps that are useful in expanding your iPad experience. You may use iPad for personal pleasure or to get your work done — or both. If you travel a great deal or use iPad to work, you'll find extra benefits in the material covered in Book VI.

Icons Used in This Book

Little pictures often found in the margin of technical books help you quickly find certain types of information, such as tips or warnings. Here are the icons you should look for in *iPad All-in-One For Dummies,* 3rd Edition:

The Tip icon points to a tiny advice column about the current topic or other useful strategies for advancing your iPad experience to the next level.

The Remember icon signals either a pertinent fact that relates to the topic you're reading about (but is also mentioned elsewhere in the book) or a reiteration of a particularly important piece of information that's, well, worth repeating.

The Warning icon alerts you to potential pitfalls, so don't ignore them. Ignoring the Warning icon might leave you with lost data, a broken iPad, or a lost connection.

 For the latest and greatest features of iPad 2 and iOS 5, hunt for the New icon. If you own a first-generation iPad, this information can help you understand where your model might differ in its functionality. (Don't worry: Except for the first-generation model not having built-in cameras, the differences aren't that great.)

 The Seriously Cool icon draws your attention to an incredible feature, an out-of-the-box way to use your iPad, or an outrageous app.

 The Technical Stuff icon marks iPad information that ventures beyond the basics.

Where to Go from Here

After you've read this book's introduction, it's time to jump into all things iPad. I hope that when you turn to any chapter in this book, you'll find something you didn't know about iPad that will increase your enjoyment of your new device.

Start by checking out the basic concepts and instructions in Book I (you might be surprised at what you discover, even if you've been tinkering with your iPad for a bit) and then jump to any book that addresses where you want to go next — to have fun, get work done, or explore more apps, for example.

Wherever you dive in, you're likely to find some advice or information that will make your iPad experience even more rewarding.

The first step you should take (and this is covered in Book I, Chapter 2) is to update to the latest operating system for iPad — iOS 5, at the time this book went to press. All steps in this book are based on iOS 5. I provide information on changes to the iOS or iPad hardware on my website (at www.ipad madeclear.com), so you can continue to use this book even if changes are introduced after you buy it. Also, if a change is very substantial we may add an update or bonus information that you can download at this book's companion website, www.dummies.com/go/ipadaio. Please check both websites periodically as Apple makes software and hardware updates to iPad.

Book I
iPad Basics

The 5th Wave   By Rich Tennant

©RICHTENNANT

Accessories

iPadPad

"It's a docking system for the iPad that comes with 3 bedrooms, 2 baths, and a car port."

1 f you're looking for basics on buying, setting up, and using features of your iPad, you've come to the right part of this book. Here you get to explore what's in the box and register your iPad. You start to get a feel for how you interact with iPad by playing around with its camera, the touchscreen, and the onscreen keyboard. This is also where I introduce you to the preinstalled apps that come with your iPad (each of which is covered in detail in later books). I also help you explore iPad settings, many of which can make iPad an even better experience, including a chapter on accessibility settings for those who need assistance interacting with the device.

This part provides basics on getting connected to the Internet and using the Mail e-mail app, as well as getting set up to sync your iPad with iTunes or by using iCloud, the great new service from Apple that automatically pushes content to all your iOS devices. Finally, I provide advice about trouble-shooting and maintaining your iPad to keep it running for years to come.

Chapter 1: Buying Your iPad

In This Chapter

- Finding out what's new in iPad 2 and iOS 5
- Picking the right iPad for you
- Knowing where to purchase your iPad
- Contemplating accessories for your iPad

*Y*ou've read about it. You've seen news reports about the lines at Apple Stores on the day the first iPad was released. You know you can't live without your own iPad to have fun, explore the online world, read e-books, organize your photos, and more.

Trust me; you've made a good decision because the iPad does redefine the computing experience in an exciting new way.

This chapter is for those of you who don't already have an iPad. Here is where you discover the different iPad models and their advantages, as well as where to buy this little gem and the accessories you can purchase to outfit your iPad.

Discovering What's New in iPad 2 and iOS 5

iPad gets its features from a combination of hardware and its software operating system, with the most current operating system being iOS 5. If you've seen the first-generation iPad in action or own one, it might be helpful to understand what new features the iPad 2 device brings to the table (all of which are covered in more detail in this book). In addition to features on the iPad first-generation device, the second-generation iPad offers

- **A thinner, lighter design:** You also now get to choose between a black or white model.
- **A dual-core A5 chip:** This chip gives your iPad much faster performance.

 ✓ **Two cameras (one front-facing; one rear-facing):** Both cameras can be used to capture still photos or HD video. If you use *FaceTime,* a video calling service, you and your caller can watch each other on live video.

 ✓ **Video mirroring capability:** You can use the Apple Digital AV Adapter (see "Considering iPad Accessories," later in this chapter) to connect the iPad to your HDTV or other HDMI-friendly devices and mirror what's on your iPad display on the other device.

 ✓ **A built-in, three-axis gyroscope:** Gamers will find this element useful to shift around in a more versatile manner as they move virtually through games that involve motion. With iPad 2, the gyroscope, accelerometer, and compass also help apps like Maps to pinpoint your location and movements as you stroll around town.

Throughout this book, I point out any features that are relevant to only those using iPad 2, so you can use this book no matter which version of the device you own.

iPad 2 may have iOS 4 *or* 5 installed, depending on when you bought it. Any iPad device can make use of iOS 5 if you update the operating system (discussed in detail in Book I, Chapter 2); this book is based on version 5 of iOS.

This update to the operating system adds many new features, including:

 ✓ **Integration with iCloud,** including the ability to back up and restore your iPad. *iCloud* is a new service from Apple that allows you to save and retrieve files from an online account, sync content with other Apple devices, and update your iPad operating system without having to sync your device to your computer.

 ✓ **Newsstand,** an app that allows you to subscribe to and read online versions of many popular magazines and newspapers that are *pushed* to your iPad so that you have the latest editions without having to do a thing once you've bought a subscription.

 ✓ **Reminders,** a great place to centralize all your upcoming events, set reminders, and organize your commitments by date or in a list format. You can also have iPad remind you to take actions when you leave or arrive at a location. (For example, when you arrive at the grocery store, it can remind you to call your spouse to ask if there's anything else for you to get!)

 ✓ Notifications delivered in the **Notification Center,** where you can control how iPad lets you know about FaceTime alerts, new messages or reminders, events in your Calendar, and items such as badges, sounds, and banners.

 ✓ **iMessage,** a new, integrated instant-messaging app for sending text messages over an Internet connection to people using other Apple devices in real time (now you send it; now they see it).

✔ A **split keyboard** allows those of you who have mastered texting with your thumbs on a mobile phone to do the same trick on the wider screen of an iPad. By splitting the keyboard with half of it on the right of the screen and half of it on the left, you can reach all keys with your thumbs from the side of the tablet. Young people of your acquaintance will be impressed.

✔ Additional **touchscreen gestures** provide shortcuts for getting things done, such as dragging e-mail addresses to address fields in Mail and multitasking.

✔ **Accessibility features** such as LED Flash and Vibration settings that help to alert those with hearing or vision challenges to incoming calls or messages.

✔ **Integration with Twitter** from several apps — Photos, Camera, Safari, YouTube, Maps, and Contacts.

✔ **E-mail tools** allow you to apply bold, italic, underlining, and indentation settings to your e-mail messages, as well as offering improved searching of messages.

✔ **PC Free** is all about liberating your device from wires so you can sync to iTunes on your computer using a wireless connection.

✔ The **Calendar app** sports a new Year view.

✔ **Game Center** offers new features such as posting profile pictures, playing turn-based games, and helping you to compare your scores with your friends'.

Choosing the Right iPad for You

iPad 2s don't come in different sizes. In fact, if you pick up an iPad 2 (see Figure 1-1), you're not likely to be able to tell one model from another except that some are black and some are white, and models including 3G have *3G* in small print on them. Their differences are primarily under the hood.

iPad 2 models have three variations:

✔ Black or white

✔ Amount of built-in memory

✔ Method used for connecting to the Internet (Wi-Fi only or Wi-Fi and 3G)

Your options in the first item in this list are pretty black and white, but if you're confused about the other two, read on as I explain these variations in more detail in the following sections.

Figure 1-1: A white iPad 2 could become your newest BF.

Because Apple upgrades and comes out with new versions of hardware and software on a somewhat regular basis (a practice that keeps tech writers on their toes), I've avoided getting too specific on memory specifications and pricing in this chapter. However, you can go to www.ipadmadeclear.com to check the latest details at any time.

Deciding how much memory is enough

Memory is a measure of how much information — for example, movies, photos, and software applications, or *apps* — you can store on a computing device. Memory can also affect your iPad's performance when handling tasks such as streaming favorite TV shows from the World Wide Web or downloading music.

Using video and audio streaming, you can enjoy a lot of content online without ever downloading the full content to your hard drive, and given the iPad has a relatively small amount of memory in any of its models, that's not a bad idea. See Book II, Chapters 1, 2 and 3 for more about getting your music and movies online.

Your memory options with an iPad are 16, 32, or 64 gigabytes (GB). You must choose the right amount of memory because you can't open the unit and add memory, as you usually can with a desktop computer. There is also no way to insert a flash drive (also known as a USB stick) to add backup capacity because iPad 2 has no USB port — or CD/DVD drive, for that matter. However, Apple has thoughtfully provided iCloud, a service you can use to back up content to the Internet. (You can read more about that in Book I, Chapter 5.)

With an Apple Digital AV Adapter accessory, you can plug into the Dock connector slot to attach an HDMI-enabled device such as an external hard drive for additional storage capacity. See Book II, Chapter 3 for more about using these AV features (most of which have not yet hit the market — but they're coming!). As of this writing, ViewSonic is offering three new HDMI projectors, DVDO is offering an HD Travel Kit for smartphones and tablets, and Belkin has introduced a new line of tools for HDTV streaming, for example.

So how much memory is enough for your iPad? Here's a rule of thumb: If you like lots of media, such as movies or TV shows, and you want to store them on your iPad (rather than experiencing or accessing this content online on sites such as Hulu or Netflix or from your Mac/PC using an app like Air Video), you might need 64GB. For most people who manage a reasonable number of photos, download some music, and watch heavy-duty media such as movies online, 32GB is probably sufficient. If you simply want to check e-mail, browse the web, and write short notes to yourself, 16GB *might* be enough, but for my money, why bother?

There is no way to expand memory in an iPad. Memory resides on a micro-SIM card (a smaller version of the SIM card in your cellphone), which is fine for saving your contacts' addresses and similar data but doesn't lend itself to video storage. Apple is banking on you wanting to stream and sync content via iTunes or iCloud. Only you can decide if that will work for you.

What's the price for larger memory? For the iPad 2, a 16GB Wi-Fi unit (see the next section for more about Wi-Fi) costs $499; 32GB jumps the price to $599; and 64GB adds another $100, setting you back a whopping $699.

Determining if you need Wi-Fi only or Wi-Fi and 3G

Another variation on price and performance for the iPad is whether your model has Wi-Fi or Wi-Fi and 3G. Because the iPad is great for browsing online, shopping online, e-mailing, and so on, obviously having an Internet connection for your device is pretty essential. That's where Wi-Fi and 3G come in. Both are technologies used to connect to the Internet, and in case you need a refresher course, here's a quick summary:

- ✔ *Wi-Fi* is what you use to connect to a wireless network at home or at your local coffee shop or an airport that offers Wi-Fi. This type of network uses short-range radio to connect devices to the Internet; its range is reasonably limited — so if you leave home or walk out of the coffee shop, you can't use it. (These limitations are changing as some towns are installing communitywide Wi-Fi networks.)

- ✔ *3G* cellphone technology allows an iPad to connect to the Internet via a cellular network that's widespread. You use it in much the same way you make calls from just about anywhere using your cellphone.

You can buy an iPad with only Wi-Fi or one with both Wi-Fi and 3G capabilities. Getting a 3G iPad costs an additional $130, but it also includes GPS so that you can get more accurate driving directions. You have to buy an iPad model that fits your data connection provider — either AT&T or Verizon as of this writing. Also, to use your 3G network, you have to pay AT&T or Verizon a monthly fee. The good news is that neither carrier requires a long-term contract, as you probably had to commit to with your cellphone and its data connection — you can pay for a connection the month you travel to Hong Kong and then get rid of it when you arrive home. But each carrier has slightly different plans. AT&T offers prepaid and postpaid options, but Verizon offers only a prepaid plan. AT&T offers plans that top out at 2GB of data per month per connection, while Verizon offers several levels, including 3GB, 5GB, and 10GB of data per month. Check out these plans before buying your iPad because you have to buy either an AT&T or Verizon version.

Sprint will be offering iPhone 5 and eventually iPad to its customers. Check their website (`http://sprint.com`) when you're ready to sign up to see what they have to offer.

Of course, AT&T and Verizon could change their pricing and options at any time, so go to these links for more information about iPad data plans: AT&T is at `www.att.com/shop/wireless/devices/ipad.jsp`, and Verizon is at `http://phones.verizonwireless.com/ipad2`.

You can use the hotspot feature on iPad, which allows you to use your iPhone's 3G connection to go online for an extra charge by your phone service carrier. See Book III, Chapter 3 for more about this feature.

So how do you choose? If you want to wander around the woods or town — or take long drives with your iPad continually connected to the Internet — get 3G and pay the price. But if you'll use your iPad mainly at home or using a Wi-Fi *hotspot* (a location where Wi-Fi access to the Internet is available), don't bother with 3G. And frankly, you can now find *lots* of hotspots out there, including restaurants, hotels, airports, and more.

You can use the hotspot feature on a smartphone, which allows iPad to use your phone's 3G connection to go online if you pay for a higher-data-use plan that supports hotspot usage with your phone service carrier. Check out the features of your phone to turn hotspot on.

Because the 3G iPad is a GPS device, it knows where you are and can act as a navigation system to get you from here to there. The Wi-Fi–only model uses a digital compass and triangulation method for locating your current position, which is much less accurate; with no constant Internet connection, it won't help you to get around town. If getting accurate directions when you're on the go is one iPad feature that excites you, get 3G and then see Book III, Chapter 2 for more about the Maps feature.

Knowing what you need to use your iPad

Before you head off to buy your iPad, you should know what other devices, connections, and accounts you'll need to work with it optimally. At a bare minimum, you need to be able to connect to the Internet to take advantage of most of iPad's features. You can open an iCloud account to store and share content online, or you can use a computer to download photos, music, or applications from non-Apple online sources such as stores or sharing sites like your local library and transfer them to your iPad through a process called *syncing*. You can also use a computer or iCloud to register your iPad the first time you start it, although you can have the folks at the Apple Store handle registration for you if you have one nearby.

Can you use iPad without owning a computer and just use public Wi-Fi hotspots to go online (or a 3G connection if you have a 3G model)? Yes. However, to be able to go online using a Wi-Fi–only iPad and to use many of its built-in features at home, you need to have a home Wi-Fi network available. You also need to use iCloud or sync to your computer to get updates for the iPad operating system.

Apple's *iPad User Guide* recommends that you have

- A Mac or PC with a USB 2.0 port and one of the following operating systems:
  - Mac OS X version 10.5.8 or later
  - Windows 7, Windows Vista, or Windows XP Home or Professional with Service Pack 3 or later
- iTunes 10.5 or later, available at www.itunes.com/download
- An iTunes Store account
- Internet access
- An iCloud account

Apple has set up its iTunes software and the iCloud service to give you two ways to manage content for your iPad — including movies, music, or photos you've downloaded — and specify how to sync your calendar and contact information. Book I, Chapter 4, covers those settings in more detail.

Finding a Place to Buy Your iPad

Apple doesn't offer iPad from every major retail store such as Sears or from all major online retailers, such as Newegg. However, with the launch of iPad 2, Apple expanded its retailer partner network quite a bit. As of this writing, you can buy an iPad at the Apple Store and from several brick-and-mortar stores such as Best Buy, Walmart, Sam's Club, and Target, and at online sites such as

MacMall.com. You can also buy 3G models, which require an account with a phone service provider, from the data providers AT&T and Verizon.

If you get your iPad from Apple, either at one of their retail stores or through their online store, here's the difference in the buying experience:

The Apple Store advantage is that the sales staff will help you unpack your iPad and make sure it's working properly, register the device (which you have to do before you can use it), and help you learn the basics. There are also occasional workshops to help people learn about iPads, and Apple employees are famous for being helpful to customers.

Apple Stores aren't on every corner, so if visiting one isn't an option (or you just prefer to go it alone), you can go to Apple Store's website (http://store.apple.com/us/browse/home/shop_ipad/family/ipad), shown in Figure 1-2, and order one to be shipped to you. Standard shipping typically is free, and if there's a problem, Apple's online store customer service reps are also known for being very helpful — they will help you solve the problem or possibly replace your iPad.

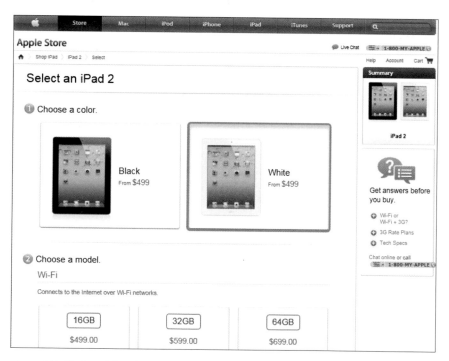

Figure 1-2: iPad model options are spelled out on Apple's site.

Considering iPad Accessories

Accessories for your iPad can make your computing life easier. You can get them from Apple or explore the broad and ever-growing world of third-party accessories.

Apple's stable of accessories

At present, Apple offers a few accessories you might want to check out when you purchase your iPad (or purchase them down the road), including:

- **iPad Case/Smart Cover:** Your iPad isn't cheap and, unlike a laptop computer, it has an exposed screen that can be damaged if you drop or scratch it. Investing in the iPad Case or Smart Cover (note that the Smart Cover works only with iPad 2) is a good idea if you intend to take your iPad out of your house — or if you have a cat or grandchildren. The iPad Smart Cover costs about $40 for polyurethane and $70 for leather, and other cases vary in price depending on design and material.

  The official Apple iPad Case has an ingenious little slot on the back. You can flip the front cover back and tuck it into the slot to make the case rest on your desk or counter at a very handy angle for viewing and typing. You can also prop the case up in a kind of U-shaped configuration to give presentations to others.

- **iPad Camera Connection Kit:** Because there's no USB port on an iPad, you can't use a USB connection to upload photos from your digital camera to your iPad. If you want to add this functionality, you can use this handy kit. It will set you back about $30 for the privilege.

- **Apple iPad Dock/Apple iPad 2 Dock:** The iPad is light and thin, which is great, but holding it all the time can get tedious. The iPad 2 Dock (see Figure 1-3) lets you prop it up so you can view it hands-free while you charge the battery and sync content to your computer. At about $30, it's a good investment for ease and comfort.

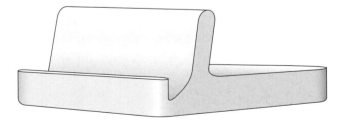

Figure 1-3: The simple, but useful, iPad 2 Dock.

✔ **iPad Keyboard Dock:** The iPad provides an onscreen keyboard that's passable, especially if you position it to view things in landscape orientation. However, if you're a touch typist who wants to write long notes or e-mails, or you want to use the iPad as a primary computing device, the iPad Keyboard Dock or a wireless keyboard could be a must-have. You get some dedicated keys for brightness and volume control, a lock key, and some iPod controls. However, you can use the Keyboard Dock with your iPad only in portrait mode and only with a first-generation iPad. You can also use an Apple Wireless Keyboard or any Bluetooth keyboard with your iPad, which costs about $70 as well.

✔ **Apple Earphones with Remote and Mic:** There are two versions of these: in-ear and not-so in-ear. They both offer remote control of your audio.

✔ **iPad 10W USB Power Adapter:** This accessory is similar to the 10W USB Power Adapter that ships with the iPad. However, this accessory makes charging easier if you need to place your iPad a bit farther from a power outlet because it sports a six-foot-long cord.

✔ **Apple VGA Adapter:** To connect devices to output media, you can buy this adapter. There are more devices coming out that use this technology, such as projectors and TVs.

✔ **Apple Digital AV Adapter:** To make use of a technology called Thunderbolt that allows you to connect devices to output high-definition media, you can buy this adapter (see Figure 1-4). Though there are hardly any devices out there that use this technology, they are coming soon.

✔ **Apple Composite AV Cable/Apple Component AV Cable:** These accessories sell for about $40 each and let you connect your iPad to a TV or stereo system.

✔ **Printers:** Apple has teamed with Hewlett-Packard (HP) to produce several printers that work with iPad's native printing capability to handle wireless printing. These printers range in price from about $100 to about $250, and you can browse all models at the online Apple Store (`http://store.apple.com`). AirPrint Activator 2 and Printopia are apps that can make any printer shared on a network accessible to AirPrint.

Checking out what others have to offer

If you want to explore third-party accessories, there are many, and more appear all the time. Just perform a search for *iPad accessories.* You'll find that there are suede, leather, neoprene, aluminum, and canvas cases; a variety of stands; carrying bags; screen protectors; and external batteries to supplement iPad's impressive 10-hour battery life. LEVO even offers an iPad stand through several online retailers such as Amazon so you can lie down and view the screen without having to use your hands; this, I assume, is for those days when you are *really* tired or suffering carpal tunnel syndrome.

Figure 1-4: Send media to other devices using this adapter.

 Want to stand out from the crowd by carrying your iPad around in a case with character? The Macally microsuede case is a good option that folds like the Apple Case so you can use your iPad as a presentation unit. If you're made of money, the Louis Vuitton model at about $400 will make you the envy of your friends. And eBags offers some nice canvas bags if your tastes, and budget, are more down-to-earth.

A good alternative to Apple's Keyboard Dock is Macally's BTKey, a fully extended keyboard with number pad, which you can use with your iPad device in portrait or landscape mode. This neat device also works with your iPhone and most Macs and Bluetooth-enabled PCs.

There are even a few clothing companies coming up with duds that can hold an iPad. (Steve Wozniak is on the board of SCOTTEVEST, shown in Figure 1-5, which offers a line of iPad-holding clothes.) iClothing and iPad Suit are following suit — excuse the pun.

 Don't bother buying a wireless mouse to connect with your iPad via Bluetooth — the iPad recognizes your finger as its primary input device, and mice need not apply.

Figure 1-5: Wear your iPad with style.

Chapter 2: Getting Started with iPad

In This Chapter

- ✔ Discovering what's in the box
- ✔ Getting your first look at the gadget
- ✔ Charging the battery
- ✔ Powering on your iPad and registering it
- ✔ Using the touchscreen
- ✔ Getting familiar with the split keyboard
- ✔ Making sure your operating system is up to date
- ✔ Using multitasking
- ✔ Taking a first look at iPad's camera
- ✔ Understanding how to customize the side switch
- ✔ Becoming familiar with the Status bar
- ✔ Locking your iPad to sleep, turning it off, and unlocking it

Once you've got your hands on an iPad, you can explore what's in the box and get an overview of the little buttons and slots you'll encounter — luckily, there are very few of them.

You also need to get comfortable with the touchscreen. If you have an iPhone or iPod touch, you're ahead of the game here, but even if you do, you should take a little time to get comfortable with using the larger-format screen.

iPad 2 has two cameras. In addition, iOS 4.3 made available a customizable side switch. As of iOS 4.2, iPad gained native printing ability, all of which I introduce you to here.

Finally, after a tough day of playing with your new gadget, you need to know how to put it to sleep. I cover all of these iPad basics in this chapter.

Exploring What's in the Box

When you fork over your hard-earned money for your iPad, you're left holding one box about the size of a package of copy paper. Here's what you'll find when you take off the shrink wrap and open the box:

- **iPad:** Your iPad is covered in two plastic sheets you can take off and toss. (Unless you think there's a chance you'll return it, in which case you might want to keep all packaging for 14 days — Apple's return period.)

- **Documentation (and I use the term loosely):** You'll find a small white envelope under the iPad itself, about the size of a half-dozen index cards. Open it up, and you'll find

  - *A tiny, useless pamphlet:* This pamphlet, named Important Product Information Guide, is essentially small print (that you mostly don't need to read) from folks like the FCC.

  - *A mysterious label sheet:* This contains two white Apple logo stickers. (Not sure what they're for, but my husband and I use one of these stickers to differentiate my iPad from his.)

  - *A small card containing the actual documentation (sort of):* This displays a picture of the iPad and callouts to its buttons on one side, and the other side contains about three sentences of instructions for setting it up and info about where to go online to find out more.

- **Dock Connector to USB Cable:** Use this cord (see Figure 2-1) to connect the iPad to your computer, or use it with the last item in the box, which is the . . .

- **10W USB Power Adapter:** The power adapter (see Figure 2-1) attaches to the Dock Connector to USB Cable so you can plug it into the wall and charge the battery.

That's it. That's all there is in the box. It's kind of the typical Apple study in Zen-like simplicity.

Taking a First Look at the Gadget

The little card contained in the documentation (see the preceding section) gives you a picture of the iPad with callouts to the buttons you'll find on it. In this section, I give you a bit more information about those buttons and some other physical features of the iPad. Figure 2-2 shows you where each of these items is located.

Dock Connector to USB Cable   10W USB Power Adapter

Figure 2-1: Some pretty simple gadgets for power and USB connections.

Here's the rundown on what these things are and what they do:

- **(The all-important) Home button:** Before the 4.2 update to iOS, you had to go back to the Home screen to do just about anything. If you were browsing online and wanted to open the calendar, you pushed the Home button and you'd exit the web browser and end up on the Home screen, where you could tap one of the application icons, such as the Calendar app (or whatever app you'd like to use), to open it. After iOS 4.2 added the ability to *multitask* (have various apps open at the same time and switch among them), you didn't have to use the Home button to first return to the Home screen and then open another app; rather, you display a multitasking bar of apps and choose one from there. However, it's still the case that no matter where you are or what you're doing, you can push Home and you're back to home base.

- **Sleep/Wake button:** You can use this button to power up your iPad, put it in sleep mode, wake it up, or power it down (more about this in the final section of this chapter).

- **Dock connector slot:** This is where you plug in the Dock Connector cord to charge your battery or sync with your computer (which you learn more about in Book I, Chapter 5). Also use this slot for the Camera Connection Kit or to connect various AV adapter cables.

- **Cameras:** The iPad 2 offers front- and rear-facing cameras that you can use to shoot photos or video. The rear one is on the top-right corner, and you need to be careful not to put your thumb over it when taking shots. (I have several very nice photos of my thumb already.)

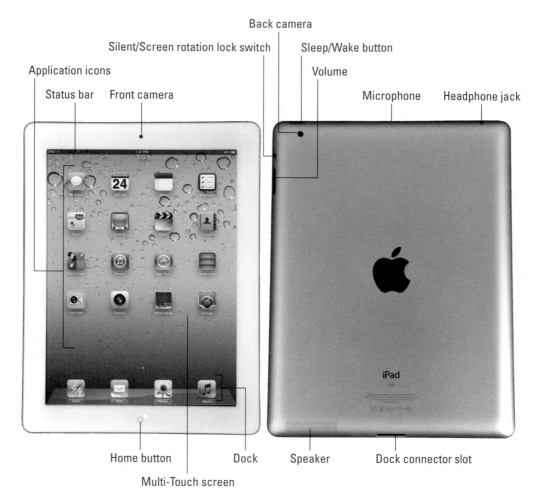

Figure 2-2: There are probably fewer gizmos to get used to on an iPad than on your cellphone.

✔ **Silent/Screen Rotation Lock switch:** In case you hadn't heard, the iPad screen rotates to match the angle you're holding it at. If you want to stick with one orientation even if you spin the iPad in circles, you can use this little switch to lock the screen, which is especially handy when reading an e-book. (Note that some apps can override this functionality if they require one orientation or the other.) You can also customize the function of this switch using iPad General Settings to make the switch mute sounds instead of locking the screen rotation.

✓ **(A tiny, mighty) mono speaker:** One of the nice surprises I had when I first got my iPad was the great little sound system it has and how much sound can come out of this little speaker. The speaker is located on the bottom edge of the screen below the Home button.

✓ **Volume:** This is a volume rocker you use like any other volume rocker: Tap up for more volume and down for less. With iOS 5, you can use this rocker as a camera shutter button when the camera is activated.

✓ **Headphone jack and microphone:** If you want to listen to your music in private, you can plug a 3.5mm minijack headphone in here (including an iPhone headset, if you have one, which gives you bidirectional sound). There's also a tiny microphone that makes it possible to speak into your iPad to do things like make phone calls using the Internet, video calling services, or other apps that accept audio input.

Charging the Battery

You've heard about the awesome 10-hour battery life on your iPad, and it's all true. My iPad showed up fully charged from the Apple Store, but even if you got yours shipped, it should have been at about 90 percent or so. But all batteries run down eventually (the little battery icon in the iPad Status bar will tell you when you're running low), so one of your first priorities is to know how to recharge your battery. This is a pretty obvious procedure, given the few items that come with your iPad, but just in case you need help, you can follow these steps to get that battery meter up to 100 percent:

1. **Gather your iPad, connector cord, and power adapter.**

2. **Gently plug the USB end (the smaller of the two connectors) of the Dock Connector to USB Cable into the USB Power Adapter.**

3. **Plug the other end of the cord (see Figure 2-3) into the cord connector slot on the iPad.**

4. **Unfold the two metal prongs on the power adapter (refer to Figure 2-3) so they extend from it at a 90-degree angle, and plug the adapter into an electrical outlet.**

If you buy the iPad Dock or the iPad Keyboard Dock accessory for a first-generation iPad, you can charge your iPad while it's resting in the dock. Just plug the larger end of the connector cord into the back of the dock instead of the bottom of the iPad.

Attach the USB connector...   Then plug this end into the iPad.

to the power adapter.

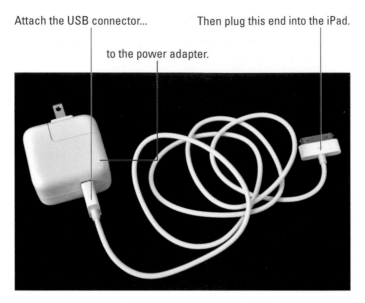

Figure 2-3: Assembling the connector cord and power adapter to charge the iPad battery.

Turning iPad On and Registering It

Apple has done a pretty nice job of getting folks to sign up for their own services, such as iTunes and iCloud, whether Apple product owners want to. In fact, the first time you turn on your iPad you have to register it using either a connection to a computer with the latest version of iTunes installed before you can get it to do anything at all, or you can use Apple's new iCloud service to register PC Free. This section covers both methods.

Registering iPad Using a Computer

Once you have an iTunes account (Book I, Chapter 5 provides details of getting set up with an iTunes account if you don't have one), hold the iPad with one hand on either side, oriented like a pad of paper, and then follow these steps to register it:

1. **Press and hold the Sleep/Wake button on the top of your iPad until the Apple logo appears.**

   In another moment a screen appears, asking if you'd like to register via iCloud or use iTunes. Tap the iTunes option and proceed. (If you prefer to register using iCloud instead, see the next section.)

2. **Plug the Dock Connector to USB Cable that came with your device into your iPad.**

3. **Plug the other end into a USB port on your computer.**

   Both your computer and iPad think for a few moments while they exchange some data.

4. **Sign in to your iTunes account in the dialog that appears on your computer's screen, and then follow the simple onscreen instructions to register your iPad and choose what content is automatically downloaded when you connect your iPad to your computer.**

   (You can change these settings later; this is covered in Book I, Chapter 4.)

   When you're done, your iPad Home screen appears, and you're in business.

5. **Unplug the Dock Connector to USB Cable.**

 If you buy your iPad at an Apple Store, the Apple Store representatives register it for you, and you can avoid getting an iTunes account right away and in fact skip this whole process (though you'll eventually probably want to get an iTunes account to get at their treasure trove of content and apps, some of which is free).

 You can choose to have the following transferred to your iPad from your computer when you sync: music, videos, downloaded apps, contacts, calendars, e-books, podcasts, and browser bookmarks. You can also transfer to your computer content you download directly to your iPad using the iTunes and App Store apps. See Book II, Chapter 1 for more about these features.

Registering PC Free Using iCloud

In Step 1 of the preceding section, you might choose to register your device via iCloud. In that case, to use this PC Free process you need to have access to a Wi-Fi hotspot or have a 3G iPad so you can connect directly to the Internet.

When you make this choice, rather than signing into iTunes you will provide an Apple ID. If you don't have an Apple ID, you're offered the option of creating one right then and there. That ID will be associated with your iCloud account, and you will use it for various iCloud-supported activities.

You'll also be asked to respond to various questions, such as your preferred language and country. When you finish answering these your iPad will be registered without ever plugging it into a computer.

Meeting the Multi-Touch Screen

When your Home screen appears (see Figure 2-4), you'll see a pretty picture in the background and two sets of icons. One set appears in the Dock along the bottom of the screen. The *Dock* contains the Safari browser, Mail, Photos, and Music app buttons by default, though you can add other apps to it. The Dock appears on every Home screen. (You start with one Home screen, but adding new apps creates additional Home screens — up to 11 in all.)

Other icons, the app icons, appear above the Dock and are closer to the top of the screen. (I give you an overview of the functionality of all these icons in the next chapter.) Different icons appear in this area on each Home screen.

Application icons

The Dock

Figure 2-4: Icons for various apps live in the Dock or on a Home screen.

This may or may not need saying, but the screen is made of glass and will smudge when you touch it and break if you throw it at the wall, and contrary to Apple's boasts, can also scratch. So, be careful and treat it nicely.

Connecting with the touchscreen

The iPad touchscreen technology allows you to swipe your finger across the screen or tap to provide input to the device. You hear more about that in the next section, but for now, go ahead and play with it for a few minutes. Just as you may have become used to with your mobile phone, you use the pads of your fingertips (not your fingernails) and do the following:

1. **Tap the Settings icon.**

   The various settings (which you hear more about throughout this book) appear. (See Figure 2-5.)

Figure 2-5: Settings is your control center for all things iPad.

2. **To return to the Home screen, press the Home button.**

3. **Swipe a finger or two from right to left on the screen.**

   Because the iPad has a few additional Home screens available (11, to be exact) that you can fill up with all the apps you'll be downloading, the screen shifts slightly to the left. (If you have more apps downloaded, filling additional Home screens, this action moves you to the next Home screen.)

   With multiple Home screens in use, you get little dots at the bottom of the screen above the Dock icons, indicating which of the Home screens you're on. You can tap to the right or left of the dots to move one screen in either direction.

4. **To experience the rotating screen feature, while holding the iPad firmly, turn it sideways.**

   The screen flips to a horizontal orientation.

5. **To flip the screen back, just turn the device so it's oriented like a pad of paper again.**

6. **Tap Music in the Dock.**

7. **Practice the multitasking feature by double-tapping the Home button.**

   All running apps appear in a bar along the bottom of the screen.

8. **Swipe to scroll through the apps and tap one to jump to it without going back to the Home screen.**

You can customize the Home screen by changing the wallpaper and brightness. Read about making these changes in Book I, Chapter 8.

Goodbye click-and-drag, hello tap-and-swipe

If you're like me, you'll fall in love with the touchscreen interface that iPad sports. It's just so intuitive using your finger as a pointing device — something you're probably already doing on your iPhone or other mobile device.

There are several methods you can use for getting around and getting things done in iPad using its Multi-Touch screen, including:

✓ **Tap once.** To open an application on the Home screen, choose a field such as a search box, select an item in a list, select an arrow to move back or forward one screen, or follow an online link, tap the item once with your finger.

✓ **Tap twice.** Use this method to enlarge or reduce the display of a web page (see Book I, Chapter 6 for more about using the Safari web browser) or zoom in or out in the Maps app.

✓ **Pinch and unpinch.** As an alternative to the tap-twice method, you can pinch or unpinch your fingers on the screen (see Figure 2-6) when you're looking at photos, maps, web pages, or e-mail messages to quickly reduce or enlarge them, respectively.

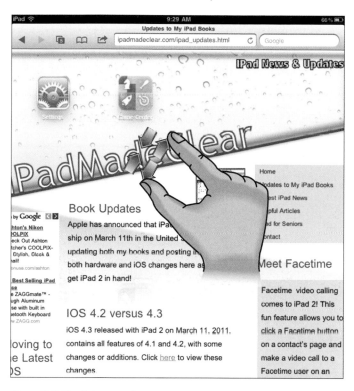

Figure 2-6: Pinch to zoom in or out on a page.

You can use a three-finger tap to zoom your screen to be even larger or use Multitasking gestures to swipe with four or five fingers. (See "Exploring Multitasking Gestures," later in this chapter.) This is handy if you have vision challenges. Go to Book I, Chapter 3, to discover how to turn this feature on using Accessibility features.

✔ **Drag to scroll (known as *swiping*).** When you press your finger to the screen and drag to the right, left, up, or down, you move around the screen. (See Figure 2-7.) Swiping to the right on the Home screen moves you to the *Spotlight screen,* Apple's term for the iPad search screen. Swiping down while reading an online newspaper moves you down the page, while swiping up moves you back up the page.

✔ **Flick.** To scroll more quickly on a page, quickly flick your finger on the screen in the direction you want to move.

Figure 2-7: Swiping gets you around a screen quickly.

✔ **Tap the Status bar.** To move quickly to the top of a list, web page, or e-mail message, tap the Status bar at the top of the iPad screen.

✔ **Press and hold.** If you're in any application where selecting text would be an option, such as Notes or Mail, or if you're on a web page, pressing and holding near text will select a word and bring up editing tools that allow you to select, cut, or copy text, and more. You can also use this method to reposition the insertion point under the magnifying glass icon that appears.

Note that with iOS 5's introduction of the Notification Center, you can swipe down from the top of the screen with one finger to display the center, which lists all messages, mail, calendar events, and more in one handy spot.

If you feel like a practice session, try out these actions by following these steps:

1. **Tap the Safari button to display the web browser. (You may be asked to enter your Wi-Fi network password to access the network to go online.)**

2. **Tap a link to move to another page.**

3. **Double-tap the page to enlarge it; then pinch your fingers together on the screen to reduce its size.**

4. **Drag one finger around the page to scroll.**

5. **Flick your finger quickly on the page to scroll more quickly.**

6. **Press and hold your finger down on text that isn't a link.**

   A magnifying glass icon appears.

7. **Release your finger.**

   The item is selected, and a Copy/Define tool is displayed, as shown in Figure 2-8.

The Copy tool

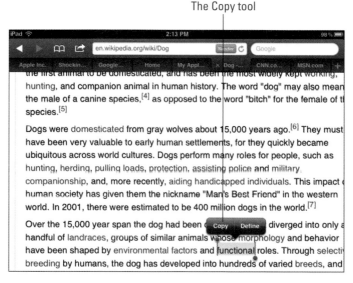

Figure 2-8: Copy text and paste it into an e-mail or document using the Copy tool.

8. **Press and hold your finger on a link or an image.**

   A menu appears with commands that allow you to open the link or picture, open it in a new page, add it to your Reading List (see Book I, Chapter 6), or copy it. The image menu also offers a Save Image command.

9. **Put your fingers slightly apart on the screen and then pinch your fingers together to reduce the page.**

10. **Press the Home button to go back to the Home screen.**

Displaying and using the onscreen keyboard

Part of the beauty of iPad is that it's highly portable, but that portability comes at a price: a physical keyboard. You can use a wireless or Bluetooth keyboard, but for short text entry, you don't really need either. That's where the onscreen keyboard comes in handy, allowing you to enter text as you may have done on a touchscreen mobile phone screen.

iPad has a built-in keyboard that appears whenever you're in a text-entry location, such as a Search field or e-mail message. Follow these steps to practice using the onscreen keyboard:

1. **Tap the Notes icon on the Home screen to open this easy-to-use notepad.**

2. **Tap the note.**

   The onscreen keyboard appears.

3. **Type a few words using the keyboard.**

   To get the widest keyboard display possible, rotate your iPad to be in landscape (horizontal) orientation. (See Figure 2-9.)

Figure 2-9: The onscreen keyboard is handiest to use in landscape orientation.

4. **If you make a mistake (and you may when you first use it), use the Delete key (the key in the top-right corner with a little *x* on it) to delete text to the left of the insertion point.**

5. **To create to a new paragraph, press the Return key, just as you would on a regular computer keyboard.**

6. **To type numbers and some symbols, press one of the number keys (labeled .?123) located on either side of the spacebar (refer to Figure 2-9).**

   Characters on the keyboard change. To return to the letter keyboard at any time, simply tap one of the letter keys (labeled ABC) on either side of the spacebar.

   If you type a number in the number/symbol keyboard and then tap the spacebar, the keyboard automatically returns to the letter keyboard.

7. **Use the Shift buttons just as you would on a regular keyboard to type uppercase letters or alternate characters.**

8. **Double-tap the Shift key to turn the Caps Lock feature on; tap the Shift key once to turn it off.**

   (You can control whether this feature is available in iPad General Settings under Keyboard.)

9. **To type a variation on a symbol (for example, to get alternate currency symbols when you hold down the dollar sign on the number keyboard), press the key and hold it until a set of alternate symbols appears (see Figure 2-10).**

   Note that displaying variations on symbols only works on some symbols.

10. **To hide the keyboard, press the Keyboard key in the bottom-right corner.**

11. **Tap the Home button to return to the Home screen.**

You can unlock the keyboard to move it around the screen. To do this, press and hold the Keyboard button on the keyboard and, from the pop-up menu that appears, choose Unlock. Now by pressing the Keyboard button and swiping up or down, you can move the keyboard up and down on the screen. To dock the keyboard again at the bottom of the screen, press and hold the Keyboard button and choose Dock from the pop-up menu.

To type a period and space, just double-tap the spacebar.

A set of alternate symbols

Figure 2-10: Only some symbols offer alternatives when you press and drag them.

Using the Split Keyboard

With iOS 5 comes the new *split keyboard* feature. This allows you to split the keyboard so that each side appears nearer the edge of the iPad screen. For those who are into texting or one-finger typing, this feature makes it easier to reach all the keys from the sides of the device.

1. **Open an application such as Notes where you can use the onscreen keyboard.**

2. **Tap in an entry field, which displays the onscreen keyboard.**

3. **Place two fingers in the middle of the onscreen keyboard and spread them toward the left and right.**

   The keyboard splits, as shown in Figure 2-11.

4. **Now hold the iPad with a hand on either side and practice using your thumbs to enter text.**

5. **To rejoin the keyboard, place two fingers on each side of the keyboard and swipe to join them together again.**

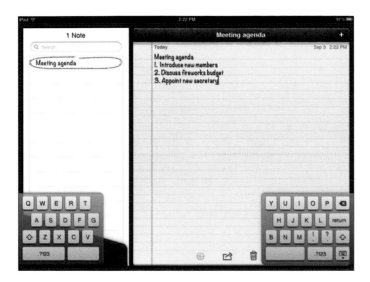

Figure 2-11: A split keyboard makes thumb entry quicker.

TIP

When the keyboard is docked and merged at the bottom of your screen, you can also simply press the Keyboard key and swipe upward. This undocks and splits the keyboard. To revert this, you can then press and swipe the Keyboard key and swipe downward. The keyboard is docked and merged.

Flicking to search

Can't find that song you downloaded or an e-mail from your boss? You'll be relieved to know that a search feature in iPad called Spotlight helps you find photos, music, e-mails, contacts, movies, and more. This search feature can be found on the screen to the left of the default Home screen.

Follow these steps to access and use Spotlight:

1. **Press and drag from left to right on the Home screen, or tap the small magnifying glass symbol farthest to the left at the bottom of the Home screen, to display the Spotlight screen.**

   You can also, from the primary Home screen, tap the left side of the Home button to move one screen to the left.

2. **Tap in the Search iPad field.**

   The keyboard appears. (See Figure 2-12.)

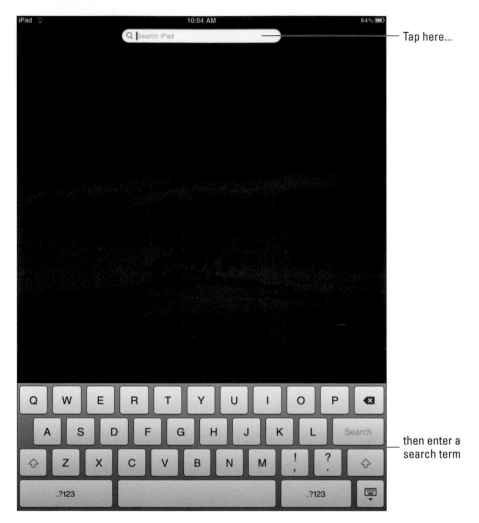

Tap here...

then enter a
search term

Figure 2-12: Use the familiar search box to enter search terms.

3. Begin entering a search term.

In the example in Figure 2-13, I typed the letter *S* and came up with a contact, a couple of built-in apps, and some music I had downloaded, as well as a few e-mail messages. As you continue to type a search term, the results are narrowed down to match.

4. Tap an item in the search results to open it in the associated app.

To close the app and go back to the search screen, tap the Home button and then tap the left side of the Home button to display the search screen again.

Figure 2-13: Narrow down your search by typing more letters.

5. **To enter a different search term, tap in the search box and tap the circled X at the right end of the box or the Delete key on the keyboard to delete the current term and then enter another.**

You can use some standard search techniques to narrow your search. For example, if you want only the e-mails that include both Bob Smith and Jane Jones, enter *"Smith, Jones" or "Bob, Jane"* as your search term. To change the search language, tap the key on the onscreen keyboard that looks like a little globe to cycle through available languages.

Updating the Operating System

This book is based on the latest version of the iPad operating system at the time, iOS 5. To make sure you get the latest and greatest features in iPad, it's a good idea to update right now (and periodically) to the latest iOS. If you've set up an iCloud account on your iPad, updates will happen automatically, or you can use a physical connection to a computer to update iOS.

The iPad may charge itself when connected to certain computers, so if you're updating the iOS from a laptop, plug it in so the battery doesn't drain before the update is complete.

Here's how to update the iOS via a connection with your computer:

1. **Plug the 30-pin end of the Dock Connector to USB Cable into your iPad, and plug the USB end into your computer.**

2. **When iTunes opens on your computer, look for your iPad name in the Devices section in the Source List on the left side of the screen (see Figure 2-14).**

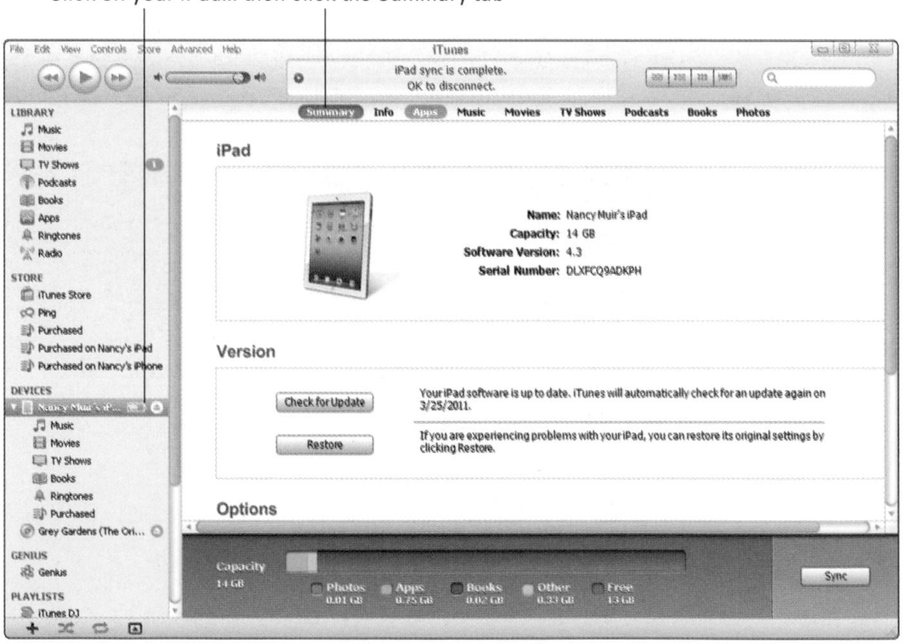

Click on your iPad... then click the Summary tab

Figure 2-14: Go to the Summary tab to find out if you need to update iOS.

3. **Click your iPad name and then click the Summary tab if it's not already displayed.**

4. **Read the note next to the Check for Update button to see whether your iOS is up to date; if it isn't, click the Check for Update button.**

   iTunes checks to find the latest iOS version and walks you through the updating procedure.

 A new iOS introduces new features for your iPad. If a new iOS appears after you've bought this book, go to the companion website, `www.ipadmade clear.com`, for updates on new features.

Multitasking Basics

Multitasking means that you can easily switch from one app to another without closing the first one and returning to the Home screen. You do this by means of a handy little scrolling menu along the bottom of the iPad screen. Follow these steps to multitask:

1. **First, open an app.**

2. **Double-tap the Home button.**

3. **On the horizontal bar that appears beneath the Dock at the bottom of the screen (see Figure 2-15), flick to scroll to the left or right until you find the second open app you want to switch to.**

Figure 2-15: The multitasking bar.

4. **Tap the app, and it displays.**

 At the left end of the multitasking bar (you may have to scroll to the left to see them) are controls for volume and playback, as well as a button that locks and unlocks screen rotation or mutes the sound, depending on which feature you've set up for the side switch to activate (you do that in the General Settings).

Exploring Multitasking Gestures

Multitasking involves jumping from one app to another. New to iOS 5 are some gestures you can tell the system to activate so you can use four or five fingers to multitask. Here are the three gestures you can make:

✔ Swipe up with four or five fingers on any Home screen to reveal the multitasking bar.

✔ Swipe down with four or five fingers to remove the multitasking bar from the Home screen.

✔ With an app open, swipe left or right using four or five fingers and you move to another app.

You can turn on these gestures by tapping Settings on the Home screen and then, in the General settings, tapping the On/Off button for Multitasking Gestures.

Examining Your iPad Cameras

iPad 2 introduced front- and rear-facing cameras to the hardware feature list. You can use the cameras to take still photos (covered in more detail in Book II, Chapter 4) or shoot videos (covered in Book II, Chapter 4). For now, take a quick look at your cameras by tapping the Camera app icon on the Home screen. An image appears, as shown in Figure 2-16.

Controls located around the screen allow you to

✔ Switch between the front and rear cameras.

✔ Change from a still camera to a video camera operation using the Camera/Video slider.

✔ Take a picture or start recording a video.

✔ Turn on a grid to help you autofocus on still photo subjects.

✔ Open the previously captured image or video.

When you view a photo or video, there are several features you can use to do things like send the image via e-mail or as a tweet, print an image, use a still photo as wallpaper or assign it to a contact, and run a slideshow or edit a video. See Book II, Chapters 3 and 4 for more details about using iPad cameras.

Switch between front and rear cameras

Options button

Take photo or start recording

Previously captured image or video   Camera/Video slider

Figure 2-16: Simple tools let you start and stop a recording or switch
between cameras.

Customizing the Silent/Screen Rotation Lock Switch

Starting with iOS 4.3, the switch on the top-right side of your iPad (holding it
in vertical orientation) became customizable. Use these steps to set it up to
either control the screen orientation or mute sound:

1. **From the Home screen, tap the Settings icon.**

2. **Under General Settings, tap either the Lock Rotation or Mute option
   under the Use Side Switch To section to choose which feature you
   want the switch to control.**

3. **Tap the Home button to return to the Home screen.**

4. **Move the side switch up or down to toggle between the settings you
   chose: screen rotation locked or unlocked, or sound muted or unmuted.**

If you choose to use the side switch to mute or unmute system sound, you can use an icon on the multitasking bar (double-tap the Home button to display this and flick to scroll all the way to the left side of the bar) to lock and unlock the screen rotation. This works the same way if you have set up the switch to handle screen rotation and want to mute or unmute the sound using the multitasking bar.

Exploring the Status Bar

Across the top of your iPad screen is a Status bar. (See Figure 2-17.) Little icons in this area can provide some useful information, such as the time, your battery charge, or the status of your wireless connection. Table 2-1 lists some of the most common items you'll find in the Status bar:

| iPad 🌐 | | 3:30 PM | | ⊕ ▶ 79% 🔋 |

Figure 2-17: The Status bar provides some handy info about your iPad.

Table 2-1	Common Status Bar Icons	
Icon	*Name*	*What It Indicates*
 📶	Wi-Fi	You're connected to a Wi-Fi network.
 ✳️	Activity	Something's in progress, such as a web page loading.
 3:30 PM	Time	You guessed it: the time.
 🔒	Screen Rotation Lock	The screen is locked and will not rotate when you turn the iPad.
 ▶	Play	A media element (such as a song or video) is playing.
 79% 🔋	Battery Life	The percentage of charge your battery has left. (It changes to a lightning bolt when the battery is charging.)

If you have GPS, 3G, Bluetooth devices, and/or a connection to a virtual private network (VPN), symbols appear on the Status bar when these are active. The GPS and 3G icons will appear only with 3G-enabled iPad models. If you have a 3G model but no 3G available, you may see an icon for EDGE. If you're out of range of both 3G and EDGE, you see GPRS. Essentially, iPad tries for the best connection and then jumps to a lesser connection if the best isn't available. Note that 3G and EDGE are the only ones of the three that allow both voice and data transmission.

Locking iPad, Turning It Off, or Unlocking It

You've seen how simple it is to turn the power on for your iPad earlier in this chapter. Now it's time to put it to *sleep* (the iPad screen goes black, but iPad can be quickly awakened again) or turn the power off to give your new toy a rest. Here are the procedures you can use:

✔ **Press the Sleep/Wake button.** iPad goes to sleep, the screen goes black, and it's locked. If iPad is asleep, pressing the Sleep/Wake button does its wake up thing.

If you bought a Smart Cover with your iPad, just fold the cover over the front of the screen, and iPad goes to sleep; open the cover to wake up the iPad. See Book I, Chapter 1, for more about iPad accessories.

✔ **Press the Home button and then use the Slide to Unlock bar.** This wakes up iPad. Swipe the onscreen arrow on the Slide to Unlock bar (see Figure 2-18) to unlock the iPad.

Figure 2-18: Use the Slide to Unlock bar to wake iPad up.

Wondering about that little flower symbol (refer to Figure 2-18) in the lower-right corner of a sleeping iPad's screen? That's the Slideshow button. Tap it if you'd like a cool slideshow of the images in Photos displayed on the sleep screen. The Slide to Unlock area disappears, but you can get it back by pressing the Home button on your iPad. See Book II, Chapter 4, for more about working with Photos.

✔ **Press and hold the Sleep/Wake button until the Slide to Power Off bar appears at the top of the screen, and then swipe the bar.** You've just turned off your iPad.

✔ **Use the Smart Cover accessory.** When you attach the Smart Cover and close it over your screen, iPad goes to sleep automatically.

iPad automatically goes into sleep mode after a few minutes of inactivity. You can change the time interval at which it sleeps by adjusting the Auto-Lock feature in Settings. (I tell you how to do that in Book I, Chapter 8.)

Chapter 3: Accessibility Features

In This Chapter

- Setting brightness and changing the wallpaper
- Using zoom, white on black text, and larger text
- Setting up VoiceOver and AutoText
- Adjusting volume and settings to help you hear more easily
- Using the touchscreen with ease

*i*Pad users are all different; some face visual, dexterity, or hearing challenges. If you're one of those folks, you'll be glad to hear that iPad offers some handy accessibility features.

To help you read your screen more easily, there's a Zoom feature that lets you enlarge the screen even more than the standard unpinch gesture does. There's even a White on Black screen option, which offers a photo-negative effective producing a dark background with white lettering that some people find easier when reading text. You can also set up a feature called VoiceOver to read onscreen elements out loud.

If hearing is your challenge, there's a setting for Mono Audio that's useful when you're wearing headphones or playing sound through an attached speaker system. Finally, Speak Auto-text is a feature that iPad uses to tell you when any autocorrections or capitalizations are made to text that you enter in any iPad application.

For those who struggle with using the touchscreen and gestures, you can take advantage of the AssistiveTouch control pane.

In this chapter, you get some highlights of the accessibility settings you're likely to need most often and advice for how to use them.

Accessibility

- VoiceOver
- Zoom
- Large Text
- White on Black
- Speak Selection
- Speak Auto-text

Automatically speak auto-corrections and auto-capitalizations.

Hearing

Mono Audio

Motor

Features to Help You See Better

You might as well set up the visual side of iPad first so your interaction with the device is easy on the eyes and battery power. There are two such settings that fall together as one category in the Settings window: Brightness & Wallpaper. In addition, you discover other settings that change how iPad appears and interacts with you using sound rather than visuals.

Setting Brightness

Especially when using iPad as an e-book reader, you may find a little less brightness in the display reduces strain on your eyes. Also, reducing the brightness can save a little on your iPad's battery life.

To modify the brightness setting, follow these steps:

1. **To begin, tap the Settings icon on the Home screen.**

2. **In the Settings dialog shown in Figure 3-1, tap Brightness & Wallpaper.**

Tap this option   then adjust brightness

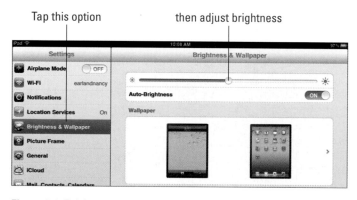

Figure 3-1: Brightness and wallpaper settings are combined in one dialog.

3. **To control brightness manually, tap the Auto-Brightness On/Off button (refer to Figure 3-1) to turn it off.**

4. **Tap and drag the Brightness slider to the right to make the screen brighter or to the left to make it dimmer.**

5. **Tap the Home button to close the Settings dialog.**

If glare from the screen is a problem for you, consider getting a screen protector. This thin film not only protects your screen from damage, but can also reduce glare. These are available from a wide variety of sources (just search for *iPad screen protector*) and cost anywhere from $2 to $24 each.

In the iBooks app, you can set a sepia tone for the page, which might be easier on your eyes. See Book II, Chapter 7 for more about using iBooks.

Changing the wallpaper

Just as your desktop computer or laptop has the ability to display a pretty picture or pattern as a desktop background called a *wallpaper,* your iPad can display an image on the Home screen and another picture when your iPad is locked.

The picture of water drops that's the default iPad image may be pretty, but it may not be the background that's best for you. Choosing different wallpaper may help you to see all the icons on your Home screen, or just allow you to display an image that appeals to your artistic sensibilities.

To change the wallpaper, do this:

1. **Tap the Settings icon on the Home screen, and then, in the Settings dialog, tap Brightness & Wallpaper.**

2. **In the Brightness & Wallpaper settings that appear, tap the arrow to the right of the iPad images displayed in the Wallpaper section (see Figure 3-2).**

Figure 3-2: Tap to reveal Wallpaper settings.

3. **In the screen that appears, tap Wallpaper to display all the built-in wallpaper images.**

You can also use your own picture for your wallpaper. Instead of choosing Wallpaper, tap Camera Roll, Photo Stream, or Photo Library or choose any listed photo library to browse your saved photos, select the picture you want to assign, and then resume with Step 5.

4. **In the Wallpaper dialog (see Figure 3-3), tap a wallpaper image.**

   A preview of that wallpaper appears onscreen (as shown in Figure 3-4).

Figure 3-3: Choose from various built-in wallpapers.

Figure 3-4: Preview your wallpaper selection.

5. **Tap either Set Lock Screen (the screen that appears when you lock the iPad by tapping the power button), Set Home Screen (to use as the wallpaper), or Set Both.**

6. **Tap the Home button.**

   You return to your Home screen with the new wallpaper set as the background.

Turning on Zoom

Normally, you can increase the size of things on your screen by double-tapping with two fingers. However, the Zoom feature enlarges the contents displayed on the iPad screen even more when you double-tap the screen with three fingers.

To turn the Zoom feature on, follow these steps:

1. **Tap the Settings icon on the Home screen and then tap General.**

2. **In General settings, swipe upward to find Accessibility and then tap it.**

   The Accessibility pane shown in Figure 3-5 appears.

Figuro 3 6: Tho Λoooooibility panc.

3. **Tap Zoom.**

4. **In the Zoom pane shown in Figure 3-6, tap the Zoom On/Off button to turn the feature on.**

Tap to turn on Zoom

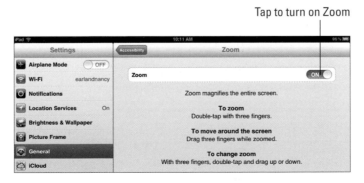

Figure 3-6: Tap and drag the Zoom On/Off button to turn it on or off.

5. **Now go to a website** (www.ipadmadeclear.com, **for example) and double-tap the screen using three fingers; it enlarges.**

6. **Press three fingers on the screen and drag to move around it.**

7. **Double-tap with three fingers again to go back to regular magnification.**

8. **Tap the Home button to close Settings.**

This Zoom feature works pretty much everywhere in iPad: in Photos, on web pages, in your Mail, and in Music and Videos. Give it a try!

Turning on White on Black

White on Black is an accessibility setting that reverses colors on your screen so that backgrounds are black and text is white. This can help people with particular vision challenges to read text more easily.

To turn this feature on:

1. **Tap the Settings icon on the Home screen and then tap General.**

2. **Tap Accessibility.**

3. **In the Accessibility dialog shown in Figure 3-7, tap the White on Black On/Off button to turn it on.**

   The colors on the screen reverse, as shown in Figure 3-8.

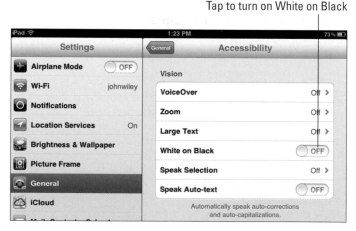

Figure 3-7: Turning on the White on Black setting can help you read text more easily.

Figure 3-8: The effect of turning on the White on Black setting.

The White on Black feature works great in some places and not so well in others. For example, in the Photos application, pictures appear almost as photo negatives. Your Home screen image will likewise look a bit strange. And don't even think of playing a video with this feature turned on! However, if you need help reading text, White on Black can be very useful in several applications.

Turning on Large Text

If having larger text in the Contacts, Mail, and Notes apps would be helpful to you, you can turn on the Large Text feature and choose the text size that works best for you. To turn on Large Text, follow these steps:

1. **Tap the Settings icon on the Home screen.**

2. **Under the General settings, tap Accessibility.**

3. **In the Accessibility pane, tap the Large Text button to turn on the feature.**

4. **In the list of text sizes shown in Figure 3-9, tap the one you prefer.**

Figure 3-9: Choose your text size here.

5. **Tap the Home button to close the Settings dialog.**

Setting up and using VoiceOver

VoiceOver reads the names of screen elements and settings to you, but it also changes the way you provide input to iPad. In Notes, for example, you can have VoiceOver read the name of the Notes app button to you, and when you enter Notes, it will read any words or characters you've entered, and tell you if features such as Auto-Correction are on.

To turn the feature on:

1. **Tap the Settings icon on the Home screen and then tap General.**

2. **Tap Accessibility.**

3. **In the Accessibility pane shown in Figure 3-10, tap the VoiceOver button.**

Tap this option

Figure 3-10: VoiceOver reads onscreen elements to you.

4. **In the VoiceOver pane shown in Figure 3-11, tap the VoiceOver On/Off button to turn it on.**

   The first time you turn on the feature, you'll see a dialog noting that turning on VoiceOver changes gestures used to interact with iPad. Tap OK once to select it and then tap OK twice to proceed.

5. **Tap the VoiceOver Practice button to select it, and then double-tap to open VoiceOver Practice.**

   (This is the new method of tapping that VoiceOver activates.)

6. **Practice using gestures such as pinching or flicking left.**

   VoiceOver tells you what action each gesture initiates.

Tap to turn on VoiceOver

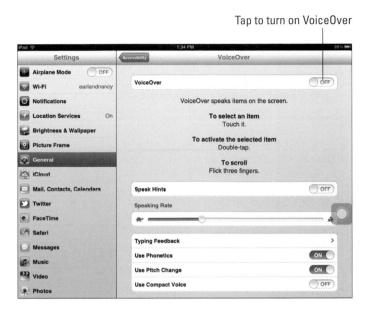

Figure 3-11: Control VoiceOver settings from this dialog.

It's important that you first single-tap to select an item such as a button, which causes VoiceOver to read the name of the button to you. Then double-tap the button to activate its function. (VoiceOver reminds you to do this if you turn on Speak Hints, which is a help when you first use VoiceOver but gets annoying after a short time.)

7. **Tap the Done button and then double-tap it to return to the VoiceOver dialog.**

8. **Tap the Speak Hints field, and VoiceOver speaks the name of the item; double-tap the slider to turn Speak Hints off.**

   If you find the rate of the voice too fast or slow, double-tap the slider and move the slider to the left to slow it down or to the right to speed it up.

9. **If you'd like VoiceOver to read words or characters to you (for example, in the Notes app), double-tap Typing Feedback.**

10. **In the Typing Feedback dialog, tap to select the option you prefer.**

    The Words option will read words but not characters such as $ (dollar sign). The Characters and Words option reads both.

You can now press the Home button and start to use other apps with the VoiceOver feature enabled. Be sure to review the next section to find out how to navigate your iPad now that you have turned VoiceOver on.

You can change the language that VoiceOver speaks. In General settings, choose International, then Language, and select another language. This will, however, also change the language used for labels on Home icons and various settings and fields in iPad.

You can use the Set Triple-Click Home setting to help you more quickly turn the VoiceOver and White on Black features on and off. In the Accessibility dialog, tap Triple-Click Home. In the dialog that appears, choose what you want a Home button triple-click to do: Toggle VoiceOver on or off; toggle White on Black on or off; toggle the Zoom feature on or off; toggle on the AssistiveTouch Control Panel; or display a menu of options using the Ask choice. Now a triple-click with a single finger on the Home button provides you with the options you selected wherever you go in iPad.

Using VoiceOver

Now that VoiceOver is turned on, you need to know how to use it. I won't kid you; using it is hard at first, but you'll get the hang of it! Here are the main onscreen gestures you should know:

- Tap an item to select it, and VoiceOver speaks its name.
- Double-tap a selected item to activate it.
- Flick three fingers to scroll.

Table 3-1 provides additional gestures that will help you use VoiceOver. I suggest that, if you want to use this feature often, you read the "VoiceOver" section of the iPad online User Guide, which goes into a great deal of detail about the ins and outs of using VoiceOver.

Table 3-1	VoiceOver Gestures
Gesture	*Effect*
Flick right or left.	Select next or preceding item.
Tap with two fingers.	Stop speaking current item.
Flick two fingers up.	Read everything from the top of the screen.
Flick two fingers down.	Read everything from the current position.
Flick up or down with three fingers.	Scroll one page at a time.
Flick right or left with three fingers.	Go to next or preceding page.
Tap three fingers.	Speak the scroll status (for example, line 20 of 100).
Flick four fingers up or down.	Go to first or last element on a page.
Flick four fingers right or left.	Go to next or preceding section (as on a web page).

Check out some new settings for VoiceOver in iOS 5, including a choice for Braille, language choices, the ability to navigate images, and a setting to have iPad speak notifications.

Utilizing iPad's Speak Auto-text

Speak Auto-text is a feature that speaks autocorrections and autocapitaliza-tions (two features that you can turn on with Keyboard settings). When you enter text in an application such as Word or Mail and the app then makes either type of change, Speak Auto-text lets you know what change was made.

To turn Speak Auto-text on, follow these steps:

1. **Tap the Settings icon on the Home screen and then tap General.**

2. **In the General settings dialog, tap Accessibility.**

3. **In the Accessibility pane shown in Figure 3-12, tap the Speak Auto-text On/Off button to turn the feature on.**

Tap to turn on Speak Auto-text

Figure 3-12: Let iPad speak to you.

Why would you want iPad to tell you when an autocorrection has been made? If you have vision challenges and you know you typed "ain't" when writing dialog for a character in your novel, but iPad corrected it to "isn't," you would want to know, right? Similarly, if you typed the poet's name e.e. Cummings and autocapitalization corrected it (incorrectly), you need to know immediately so you can change it back again!

Hearing Better

In the hearing category, you can do two things: Adjust the volume level for all apps on your iPad and modify how sounds play when you're using head-phones or an attached speaker system.

Adjusting the volume

Though individual applications such as Music and Videos have their own volume settings, you can set your iPad system volume as well to control the level of system sounds and sounds in apps that don't have their own volume control. This system setting is the max against which Music volume settings work; if you set volume to 80 percent here, for example, Music's 100 percent volume setting will actually be the maximum system volume, or 80 percent.

To adjust the system volume from the Settings dialog, in General settings, tap Sounds. In the Sounds pane that appears (see Figure 3-13), tap and drag the slider to the right to increase the volume, or to the left to lower it.

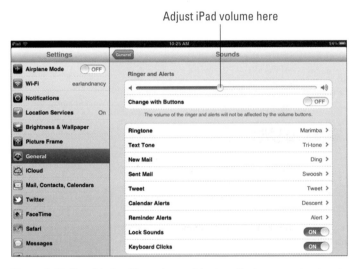

Figure 3-13: Use this familiar volume slider to adjust your system's volume.

In the Sounds pane, you can turn on or off the sounds that iPad makes when certain events occur (such as receiving new mail or Calendar alerts). These sounds are turned on by default. Conversely, if you need the audio clue and this feature has been turned off, just tap the On/Off button for the item to turn it back on.

Using Mono Audio

Stereo used in headphones breaks up sounds so that you hear a portion in one ear and a portion in the other to simulate the way our ears actually process sounds. However, if you're hard of hearing or deaf in one ear, you're getting only a portion of a sound in your hearing ear, which can be difficult.

If you have hearing challenges and wear headphones, turn on Mono Audio, and iPad plays all sounds in each ear.

Follow these steps to turn Mono Audio on:

1. **Tap the Settings icon on the Home screen and then tap General.**

2. **In the General settings, tap Accessibility.**

3. **In the Accessibility pane shown in Figure 3-14, tap the Mono Audio On/Off button to turn it on.**

Tap to turn on Mono Audio

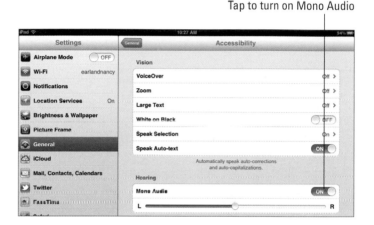

Figure 3-14: Mono audio helps people who hear better in one ear than the other.

4. **Tap and drag the slider to L for sending sound to only your left ear or R for the right ear.**

If you have hearing challenges, another good feature that iPad provides is support for closed captioning. In the Videos player, you can use a closed-captioning feature to provide onscreen text for dialogue and actions in a movie as it plays if the movie format supports closed captioning. For more about playing videos, see Book II, Chapter 3.

Using AssistiveTouch

The AssistiveTouch Control Panel helps those who have challenges working with buttons to provide input to iPad using the touchscreen. When turned on, this feature makes onscreen menus of common tasks available to you to get things done with a single tap.

To turn on AssistiveTouch:

1. **Tap Settings on the Home screen and then tap General and Accessibility.**

2. **In the Accessibility pane, tap AssistiveTouch.**

3. **In the pane that appears, tap the On/Off button for AssistiveTouch to turn it on (see Figure 3-15).**

   Note the gray square that appears on the right side of the pane. This square now appears on the screen in whatever apps you display on your iPad.

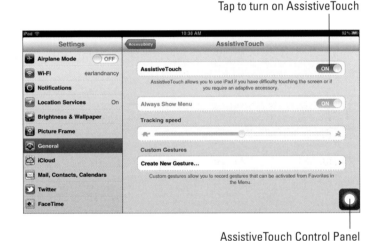

Figure 3-15: The AssistiveTouch Control Panel looks like a small gray square.

4. **Tap the AssistiveTouch Control Panel to display options, as shown in Figure 3-16.**

5. **You can tap Gestures, Favorites, or Device on the panel to see additional choices, or tap Home to go directly to the Home screen.**

   Once you've chosen an option, tapping the Back arrow takes you back to the main panel.

Figure 3-16: These options help you perform actions with a simple tap or two.

Table 3-2 shows the major options available in the AssistiveTouch Control Panel.

Table 3-2	AssistiveTouch Controls
Control	*Purpose*
Gestures	Choose the number of fingers to use for gestures on the touchscreen.
Favorites	Displays a set of gestures with only the Pinch gesture preset; you can tap any of the other blank squares to add your own favorite gestures.
Device	You can rotate the screen, lock the screen, turn volume up or down, mute or unmute sound, or shake iPad to undo an action using the presets in this option.
Home	Sends you to the Home screen.

Chapter 4: Overview of Bundled Apps

In This Chapter

⮥ **Getting the most out of the Internet with Safari, iMessage, and Mail**

⮥ **Organizing your photos**

⮥ **Getting organized with Calendar, Contacts, Notes, Reminders, and Maps**

⮥ **Using built-in apps for playing music and videos**

⮥ **Shopping for content at iTunes and apps at the App Store**

⮥ **Reading periodicals with Newsstand**

⮥ **Playing around with Game Center**

⮥ **Making video calls with FaceTime**

⮥ **Using Camera**

⮥ **Manipulating photos with Photo Booth**

*i*Pad comes with certain functionality and applications (which you probably know as *apps,* for short) already installed. When you look at your Home screen (one of eleven possible Home screens you can fill up with other apps), you'll see fifteen icons for apps, plus one for accessing iPad Settings. Four icons are displayed across the bottom in iPad's Dock: Safari, Mail, Photos, and Music. The other apps (Messages, Calendar, Notes, Reminders, Maps, YouTube, Videos, Contacts, Game Center, iTunes, App Store, Newsstand, FaceTime, Camera, Photo Booth, and Settings) are nearer the top of your screen and include apps for organizing your time and contacts, playing videos and reading periodicals, gaming, and shopping for content and yet more apps. The Dock icons will appear on every Home screen, but the others you can access on only the first Home screen unless you move them elsewhere.

This chapter gives you a quick overview of what each bundled app does. You'll find out more about every one of them as you move through the chapters in this book.

Settings isn't exactly an app, but it's an icon you should know about: It's the central location in iPad where you can adjust settings for various functions, change settings for how apps function, and perform administrative tasks like setting up e-mail accounts or a password. Read more about using Settings in Book I, Chapter 8. There is also advice about using settings for various apps in Books II, III, and V, and information about e-mail settings in Book I, Chapter 7.

Getting Online with iPad

iPad would kind of be an expensive calendar, address book, and music player if you couldn't go online to browse, buy things, get e-mail, stream video and audio, and more. Two bundled apps, Safari and Mail, help to open iPad up to the whole world of the Internet.

Going on Safari

Safari is Apple's web browser. If you've owned a Mac computer, iPhone, or iPod touch, you've already used Safari (see Figure 4-1) to navigate around the Internet, create and save bookmarks of favorite sites, and add web clips to your Home screen so you can quickly visit favorite sites from there.

 If you've been a Windows user in the past, you may also have used Safari, or you may be more familiar with browsers such as Internet Explorer or Firefox. If you haven't used Safari, don't worry; the browser should be pretty easy for you to get the hang of, with its familiar address field, Search field, tabs, navigation buttons, and bookmarks.

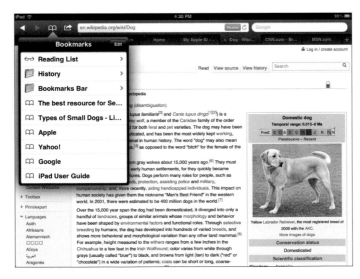

Figure 4-1: Find what you need on the web with Safari.

Using a browser on iPad is a lot of fun because of the touchscreen function-ality and the ability to zoom in or out on a page by flicking two fingers inward or outward. Tabbed browsing allows you to move easily among open websites. You can read more about using Safari in Book I, Chapter 6.

Getting Mail

iPad lets you get all your mail in one place through the Mail app — the program you use to access e-mail accounts you set up in iPad. You can set up accounts you have with popular e-mail providers such as Gmail, Yahoo!, AOL, and Windows Live. You can also access accounts through iCloud or Microsoft Exchange. (Your work e-mail account might use Microsoft Exchange, for exam-ple.) Most any IMAP- or POP3-type account (the two most common mail proto-cols out there) is supported. You can also arrange to access the e-mail accounts you have with your Internet service provider (ISP).

Once you set up an account, when you tap the Mail icon, your e-mail will dis-play without you having to browse to the site or sign in. Then you can use tools to move among a few preset mail folders, read and reply to mail, and download attached photos to iPad. You can also use the Print feature in Mail to print your e-mail messages to a wireless printer. You can read more about setting up and using e-mail accounts in Book I, Chapter 7.

In portrait orientation, e-mails are displayed full screen, and you can use a drop-down menu to view your inbox. In landscape orientation, the inbox stays put on the left side of your screen.

Using iMessage to connect

With iOS 5 comes an instant messaging app called Messages. This app allows you to use the iMessage service to swap text messages with others in real time using a cellphone number or e-mail address. You can forward your con-versations to others as well.

You can use Messages settings to turn the app on or allow others to get a read receipt when you've read their messages. You can also use the data in your Contacts app to make addressing messages quick and easy.

Playing with Photos

Photos isn't exactly Photoshop or any other sophisticated photo-imaging program — it's just a pretty simple app for organizing and viewing photos with a few very simple editing tools. Still, though it doesn't do much, what it does, it does in a very cool way.

Photos (see Figure 4-2) allows you to organize pictures in folders; e-mail, message, or tweet photos to others; use a photo as your iPad wallpaper; or upload someone's picture to a contact record. You can use tools to rotate, enhance, remove red eye, or crop photos. You can also run slideshows of your photos. You can open albums, pinch or unpinch to shrink or expand photos, and scroll through photos with a swipe.

Figure 4-2: A simple but fun way to view your photos.

The sexy part of Photos is the way you interact with the photos with your fingers on the touchscreen. You can also use Photos to convert iPad into a digital photo frame while you have it docked or charging, and you can run slideshows of your photo albums as well. If Photos sounds like fun (and it is), you should read more about how it works in Book II, Chapter 4.

Using Apps to Stay Organized

Scheduling your time, tracking contacts, jotting down notes — they're all a part of keeping organized in today's hectic world. iPad offers four apps to help you do just that: Calendar, Contacts, Reminders, and Notes.

 Note that from iOS 4.2 on, iPads have native print capability. In Photos, that means that you can select a photo or photos, tap to display the main menu, tap the Print option, select your printer, and print. You have to have a printer that supports AirPrint wireless printing to use this method. See Book V, Chapter 1 for more about printing.

 Version 4.2 and later of the iOS for iPad made multitasking available. That means that you don't have to return to the Home screen every time you want to switch among all these great apps. As on the iPhone, multitasking is dead simple. With one app open, just double-tap the Home button, and a

horizontal bar with app icons for any open apps appears along the bottom of the screen. Scroll to find the one you want, tap it, and it is displayed.

Staying on schedule with Calendar

What would any computing device today be without a calendar feature, given our hectic lives? If the calendar features on your computer and mobile phone don't already keep you on track, try iPad's Calendar. This app provides a handy onscreen daybook you can use to set up appointments and send alerts to remind you about them. You can also sync Calendar with other calendars you maintain online via iTunes or iCloud.

See the next chapter for more about syncing and Book V, Chapter 3 for details on using Calendar.

Keeping in touch with Contacts

Today, it's all about who you know and staying in touch. Contacts is the built-in address book feature (see Figure 4-3) for iPad that lets you do just that. You can use Contacts to enter contact information (including photos, if you like, from your Photos app) and share contact information via e-mail. You can also use a search feature to find contacts easily.

Figure 4-3: Keep the basics about all your contacts in this handy app.

Contacts is another app you can sync with your iPhone or computer to save you tedious reentry of information. Read more about this in Book V, Chapter 5.

Want to find your contact in the real world? Tap that person's address in Contacts and the iPad Maps app shows you how to get there! You can also tap an address you find in Maps and add it to Contacts.

Making Notes

Notes is a simple notepad app where you can enter text or cut and paste text from a website or e-mails. You can't do much except save your notes or e-mail them — there are no features for formatting text or inserting objects. You'll find Notes handy, though, for simple notes on-the-fly.

You'll feel right at home with the familiar yellow pad interface that Notes sports. The font has a casual handwritten look, and the icons along the bottom are pretty straightforward, though you can switch among three fonts by changing Notes options in iPad Settings. You can move to the previous note, e-mail a note, trash a note, or move to the next note.

If this simple note-keeper appeals to you, read more about the Notes app in Book V, Chapter 2.

You enter info into Notes using the onscreen keyboard. If you are a heavy note taker, consider buying a compatible Bluetooth keyboard for easier typing.

Staying on track with Reminders

A new app included starting with iOS 5 is Reminders. This is a handy electronic to-do list where you can enter tasks or pull tasks from the Calendar app. You can organize reminders into custom categories and see them in a list or organized by date, which also displays a useful monthly calendar on one side of the screen.

Of course, an obvious feature of an app called Reminders is that you can set it up to remind you of an event. Location-based reminders (which work most efficiently with the always-on 3G connection on iPad 3G models) prompt your iPad to remind you about an event based on your location; for example, set a reminder to buy milk at a specific location, and you receive the alert when you're walking by the market. This feature uses Location Services to track your whereabouts at any point in time.

Going Places with Maps

This app is a very cool iPad version of Google Earth. You can view classic maps or aerial views of addresses, get directions from one place to another by car, foot, or public transportation, and even view an address as if you were standing in front of the building at street level.

If you own a Wi-Fi iPad, a less sophisticated system than 3G can identify your current location and help you find directions from there to other places. 3G iPad owners enjoy a much more targeted location system, but all models can take advantage of the ability to bookmark or share locations, or add an address to Contacts.

See Book III, Chapter 2 for step-by-step procedures for using the Maps app.

Being Entertained by iPad

One of the joys of iPad is its use as a media consumption tool. Playing music and watching videos is a very entertaining use of iPad, indeed. The bundled Music and Videos apps make playing media easy to do.

Playing around with Music

Unless you've been living in a cave without 3G or satellite TV for the last several years, you know perfectly well that iPod is the Apple preferred player. On your iPad, the Music app is your media player with a heavy emphasis on music. You can use Music to play music, podcasts, or audiobooks.

One of the nicest things about Music on iPad is the fact that iPad comes with a very nifty sound system and speaker, so the experience of listening with or without headphones will be a pleasing experience for all of you who have become addicted to MP3 listening devices. You can also browse your music by a variety of criteria, such as artist, album, song, or genre.

You can also use the Videos app to play TV or movies, as well as iTunes U online courses and podcasts, and it offers some great features for controlling video playback.

Watching videos and browsing YouTube

The Videos app is a media player like Music, but it specializes in playing videos and offers a few more features, such as chapter breakdowns and information about movie plots and casts for media you got from iTunes. You can move between widescreen and full-screen display, and it shines at showing high-definition content. See Book II, Chapter 3 for more on the Videos app.

YouTube is the app you should use to access all those videos, good and bad, that people upload to this popular video-sharing site. Tap the YouTube icon on your iPad Home screen, and you're taken to the YouTube site. Here you can watch videos people have posted, comment on them, share them with others, and so on.

Going Shopping at iTunes and the App Store

The iTunes app takes you to the iTunes Store, where you can shop till you drop (or your iPad battery runs out of juice) for music, movies, TV shows, audiobooks, university lectures, and podcasts and download them directly to your iPad. You can also preview content before you download it. See Book I, Chapter 5, for more about how to buy apps, and Book VI for a listing of some of the very best apps out there.

Ready for more shopping? Tapping the App Store icon takes you directly to an Apple online store, where you can buy and download apps that do everything from enabling you to play games to building business presentations. At last count, there were over 400,000 apps available for iPad, with more being added all the time. Some were created for iPhone/iPod touch and run on iPad; some were created especially for the iPad. And some are even free!

Reading Periodicals with Newsstand

Similar to an e-reader for books, Newsstand is a handy app for subscribing to and reading magazines, newspapers, and other periodicals.

Are you more into books than magazines? Then you'll be glad to know about iBooks, an e-reader application that isn't supplied with iPad out of the box. It's free (like many other apps out there), but you'll have to download it from the App Store. Because iPad has been touted as a great e-reader, you should definitely consider getting the iBooks app and/or another e-reader app, such as Kindle or Stanza, as soon as possible. For more about downloading apps for your iPad, see Book II, Chapter 1, and to work with the iBooks' e-reader app itself, go to Book II, Chapter 7.

Playing with Game Center

Apple's iOS 4.2, released in November 2010, added the Game Center app to the iPad mix. Game Center is a way to essentially browse game apps in the App Store by best-selling titles. Tap Game Center on your Home screen, tap one of the sets of colorful icons that appears on the Game Center screen, and you're taken to the App Store, with information about a game displayed.

From then on, it's about obtaining the game (either free or for a price through your iTunes account) and playing it. You can add friends to build your gaming social network and play and track scores for interactive games. See Book I, Chapter 5 for more about buying apps, and Book II, Chapter 8 for more about gaming with your iPad.

Facing Up to Things with FaceTime

iPad 2 shipped with front- and back-facing cameras, which unleashed all kinds of possibilities. One of the coolest is an app called FaceTime, a video calling app that lets you use the video cameras on iPad 2 to talk to others with an iPad 2, iPod touch, Mac, or iPhone 4 face to face. (See Figure 4-4.) You can call someone via their iPhone 4 or 4S cellphone number or e-mail address.

You'll want to start trying FaceTime with all your friends who own a compatible Mac device, so head straight to Book II, Chapter 4, to get up to speed on FaceTime features.

Figure 4-4: Talk face to face using FaceTime.

Taking Snapshots and Videos with Camera

Camera is the app that serves as control central for the still and video cameras built into iPad 2. You can take still pictures or videos using either the front or back camera. The front-facing camera is especially useful for talking face to face on video calls with slightly higher resolution (see the previous section), and the back camera provides an easy way to capture an image of what you're looking at.

You can also work with slideshows and share content with others using e-mail. See Book II, Chapter 4 for more about working with the cameras.

Changing Photos with Photo Booth

The very fun Photo Booth app has been included with Mac OS X for some time. It lets you take photos with weird and wonderful results. (See Figure 4-5.) You can use the built-in effects, such as Kaleidoscope, Mirror, and Thermal Camera, along with your iPad camera to take photos that turn out unlike any others.

The photos you take using Photo Booth are stored in your Camera Roll album of Photos. You can easily share them with others or use iPad's native printing capability to print them to an AirPrint-compatible wireless printer.

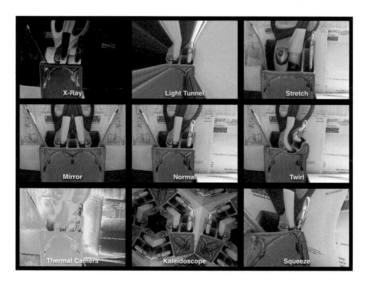

Figure 4-5: Manipulate photos in a variety of ways with Photo Booth.

Chapter 5: Setting Up iTunes to Sync and Buy Apps

In This Chapter

- ✓ **Getting connected to the Internet**
- ✓ **Downloading iTunes and creating an account**
- ✓ **Making iPad settings in iTunes**
- ✓ **Syncing iPad to your computer**
- ✓ **Using iCloud**
- ✓ **Purchasing apps from the App Store**
- ✓ **Updating apps**

Apple made its iTunes desktop application one way for you to manage settings for how your iPad *syncs* with your computer so you can share information and content such as calendar events, pictures, music, movies, and contacts. Before you can use iTunes to sync, you have to download the software, and if you want to make purchases from the store, you need to open an iTunes account, both of which I cover in this chapter. You can also use the new iCloud service to store and share content online using a Wi-Fi connection. In this chapter, I cover how to set up an iCloud account and make settings to back up and share content in the cloud.

Some apps, such as Contacts and Videos, come pre-installed on your iPad. But as you know if you're an iPhone user, there's a world of other apps out there, including many that you can get for your iPad. Once you've set up iTunes, you can buy apps (or download free ones) in the iPad App Store using your iTunes account. Some are free, such as iBooks, and some you can get for a price (typically from 99 cents to about $10, though a few go up to $50 or more).

In this chapter, I tell you how to connect to the Internet (you need an Internet connection to access the App Store), and then I tell you how to set iTunes and iCloud to sync your iPad with other devices and how you can acquire apps for your iPad through the App Store.

Once you have an iTunes account, you can also shop iTunes for music, videos, audiobooks, and more. See Book II, Chapter 1, for more about shopping for multimedia content.

Connecting to the Internet

In order to browse the web, access Mail, and shop online, you have to first be connected to the Internet, so I'm putting this information right up front. How you connect to the Internet depends on which iPad model you own:

- ✔ The **Wi-Fi–only iPad** connects to the Internet via a Wi-Fi network. You may already have set up this type of network in your own home using your computer and some equipment from your Internet provider. You can also connect through public Wi-Fi networks *(hotspots)*. You probably have already noticed how many hotspots your town or city has: Look for Internet cafes, coffee shops, hotels, libraries, and transportation centers such as airports or bus stations. In fact, once you start looking, you'll notice lots of signs alerting you to free Wi-Fi locations — they're everywhere.

- ✔ If you own a **Wi-Fi and 3G-enabled iPad,** you can still use a Wi-Fi connection (which is usually much faster if you have a good connection), but you can also use a paid data network through AT&T or Verizon to connect via a cellular network just about anywhere you can get cellular phone coverage.

See Book I, Chapter 1, for more about the capabilities of different iPad models and the costs associated with 3G.

When you're in range of a hotspot, a pop-up may display automatically; if it doesn't, tap Settings, then tap Wi-Fi, and then tap Choose a Network. (Note that secure networks, which require a password, will display a little padlock icon.) If access to several nearby networks is available, you may see a message asking you to tap a network name to select it. After you select one (or if only one network is available), you see a message similar to the one shown in Figure 5-1 if a password is required. Enter a network password and then tap the Join button.

Free public Wi-Fi networks typically don't require passwords. However, it's therefore possible for someone else to track your online activities over these unsecured networks. No matter how much you might be tempted, you might want to avoid accessing financial accounts or sending unencrypted sensitive e-mail when connected to a public hotspot.

Enter the network password...

then tap Join

Figure 5-1: Joining a Wi-Fi network.

Setting Up iTunes

Think of iTunes as Apple's version of the Mall of America. It's both the place from which you can manage your iPad settings for syncing content and a great big online store where you can buy content and apps for your PC or Mac, iPod touch, iPhone, and iPad. It's also the place where you can make settings for several of these devices to control how they download and share content. Even if you find some other sources of content for your iPad, it's worth having an iTunes account, if only to use the settings it provides.

You can use iTunes account or an Apple ID and iCloud to register your iPad when you first buy it before you can use it. In my case and perhaps in yours, the nice man at the Apple Store activated my iPad before I left the store with it, so I set up my own iTunes account the first time I wanted to buy a hot movie title.

Downloading iTunes to your computer

If you own a Mac, iTunes is already installed. If you own a Windows-based PC, your first step in connecting to iTunes is simply to download the software. You should do this on your old-fashioned computer or laptop. As of this writing, iTunes 10.5 is the latest version of this software and requires that you have Windows XP Service Pack 3 or later on your PC, or Mac OS X version 10.5 or later on your Apple computer. You'll also need a broadband Internet connection, 512MB of RAM (1GB for playing HD video), and at least a 1024 x 768 screen resolution for viewing content.

You can probably handle this one yourself and, if you're a Mac user, you've already got iTunes (although maybe not the latest version) — but just in case, here are the steps involved in downloading iTunes:

1. **On your computer, go to** www.apple.com/itunes **using your browser of choice.**

2. **Click the iTunes Free Download link (shown in Figure 5-2) and in the screen that follows, click the Download Now button.**

Click this button

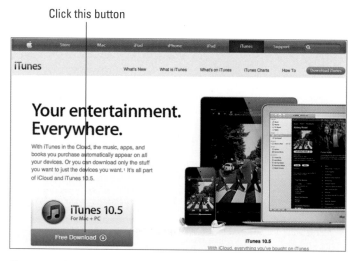

Figure 5-2: Get the free iTunes download.

3. **In the dialog that appears (see Figure 5-3), or using the Internet Explorer 9 download bar if you have that version, click Run.**

The iTunes application downloads.

Click Run

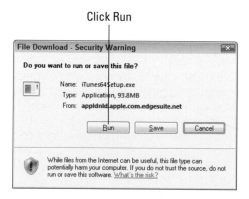

Figure 5-3: Your garden-variety download dialog.

4. **When the download is complete, another dialog appears, asking whether you want to run the software; click Run.**

   The iTunes Installer appears. (See Figure 5-4.)

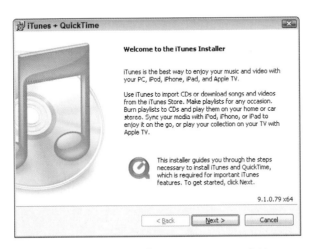

iTunes + QuickTime

Welcome to the iTunes Installer

iTunes is the best way to enjoy your music and video with your PC, iPod, iPhone, iPad, and Apple TV.

Use iTunes to import CDs or download songs and videos from the iTunes Store. Make playlists for any occasion. Burn playlists to CDs and play them on your home or car stereo. Sync your media with iPod, iPhone, or iPad to enjoy it on the go, or play your collection on your TV with Apple TV.

This installer guides you through the steps necessary to install iTunes and QuickTime, which is required for important iTunes features. To get started, click Next.

9.1.0.79 x64

< Back   Next >   Cancel

Figure 5-4: The iTunes Installer gets you set up quickly.

5. **Click Next.**

6. **Select the I Accept the Terms of the License Agreement check box in the next dialog and click Next.**

7. **Review the installation options, click to deselect ones you don't want to use, and then click the Install button shown in Figure 5-5.**

   A dialog appears, showing the installation progress.

8. **When a dialog appears telling you that the installation is complete, take it at its word and click Finish.**

You've probably already guessed that you'll have to restart your computer if it's a Windows machine for the configuration settings made during the installation to take effect. Once your computer restarts, you can use the iTunes desktop shortcut (if you decided to create one) to open iTunes.

Apple updates things all the time, so with iTunes open on your computer, click Help and select Check for Updates to get an updated version. Also, when you connect your iPad to your computer and open iTunes, it will alert you if there is an update to your iPad operating system and, if you choose to update, will download the update and sync it to your iPad.

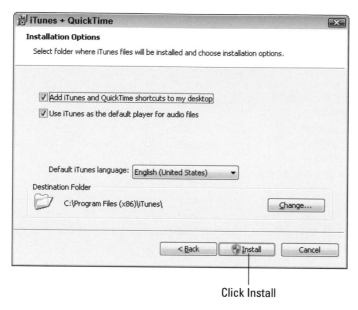

Click Install

Figure 5-5: Make a choice about adding desktop shortcuts on your computer here.

Opening an iTunes account

To be able to buy and download items from the Apple Store (even free apps and content) on your iPad, you have to open an iTunes account. (Don't worry. It's free, though to buy items you'll have to provide a credit card, iTunes gift card, or get credits on your iTunes account.)

Follow these steps to get your iTunes account:

1. **Open iTunes.**

   This is the application you downloaded to your computer in the preceding section. If you didn't create a desktop shortcut, you can open iTunes from your computer's Start menu in Windows or by clicking the iTunes item in the Mac Dock or Launchpad on your Mac.

2. **Click the Store tab to open the Store menu and choose Create Account from the menu that appears (see Figure 5-6).**

3. **On the Welcome to the iTunes Store screen that appears, click Continue.**

Select this option

Figure 5-6: Start the process to create an account.

4. **On the following screen (see Figure 5-7), click to select the I Have Read and Agree to the iTunes Terms and Conditions check box and then click the Continue button.**

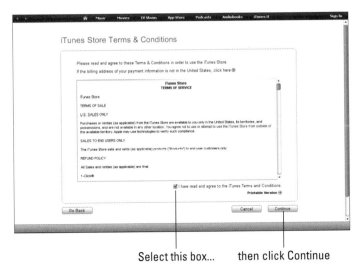

Select this box...   then click Continue

Figure 5-7: Click the usual check box for agreeing to terms, and proceed!

5. **In the Create iTunes Store Account (Apple ID) screen that follows (see Figure 5-8), fill in the information fields, click the last two check boxes to deselect them (if you don't want to receive e-mail from the Apple Store), and then click the Continue button.**

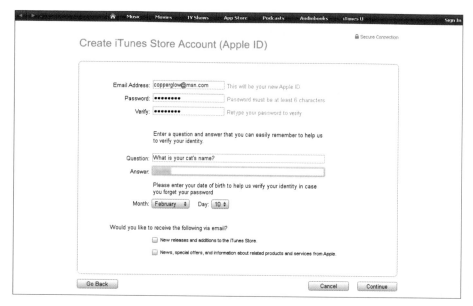

Figure 5-8: Choose any question and fill in the answer you want (cats optional).

6. **On the Provide a Payment Method screen that appears (see Figure 5-9), enter your payment information and then click the Continue button.**

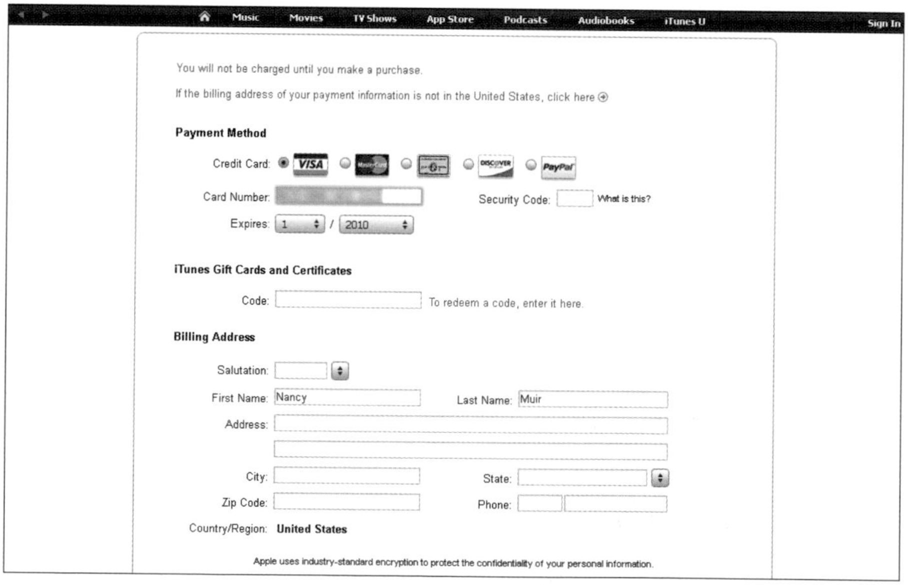

Figure 5-9: Okay, you know the routine: fill in your payment information. . . .

The screen shown in Figure 5-10 appears, confirming that your account has been opened.

7. **Click the Done button to return to the iTunes Store.**

Click Done to return to the store

Figure 5-10: Success — you are an official iTunes person.

Making Settings and Syncing

Remember that great photo of your promotion party you have on your hard drive? How do you get that onto iPad so you can show it off at the next family reunion? Or how about that audiobook on career success you bought and downloaded to your laptop on your last business trip? It would sure be handy to get that sucker onto your iPad. Never fear: By making a few easy settings and syncing with your computer, you can bring all that content over in a (pardon the term, Steve Jobs) flash.

Remember that you can also sync content using iCloud. See the next section for more about that option.

Making iPad settings using iTunes

When you plug your Dock Connector to USB Cable into your iPad and computer and then open iTunes, you'll find a whole group of settings becomes available. These help you determine how content will sync between the two devices.

Note that you can sync wirelessly to your computer by tapping Settings on the Home screen, opening General settings, and tapping iTunes Wi-Fi Sync. In the dialog that appears, tap Sync Now. This works only if your iPad is plugged in and both iPad and your computer are connected to the same Wi-Fi network.

Here's how to use the iTunes settings for your iPad:

1. **Connect your iPad to your computer using the Dock Connector to USB Cable.**

   Plug the data connection cord into your iPad (using the wider connector) and plug the other end of the cord into a USB port on your computer.

2. **Open your iTunes software.**

   (On a Windows computer, choose Start⇨All Programs⇨iTunes; on a Mac, click the iTunes icon in the Dock.)

   iTunes opens, and your iPad is listed in the Devices section of the Source List.

3. **Click the name of your iPad in the Devices section of the Source List.**

   A series of tabs displays, as shown in Figure 5-11. The tabs offer information about your iPad and settings to determine which content such as music, movies, or podcasts to download, and for some content types when to download. (You can see the simple choices on the Music tab in Figure 5-12.) The settings relate to the kind of content you want to download and whether you want to download it automatically when you sync or do it manually. See Table 5-1 for an overview of the settings that are available on each tab.

4. **Make all settings for the types of content you plan to obtain on your computer and sync to your iPad, and then click the Sync button in the bottom-right corner to sync files with the iPad.**

Be alert to warnings when you sync your iPad and computer because, depending on your settings, you may overwrite or erase content you've downloaded when you sync. You may want to copy content you've downloaded to your iPad directly to your iTunes library before syncing so your computer doesn't erase what you've downloaded during the sync.

Click on your iPad...   to display this series of tabs

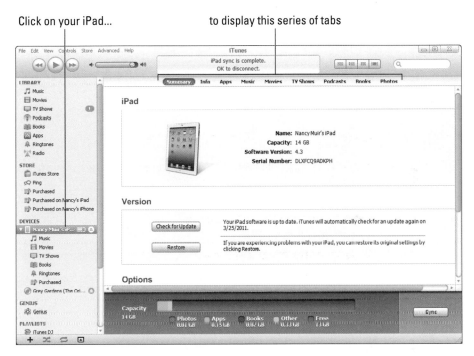

Figure 5-11: The various tabs you can use to control iPad from iTunes.

Figure 5-12: Settings to control how music syncs to your iPad.

Table 5-1	iPad Settings in iTunes
Tab Name	*What You Can Do with These Settings*
Summary	Perform updates to iPad software and set general syncing options.
Info	Specify which information to sync: Contacts, Calendars, E-mail, Bookmarks, or Notes.
Apps	Sync apps and data you've downloaded to your computer to iPad and manage the location of those apps and folders.
Music	Choose which music to download to your iPad when you sync.
Movies	Specify whether to automatically download movies.
TV Shows	Choose which shows and episodes to sync automatically.
Podcasts	Choose which podcasts and episodes to sync automatically.
Books	Choose to sync all or only selected audio and electronic books to your iPad.
Photos	Choose the folders from which you want to download photos or albums.
iTunes U	Choose to sync class content you've downloaded via iTunes U.

Syncing iPad to your computer

After you specify which content to download in iTunes (see the preceding section), you use the Dock Connector to USB Cable to connect your iPad and computer to sync info like contacts and calendar settings.

With iTunes installed on your computer and an iTunes account set up, follow these simple steps to sync to your iPad:

1. **Plug the data connection cord into your iPad.**

2. **Plug the other end of the data connection cord into your computer.**

   iTunes opens and shows an iPad item in the Source List. (See Figure 5-13.) Your iPad screen shows the words *Sync in Progress.*

   When the syncing is complete, the Lock screen returns on the iPad, and iTunes shows a message indicating that the iPad sync is complete and that you can disconnect the cable. Any media you chose to transfer in your iTunes settings, and any new photos on your computer, have been transferred to your iPad.

3. **After syncing, unplug the data connection cord from your iPad and your computer.**

Your iPad is listed here

Figure 5-13: Syncing connects your computer and iPad so you can share data.

 If you're into social networking, you might try tapping the Ping button at the bottom of the iTunes screen to check out Apple's new entry in the social networking world. It's described as a great way to follow your favorite artists or friends and keep tuned to the music everybody's listening to. As of this writing, Ping really hasn't taken off, but as with all things social on the Internet, it could grow very quickly or fall on its face!

Understanding iCloud

There's an alternative to syncing content by using iTunes. At the time that Apple launched iOS 5, it also introduced iCloud, a service that allows you to back up all your content and certain settings such as bookmarks to online storage. That content and those settings are then pushed automatically to all your Apple devices through a wireless connection.

All you need to do is get an iCloud account, which is free, and then make settings on each device for which types of content you want pushed to each device. After you've done that, any content you create or purchase on one device — such as music, apps, books, and TV shows, as well as documents created in Apple's iWork apps, photos, and so on — can be synced among your devices automatically.

When you get an iCloud account, you get 5GB of free storage; content you purchase (such as apps, books, music, and TV shows) won't be counted against your storage. If you want additional storage, you can buy an upgrade from one of your devices. 10GB costs $20 per year; 20GB is $40; and 50GB is $100 a year. Most people will do just fine with the free 5GB of storage.

To upgrade your storage, go to iCloud in Settings, tap Storage & Backup, and then tap Manage Storage. In the dialog that appears, tap Buy More Storage. Tap the amount you need and then tap Buy.

You can make settings for backing up your content to iCloud in the iCloud section of Settings. You can have content backed up automatically, or do it manually. See Book I, Chapter 9, for more about this topic.

Getting an iCloud Account

Before you can use iCloud, you need an iCloud account, which is tied to the Apple ID you probably already have. You can turn on iCloud when first setting up your iPad or use Settings to sign up using your Apple ID.

1. **When first setting up your phone after upgrading to iOS 5, in the sequence of screens that appear you'll see the one in Figure 5-14. Tap Use iCloud.**

2. **In the next dialog, tap Backup to iCloud.**

   Your account is now set up based on the Apple ID you entered earlier in the setup sequence.

Here are the steps to set up iCloud on your iPad if you didn't do so on first setting up iPad:

1. **Tap Settings and then tap iCloud.**

2. **Tap the On/Off button to turn on iCloud.**

3. **Enter your Apple ID and password and tap the Sign In button (see Figure 5-15).**

   If you don't have an Apple ID, tap the Get a Free Apple ID button and follow the instructions to get your ID.

   A dialog appears, asking whether you'd like to merge your iPad calendars, reminders, and bookmarks with iCloud.

4. **A dialog may appear asking if you want to allow iCloud to use the location of your iPad. Tap OK.**

   Your account is now set up.

Figure 5-14: Set up iCloud while setting up your iPad

Figure 5-15: Use your Apple ID to access iCloud.

Making iCloud Sync Settings

When you have an iCloud account up and running (see the preceding section), you have to specify which type of content should be synced with your iPad via iCloud. Note that content that you purchase and download will be synced among your devices automatically via iCloud.

1. **Tap Settings and then tap iCloud.**

2. **In the iCloud settings shown in Figure 5-16, tap the On/Off button for any item that's turned off that you want to turn on (or vice versa).**

   You can sync Mail, Contacts, Calendars, Reminders, Bookmarks, and Notes.

3. **To turn Photo Stream, Documents & Data, or Storage & Backup on or off (so you can sync photos, documents created in iWork, or settings data, respectively), tap those options on the list (refer to Figure 5-14) and then tap the On/Off button for each particular setting in the subsequent screen.**

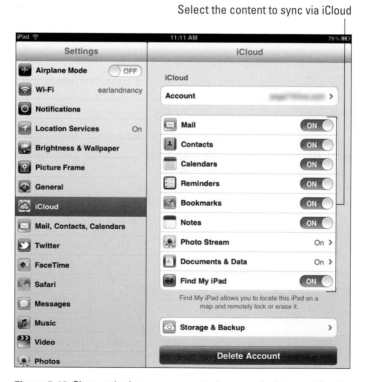

Select the content to sync via iCloud

Figure 5-16: Choose the items you want to have pushed to your iPad here.

4. **To enable automatic downloads of music, apps, and book, tap Store in the Settings pane.**

5. **Tap the On/Off button for Music, Apps, or Books to set up automatic downloads of any of this content to your iPad via iCloud.**

If you want to allow iCloud to provide a service for locating a lost or stolen iPad, tap the On/Off button in the Find My iPad field to activate it. This service helps you locate, send a message to, or delete content from your iPad if it falls into other hands.

Buying Apps or Downloading Free Apps

Apps are the technology equivalent of all the sports paraphernalia (caps, t-shirts, beer-can cooler sleeves, and so on) that you might buy to support your favorite team. However, apps also provide all kinds of functionality, from the ability to plan travel, manage finances, and find local restaurants and gas stations to hard-core business productivity and serious gaming fun.

Most iPhone apps will work on your iPad, so if you own the pricey mobile phone and have favorite apps on it, you might want to use them on your iPad! Also, for more about my recommended apps, see Book VI.

Searching the App Store

Apple isn't one to miss a profit opportunity, so naturally, one of the iPad built-in apps is the App Store. This is the apps portal that will get you to thousands of great apps for everything from games to bean counting.

If you want to get non-Apple apps, such as Google Voice, you can join the estimated 4 million people who have done what's called *jailbreaking* to liberate their iPhones or iPads from the tyranny of getting apps solely through iTunes. Check out this article for details about jailbreaking, but be forewarned that jailbreaking voids your iPad warranty, impedes your access to Apple updates, and could even make it hard to download and use legitimate Apple-approved apps: `http://gizmodo.com/5530906/jailbreaking-your-ipad-how-you-can-and-why-you-should`.

Here's your quick introduction to using the App Store to obtain whatever apps your heart desires:

1. **Tap the App Store icon on your iPad Home screen.**

    The site shown in Figure 5-17 appears.

Previous and Next arrows   New, What's Hot, and Release Date tabs   Search Field

Top Charts button   Categories button

Figure 5-17: Welcome to the App Store!

2. **At this point, you have several options for finding apps:**

- Tap in the Search field, enter a search term, and tap the Search button on the onscreen keyboard to see results.

- Tap either the Previous or Next arrow to see more selections, or tap the See All link to display all selections.

- Tap the New, What's Hot, or Release Date tab at the top of the screen to see a categories of apps.

- Tap the Top Charts button at the bottom of the screen to see which free and paid apps other people are downloading most.

- Tap the Categories button to search by type of app, as shown in Figure 5-18.

Figure 5-18: Find the apps that fit your needs.

Getting apps from the App Store

Buying apps requires that you have an iTunes account, which I cover earlier in this chapter. After you have an account, you can use the saved payment information there to buy apps in a few simple steps, or download free apps. I strongly recommend that you install the free iBooks app, so in this section, I walk you through the steps for getting it.

1. **With the App Store open, tap the Search field, enter** iBooks, **and then tap the Search button on the onscreen keyboard.**

2. **Tap the price button (which in this case reads** *Free*) **for iBooks in the results that appear, as shown in Figure 5-19.**

   Note that to get a paid app, you'd tap the price button, which displays the cost of the app.

   The price button changes to read Install App (or in the case of a paid app, the button changes to read Buy App).

Tap this button

Figure 5-19: Tap the app you need.

3. **Tap the button.**

   You may be asked to enter your iTunes password and tap the OK button to proceed.

   The app downloads; if you purchase an app that isn't free, at this point your credit card is charged for the purchase price or your Store credit is reduced by the amount of the purchase price.

 Out of the box, only preinstalled apps are located on the first iPad Home screen of your iPad by default. Apps you download are placed on additional Home screens, and you have to scroll to view and use them. See the next section for help in finding your newly downloaded apps using multiple Home screens.

 If you have opened an iCloud account, anything you purchase on your iPad can be set up to automatically be pushed to other Apple iOS devices. See earlier sections in this chapter for more about iCloud.

 If you're a road warrior, you'll be glad to hear that the travel industry is all over apps to help you get around, as the iPad is such a logical travel companion. Lonely Planet has released country guides for the iPad, and iPhone apps for travelers are being re-created for iPad. See Book III, Chapter 3, if you're someone who hits the road on a regular basis and want to make the most of your iPad.

Organizing your apps

iPad can display up to 11 Home screens. By default, the first contains preinstalled apps; other screens are created to contain any apps you download or sync to your iPad. At the bottom of any iPad Home screen (just above the Dock), a magnifying glass icon represents the Search screen to the left of the primary Home screen; dots that appear to the right of the magnifying glass icon indicate the number of Home screens, as shown in Figure 5-20.

Here's some advice on how to organize your apps:

1. **Tap the Home button to open the last displayed Home screen.**

2. **Flick your finger from right to left or tap either end of the Home screen dots to move to the next or previous Home screen.**

    Note that the dots near the bottom of the screen indicate which Home screen you're on. To move back, flick from left to right.

3. **To reorganize apps on a Home screen, press and hold any app on that page.**

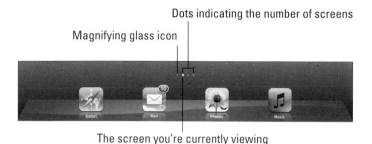

Dots indicating the number of screens

Magnifying glass icon

The screen you're currently viewing

Figure 5-20: Finding apps on the various iPad Home screens.

The app icons begin to jiggle, and any apps you installed will sport a Delete button (a black circle with a white X on it). (See Figure 5-21.)

Figure 5-21: Move an app to another location on a Home screen.

4. **Press, hold, and drag an app icon to another location on the screen to move it.**

5. **Tap the Home button to stop all those icons from jiggling!**

To move an app from one page to another, while things are jiggling, you can press, hold, and drag an app to the left or right to move it to the next Home screen. You can also manage what app resides on what Home screen from iTunes when you've connected iPad to iTunes via a cable or wireless sync.

Organizing apps in folders

As with iPhone, iPad lets you organize apps in folders (if you have iOS version 4.2 or later). The process is simple and specific to each device. For iPad, follow these steps to get more organized:

1. **Tap and hold an app till all apps do their jiggle dance.**

2. **Drag an app on top of another app.**

   A bar appears across the screen showing the two apps and a folder name field that contains a placeholder name. (See Figure 5-22.)

3. **To delete the placeholder name and change the folder name, tap in the field at the end of the placeholder name.**

   The placeholder text is deleted, and the keyboard appears.

Figure 5-22: Collect apps in logical folders to help you save Home screen space.

4. **Tap the Delete key to delete the placeholder name and then type one of your own.**

   (If you change your mind and want to put the app back on the Home screen, you can easily drag it out of the folder.)

5. **Tap anywhere outside of the bar to save the name.**

6. **Tap the Home button to stop all that jiggling!**

   The folder appears on the Home screen where you began this process.

To get to the items stored in your folder, just double-tap it.

Deleting apps you no longer need

Not all apps are endlessly entertaining or useful. When you no longer need an app you have installed, it's time to get rid of it to save some space on your iPad. (Note, however, that you can't delete apps that were preinstalled on the iPad.) If you use iCloud to push content across all Apple iOS devices, note that deleting an app on your iPad won't affect that app on other devices.

To send an app on its way, do this:

1. **Display the Home screen that contains the app you want to delete.**

2. **Press and hold the app until all apps begin to jiggle.**

3. **Tap the Delete button for the app you want to delete (see Figure 5-23).**

Delete buttons

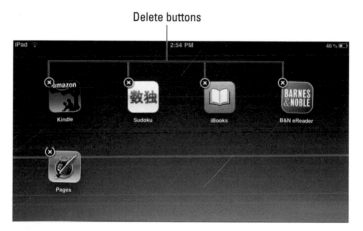

Figure 5-23: Tap Delete on the jiggling app.

4. **In the confirmation dialog shown in Figure 5-24, tap Delete to proceed with the deletion.**

   A dialog asking you to rate an app before deleting it appears.

Figure 5-24: Tap Cancel if you have regrets; otherwise, tap Delete to send the app on its way.

5. **Tap the Rate button to rate the app or No Thanks to opt out of the survey.**

Don't worry about wiping out several apps at once by deleting a folder. You can't delete full folders, only individual apps within them.

Updating Apps

App developers update their apps all the time, so you might want to check for those updates. Assuming Notification Center is set up to alert you to updates, the App Store icon on the Home screen will display the number of available updates. If you've turned this setting off, tap the App Store icon on the Home screen. At the bottom right of the App Store screen is an Updates icon that indicates the number of updates available in a red circle. Now proceed with these steps to update your apps:

1. **Tap the Updates icon to access the Updates screen (see Figure 5-25) and then tap any item you want to update.**

   To update all, tap the Update All button.

2. **On the app screen that appears, tap Update.**

   You may be asked to confirm that you want to update, or to enter your Apple ID password and then tap OK to proceed. You may also be asked to confirm that you are over a certain age or agree to terms and conditions; if so, scroll down the terms dialog and at the bottom, tap Agree.

In iOS 5, Apple introduced the capability to download multiple apps at once. If you choose more than one app to update instead of them downloading sequentially, all items will download simultaneously.

If you have an iCloud account and update an app on your iPad, it's also updated on any other Apple iOS devices automatically, and vice versa.

The Updates icon

Figure 5-25: Choose what you want to update here.

Chapter 6: Browsing the Web

In This Chapter

- ✓ Discovering Safari
- ✓ Creating and utilizing bookmarks
- ✓ Using Safari Reading List and Reader
- ✓ Saving web clips to the Home screen
- ✓ Adding an image to your photo library
- ✓ E-mailing a link to a website
- ✓ Making private browsing and cookie settings

Getting on the Internet with your iPad is easy, using its Wi-Fi or 3G capabilities. After you're online, the built-in browser, Safari, can take you all around the web. Safari will be familiar to you if you've used an Apple device before or used the browser on your Mac or PC. On iPad, you're actually using a hybrid of the mobile version of Safari also used on iPhone and iPod touch and the desktop Safari.

If you've never used Safari, this chapter helps you get up to speed quickly. In this chapter, you discover how to connect your iPad to the Internet and navigate among web pages using tabbed browsing. Along the way, you see how to place a bookmark for a favorite site or web clip on your Home screen. You can also view your browsing history, save online images to your Photo library, and e-mail a hotlink to a friend. You explore the Safari Reader and Safari Reading List features and find out how to keep yourself safer while online using private browsing. Finally, you review the simple steps involved in printing what you find online.

All-new design
Less in your hands.
More at your fingertips.

Exploring Safari

If you need to know how to connect to the Internet, see the preceding chapter. After you're connected, you're ready to browse with Safari.

Just in case you've never used Safari, here's a quick rundown of how it works on your iPad. It offers all the typical browser tools, but an important iPad twist is how you can use gestures on the touchscreen to manipulate pages and navigate the web.

Though Safari is a fine browser, you aren't limited to it. You can download other browsers to iPad, such as Atomic Web Browser and Duo Browser. Check out the App Store for the latest available browsers.

Try the following steps to get practice using Safari:

1. **After you're connected to a network, tap the Safari icon on the Home screen.**

   Safari opens, probably displaying the Apple iPad home page the first time you go online. (See Figure 6-1.)

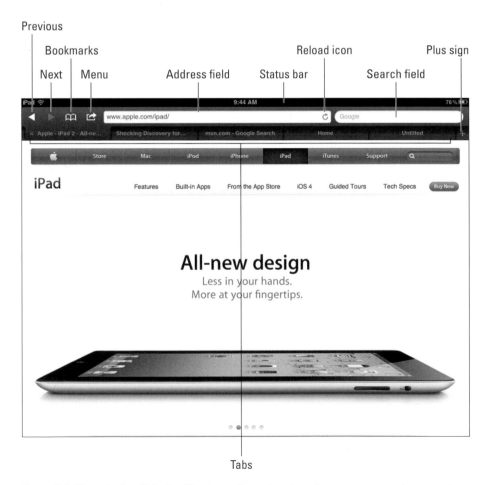

Figure 6-1: These tools will be familiar to you from almost any browser you may have used.

2. **Put two fingers together on the screen and swipe outward to enlarge the view, as shown in Figure 6-2.**

   Double-tap the screen with a single finger to restore the default screen size.

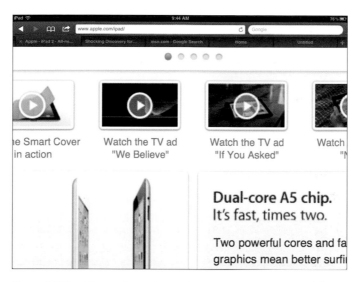

Figure 6-2: Double-tapping enlarges the screen so you can read the fine print.

3. **Put your finger on the screen and flick upward to scroll down the page.**

4. **To return to the top of the web page, put your finger on the screen and drag downward, or tap the Status bar at the top of the screen.**

Using the pinch method (see Book I, Chapter 2) to enlarge or reduce the size of a web page on your screen allows you to enlarge or reduce the screen to various sizes, giving you more flexibility and control than the double-tap method.

When you enlarge the display, you gain more control using two fingers to drag from left to right or from top to bottom on the screen. On a reduced display, one finger works fine for making these gestures.

Navigating among web pages

I expect that you have entered URLs and used the Next and Previous buttons in a browser to navigate around the web. However, the iPad's onscreen keyboard differs slightly from a standard keyboard, and it might help you to run through how you navigate with the mobile version of Safari.

Follow these steps for a bit of navigating practice:

1. **Tap in the Address field.**

   The onscreen keyboard appears, as shown in Figure 6-3.

Go key

Figure 6-3: This keyboard requires you do a few unique things to use numbers and symbols.

2. **To clear the field, press the Delete key on the keyboard. Enter a web address, using the .com key to make entry faster.**

   If you have no website in mind, go to this book's companion site, `www.ipadmadeclear.com`.

   By holding down the .com key, you get access to options like `.edu`, `.gov`, and `.net`.

3. **Tap the Go key on the keyboard (refer to Figure 6-3).**

   The website appears.

   • If, for some reason, a page doesn't display, tap the Reload icon on the end of the Address field.

   • If Safari is loading a web page and you change your mind about viewing the page, you can tap the Cancel icon (the *X*) that appears at the end of the Address field during this process to stop loading the page.

4. **Tap the Previous arrow to go backward to the last page Safari displayed.**

5. **Tap the Next arrow to go forward to the page you just came from by tapping Previous.**

6. **To follow a link to another web page, tap the link with your finger.**

   To view the destination web address of the link before you tap it, just touch and hold the link, and a menu appears that displays the address at the top, as shown in Figure 6-4.

The link's web address

Figure 6-4: You can open a link in a new page using this menu.

By default, AutoFill is turned on in iPad, causing entries you make in fields such as the address field to automatically display possible matching entries. You can turn off AutoFill by using iPad Settings.

You probably know that Apple doesn't support Flash, the technology that *lots* of sites use to play videos. That's because Steve Jobs considers Flash a poor technology, and who am I to disagree with him? You have a couple of options for getting content. There are some sites posting non-Flash versions of content, and you can search these out using the keywords *non-Flash movies.* You can stream content using a conversion app such as AirVideo or AirVideo Server on your Mac or PC. Or you can convert a Flash file to AVI or MPG movie format using your computer. To do this, you can download a free tool, such as one of these:

✔ **HandBrake:** www.handbrake.fr

✔ **swf>>avi:** www.avi-swf-convert.com

✔ **SWF to Video Scout:** http://tinyurl.com/28a4g7f

Using tabbed browsing

With iOS 5 comes *tabbed browsing*, a feature that allows you to have several websites open at once on separate tabs so you can move easily among those sites. You may have used tabbed browsing in other popular browsers such as the desktop version of Safari, Internet Explorer, or Mozilla Firefox. This is a welcome addition to Safari that's worth exploring.

To add a tab:

1. **With Safari open, tap the plus sign near the upper-right corner of the screen (refer to Figure 6-1).**

   The search field becomes active and a drop-down list and the onscreen keyboard appear. (See Figure 6-5.)

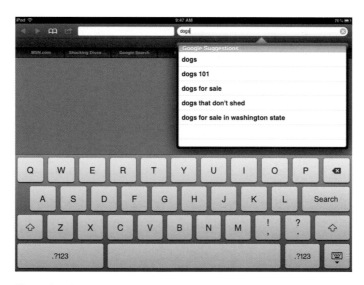

Figure 6-5: Search tools help you find online content using Safari.

2. **You can tap an item from a recent search, or tap in the search field and enter the name of a site to open.**

   The site opens on a new tab.

3. **You can now switch among open sites by tapping another tab.**

Using tabbed browsing, you can not only place a site on a tab but also place a search results screen on a tab. If you recently searched for something, those search results will be on your Recent Searches list. Also, if you're displaying a search results page when you tap the plus sign to add a tab, the first ten suggested sites in the results will be listed there for you to choose from.

Viewing browsing history

As you know, when you move around the web, your browser keeps a record of your browsing history. This record can be handy when you visit a site that you want to view again but you've forgotten its address. (We've all done it.) On your iPad, you use the Bookmarks menu to get to your history.

Follow these steps to browse your browsing history:

1. **With Safari open, tap the Bookmarks icon.**

2. **In the menu shown in Figure 6-6, tap History.**

Tap this option

Figure 6-6: In addition to bookmarks, this menu is your gateway to your browsing history.

3. **In the History list that appears (see Figure 6-7), tap a date if available and then tap a site to navigate to it.**

To clear the history, tap the Clear History button. (Refer to Figure 6-7.) This button is useful when you don't want your spouse or children to see where you've been browsing for birthday or holiday presents!

You can tap and hold the Previous button to quickly display a list of your browsing history.

Figure 6-7: Use your finger to scroll down to view more of this list.

Searching the web

If you don't know the address of the site you want to visit (or you want to do research on a topic or find information you need online), get acquainted with Safari's Search feature on iPad. By default, Safari uses the Google search engine.

1. **With Safari open, tap in the Search field (see Figure 6-8).**

   The onscreen keyboard appears.

2. **You can tap one of the suggested sites or enter a search word or phrase and then tap the Search key on your keyboard.**

3. **In the search results that are displayed, tap a link to visit that site.**

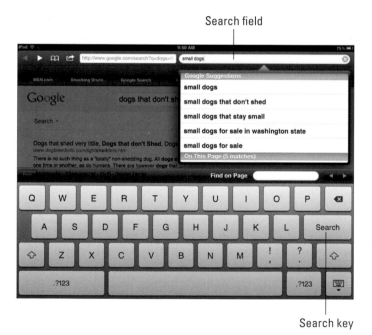

Figure 6-8: Use Search to locate a word or phrase on any site.

You can change your default search engine from Google to Bing or Yahoo! In iPad Settings, tap Safari and then tap Search Engine. Tap Yahoo! or Bing, and your default search engine changes.

 You can browse for specific items such as images, videos, or maps by tapping the corresponding link at the top of the Google results screen. Also, tap the More button in this list to see even more options to narrow your results, such as searching for books or YouTube videos on the subject.

Adding and Using Bookmarks

Bookmarks, which you have probably used in other browsers, are a way to save sites you visit often so that you can easily go to them again. Follow these steps to add bookmarks:

1. **With a site you want to bookmark displayed, tap the Menu icon.**

2. **On the menu that appears (see Figure 6-9), tap Add Bookmark.**

Tap this option

Figure 6-9: Choose to add a bookmark in this menu.

3. **In the Add Bookmark dialog shown in Figure 6-10, edit the name of the bookmark (if you want) by tapping the name of the site and using the onscreen keyboard to edit its name.**

4. **Tap the Save button.**

5. **To go to the bookmark, tap the Bookmarks icon.**

6. **On the Bookmarks menu that appears (see Figure 6-11), tap the bookmarked site you want to visit.**

Enter the name here

Figure 6-10: Give your bookmark a name that makes sense to you.

Tap a bookmarked site to visit it

Figure 6-11: Tap to go to a favorite bookmark.

If you want to sync your bookmarks on your iPad browser to your computer, connect your iPad to your computer and make sure that the Sync Safari Bookmarks setting on the Info tab is activated.

When you tap the Bookmarks button, you can use the Bookmarks Bar option to create folders to organize your bookmarks. First, turn on the Always Show Bookmarks Bar in iPad Settings for Safari. When you next add a bookmark, you can then choose, from the dialog that appears, to add the new bookmark to any folder by tapping the Bookmarks button.

Using Safari Reading List

Remember when you were in school and had lots of reading assignments to keep track of from all your classes? Well, after graduation, reading lists don't go away; whether staying up to date in your chosen field or just keeping up with the latest articles and information, being able to assemble a list of online reading can be a great help. The Safari Reading List provides a way to save links to content you want to read at a later time so you can easily visit them again.

To use Reading List, follow these steps:

1. **With a site you want to add to your Reading List displayed, tap the Menu icon.**

2. **On the menu that appears (refer to Figure 6-9), tap Add to Reading List.**

   The site is added to your list.

3. **To view your Reading List, tap the Bookmarks icon and tap Reading List.**

4. **On the Reading List that appears (see Figure 6-12), tap the content you want to revisit and resume reading.**

Figure 6-12: It's so easy to find where you left off reading with Safari Reading List.

If you want to see both the Reading List material you've read and that material you haven't read, tap the All tab in the Reading List pane. (Refer to Figure 6-12.) To see just the material you haven't read, use the Unread tab. Be aware, however, that with websites that change content frequently, the content you placed on your Reading List may not be available at a later date.

To save an image on a web page to your Reading List, tap and hold the image until a menu appears and then tap Add to Reading List. To delete an item, with the Reading List displayed swipe left or right, and a Delete button appears. Tap it to delete the item from Reading List.

Utilizing Safari Reader

Reading content on the web isn't always user friendly. The ads, sidebars, and various distractions can take away from your reading experience. Happily, the Safari Reader feature now gives you an e-reader type of experience right within your browser, removing other stories and links as well as those distracting advertisements.

1. **When you're on a site where you're reading content such as an article, Safari displays a Reader button on the right side of the address field (see Figure 6-13). Tap the Reader button.**

   The content appears in a reader format. (See Figure 6-14.)

   Reader button

   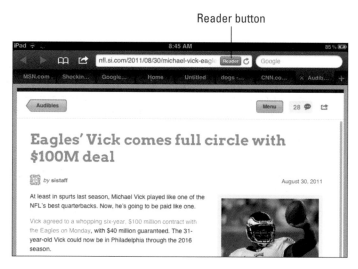

   Figure 6-13: The Reader button appears when the feature is available for the site you're viewing.

2. **Scroll down the page.**

   The entire content is contained in this one long page.

3. **When you finish reading the material, just tap the Previous button to go back to its source.**

To enlarge the text in the Reader, tap the large *A* in the top-left corner. (Refer to Figure 6-14.)

If there's a video contained in an article you're perusing in Reader, it will still appear in Reader with the standard play button. Tap the button, and the video plays right within Reader.

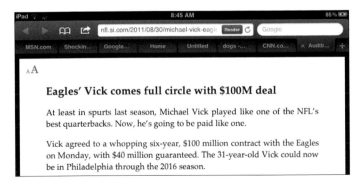

Figure 6-14: At last . . . an easy-on-the-eyes reading experience on the web!

Adding Web Clips to the Home Screen

The web clips feature allows you to save a website as an icon on your Home screen so that you can go to the site at any time with one tap. You can then reorganize those icons just as you can reorganize apps icons. (See Book I, Chapter 2 for information on organizing apps on Home screens.)

Here are the steps for adding web clips:

1. **With Safari open and displaying the site you want to add, tap the Menu icon.**

2. **On the menu that appears (see Figure 6-15), tap Add to Home Screen.**

Tap this option

Figure 6-15: Set up a web clip to go to a favorite site from your Home screen.

3. **In the Add to Home dialog that appears (see Figure 6-16), you can edit the name of the site to be more descriptive (if you like) by tapping the name of the site and using the onscreen keyboard to edit its name.**

Edit the name here

Figure 6-16: Give your web clip a descriptive name or use the site's URL.

4. **Tap the Add button.**

The shortcut to the site is added to your Home screen.

You can have up to 11 Home screens on your iPad to accommodate all the web clips and apps you download (though there is a limit to how many will fit). You can also use folders to organize your web clips and save space on your Home screens. If you want to delete an item from your Home screen for any reason, press and hold the icon on the Home screen until all items on the screen start to jiggle and Delete badges appear on all items except prein-stalled apps. Tap the Delete button on the item you want to delete, and it's gone. (To get rid of the jiggle, tap the Home button again.)

Saving an Image to Your Photo Library

Have you found a photo you like online? Maybe your BF's Facebook image, or a picture of your upcoming vacation spot? You can easily save images you find online to the iPad Photos app library. Here's how:

1. **Display a web page that contains an image you want to copy.**

2. **Press and hold the image.**

The menu in Figure 6-17 appears.

Tap this option

Figure 6-17: Quickly saving an online image into Photos.

3. **Tap the Save Image option (refer to Figure 6-17).**

   The image is saved to your Photos library.

Be careful about copying images from the Internet and using them for business or promotional activities. Most images are copyrighted, and you may be violating that copyright if you use an image in (say) a brochure for your association or a flyer for your community group. Note that some search engines offer the option of browsing only for images that aren't copyrighted.

Sending a Link

If you find a great site that you want to share, you can do so easily by sending a link in an e-mail. Follow these steps to do so:

1. **With Safari open and the site you want to share displayed, tap the Menu icon.**

2. **On the menu that appears (refer to Figure 6-15), tap Mail Link to This Page.**

3. **In the message form that appears (see Figure 6-18), enter a recipient's e-mail address, a subject, and your message.**

Figure 6-18: Use this simple e-mail form to send an image and message.

4. **Tap Send.**

    The e-mail goes on its way.

 The e-mail is sent from the default e-mail account you have set up on iPad. For more about setting up an e-mail account, see Book I, Chapter 7.

 When entering text in any online form, such as an e-mail message or search box, you can take advantage of Safari's AutoFill feature. Turn this on in the Safari area of iPad's Settings. Safari can then use information from iPad's Contacts app and remember names and passwords you've entered before to offer options for completing text entries as you type.

 To tweet the link using your Twitter account, in Step 2 of this task choose Tweet, enter your tweet message in the form that appears, and then tap Send. For more about using Twitter with iPad, see Book II, Chapter 5.

Making Private Browsing and Cookie Settings

Apple has provided some privacy settings for Safari that you should consider using. Private Browsing automatically removes items from the download list, stops Safari from letting AutoFill save information used to complete your entries in the search or address fields as you type, and doesn't save some browsing history information. These features can keep your online activities more private. The Accept Cookies setting allows you to stop the downloading of *cookies* (small files that document your browsing history so you can be recognized the next time you go to or move within a site) to your iPad.

You can control both settings by choosing Safari in the Settings window. Tap to turn Private Browsing on or off. (See Figure 6-19.) Tap the arrow on Accept Cookies and choose to never save cookies, always save cookies, or save cookies only from visited sites.

Make cookies settings here

Turn on Private Browsing

Figure 6-19: Protect your private information and activities from prying eyes with these settings.

You can also use those two settings to clear your browsing history, saved cookies, and other data manually. (Refer to Figure 6-19.)

Printing from Safari

If you have a wireless printer that supports Apple's AirPrint technology (Hewlett-Packard is the only manufacturer that makes these at present), you can print web content using a wireless connection. Here's how:

1. **With Safari open and the site you want to print displayed, tap the Menu icon.**

2. **On the menu that appears, tap Print.**

3. **In the Printer Options dialog that appears (see Figure 6-20), tap Select Printer.**

Figure 6-20: Print directly from your iPad if you have a compatible wireless printer.

4. **In the list of printers that appears, tap the name of your wireless printer.**

5. **Tap either the plus or minus button in the Copy field to adjust the number of copies to print.**

6. **Tap Print to print the displayed page.**

If you don't have an AirPrint–compatible wireless printer or don't wish to use an app to help you print wirelessly, just e-mail a link to the web page to yourself, open the link on your computer, and print from there.

The apps Printopia and AirPrint Activator 2 make any shared or network printer on your home network visible to your iPad. Printopia has more features, but is more expensive, whereas AirPrint Activator is free.

Chapter 7: Working with E-mail in Mail

In This Chapter

✔ Adding a Gmail, Yahoo!, or AOL account

✔ Setting up a POP3 e-mail account

✔ Opening Mail and reading messages

✔ Formatting e-mail

✔ Searching e-mail

✔ Deleting an e-mail

✔ Organizing e-mail

*W*hat use would an iPad be if you couldn't stay in touch with your friends online? You can access an existing e-mail account using the handy Mail app supplied with your iPad, or you can sign into your e-mail account using the Safari browser. Using Mail involves adding an existing e-mail account using iPad Settings. Then you can use Mail to write, format, retrieve, and forward messages from that account.

Mail offers the capability to mark the messages you've read, delete messages, and organize your messages in a small set of folders, as well as use a handy search feature. In this chapter, you find out about Mail and its various features.

If you're wondering about IM (instant messaging) and iPad, check out Book II, Chapter 5 to discover the new IM app, Messages, newly available with iOS 5.

Adding a Gmail, Yahoo!, or AOL Account

To use the Mail app to access e-mail on iPad, you first have to make settings for an existing e-mail account on your iPad. You can add one or more e-mail accounts using iPad Settings, including any e-mail account that you've associated with an iCloud account. If you set up multiple accounts, you can then switch between accounts by tapping an account name in the upper-left corner of the displayed inbox, and then tapping Accounts and choosing which account to display. Or you can use the consolidated inbox and check your mail from all active accounts on one page.

If you have a Gmail, Yahoo!, Windows Live Hotmail, or AOL account, iPad pretty much automates the setup. Here are the steps to get you going with any of these e-mail providers:

1. **Tap the Settings icon on the Home screen.**

2. **In the Settings dialog, tap Mail, Contacts, Calendars.**

   The settings shown in Figure 7-1 appear.

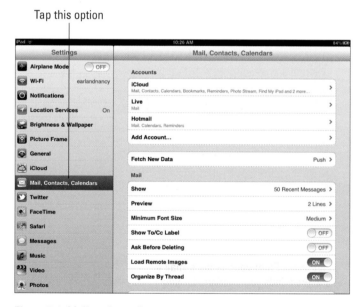

Figure 7-1: Mail settings allow you to set up multiple e-mail accounts.

3. **Tap Add Account.**

   The options shown in Figure 7-2 appear.

4. **Tap iCloud, Gmail, Yahoo!, AOL, or Windows Live Hotmail and then enter your account information in the form that appears (see Figure 7-3).**

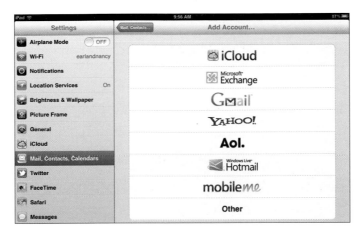

Figure 7-2: Choosing built-in e-mail providers is a quick way to get set up, if you have an account with one.

Enter your account info

Figure 7-3: Enter your name, e-mail address, and password, and iPad finds your settings for you.

5. **After iPad takes a moment to verify your account information, you can tap any On/Off button to have Mail, Contacts, Calendars, or Reminders from that account synced with iPad.**

6. **When you're done, tap Save.**

   The account is saved, and you can now open it using Mail.

If you have a Microsoft Exchange or MobileMe account, you can also sync to your computer to exchange contact and calendar information as well as e-mail. See the iPad User Guide for more about these options. See Book III, Chapter 1, for more about working with Microsoft Exchange accounts.

Setting Up a POP3 E-mail Account

You can also set up most e-mail accounts, such as those available through Earthlink or a cable provider, by obtaining the host name from the provider. To set up an existing account with a provider other than Gmail, Yahoo!, Windows Live Hotmail, or AOL, you may need to enter the account settings yourself.

Follow these steps to set up an IMAP or POP3 account:

1. **Tap the Settings icon on the Home screen.**
2. **In Settings, tap Mail, Contacts, Calendars and then tap Add Account.**
3. **In the screen that appears (refer to Figure 7-2), tap Other.**
4. **In the screen that appears (see Figure 7-4), tap Add Mail Account.**

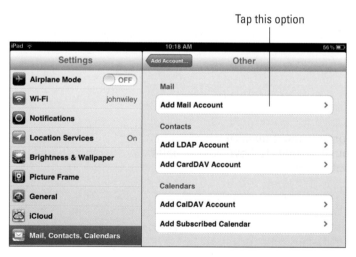

Figure 7-4: Proceed by choosing to add an e-mail account on this screen.

5. **In the form that appears, enter your name, the account Address, Password, and Description, and tap Next.**

iPad takes a moment to verify your account and then returns you to the Mail, Contacts, Calendars page with your new account displayed.

iPad will probably add the outgoing mail server information for you, but if it doesn't, tap SMTP and enter this information.

6. **To make sure the Account field is set to On, under Settings tap Mail, Contacts, Calendars and tap the account. In the dialog that appears, tap the On/Off button and then tap Done to save the setting.**

You can now access the account through Mail.

You can have more than one account set to On for receiving e-mail, tap the account name in Settings. When you do, you can then open different accounts to view their inboxes from within the Mail app. If you don't want a particular account's e-mails to be downloaded, you can turn any active e-mail account off by opening it in Settings and tapping the On/Off button.

If you turn on Calendars in the Mail account settings, any information you've put into your calendar in that e-mail account will be brought over into the Calendar app on your iPad and reflected in the Notification Center (discussed in more detail in Book V, Chapter 4).

Opening Mail and Reading Messages

The whole point of e-mail is to send and receive messages. Mail offers a pretty simple interface for reading your e-mail. It displays an open message and a pane that you can use to show inbox contents or change to a different folder. In landscape orientation, the Mailboxes/Inbox pane is always displayed, but in portrait orientation, you display it by tapping the Inbox button.

When you tap the Mail app to open it, it automatically heads out and checks for any new e-mail. (If you use Microsoft Exchange or iCloud, you can turn on push settings to have your e-mail host send messages to your iPad automatically.)

Here are some common actions in Mail:

✔ To follow a link in a message, you simply tap it. Note that tapping web links opens them in Safari, and tapping address links opens the Maps app with a map to that address displayed.

✔ To open an attachment, tap it, and it downloads and opens in the appropriate iPad app or viewer.

✔ To open a meeting invitation, tap the meeting icon (what it looks like depends on the originating application; for example, Windows Live Hotmail uses a little calendar symbol).

iPad supports many common file types — including those that run on multiple platforms, such as PDF and text; those available on Macs, including iWork Pages and Numbers; those familiar to Windows users (though also available in Mac versions), including Microsoft Word and Excel; as well as most common graphics and audio file formats.

 When your iPad gets an e-mail, it alerts you with a chime. If those e-mail–received alerts are driving you nuts, you can go to Settings and under General, Sounds, use the slider to lower the volume or tap the On/Off button to turn off the chimes.

These steps take you through the simple process of using Mail to open and read e-mails if you have a single e-mail account set up on iPad:

1. **Tap the Mail app icon located in the Dock on the Home screen (see Figure 7-5), which displays the number of unread e-mails in your inbox in a red circle.**

Tap this icon

Figure 7-5: Without having to open Mail, you can see how many unread messages you have.

2. **If you have only one e-mail account set up on your iPad, a list of messages displays (see Figure 7-6); if the list doesn't display, tap the button to the left of the word *Inbox* (refer to Figure 7-6) to display a list of inboxes. Tap the inbox whose contents you want to display.**

Tap here to display the list of Inboxes   List of messages

Figure 7-6: Open your Inbox and view its contents.

Note that in landscape orientation, the Mailboxes/Inbox panel is always displayed; in portrait orientation, you display it by clicking the button to the left of the word *Inbox*.

3. **Tap a message to read it.**

    The message opens, as shown in Figure 7-7.

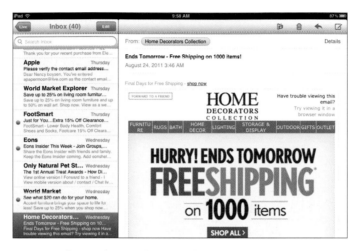

Figure 7-7: Open your e-mail and read it.

4. **If you need to scroll to see the entire message, just place your finger on the screen and flick upward to scroll down.**

    You can also swipe right while reading a message to open the Inbox list of messages, and then swipe left to hide the list.

If you have multiple e-mail accounts set up, you can choose which inbox to display. From the inbox that appears when you open Mail, tap the Back button to view the list of your mailboxes. (See Figure 7-8.)

With several accounts set up, in addition to each account listed on the Mailboxes screen, there's an All Inboxes item listed. Tapping this takes you to a consolidated Inbox containing all messages from all accounts in one place.

You can tap the Hide button (top-right corner of a message) to hide the address details (the To field) so more of the message appears on your screen. To reveal the field again, tap the Details button (which becomes the Hide button when details are displayed).

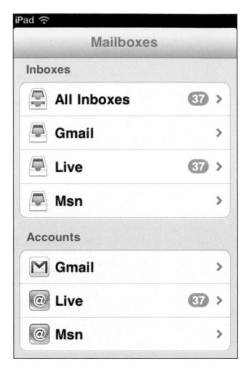

Figure 7-8: Mailboxes for various accounts and the consolidated Inbox are listed here.

E-mail messages you haven't read are marked with a blue circle in your inbox. After you read a message, the blue circle disappears. If you like, you can mark a read message as unread. This can help remind you to read it again later. With a message open and details about it displayed, tap the Mark link on the right side and then tap Mark as Unread. To flag a message — which places a little flag next to it in your inbox, helping you to spot items of more importance or to read again — tap Mark and then tap Flag.

You can use gestures such as double-tapping and pinching to reduce or enlarge an open e-mail.

Replying to or forwarding e-mail

Replying to or forwarding e-mails is pretty darn easy with iPad as well. In fact, there's a handy button for replying or forwarding. There's also a Print command on this menu to make printing your e-mails to a compatible wireless printer easy.

One thing you need to know right now: You can't attach anything to e-mail messages when you create, reply to, or forward them. Instead, you can use features in apps such as Photos, Contacts, Notes, iWork Pages, and Maps to share individual documents via e-mail.

Here's how to use the simple Reply/Forward functions in iPad:

1. **With an e-mail message open (see the previous section), tap the Reply/ Forward/Print button shown in Figure 7-9.**

Tap the Reply/Forward/Print button

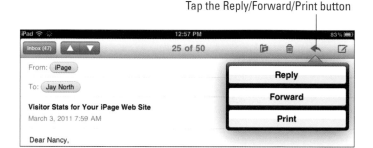

Figure 7-9: The Reply/Forward/Print button sports a left-pointing arrow.

2. **Now for the simple part. Do one of the following:**

   • *Tap Reply to respond to the message sender.* The reply message form shown in Figure 7-10 appears. Tap in the message body and jot down your inspired thoughts. If the message has more than one recipient, a Reply to All option is included on the menu.

   • *Tap Forward to send the message to somebody else.* If the e-mail has an attachment, you can choose Include or Don't Include in the dialog that appears. The form in Figure 7-11 then appears. Enter a recipient in the To field, and then tap in the message body and enter a message.

   To find out how to print an e-mail, see "Printing E-mails," later in this chapter.

3. **Tap Send.**

   The message goes on its way.

If you want to copy an address from the To field to the Cc/Bcc field, tap and hold the address and drag it to the other field.

Tap here to enter a reply

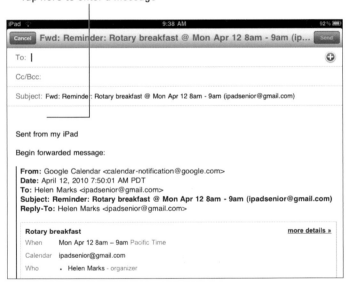

Figure 7-10: What you reply is up to you!

Tap here to enter a message

Figure 7-11: When you forward a message, all previous contents are included.

Although you can include whether to keep original attachments when *forwarding* an e-mail, any attachments to the original e-mail can't be included in a *reply*.

Creating and sending a new message

You're probably an old pro at creating and sending e-mail messages, but it's worth a quick trip through iPad's Mail feature and its approach to writing an e-mail using the onscreen keyboard.

Note that, by default, your e-mails have a signature that says, "Sent from my iPad." This will definitely impress your geekiest friends, but if you want to change it to something a little more useful, just go to Settings. In the Mail settings, choose Signature. You can then enter any signature text you want.

Follow these steps to create and send e-mail:

1. **With Mail open, tap the New Message icon.**

   A blank message form (see Figure 7-12) appears.

Figure 7-12: A very basic e-mail message form.

2. **Enter a recipient's address in the To field.**

   If you have saved addresses in Contacts, tap the plus symbol in an address field to choose an addressee from the Contacts list.

3. **If you want to copy other people on the message, enter other addresses in the Cc/Bcc field.**

   When you tap the Cc/Bcc field, both Cc and Bcc fields are displayed.

4. **Enter a subject for the message in the Subject field.**

5. **Tap in the message body and type your message.**

6. **Tap (you guessed it) Send.**

Depending on your e-mail provider, Mail may keep a copy of all deleted messages for a time in a Trash folder. To view deleted messages, go to the list of all mailboxes. Tap the account name in the Accounts list, and a list of folders appears. Tap the Trash folder, and all deleted messages are displayed.

Want to shout at somebody in an e-mail (not, of course, a practice I advocate)? You can activate Caps Lock when using the onscreen keyboard on your iPad by double-tapping either Shift key. To turn Caps Lock off, tap either Shift key once. To use this functionality, first be sure to use the General, Keyboard settings to enable Caps Lock.

Formatting E-mail

A new feature that comes with iOS 5 is the capability to apply formatting to e-mail text. You can use bold, underline, and italic formats, and indent text using the Quote Level feature.

1. **Tap the text and choose Select or Select All to select a single word or all the words in the e-mail.**

   Note that if you select a single word, handles appear that you can drag to add adjacent words to your selection.

2. **Tap the arrow at the far end of the toolbar that appears.**

3. **To apply Bold, Italic, or Underline formatting, tap the BIU button (see Figure 7-13).**

Figure 7-13: Use BIU to add emphasis or standard styles such as italicized book titles.

4. **In the toolbar that appears (see Figure 7-14) tap Bold, Italics, or Underline to apply formatting.**

Make your selection here

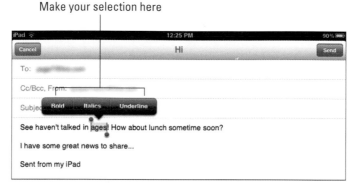

Figure 7-14: Choose the style that works for your message.

5. **To change the indent level, tap at the beginning of a line and then tap the arrow at the far end of the toolbar.**

6. **In the toolbar that appears, tap Quote Level.**

7. **Tap Increase to indent the text or Decrease to move indented text farther toward the left margin.**

To change the minimum size of text in e-mails, use the iPad Settings. Tap Mail, Contacts, Calendars, and then tap the Minimum Font Size setting. Choose from Small, Medium, Large, Extra Large, and Giant in the list that appears.

Searching E-mail

I'm sure you've never mislaid an e-mail, but most of the rest of us do it all the time. Say you want to find all messages from a certain person or with a certain word in the Subject field. You can use Mail's handy Search feature to find that e-mail. You can search To, From, and Subject fields.

Follow these steps to practice using Mail's Search feature:

1. **With Mail open, tap the Inbox button.**

2. **In the Inbox, tap in the Search field.**

   The onscreen keyboard appears.

3. Enter a search term or name as shown in Figure 7-15.

Enter a search term here   Search results

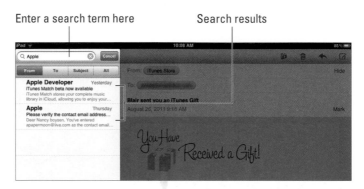

Figure 7-15: Tapping in the Search Inbox field opens the onscreen keyboard.

4. Tap the From, To, or Subject tab to view messages that contain the search term in one of those fields, or tap the All tab to see messages in which any of these three fields contains the term.

Matching e-mails are listed in the results, as shown in Figure 7-16.

 To start a new search or go back to the full inbox, tap the Delete key in the upper-right corner of the onscreen keyboard to delete the term, or tap the Cancel button.

Search results

Figure 7-16: Any e-mail that contains your search term in the To, From, or Subject field is listed.

If you have a mail account set up to download messages to your device instead of accessing them from the mail server, you can use Mail to search the entire content of the messages in that account.

Printing E-mails

As of iOS version 4.2, iPad has had native printing capabilities that can be used by certain apps, including Mail. You need an AirPrint-compatible wireless printer setup to use this feature. For more about other options for printing from your iPad, see Book V, Chapter 1.

With an e-mail message open, follow these steps to print:

1. **Tap the Reply/Forward/Print button and then tap Print (refer to Figure 7-9).**

2. **In the Printer Options dialog that appears (if you haven't used this feature with your printer before), tap Select Printer.**

   iPad searches for any available wireless printers.

3. **Tap your printer to select it.**

4. **Tap Printer Options to return to the Printer Options dialog and use the + or – buttons in the Copies field to adjust the number of copies.**

5. **Tap Print.**

   Your print job goes on its way.

Deleting an E-mail

I have friends who never delete e-mails, but that, frankly, drives me nuts. When you no longer want an e-mail cluttering up your inbox, you can delete it. When you delete an e-mail on your iPad, it's gone from your inbox, including the inbox you access through your mobile phone or computer e-mail setup. However, for a time, you can retrieve it if your e-mail provider offers a Trash folder for your e-mail account and if the provider's settings don't cause e-mails to be deleted from their server on download.

Here's how to delete those e-mails you no longer want:

1. **With the inbox displayed, tap the Edit button.**

   Circular check boxes are displayed to the left of each message. (See Figure 7-17.)

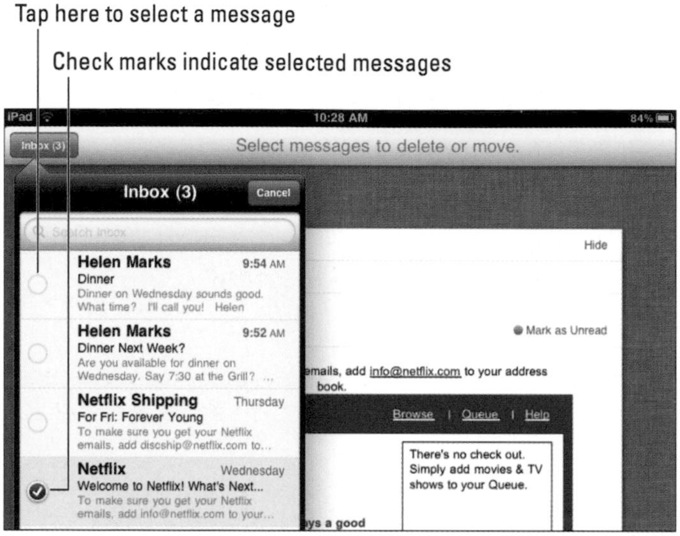

Tap here to select a message

Check marks indicate selected messages

Figure 7-17: Delete several messages at once using the Delete feature.

2. **Tap the circle next to the message you want to delete.**

You can tap multiple items if you have several e-mails to delete. Messages marked for deletion show a check mark displayed in the circular check box. (Refer to Figure 7-17).

3. **Tap the Delete button.**

The message(s) is moved to the Trash folder.

You can also delete an open e-mail by tapping the trashcan icon in the tool-bar that runs across the top of Mail or swiping left or right on a message displayed in an inbox and tapping the Delete button that appears.

Organizing E-mail

I won't kid you; the message-management features in Mail aren't super-robust. In most email accounts (iCloud, Mobile, Me, and Gmail being the exceptions) you can't create your own folders, though I'm hoping that will be a feature added to the next version of iPad. Here's what you can do: Depending on your e-mail provider, you may be able to move messages into any of a few predefined folders in Mail. With the folder containing the message you want to move (for example, the Trash or Inbox if you have a

Windows Live Hotmail account) displayed, tap the Edit button. Circular check boxes are displayed to the left of each message. (Refer to Figure 7-17.)

Now follow these steps to move any message into another folder:

1. **Tap the circle next to the message you want to move.**

2. **Tap the Move button.**

3. **In the Mailboxes list that appears (see Figure 7-18), tap the folder where you'd like to store the message.**

   The message is moved.

If you get a junk e-mail, you might want to move it to the Spam or Junk E-mail folder. Once you do, any future mail from that same sender is automatically placed in that folder.

Figure 7-18: There aren't many folders here, but you'll probably make do.

If you have an e-mail open, you can move it to a folder by tapping the Folder icon on the toolbar that runs along the top. The Mailboxes list displays; tap a folder to move the message.

Chapter 8: Managing iPad Settings

In This Chapter

↙ **Setting brightness and changing the wallpaper**

↙ **Managing Picture Frame settings**

↙ **Controlling general settings**

↙ **Setting up Notifications**

↙ **Managing iCloud**

↙ **Getting an overview of apps settings**

*i*Pad Settings is a control center for the device, offering settings that let you adjust things like the screen brightness and wallpaper, sound volume, and security features. You can also set up e-mail accounts (which I tell you about in the preceding chapter) and control how the Calendar and Contacts apps manage their respective details. Finally, there are settings for each of the individual pre-installed apps, as well as many apps designed for the iPad that you've downloaded to your device.

In this chapter, you get some highlights of the settings you're likely to need most often, and advice for how to use them.

TIP

You can control the Apple Push Notification Service, used to push alerts at your Apple device, via the Notifications item in Settings. This lets you control the alerts sent to you. You can turn alerts on and off, for example, which can save you battery life. You can also control alerts in a specific app's settings.

Making Brightness and Wallpaper Settings

You might as well set up the visual side of iPad first so your interaction with the device is easy on the eyes and battery power. There are two such settings that fall together as one category in the Settings window: Brightness & Wallpaper.

Setting brightness

Especially when using iPad as an e-book reader, you may find a little less brightness in the display reduces strain on your eyes. Also, reducing the brightness can save a little on your iPad's battery life.

To modify the brightness setting, follow these steps:

1. **To begin, tap the Settings icon on the Home screen.**

2. **In the Settings dialog shown in Figure 8-1, tap Brightness & Wallpaper.**

Tap this option...   then adjust brightness

Figure 8-1: Brightness and wallpaper settings are combined in one dialog.

3. **To control brightness manually, tap the Auto-Brightness On/Off button (refer to Figure 8-1) to turn it off.**

4. **Tap and drag the Brightness slider to the right to make the screen brighter, or to the left to make it dimmer.**

5. **Tap the Home button to close the Settings dialog.**

If glare from the screen is a problem for you, consider getting a screen protector. This thin film not only protects your screen from damage, but can also reduce glare. These are available from a wide variety of sources (just search for *iPad screen protector*) and cost about $2 each.

In the iBooks app, you can set a sepia tone for the page, which might be easier on your eyes. See Book II, Chapter 7 for more about using iBooks.

Changing the wallpaper

Just as your desktop computer or laptop has the ability to display a pretty picture or pattern as a desktop background called a *wallpaper,* your iPad can display an image on the Home screen and another picture that displays when your iPad is locked.

The picture of water drops that's the default iPad image may be pretty, but it may not be the background that's best for you. Choosing different wallpaper may help you to see all the icons on your Home screen, or just allow you to display an image that appeals to your artistic sensibilities.

To change the wallpaper, do this:

1. **Tap the Settings icon on the Home screen, and then, in the Settings dialog, tap Brightness & Wallpaper.**

2. **In the Brightness & Wallpaper settings that appear, tap the arrow to the right of the iPad images displayed in the Wallpaper section.**

3. **In the pane that appears, tap Wallpaper to display all the provided wallpaper images.**

   You can also use your own picture for your wallpaper. Instead of choosing Wallpaper, tap Camera Roll or choose a photo library to browse your saved photos, select the picture you want to assign, and then resume with Step 5.

4. **In the Wallpaper dialog (see Figure 8-2), tap a wallpaper image.**

   A preview of that wallpaper appears onscreen.

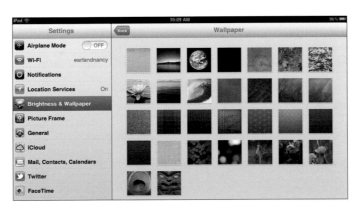

Figure 8-2: Choose from various built-in wallpapers.

5. **Tap Set Lock Screen (the screen that appears when you lock the iPad by tapping the power button), Set Home Screen (to use as the wallpaper), or Set Both.**

6. **Tap the Home button.**

You return to your Home screen with the new wallpaper set as the background.

Controlling the Picture Frame

The *Picture Frame* is a feature of iPad that allows you to play a slideshow of images from the Lock screen. When the Lock screen is displayed, you just tap the little flower-like icon in the bottom-right corner to start the show. It's a great way to show a presentation to a customer or dazzle somebody with the pictures from -your latest vacation.

To turn on Picture Frame and select the images it displays, follow these steps:

1. **Tap the Settings icon on the Home screen.**

2. **From the Settings dialog, tap Picture Frame.**

The settings shown in Figure 8-3 appear.

Tap this option

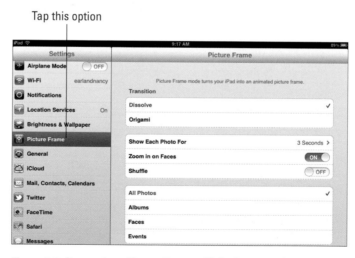

Figure 8-3: Choose how Picture Frame will display your pictures here.

3. **Tap either Dissolve or Origami to choose a transition style.**

    • *Dissolve:* Has one picture fade away, and another replaces it.

    • *Origami:* Displays several pictures on the screen and folds them together in an interesting way to change the picture display.

4. **Tap the Show Each Photo For feature to choose a time increment.**

    You can set this for 2, 3, 5, 10, or 20 seconds.

5. **Tap the Zoom in on Faces feature to have iPad zoom in on faces that appear in images.**

    This mode allows iPad to work with iPhoto-captured images on which you have used your computer's photo-imaging software facial recognition feature.

6. **Tap Shuffle to move randomly among the pictures in your library.**

    Without shuffle, Picture Frame moves through the pictures in sequence.

7. **Tap All Photos, Albums, Faces, or Events to choose which photos to display.**

    If you tap Albums, all the albums in Photos appear in a list, and you can tap to select or deselect the ones you want to include. If you tap Faces, only photos showing people's faces are displayed. If you tap Events, photos are listed by date.

8. **From the Lock screen, you can now tap the pretty flower icon and watch your slideshow play back in Picture Frame.**

Note that if you enable Passcode Lock to allow your iPad to be turned on only when you enter a passcode (see the "Handling security" section, later in this chapter, for more about this), you can choose to enable or disable the Picture Frame.

To pause a slideshow, just tap the screen. Tap it again to resume. To stop the show, drag the slider, which unlocks iPad.

Managing General Settings

A great many of the iPad settings are tucked into the General category. These include sounds, network, security, and settings for things like date and time, keyboard, and accessibility.

Here's a rundown of settings you'll find tucked under the General category in Settings.

Sounds

In this category, you can do two things: Adjust the volume level for all apps on your iPad and modify whether system sounds play for events such as new e-mail, calendar alerts, and keyboard clicks.

Adjusting the volume

Though individual applications such as Music and Videos have their own volume settings, you can set your iPad system volume as well to control the level of system sounds and sounds in apps that don't have their own volume control. This system setting is the max against which Music volume settings work; if you set volume to 80% here, for example, Music's 100% volume setting will actually be the maximum system volume, or 80%.

To adjust the system volume from the Settings dialog, in General settings, tap Sounds. In the Sounds dialog that appears (see Figure 8-4), tap and drag the slider to the right to increase the volume, or to the left to lower it.

Adjust iPad volume here

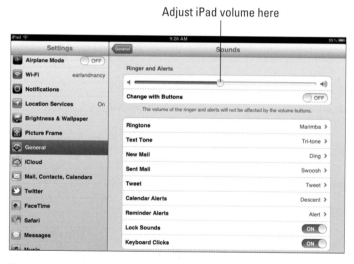

Figure 8-4: Use this familiar volume slider to adjust your system's volume.

Under General settings, make a choice from the Use Side Switch To settings to set the side switch on your iPad to mute all sounds. If you prefer to use that switch to lock screen rotation, another way to mute your iPad is to hold down the volume switch (below the side switch on the top-right corner of the device) until the sound is effectively off. This method assumes you have set this switch to control volume.

Turning system sounds on and off

In my experience, people are either big fans or big haters of system sounds on computers. You know, that annoying bleep you get when a new e-mail arrives or whatever? iPad also makes sounds when certain events occur, if you want it to. You can turn on and off the following system sounds:

- Ringtone
- Text Tone
- New Mail
- Sent Mail
- Tweet
- Calendar Alerts
- Reminder Alerts
- Lock Sounds
- Keyboard Clicks

To turn any of these off or on, from the Settings dialog, tap General, and then tap Sounds and use the On/Off feature for any of these sounds.

Making network and Bluetooth settings

There are a few settings you can make for your networks and Bluetooth under the General settings: ones for virtual private networks (VPNs), ones for Wi-Fi networks, and finally, settings for 3G networks.

You may have read in the news that your iPad and iPhone save a record of your every move. If you don't like that idea, plug your iPad or iPhone into your computer and, when iTunes opens, click on your device. Then, with the Summary tab selected, click the Encrypt iPhone/iPad Backup option. Apple can't find you anymore!

Another setting you can make in Settings is to turn Location Services on or off. Turning this on lets apps like Maps find your current physical location. If you turn this feature off and an app needs Location Services to function, it will prompt you to turn it on.

If you want to have iTunes use a feature called Wi-Fi Sync to sync to your iPad over a Wi-Fi network without having to plug a cable into your iPad and computer, tap the iTunes Wi-Fi Sync item under General settings and then tap Sync Now.

Setting up a VPN

A *virtual private network* (VPN) allows you to access a private network, such as one at your office, over the Internet. A VPN lets you make such a connection securely, and your iPad allows you to make settings for activating your connection.

In Settings you can do two things: turn VPN on or off, and configure a VPN network. In this chapter, I handle the on/off task only, as configuring a VPN network is covered elsewhere.

For more about connecting to your company network remotely and configuring a VPN, see Book III, Chapter 1.

To turn VPN on, follow these steps:

1. **Tap the Settings icon on the Home screen.**

2. **Tap General and then tap Network.**

3. **Tap VPN, and in the following dialog (see Figure 8-5), tap the Off button till it reads On.**

   Note that if you haven't yet configured your VPN, an Add Configuration dialog appears. See Book III, Chapter 1, for more about configuring a VPN connection.

Figure 8-5: Turn your VPN connection on from this dialog.

Making Wi-Fi settings

The Wi-Fi settings include simply turning Wi-Fi on or off, choosing which network to connect to, and activating a feature that joins recognized networks automatically.

To make Wi-Fi settings, follow these steps:

1. **Tap the Settings icon on the Home screen.**

2. **Tap General and then tap Network.**

3. **Tap Wi-Fi.**

    You see the settings shown in Figure 8-6. Here you can do the following:

    *   *Tap the Off button and slide it to turn Wi-Fi on or off.*

    *   *Tap the arrow on a listed network to see its details, as shown in Figure 8-7.* Because you are connecting with a network set up on another device, you can't edit this information from your iPad.

    *   *Tap the Ask to Join Networks button and slide it to turn this feature on or off.* If you turn it off, iPad won't join available networks automatically.

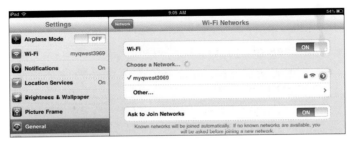

Figure 8-6: Get Wi-Fi set up for easy connections.

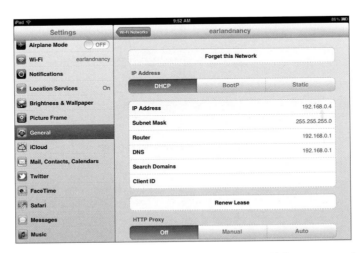

Figure 8-7: These settings come from the device on which your network has been set up.

If you have the Ask to Join Networks feature turned on and there are no known networks out there, iPad will ask you whether you want to join any new networks that surface.

Going 3G

Let's not forget 3G. If you have a 3G iPad, you can make some settings for your 3G connections by tapping the Settings icon and then tapping Cellular Data. The 3G connection settings include:

- **Turning a data network on or off:** If you don't want to connect to your data provider, turn this setting off.

- **Turning data roaming on or off:** If you don't want to allow your iPad to use roaming signals, which might cost you more, turn this one off.

- **Viewing your account information:** You can both view and change your 3G account information from your iPad.

- **Adding a SIM PIN:** To protect the data on your iPad's micro-SIM card, you might want to add a PIN to it. If somebody doesn't have the PIN, the SIM card stays locked so nobody can hack it to get data like your Contacts information.

Note that you can also use Airplane mode settings to turn your Wi-Fi and Bluetooth signals off when in flight, and quickly turn them back on again when you're safely on terra firma.

Handling security

Because you are likely to take your iPad on the road on a regular basis, it's a good idea to consider a few security features. Some save battery life and protect your data or access to certain apps.

Security settings involve three features, which you access through the General settings:

- **Auto-Lock:** Turns your display off to save battery power. You can set the amount of time you'd like to expire before Auto-Lock locks your iPad.

- **Passcode Lock:** Assigns a password to the Lock screen. You can set a passcode, turn it on or off, change the passcode, and set the time interval at which your passcode is required. This is useful if you don't want to bother with a passcode for only brief periods of locking your iPad. Finally, you can use the Erase Data after Ten Failed Passcode Attempts setting so that multiple failed attempts to access your device results in your iPad erasing all data on it. This could protect, for example, your contacts' information or map data that shows your location from prying eyes. Note that if Simple Passcode is turned on, you're limited to a four-character passcode.

✓ **Restrictions:** Allows you to restrict access to certain apps and content using a passcode. (See Figure 8-8.) This is useful if you don't want your kids to access a particularly adult app or simply don't want them browsing with Safari or buying things with iTunes, for example.

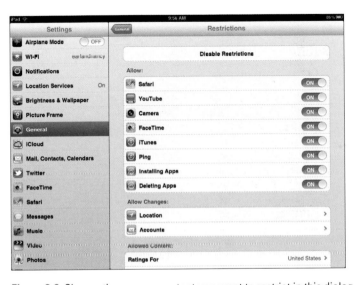

Figure 8-8: Choose the apps or content you want to restrict in this dialog.

If you forget a passcode, the only thing to do is restore iPad software, which can be a headache. The obvious advice here: Don't forget your passcode!

Setting the date and time

By default, your iPad is set to Cupertino time — Cupertino, California, that is, home to Apple Computer. If you have occasion to reset the time zone or date and time, either because you live somewhere other than Apple headquarters or you travel around with your iPad, here's how you control the time setting on your iPad:

1. **Tap the Settings icon on the Home screen.**

2. **Tap General.**

3. **Tap Date & Time.**

   The settings in Figure 8-9 appear.

4. **Do any of the following:**

   - *Tap the Off button to turn 24-hour time on.* This is military time, so that 2 p.m. is 14:00, and so on.

   - *Tap Time Zone, and a text entry field displays along with your onscreen keyboard.* Press the Delete key to delete Cupertino, and type your location. (If you type a major city near you, it will come up on a list as you type, and you can just tap to select it.)

   - *Tap the On/Off button for Set Automatically.* This feature sets your time and date based on your current location.

Figure 8-9: Choose the time format or time zone, or let iPad set things up for you.

Controlling keyboard settings

Your keyboard is one of the most important ways you interact with iPad, so it's helpful if you have all the onscreen keyboard settings just the way you want them. You can access these under the Keyboard option in the General settings (see Figure 8-10), and they include the following:

- **Auto-Capitalization** and **Auto-Correction:** Allows iPad to help you avoid mistakes by automatically suggesting corrections to what it perceives as spelling errors, based on a built-in dictionary, or correcting capitalization mistakes you make after you finish entering a sentence.

- **Check Spelling:** If you want iPad to automatically check spelling, turning this feature on causes two things to happen: A jagged red line appears under text in apps such as Notes and Mail; and as you type a word with a misspelling, a suggested correct spelling appears in a little bubble. If you also have Auto-Correction turned on, the word will automatically be corrected when you finish typing it and add a space or punctuation mark such as a period. Note that you can use the Undo key on the onscreen keyboard with numbers displayed to undo automatic changes.

✔ **Enable Caps Lock:** Activates a feature that lets you double-tap the Shift key to activate Caps Lock. Note that when Caps Lock is activated, the Shift key on the onscreen keyboard is blue. This setting is turned off by default.

✔ **"." Shortcut:** Turning this on activates a shortcut that allows you to enter a period and a space by double-tapping the spacebar.

✔ **Split Keyboard:** Turns on a feature that allows you to break the onscreen keyboard into two pieces, one on each side of your screen, to make a more texting-like experience for those who like to type mainly with their thumbs.

✔ **International Keyboards:** Gives you access to the choice of two built-in keyboards: French and English. If you tap Add New Keyboard in this dialog, you are offered nine more language options, including German, Italian, Russian, Spanish, and (my personal favorite) Flemish.

✔ **Shortcuts:** Use these two settings to have iPad automatically convert common texting phrases such as "on my way" into shortcuts, or add new shortcuts to its repertoire.

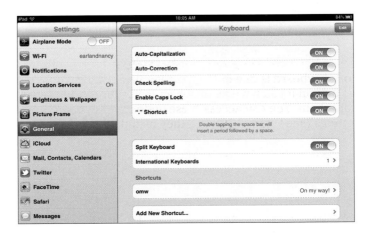

Figure 8-10: Set up your keyboard to work the way you want it to.

Working with the Reset feature

If only life had a reset button to put some things back the way they were. Well, it doesn't, but iPad does. The last item under General settings is Reset. When you tap it, you get options for resetting the following:

- **Reset All Settings:** Every one of the preferences and settings are reset, though information you've added to apps like Calendar and Contacts doesn't change at all.

- **Erase All Content and Settings:** This one both resets your settings and erases information you've added to apps like Calendar and Contacts. This is useful if you plan to sell your iPad.

- **Reset Network Settings:** By choosing this, any networks you've set up are removed. iPad will also turn off Wi-Fi and then turn it on again, which disconnects you from any network you're connected to. Note that the Ask to Join Networks setting stays on.

- **Reset Keyboard Dictionary:** When you turn down iPad suggestions of words as you type, you can add words to the keyboard dictionary. You do this by tapping a suggested word, which rejects it but adds the current spelling of the word to the dictionary. If you don't want to keep all those added words, use this reset option.

- **Reset Home Screen Layout:** If you want to get back to the original home screen you saw when you took iPad out of its box, choose this reset option.

- **Reset Location Warnings:** When you use an app like Maps that checks your location, it asks you if it's okay to do that. When you tap OK two times to let it proceed, it stops asking. If you want it to start asking again, tap this reset option.

Managing iCloud Settings

Book I, Chapter 5 takes you through the steps in setting up an iCloud account, one of four things you can do using the iCloud item in Settings. (See Figure 8-11.) Here are the other three things you can control for Apple's online storage and sharing service from within Settings:

Figure 8-11: Choose which type of content to sync via iCloud here.

✔ **Turn various apps on or off for inclusion in iCloud syncs.** For example, you can set Contacts to sync contacts stored in e-mail accounts, Calendars to sync with online calendars, and Documents and Data or Photo Stream to back up and share content via iCloud.

✔ **Control Storage & Backup.** This includes checking your available storage, buying additional storage, or turning iCloud Backup on or off.

✔ **Delete an account.** You would do this if you no longer want to use a certain iCloud account or want to change accounts.

Settings for Individual Apps

Most bundled apps have a corresponding group of settings in iPad. Rather than bore you by taking you through each and every one, I provide Table 8-1, which gives you an overview of the types of settings you can control. If there's a particular app you like to work with often, it's worth your while to explore the settings for it to see if there's one that might make your life with that app a bit easier.

Table 8-1	Built-in Apps Settings Overview
App	*Types of Settings*
Mail	Add Accounts, Fetch New Data Frequency, and Display Settings (how many messages to show, font size, and so on)
Contacts	Display Settings (sort order and display order)
Calendars	Turn on Alerts, Time Zone, and Default Calendar
Twitter	Add Account, Update Contacts, and Allow Apps to Use Twitter
FaceTime	Turn On/Off and Set Email Account
Safari	Search Engine, Turn AutoFill On/Off, Show Bookmarks Bar, and Security and History
Messages	Turn On/Off, Make Receive Settings, and Show/Hide Subject Field
Music	Sounds and Volume Settings and Display Lyrics and Podcast Information
Video	Start Playing (where you left off or from the beginning), Closed Captioning, Widescreen On/Off, and Type of TV Signal
Photos	Slideshow Settings
Notes	Set Font
Store	Set Automatic Download Types

Also note that apps that you download, which have been designed for iPad, will often appear in your Settings under the heading of Apps. Non-iPad apps (for example, iPhone apps) don't seem to appear. The settings vary based on the app, so go exploring and see what you find!

Chapter 9: Maintaining and Troubleshooting

In This Chapter

✔ Taking care of your iPad

✔ Solving common iPad problems

✔ Finding technical support

✔ Finding a missing iPad

✔ Backing up to iCloud

*i*Pads don't grow on trees — they cost a pretty penny. That's why you should know how to take care of your iPad and troubleshoot any problems that it might have so you get the most out of it.

In this chapter, I provide some advice about the care and maintenance of your iPad, as well as tips about how to solve common problems, update iPad system software, and even reset iPad should something go seriously wrong. In case you lose your iPad, I even tell you about a feature that helps you find it — or even disable it if it's fallen into the wrong hands. Finally, you get information about backing up your iPad settings and content using iCloud.

Maintaining Your iPad

You've got a great gadget and an investment to protect in your iPad. A few simple precautions can keep it damage-free — at least until you rush out and buy the next version.

It's wise to keep the screen clean and safe from damage, as well as maximize your battery use. The following sections tell you how.

Keeping the iPad screen clean

If you've been playing with your iPad, you know — despite Apple's claim that iPads have fingerprint-resistant screens — that iPads are fingerprint magnets. They are covered with an oil-resistant coating, but that definitely doesn't mean they're smudge-proof.

Here are some tips about cleaning your iPad screen:

- ✔ **Use a dry, soft cloth.** You can get most fingerprints off with a dry, soft cloth such as the one you use to clean your eyeglasses or a cleaning tissue that's lint- and chemical-free. Or try products used to clean lenses in labs, such as Kimwipes or Kaydry, which you can get from several major retailers such as Amazon.

- ✔ **Use a slightly dampened soft cloth.** To get the surface even cleaner, slightly dampen the cloth before you use it to clean the screen. Again, make sure whatever cloth material you use is free of lint.

- ✔ **Remove the cables.** This may go without saying, but I'll say it anyway: If you don't want a fried iPad, turn it off and unplug any cables from it before cleaning the screen with a moistened cloth.

- ✔ **Avoid too much moisture.** Avoid getting too much moisture around the edges of the screen where it can seep into the unit.

- ✔ **Never use any household cleaners on your iPad screen.** They can degrade the coating that keeps the screen from absorbing oil from your fingers.

Do *not* use premoistened lens-cleaning tissues to clean your screen. Most of these wipe products contain alcohol, which can damage the screen's coating.

Protecting your gadget with a case

Your screen isn't the only element on the iPad that can be damaged, so consider getting a case for it so you can carry it around the house or around town safely. Besides providing a bit of padding if you drop the device, a case makes the iPad less slippery in your hands, offering a better grip when working with it.

Several types of cases came out pretty much the day iPad shipped, and more are showing up all the time. You can choose the Smart Cover from Apple, for example ($39 for polyurethane finish or $69 for leather), or covers from other manufacturers such as Tuff-Luv (www.tuff-luv.com) and Griffin (www.griffintechnology.com) that come in materials ranging from leather (see Figure 9-1) to silicone. (See Figure 9-2.)

Figure 9-1: A lovely leather case, with a built-in
stand mechanism for better viewing.

A silicone "skin" case

Figure 9-2: A less-expensive option is a
silicon skin.

Cases range in price from a few dollars to $70 or more for leather; some will cost you hundreds of dollars. Some provide a cover (refer to Figure 9-1), and others protect only the back and sides or, in the case of Smart Cover, only the screen. (Refer to Figure 9-2.) If you carry your iPad around much at all, consider a case with a screen cover to provide better protection for the screen or use a screen overlay such as the InvisibleShield from ZAGG (www. zagg.com).

Extend your iPad's battery life

The much-touted, 10-hour battery life of the iPad is a wonderful feature, but you can take some steps to extend that battery life even further. You can estimate how much battery life you have left by looking at the Battery icon in the far-right end of the Status bar at the top of your screen. Here are a few tips to help that little icon stay full up:

✓ **Use a wall outlet to charge.** Though it can vary depending on your computer model, generally when connected to a Mac computer, iPad can slowly charge; however, some PC connections slowly drain the battery. Even so, the most effective way to charge your iPad is to plug it into the wall outlet using the Dock Connector to USB Cable and the 10W USB Power Adapter that came with your iPad. (See Figure 9-3.)

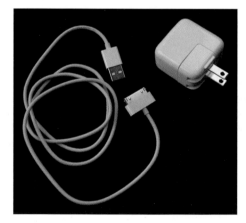

Figure 9-3: The provided cord and power adapter.

✓ **Turn the iPad off.** The fastest way to charge the iPad is to turn it off while charging it.

✓ **Avoid USB ports on keyboards.** Your battery may lose some power if you leave it connected to the USB port on a keyboard or other device.

The fastest way to charge your iPad is with the included cord. Using your computer to charge it can take a great deal longer.

✔ **Limit the screen's impact on the battery.** Turn the screen off when not in use, as the display eats up power. Also, reduce the screen brightness in Settings to save power.

✔ **Turn off Wi-Fi.** If you're not using Wi-Fi, turn it off under Settings. Constantly maintaining a Wi-Fi connection or searching for a signal can use up a bit of power.

Your iPad battery is sealed in the unit, so you can't replace it as you can with many laptops or your cellphone battery. If the battery is out of warranty, you'll have to fork over the money, possibly more than $100, to get a new one. If you use your phone a great deal, consider getting the AppleCare service contract for free replacement. See the "Getting Support" section, later in this chapter, to find out where to get a replacement battery.

Troubleshooting Your iPad

Though we'd all like to think that our iPads are perfect magical machines, unburdened with the vagaries of crashing Windows PCs and system software bugs, that's not always the case.

Here are some common issues that can come up with iPad, and ways around them.

Dealing with a nonresponsive iPad

If your iPad goes dead on you, it's most likely a power issue, so the first thing to do is to plug the Dock Connector to USB Cable into the 10W USB Power Adapter, plug the 10W USB Power Adapter into a wall outlet, plug the other end of the Dock Connector to USB Cable into your iPad, and charge the battery.

Another thing to try — especially if you think that an app might be hanging up the iPad — is to press the Sleep/Wake button for a few seconds. Then, press and hold the Home button. The app you were using should close.

You can always try the old reboot procedure, which in the case of an iPad means pressing the Sleep/Wake button on the top until the red slider is displayed. Drag the slider to the right to turn your iPad off. After a few moments, press the Sleep/Wake button to boot up the little guy again. Be sure your battery has a decent charge as this procedure can eat up battery power.

If the situation seems drastic and none of these ideas works, try to reset your iPad. To do this, press the Sleep/Wake button and the Home button at the same time until the Apple logo appears onscreen.

When you're using a Bluetooth keyboard, your onscreen keyboard won't appear. The physical keyboard has, in essence, co-opted keyboard control of your device. To use your onscreen keyboard with a Bluetooth keyboard connected, you have a few options: You can turn the Bluetooth keyboard off, turn off Bluetooth in iPad's General settings, switch the keyboard off, or move the keyboard out of range. Your onscreen keyboard should reappear.

Are you accidentally tapping extra keys on the onscreen keyboard as you type? Wearing a wrist support can keep you from hitting extra characters with your wrists. Also, it's much easier to use the onscreen keyboard in landscape mode where it's just plain wider.

Updating software

Just as software manufacturers provide updates for your main computer, Apple occasionally updates the iPad system software to fix problems or offer enhanced features. You should occasionally check for an updated version (say, every month).

Note that if you've chosen to back up and restore iPad via iCloud when you first set up the device or later using Settings, restoring and updating your device happens automatically (see Book I, Chapter 5 for more about iCloud).

If you choose not to use iCloud, follow these steps to update the iPad system software using a connection to your computer:

1. **Start by connecting your iPad to your computer.**

2. **On your computer, open the iTunes software you installed.**

   (See Book I, Chapter 4 for more about this topic.)

3. **Click your iPad's name in the iTunes Source List on the left.**

4. **Click the Summary tab shown in Figure 9-4.**

5. **Click the Check for Update button.**

   iTunes displays a message telling you if a new update is available.

6. **Click the Update button to install the newest version.**

Click on your iPad...   then click the Summary tab

Figure 9-4: Get system updates for iPad through your iTunes account.

If you're having problems with your iPad, you can use the Update feature to try to restore the current version of the software. Follow the preceding set of steps, and then click the Restore button instead of the Update button in Step 6. Typically, restoring an OS to another version does run the risk of going back to original settings, so be aware of that going in.

Restoring sound

Coincidentally, the very morning I wrote this chapter, my husband was puttering with his iPad. Suddenly, the sound stopped. We gave ourselves a quick course in recovering sound, so now I can share these tips with you. Make sure that:

- **You haven't touched the volume control keys on a physical keyboard connected to your iPad via Bluetooth.** They're on the right side of the top-right side of your iPad when holding it in portrait orientation. (See Figure 9-5.) Be sure not to touch one and inadvertently lower the sound till it's essentially muted.

✓ **You haven't flipped the Silent switch.** If you have the Screen Rotation/Silent switch set to control sound, moving the switch mutes sound on your iPad.

✓ **The speaker isn't covered up.** Make sure you haven't covered up the speaker in a way that muffles the sound.

✓ **A headset isn't plugged in.** Sound won't play through the speaker and the headset at the same time.

✓ **The Volume Limit is set to Off.** You can set up the Volume Limit in Music Settings to control how loudly the Music app can play (which is useful if your partner's into loud Rap music). Tap the Settings icon on the Home screen, and then on the left side of the screen that displays, tap Music and use the Volume Limit controls (see Figure 9-5) to turn down the Volume Limit.

Make sure this is set to Off

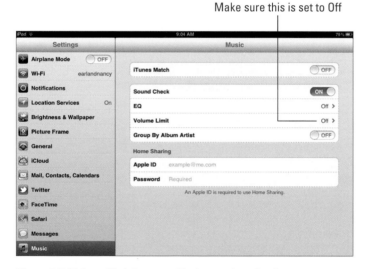

Figure 9-5: Volume Limit lets your iPad get only so loud.

If all else fails, reboot. That's what worked for us — just press the Sleep/Wake button until the red slider appears. Press and drag the slider to the right. After iPad turns off, press the Sleep/Wake button again until the Apple logo appears, and you may find yourself back in business sound-wise.

Getting Support

As you may already know if you own another Apple device, Apple is known for its great customer support, so if you're stuck, I definitely recommend that you try them out. Here are a few options you can explore for getting help:

✔ **The Apple Store:** Go to your local Apple Store if one is handy to find out what the folks there might know about your problem.

✔ **The Apple support website:** Visit this site at `www.apple.com/support/ipad`. (See Figure 9-6.) Here you'll find online manuals, discussion forums, downloads, and the Apple Expert feature, which enables you to contact a live support person by phone.

Figure 9-6: Don't forget to check out the manuals and discussions for help.

✔ **The iPad User Guide:** You can use the bookmarked manual on the Safari browser or visit `http://manuals.info.apple.com/en_us/ipad_user_guide.pdf`. This is a more robust version of the bookmarked User Guide. You can also download the manual and read it in most popular e-reader programs.

✔ **The Apple battery replacement service:** If you need repair or service for your battery, visit `www.apple.com/batteries/replacements.html`.

Note that your warranty provides free battery replacement if the battery level dips below 50 percent and won't go any higher during the first year you own it. If you purchase the AppleCare service agreement, this is extended to two years. Also note that Apple recommends that the iPad battery should be replaced only by an Apple Authorized Service Provider.

Finally, here are a few useful non-Apple discussion forums that may help provide some answers:

- MacRumors at `http://forums.macrumors.com/forumdisplay.php?f=137`

- The iPad Guide discussions at `www.theipadguide.com/forum`

- iPad.org provides several useful threads at `http://ipad.org/forum`

Finding a Missing iPad

Starting with iOS 4.2, you can take advantage of the Find My iPad feature to pinpoint the location of your iPad. This is a very handy feature if you forget where you left your iPad or it is stolen. Find My iPad not only lets you track down the critter, but also lets you wipe off the data contained in it if you have no way to get the iPad back.

Follow these steps to get this feature set up:

1. **Tap the Settings icon on the Home screen.**

2. **In the Settings pane, tap iCloud.**

3. **In the iCloud settings, tap the On/Off button for Find My iPad to turn the feature on (see Figure 9-7).**

Figure 9-7: Turn the feature on or off to locate your iPad from your computer.

4. **From now on, if your iPad is lost or stolen, you can go to** `http://iCloud.com` **and enter your ID and password.**

5. **The Find My iPad screen appears with your iPad's location noted on a map.**

Additionally, if you feel like your iPad is in the hands of someone who might misuse the data on it, you can use this feature to lock the device and even delete all data you've added to your iPad manually or by syncing. Just know, though, that the latter isn't reversible. To wipe information from the iPad, click Remote Wipe button. (See Figure 9-8.) To lock the iPad from access by others, click the Remote Lock button.

Figure 9-8: To protect data on your iPad, as a last resort you can wipe it clean.

You can also tap Display a Message or Play a Sound to send whoever has your iPad a note saying how to return it to you — or a note that the police are on their way if it's been stolen! If you choose to play a sound, it plays for two minutes, helping you track down your iPad or anybody holding it within earshot.

Backing Up to iCloud

You used to be able to back up your iPad content using only iTunes, but with Apple's introduction of iCloud, you can back up via a Wi-Fi network to your iCloud storage. You get 5GB of storage (not including iTunes-bought music, video, apps, and electronic books or content pushed automatically among your Apple devices by iTunes Match) for free, or you can pay for increased levels of storage (10GB for $20 per year, 20GB for $40 per year, or 50GB for $100 per year).

1. **To perform a backup to iCloud, first set up an iCloud account (see Book I, Chapter 5 for details on creating an iCloud account) and then tap Settings on the Home screen.**

2. **Tap iCloud and then tap Storage and Backup (see Figure 9-9).**

Tap this option

Figure 9-9: Backing up to the cloud.

3. **In the pane that appears (see Figure 9-10), tap the iCloud Backup On/ Off switch to enable automatic backups, or to perform a manual backup, tap Back Up Now.**

   A progress bar shows how your backup is moving along.

Set this to On

Figure 9-10: Automatic backups ensure your data is saved.

Book II
Just for Fun

The iPad is made for soaking up media and other fun stuff, so in this part, the focus is on fun. First, you explore how and where to buy content from music to movies. Once you have music on your iPad, you get to try out the iPad music player (the Music app) and even make music of your own using the GarageBand app. Movie time? Play around with the Videos app and the built-in video camera, and try some video editing with iMovie. You can even videoconference using FaceTime.

In this part, you also find out all about the iPad camera and the Photos app, as well as how to get wonderful photo effects with Photo Booth. To round out the fun, I introduce you to using your iPad as an e-reader for both books and periodicals, and playing some very cool games on your very magical device.

Chapter 1: Buying Content at iTunes and Beyond

In This Chapter

✓ **Exploring the iTunes Store**

✓ **Previewing music, a movie, or an audiobook**

✓ **Buying a selection**

✓ **Renting movies**

✓ **Shopping beyond iTunes**

✓ **Using iCloud to push purchases to all devices**

*i*Pad is set up with a preinstalled iTunes app that makes it easy to shop for music, movies, TV shows, audiobooks, podcasts, and even online classes at Apple's iTunes Store.

In this chapter, you discover how to use your iPad to find content on the iTunes website. That content can be downloaded directly to your iPad, or downloaded to another device and then synced to your iPad. In addition, I cover a few options for buying content from other online stores and how to download purchases automatically using iCloud.

I cover opening an iTunes account and downloading iTunes software to your computer in Book I, Chapter 5. If you need to, go back and handle those two tasks before digging into this chapter.

Exploring the iTunes Store

Like it or not, the iTunes Store is set up to be your most convenient source for content on your iPad at the moment. Sure, you can get content from other places, but the iTunes app comes preinstalled on your iPad — and Apple makes it easy to access it from various Apple devices or your PC.

So, it's time you got to know the iTunes Store: the easiest way to grab all those movies, TV shows, and music that you love for viewing and listening to on your iPad.

Visiting the iTunes Store

Using the iTunes Store from your iPad is easy with the built-in iTunes app. You just tap the iTunes icon on the Home screen. If you're not already signed in, the dialog shown in Figure 1-1 appears, asking for your iTunes password. Enter your password and tap OK.

Tap here and enter your password

Figure 1-1: Log in to the iTunes Store.

Now you can roam around trying different options out. You have music, podcasts, movies, TV shows, audiobooks, and online courses to choose from.

Start exploring musical selections by tapping the Music button in the row of buttons at the bottom of the screen, if it's not already selected. To scroll through featured and New and Noteworthy selections, tap the Next or Previous arrow, as shown in Figure 1-2.

Tap the Top Charts tab at the top of the screen to display top-selling songs and albums. Tap any of the other musical items listed to see more detail about them, as shown in Figure 1-3.

The navigation techniques in these steps work essentially the same in any of the content categories (the buttons at the bottom of the screen), which include Music, Movies, TV Shows, Podcasts, Audiobooks, and iTunes U. Just tap one to explore it.

If you want to use the Genius playlist feature, which recommends additional purchases based on the contents of your iTunes libraries, turn this feature on in iTunes on your computer, and then on your iPad, tap the Genius tab at the top of the screen. Song and album recommendations appear. Note that this service seems to work best on mainstream music genres such as pop and rock, not so well on narrower genres like swing music and show tunes.

Tap these arrows to scroll through the selections

Figure 1-2: Browse selections in the iTunes Store.

Figure 1-3: Detailed information may include the genre, release date, and song list.

Finding a selection

There are several ways to look for a selection in the iTunes Store. You can use the Search feature, search by genres or categories, or view artists' pages. Here's how these work:

✓ **Search:** Tap in the Search field shown in Figure 1-4 and enter a search term using the onscreen keyboard. Tap the Search button on the keyboard or, if one of the suggestions given appeals to you, just go ahead and tap it. Search results will be divided into categories such as Music and Podcasts. Flick down to scroll through them and find what you need.

✓ **Genre:** Tap the Genre button. (In some content types, such as Audiobooks, this is called the Categories button.) A list of genres/categories like the one shown in Figure 1-5 appears.

Enter a search term here

Figure 1-4: Search by composer, artist, or album title.

Tap here to view the list

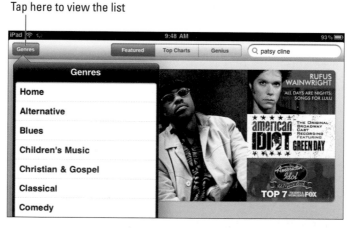

Figure 1-5: Find a genre of music to help you narrow down your search.

✔ **Link:** In a description page that appears when you tap a selection, you can find more offerings by the people involved. For example, for a music selection, tap the Artist Page link to see all of that artist's selections. For a movie, tap the name of someone in the movie credits to see more of that person's work, as shown for Kate Winslet in Figure 1-6.

Figure 1-6: If you have an artist you favor, search for him or her.

If you find a selection you like, tap the Tell a Friend link on its description page to share your discovery with a friend via e-mail. A message appears with a link to the selection. Enter an address in the To field and tap Send. Your friend is now in-the-know.

Want to see every option? When displaying items on the Featured tab for any type of content, tap the See All link to see all featured selections rather than only the top New and Noteworthy selections.

Sorting movie selections

When you're out to find a movie to watch or music to listen to on your iPad some Tuesday or Saturday night and you don't know what you want to experience, using a sort feature can help you find something that might appeal to you. You can sort movie selections by best sellers, name, or release date when you have an Artist Page displayed for movies or music.

With iTunes open, tap the Sort By field. In the menu shown in Figure 1-7, tap the criteria you want to sort by.

Selections are sorted by the criteria you chose (for example, alphabetically if you chose Name or with the latest release first if you chose Release Date). Find the item that interests you and tap it for more info, or tap the price button to buy it.

Tap here to select a sort criteria

Figure 1-7: Choose search criteria from this menu.

Previewing music, a movie, or an audiobook

Because you've already set up an iTunes account (if you haven't done so yet, refer to Book I, Chapter 5), when you choose to buy an item, it's automatically charged to the credit card you have on record or against a store credit if you have one.

However, you might just want to preview an item before you buy it to be sure it's a good fit. If you like it, buying and downloading are then easy and quick.

Follow these steps to preview your content:

1. **Open iTunes and locate a selection you might want to buy using any of the methods I outline in earlier sections.**

2. **Tap the item to see detailed information about it, as shown in Figure 1-8.**

3. **If you're looking at a music selection, tap the track number or name of a selection (refer to Figure 1-8) to play a preview. For a movie or audiobook selection, tap the Preview button shown in Figure 1-9.**

If you like what you hear or see, you're ready to buy. Which brings you to the next section.

The iTunes Store offers several free selections, especially in the Podcast and iTunes U content categories. If you see one you want to try out, download it by tapping the button labeled Free and then tapping the Get Episode or similarly named button that appears.

Tap a track number or name to listen to a preview

Patsy Cline
Patsy Cline's Greatest Hits (Remastered)

Artist Page >

Tell a Friend >

Genre: Country
Released: 1967
12 Songs
★★★★★ 61 Ratings

$9.99

iTunes Review

Considering her legendary status, it's amazing that Patsy Cline only recorded 104 tracks over a span of eight years. Her ability to convey romantic torment without ever losing her grace or dignity remains unmatched, and for those looking for the essence of Cline's music, *Greatest* ... More ▼

Tap to Preview

	Name	Time	Popularity	Price
1	**Walkin' After Midnight (1961 Remake)**	1:59	▮▮▯▯▯▯▯▯▯▯	$1.29
2	**Sweet Dreams (Single Version)**	2:33	▮▮▮▯▯▯▯▯▯▯	$0.99
3	**Crazy (Single Version)**	2:41	▮▮▮▮▮▮▯▯▯▯	$1.29

Figure 1-8: Why not preview before you buy?

Tap here to preview the selection

The Blind Side PG-13

Tell a Friend >

Warner Bros.
Genre: Drama
Released: 2010
Run Time: 2:08:31
★★★★★ 2325 Ratings

Language: English
Format: Widescreen
Dolby Digital 5.1 surround sound

iTunes Extras

PREVIEW

RENT $4.99

HD   Standard Def.

Learn About Rentals >

iTunes Extras

Includes a one-on-one "Sideline Conversation" with Sandra Bullock and more. Enjoy them on your Mac, PC, or Apple TV. iTunes Extras are available with purchase only.

Figure 1-9: You can also preview movies before you rent or buy.

Buying a selection

There is free content out there, but for all but movie selections that you can also rent, other types of content often require that you buy what you want to consume. Buying involves authorizing the purchase and downloading the content to your iPad (which is done automatically once the purchasing part is complete).

When you find an item you want to buy, here's how to make your purchase:

1. **Tap the button that shows either the price (if it's a selection available for purchase; see Figure 1-10) or the word *Free* (if it's a selection available for free).**

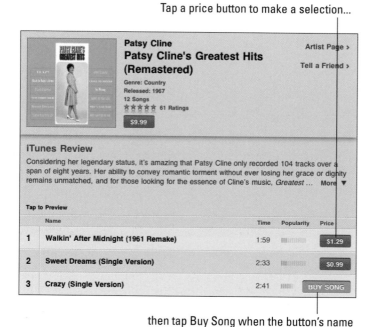

Tap a price button to make a selection...

then tap Buy Song when the button's name changes to purchase the selection

Figure 1-10: Buy the content you want using these buttons.

The button label changes to Buy *X*, where *X* is the particular content you're buying, such as a song or album. (Refer to Figure 1-10.)

2. **Tap the Buy *X* button.**

The iTunes Password dialog appears. (Refer to Figure 1-1.)

3. **Enter your password and tap OK, or if you have a credit tap the Redeem link and enter the code provided.**

The item begins downloading (see Figure 1-11) and is automatically charged to your credit card or against a store credit. When the download finishes, you can view the content using the Music or Videos app, depending on the type of content you bought.

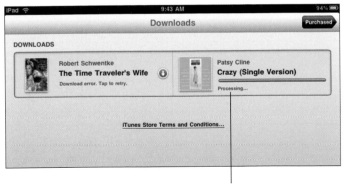

The selection being downloaded

Figure 1-11: iTunes shows you the progress of your download.

If you want to buy music, you can open the description page for an album and buy individual songs rather than the entire album. Tap the price for a song, and then proceed to purchase it.

Note the Redeem button on many iTunes screens. Tap this button to redeem any iTunes gift certificates you might get from your generous friends, or from yourself.

If you don't want to allow purchases from within apps (for example, Music or Videos) but rather want to allow purchases only through the iTunes Store, you can go to the General Settings, tap Restrictions, then tap Enable Restrictions, and enter a passcode. Once you've set a passcode you can tap individual apps to turn on restrictions for them.

If you have a 3G-model iPad, you can allow content to be downloaded over your 3G cellular network. Be aware, however, that downloading larger items such as video or audiobooks could incur hefty data charges with your provider. However, if you aren't near a Wi-Fi hotspot, it might be your only option. Go to Settings, Store, and tap the On/Off button for the Cellular setting.

Renting movies

In the case of movies, you can either rent or buy content. If you rent, which is less expensive, you have 30 days from the time you rent the item to begin to watch it. Once you have begun to watch it, you have 24 hours from that time left to watch it as many times as you like.

1. **With the iTunes app open, tap the Movies button.**

2. **Locate the movie you want to rent and tap the View button shown in Figure 1-12.**

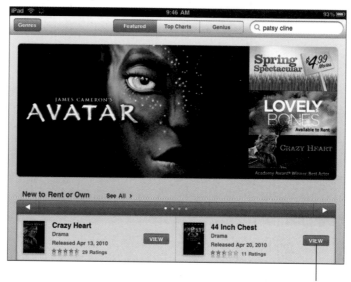

Tap this button

Figure 1-12: To rent, start by viewing details about the content.

3. **In the detailed description of the movie that appears, tap the Rent button shown in Figure 1-13.**

   The gray Rent button changes to a green Rent Movie button.

4. **Tap the Rent Movie button to confirm the rental.**

   The movie begins to download to your iPad immediately, and your account is charged the rental fee.

5. **To check the status of your download, tap the Downloads button.**

   The progress of your download is displayed. Once the download is complete, you can use either the Music or Videos app to watch it. (See Book II, Chapters 2 and 3 to read about how these apps work.)

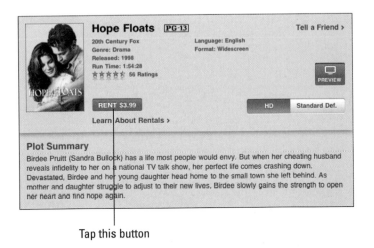

Tap this button

Figure 1-13: If you want to watch it only once, rent and save money.

Some movies are offered in high-definition versions. These HD movies look great on that crisp, colorful iPad screen. It's best to download these over a Wi-Fi connection as a 3G connection could incur hefty charges.

You can also download content to your computer and sync it to your iPad. Refer to Book I, Chapter 5 for more about this process.

Listening to Podcasts

Podcasts are audio (and sometimes video) broadcasts you can listen to on your iPad. Most of these are free (at least I haven't found any that aren't, yet!), and iTunes features a wide variety of broadcast topics. They're usually informative rather than strictly entertaining, and great for listening to on that long drive to your friend's cabin in the woods.

It's simple to find podcasts. With iTunes open, tap the Podcast button in the row of buttons at the bottom of the screen. Tap a podcast selection, and a detailed listing of podcasts like the one shown in Figure 1-14 appears.

Now you can tap the name or number of a podcast for additional information, or simply tap the Free button, and then tap the Get Episode button (refer to Figure 1-14) to download the podcast. After it downloads, you can play it using the Music app.

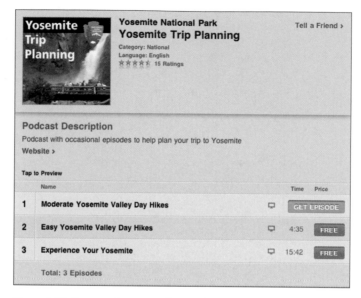

Figure 1-14: Many podcasts are free and provide useful and entertaining information.

To save you some work, you might consider using the subscription feature in iTunes. First, locate a podcast and tap the Subscribe button. A URL for the podcast is displayed. Copy the URL, and then, with iTunes open, tap the Advanced menu and choose Subscribe to Podcast. In the dialog that opens, enter the URL of a podcast you like. Now you'll get all episodes of that podcast delivered to iTunes as they become available, and they'll be available to all your devices through iCloud. (See more about setting up iCloud for automatically pushing purchases from one device to your other Apple devices in the final section of this chapter.)

Going to School at iTunes U

Feel like you could use a little more learning? Who couldn't? One very cool feature of iTunes is *iTunes U,* a compilation of free online courses from universities and other providers. This is a great way to fill in the blanks in your knowledge. The quality and sources may vary, but most content is outstanding — so it's worth a look.

To explore what's available on the iTunes U campus:

1. **Tap the iTunes U button in the row of buttons at the bottom of the screen to display selections.**

2. **Tap one of the three tabs shown in Figure 1-15: Universities & Colleges, Beyond Campus, or K-12.**

Tap one of these tabs

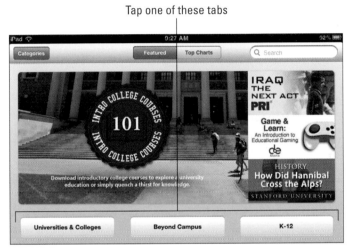

Figure 1-15: Choose the educational category that's of interest to you.

3. **On the list that appears, tap an item to select the source for a course.**

That provider's page appears.

4. **Tap the Next or Previous button to scroll through offerings.**

5. **When you find a topic of interest, tap a selection and it opens, displaying a list of segments of the course, as shown in Figure 1-16.**

6. **Tap the Free button next to a course and then tap the green Download/Get Episode button that appears.**

If there's only one session, the button in this step says Download, but if there's more than one session, it says Get Episode. The course begins downloading.

Once you're on a provider's page, to return to iTunes U, just tap the back button labeled iTunes U (located in the upper-left corner of the screen), and you return to the page with the three provider tabs. (Refer to Figure 1-15.)

Figure 1-16: Click to download the course that you need.

 You can also make selections of courses from the Featured or Top Charts tabs of iTunes U. Narrow these down by tapping the Categories button and choosing a category of courses to browse.

Shopping Anywhere Else

As mentioned earlier in this chapter, one feature that's missing from iPad is support for Flash, a format of video playback that many online video-on-demand services use. However, many content stores are hurriedly adding iPad-friendly videos to their collections, so you do have alternatives to iTunes for your choice of movies or TV shows. You can also shop for music from sources other than iTunes, such as Amazon.com.

You can open accounts at these stores by using your computer or your iPad's Safari browser and then following a store's instructions for purchasing and downloading content. Keep in mind that costs will vary. For example, one such provider is Hulu. (See Figure 1-17.) To get iPad-friendly content from Hulu, you have to sign up for Hulu Plus service and pay $9.99 a month. Then, download the app directly from Hulu.com and start watching content.

Here are some of the other online stores that are looking at offering iPad-compatible content, with more coming all the time:

- **Clicker** (www.clicker.com) is working on providing its online television and movie content to iPad.

✔ **Ustream** (www.ustream.tv) has a mobile app for streaming sports and entertainment programs to mobile devices.

✔ **ABC** (http://abc.go.com) and **CBS News** (www.cbsnews.com) stream live TV programming to the iPad.

✔ **Netflix** (www.netflix.com) makes non-Flash movies available that can be played on iPad.

Book II
Chapter 1

Buying Content at
iTunes and Beyond

Figure 1-17: Hulu has jumped on the iPad wagon through its paid Hulu Plus service.

Additionally, if you can get Flash-based content onto your Mac or Windows machine, you can stream it to your iPad using Air Video and Air Video Server, and it will do an on-the-fly conversion.

There are also apps that stream content if you pay a subscription fee or are an existing customer. Two good ones are Xfinity TV from Comcast and TWCable from Time Warner.

Enabling Auto Downloads of Purchases from Other Devices

With iCloud, once you set up an iCloud account, either during the initial setup of your device or through iPad Settings, you can make a purchase or download free content on any of your Apple devices and have those purchases automatically copied onto all your Apple devices. To enable this autodownload feature on iPad, follow these steps:

1. **Start by tapping Settings on the Home screen.**

   To use iCloud, first set up an iCloud account. See Book I, Chapter 5 for detailed coverage of iCloud, including setting up your account.

2. **Tap Store.**

3. **In the options that appear, tap the On/Off button for any category of purchases you want to autodownload to your iPad from other Apple devices: Music, Apps, or Books (see Figure 1-18).**

Figure 1-18: Authorize purchases from an app by turning it on here.

At this point, Apple doesn't offer an option of autodownloading video content using these settings. You can always download video directly to your iPad through the iTunes app or sync to your computer using iTunes to get the content.

Chapter 2: Playing Music on iPad

In This Chapter

✓ **Creating playlists**

✓ **Searching for audio**

✓ **Playing music and other audio**

✓ **Shuffling music**

✓ **Using AirPlay**

✓ **Playing around with GarageBand**

Almost everybody on Earth has heard of the iPod — that small, portable, music-playing device from Apple that's seemingly glued into the ears of many kids and teens. iPad includes an iPod-like app called Music that allows you to take advantage of its pretty amazing little sound system to play your own style of music or podcasts and audiobooks.

In this chapter, you can get acquainted with the Music app and its features that enable you to sort and find music and control playback from your iPad. You also get an overview of the Ping feature of iTunes that you can use to share your musical preferences with others; the AirPlay feature to access and play your music over a home network; and GarageBand, an app that lets you take the spotlight as musician, composer, or arranger.

Looking over Your Library of Music

In the previous chapter, I guide you through the process of getting content onto your iPad. After you have some audio content in the form of music, podcasts, or audiobooks, it's organized into collections, and you can find that content by categories such as artist or genre with predefined category buttons along the bottom of the Music app screen.

Viewing the library contents

You can easily view the contents of your library collections, which you may have synced from your computer, pushed to your device through iCloud, or downloaded directly using iPad's Wi-Fi (or 3G, if you have a 3G iPad) capability. (See Book II, Chapter 1 for details.)

Take a tour of your Music library collections by following these simple steps:

1. **Tap the Music app icon located in the Dock on the Home screen.**

   The Music library appears. (See Figure 2-1.)

Tap a criteria to use

Figure 2-1: The Music library showing your downloaded music.

2. **Tap the Playlists, Songs, Artists, or Albums buttons at the bottom of the library to view your music according to these criteria (refer to Figure 2-1).**

3. **Tap the More button (see Figure 2-2) to view music by genre or composer, or to view any audiobooks you've acquired.**

   The Purchased button appears only if you have already obtained content on iTunes.

Tap this button

Figure 2-2: View selections by various criteria using the More button.

iTunes has several free items you can download and use to play around with the features in Music, including music and podcasts. You can also sync content stored on your computer or other Apple devices to your iPad and play it using the Music app. See Book I, Chapter 5 for more about syncing.

Apple offers a service called iTunes Match. You pay $24.99 per year for the capability to match the music you've bought from other providers or ripped from CDs (and stored on your computer) to what's in the iTunes library. If there's a match (and there often is), that content is added to your iTunes library. Then, using iCloud, you can sync the content among all your Apple devices.

You can use the iTunes Summary tab to make a setting to sync music at 128 Kbps. Doing this saves space on your iPad if you're an avid music downloader. You can also make a setting for whether to download album covers in iTunes.

Creating Playlists

Everybody loves playlists. They let you compile your very own music mix to match your mood or the occasion. You can easily create your own playlists with the Music app to put tracks from various sources into collections of your choosing.

You can create your own playlists to put tracks from various sources into collections of your choosing. With the Music app open, follow these steps to create your own playlists:

1. **Tap the Playlists button in the bottom of the iPad screen.**
2. **Tap New.**
3. **In the dialog that appears, enter a name for the playlist and tap Save.**
4. **In the list of selections that appears (see Figure 2-3), tap the plus sign next to each item you want to include.**

   Selected items turn gray.

Tap this symbol to include a song in the playlist

Figure 2-3: Personalize your Music experience with custom playlists.

5. **Tap the Done button, and then tap Done again on the list of songs that appears.**
6. **Tap the Playlists button.**

   Your playlist appears in the Library list, and you can now play it by tapping the list name and then the Play button.

You can use the Genius Playlist feature in iTunes to set up playlists of recommended content in your iPad library. Based on items you've purchased, iTunes suggests other purchases that would go well with your collection. Okay, it's a way to get you to buy more music, but if you are building your music collection, it might be worth a try! Visit the iTunes site at www.apple.com/itunes for more information.

Searching for audio

If you can't find what you want by going through collections or categories, you can search for an item in your Music library by using the Search feature.

You can enter an artist's, author's, or composer's name or a word from the item's title in the Search field to find what you're looking for.

With the Music app open, tap in the Search field in the lower-right corner. (See Figure 2-4.) The onscreen keyboard opens.

Tap here to search for audio

Figure 2-4: Enter your search terms and see what you find!

Enter a search term in the Search field. Results are displayed, narrowing the search as you type, as shown in Figure 2-5. Now just tap any item in the Search results to play it.

Results display as you type

Amazing Grace	Susan Boyle	I Dreamed a Dream	3:34
Boulevard Of Broken Dreams	Diana Krall	All For You: A Dedication To The Nat King...	6:28
Cry Me a River	Susan Boyle	I Dreamed a Dream	2:42
Daydream Believer	Susan Boyle	I Dreamed a Dream	3:19
The End of the World	Susan Boyle	I Dreamed a Dream	3:14
How Great Thou Art	Susan Boyle	I Dreamed a Dream	3:13
I Dreamed a Dream	Susan Boyle	I Dreamed a Dream	3:11

Figure 2-5: Music search results.

Playing Music and Other Audio

You've got all that music and other audio content to listen to, and beyond downloading and organizing your selections, that's what Music is mainly for. You'll find the typical playback tools in the Music app, but in case you want a refresher, here's the quick rundown on how to use Music as a player.

Playing your tunes

Playing an audio file is simple, and you'll be glad to hear Music can continue to play in the background while you go about using other apps. If you're browsing in Safari, for example, with music playing in Music, you can double-tap the Home button and a mini toolbar opens where you can control playback without leaving the browser.

The procedure for playing music is to basically find what you want to play, and then use the playback tools to play it. Here's how:

1. **Locate the item you want to play using the methods I describe in previous sections of this chapter.**

2. **Tap the item you want to play from the list that appears (see Figure 2-6).**

   It begins playing. If you're displaying the Songs tab or the Purchased library, you need only tap a song to play it without first starting the album.

Tap an item to play it

Figure 2-6: Choose your musical poison here.

3. **If you want to go a specific item, such as a song in the album that's playing, tap the item you want to play from the list that appears.**

   It begins to play.

4. **Use the Previous and Next buttons at the top of the screen, shown in Figure 2-7, to navigate the audio files.**

   The Previous button takes you back to the beginning of the item that's playing or the previous track if nothing's playing; the Next button takes you to the next item.

Previous Next   Genius Playlist symbol

Pause   Progress bar   Volume slider

Back to Library arrow   Album List button

Figure 2-7: Your typical playback tools displayed in the Music app.

Book II
Chapter 2

Playing Music
on iPad

5. **Tap the Pause button to pause playback.**

6. **Tap and drag the line that indicates the current playback location on the Progress bar left or right to "scrub" to another location in the song.**

7. **Don't like what's playing? Tap the Back to Library arrow in the bottom-left corner to return to the Library view, or tap the Album List button in the bottom-right corner to show other tracks in the album that's playing and make another selection.**

Shuffling music

If you want to play a random selection of the music you've purchased or synced through iCloud or from your computer to your iPad, use the Shuffle feature. With the Music app open, tap the Music, Playlist, or Purchased button in the Source List on the left and then tap the Songs button on the bottom of the screen.

Tap the Shuffle button shown in Figure 2-8. Your content plays in random order.

Tap this button

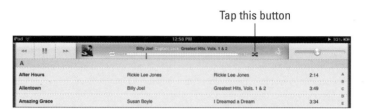

Figure 2-8: Shuffle your music for a varied musical experience.

Adjusting the volume

Music offers its own volume control that you can adjust during playback. With Music open, tap a piece of music or a podcast to play it. In the controls that appear onscreen (see Figure 2-9), press and drag the button on the Volume slider to the right for more volume or to the left for less volume. To mute iPad's speaker at any time, press the Mute button or, if it's set up to control volume, slide the Silent switch on the side of your iPad to the mute setting.

Use the Volume slider to adjust the volume

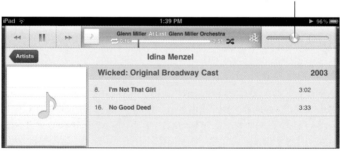

Figure 2-9: Louder or softer, just use the slider to get the effect you want.

If you've got volume set at high and you're still having trouble hearing, consider getting a headset. These devices cut out extraneous noises and should improve the sound quality of what you're listening to, as well as adding stereo to iPad's mono speaker setup. Preferably, you should use a 3.5mm stereo headphone; insert it in the headphone jack at the top of your iPad. You can also use Apple's iPod or iPhone earbuds, which work just fine with iPad. The iPhone buds include a microphone as well.

Understanding Ping

Ping is a social network for music lovers. If you think of Facebook or other social networking sites and imagine that they focus on musical tastes, you get a good idea of what Ping is all about.

After you join Ping, you can share the music you like with friends, take a look at the music your friends are purchasing, and follow certain artists. (See Figure 2-10.) You can also access short previews of the sounds your friends like.

Figure 2-10: Ping makes sharing music with friends fun.

If you have a few musical friends with whom you'd like to connect, Ping can be great fun.

To use Ping, you need to activate it using iTunes on a PC or Mac by clicking the Ping link in the Source List and then clicking the Turn On Ping button. You're then asked to fill in profile information such as your name, gender, town, and musical preferences. (See Figure 2-11.) After you save that information, you have a Ping home page and can start inviting friends to share musical inspirations with you.

One cool feature of Ping is that, on your Ping page, a list of concerts near you is displayed. Even in my small town, Ping alerted me to some interesting events to check out.

Figure 2-11: Build your Ping profile.

Using AirPlay

AirPlay gives you the ability to stream audio to externally powered speakers that are included on your wireless network. Several speaker manufacturers are building AirPlay hardware into their systems. AirPlay streaming technology is built into the iPhone, iPod touch, and iPad. With AirPlay, you can send media files from one device to be played on another. You can send (say) a movie you purchased on your iPad or a slideshow of photos to be played on your TV — and control the playback from your iPad. You can also send music to be played over speakers.

There are a few ways to do this. You can purchase Apple TV and stream video, photos, and music to the TV, or you can purchase AirPort Express and attach it to your speakers to play music. Finally, if you buy AirPlay-enabled wireless speakers, you can stream audio directly to them. Because this combination of equipment varies, my advice — if you're interested in using AirPlay — is to visit your nearest Apple Store and find out which hardware combination will work best for you.

If you get a bit antsy watching a long movie, one of the beauties of AirPlay is that you can still use your iPad to check e-mail, browse photos or the Internet, or check your calendar while the media is playing.

Playing around with GarageBand

GarageBand is a music composition and playing app that has been pre-installed on Mac computers for a while, and now it's available for iPad. You have to buy the app for about $5 from the App Store. After you install it, you can start making music as follows:

1. **Tap GarageBand on the Home screen where it appears.**

   A menu of virtual instruments appears, as shown in Figure 2-12. Swipe left or right to scroll through them.

Figure 2-12: What instrument did you study in high school? Pick it from this list.

2. **Tap an instrument name, such as Keyboard, to display it (as shown in Figure 2-13).**

   Each instrument has slightly different options, but all allow you to record what you play on the virtual instrument; you can also play it back, visit any songs you've saved, control volume, and return to the main menu of Instruments. Tapping the Instruments button allows you to change to a different instrument.

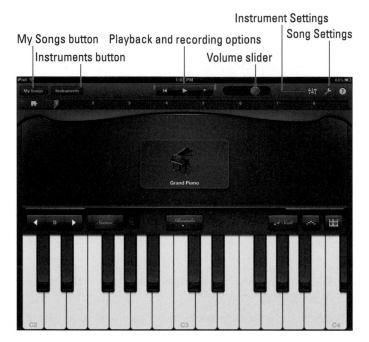

Figure 2-13: The options here allow you to be a musician, composer, or arranger.

3. **Tap the Instrument Settings button to control settings such as echo and reverb (see Figure 2-14), or tap the Song Settings button to add sounds or adjust the tempo (see Figure 2-15).**

Figure 2-14: Give your music cool effects.

Play button   Record button

Figure 2-15: Keep your song jumping by adjusting the tempo.

4. **With the instrument displayed, tap it (whether it's a drum or keyboard), to produce sounds.**

5. **If you want to record what you're playing, tap the Record button to start playing, and tap it again when you're done.**

6. **Play back what you've recorded by tapping My Songs, tapping an item, and then tapping the Play button (refer to Figure 2-15).**

There's no room here for an exhaustive tutorial on using all GarageBand instruments, but feel free to play with this fun app. You can't break anything, and the great built-in help system can help you figure most features out!

Chapter 3: Watching Videos

In This Chapter

✔ **Playing movies, podcasts, or TV shows with Videos**

✔ **Going to a movie chapter**

✔ **Deleting an item from iPad**

✔ **Finding videos on YouTube**

*i*Pad 2 sports two video cameras you can use to capture your own videos. By purchasing the iMovie app (a longtime mainstay on Mac computers), you add the capability to edit those videos.

In addition, two included applications on your iPad help you view videos. The Videos app is a player with which you can watch downloaded movies, TV shows, or media you've synced from iCloud or your Mac or PC. The YouTube app takes you online to the popular video-sharing site. As you probably know, videos here range from professional music videos to clips from news or entertainment shows and personal videos of cats dancing and other news making events as they happen. If you like to view things on a bigger screen, you can use iPad's AirPlay technology and Apple TV, a device that will cost you $99 to send your iPad movies and photos to your TV; the Apple Digital AV Adapter, a $39 accessory; or Apple TV, a device that will cost you $99.

In this chapter, I explain all about watching, editing, rating, and sharing video content from a variety of sources. You might want to refer to Book II, Chapter 1 first to purchase or download one of many free TV shows or movies you can practice with.

Getting Visual with Videos

Note that you can get video content through iTunes and some third-party companies that support iPad, including Netflix and ABC TV. You can also use an app like Air Video to send content from your Mac or PC to your iPad via a wireless connection, or use the EyeTV app from your Mac to send live TV or recordings. Some of the content you find online is free, and some shows or movies will cost you a few bucks.

You can also view videos you stream from a Home Sharing iTunes library over a home network, which can really save space on your iPad because the content can be stored on another device. Turn on Home Sharing in the Video section of iPad Settings.

This chapter focuses mainly on the bundled Videos and YouTube apps, but you should also note that more and more online content providers are making it possible to view videos on their sites. For example, you can go to Flickr and use their HTML5 player for video playback.

See Book II, Chapter 1 for more about buying or renting movies or TV shows using the iTunes Store.

Playing movies, podcasts, or TV shows with Videos

Did you realize your iPad is a miniature home entertainment center? The built-in Videos app can play TV shows, movies, and podcasts.

Use the steps in Book II, Chapter 1 to download video content to your iPad. After you've downloaded content, use these steps to work with Video's pretty familiar playback tools to play it:

1. **Tap the Videos app icon on the Home screen to open the application.**

2. **On a screen like the one shown in Figure 3-1, tap the Movies, TV Shows, or Podcasts tab, depending on which one you want to watch.**

Tap the Movies or TV Show tab

Figure 3-1: Choose the type of content you want to view.

3. **Tap an item to open it.**

A description appears, as shown in Figure 3-2.

Play button

Figure 3-2: You can get information about the media on this opening screen.

4. **Tap the Play button.**

The movie, TV show, or podcast opens and begins playing. The progress of the playback is displayed in the progress bar, showing how many minutes you've viewed and how many remain. (See Figure 3-3.) If you don't see this bar, tap the screen once to display it briefly along with a set of playback tools at the bottom of the screen.

Done button   Progress bar

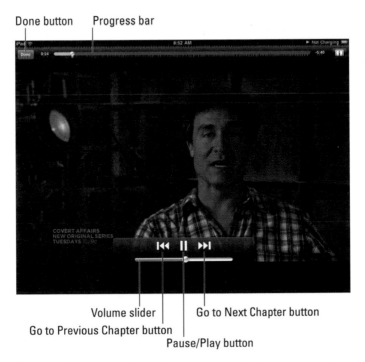

Volume slider   Go to Next Chapter button

Go to Previous Chapter button

Pause/Play button

Figure 3-3: Use the standard playback controls to play your content.

Watching non-iTunes videos

Are you limited to iTunes video content on your iPad or viewing all your downloaded content on the smaller screen? Not at all. You can connect iPad to your television, so you can watch videos on the more vision-friendly larger screen. To do this, you have to buy an Apple iPad Dock, an Apple Digital AV Adapter, or a Component and Composite Adapter at the Apple Store. You also need any other appropriate cables for your TV to complete the connection.

Note that iPad supports only the following video formats: H.264 video up to 720p, 30 frames per second; MPEG-4 video, up to 2.5 Mbps, 640 by 480 pixels, 30 frames per second; and Motion JPEG (M-JPEG) up to 35 Mbps, 1280 by 720 pixels, 30 frames per second. If you want to play AVI videos, you can use conversion software such as Mac AVI to iPad Video Converter to be able to convert, edit, and play AVI movies

on your iPad. You can also stream with Air Video Live Conversion, or use the free HandBrake app to convert to an iPad-friendly format.

In addition, you can rip Blu-ray video disc content to an iPad-compatible format and then transfer the content by syncing to your computer using iTunes. You can use the free Windows-only Aiseesoft Blu-ray to iPad Ripper at www.softdiggs.com/blu-ray-ripper.php to handle the transfer. You'll find the Mac version, under a different brand name, here: www.softdiggs.com/blu-ray-ripper-for-mac.php.

Finally, check out an app called Air Video from InMethod. Using this app, you can stream content to your iPad, convert content, or save content to iTunes, which you can then sync to your iPad.

5. **With the playback tools displayed, take any of these actions:**

   - *Tap the Pause button to pause playback.*

   - *Tap either Go to Previous Chapter or Go to Next Chapter to move to a different location in the video playback if the video supports chapters.*

   - *Tap the circular button on the Volume slider and drag it left or right to decrease or increase the volume, respectively.*

6. **To stop the video and return to the information screen, tap the Done button to the left of the progress bar.**

You can set up widescreen viewing options in the Videos section of iPad Settings. For more about using Settings, see Book I, Chapter 8.

Note that if you've watched a video and stopped it partway through, the next time you open the video in iPad it opens, by default, at the last spot you were viewing. To start a video from the beginning, just as with most players, you simply tap and drag the circular button on the progress bar all the way to the left. You can also change the default setting to start where you left off to starting from the beginning in iPad's Settings under Video.

Turning on closed-captioning

If you have hearing challenges or are a fan of foreign flicks, you'll be glad to hear that iPad offers support for closed-captioning and subtitles. This feature requires that you have content that supports closed-captioning (not all shows or movies do) and that you use iPad Settings to turn on the feature. Look for the CC logo on media you download to use this feature; be aware that video you record using the iPad video camera won't have this capability.

Turn on the feature in iPad Settings by following these steps:

1. **Tap the Settings icon on the Home screen.**

2. **On the screen that appears (see Figure 3-4), tap Video in the Settings section on the left side of the screen.**

Tap Video...   then tap here to turn on Closed Captioning

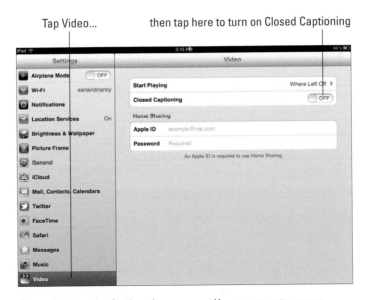

Figure 3-4: Use the Settings icon on your Home screen to access video settings.

3. **In the menu that displays on the right side of the screen (refer to Figure 3-4), tap the Closed Captioning On/Off button to turn on the feature.**

 Now when you play a movie with closed-captioning, you can click the Audio and Subtitles button to the left of the playback controls to manage these features.

Going to a movie chapter

You know that movies you view on a DVD or online are divided into chapters, so you can jump from one part to another quickly. Jumping to another chapter using the Videos app is a pretty simple procedure:

1. **Tap the Videos app icon on the Home screen.**

2. **Tap the Movies tab if it isn't already displayed.**

3. **Tap the title of the movie you want to watch.**

   Information about the movie is displayed. (Refer to Figure 3-2.)

4. **Tap the Chapters tab.**

   A list of chapters is displayed, as shown in Figure 3-5.

Chapters tab

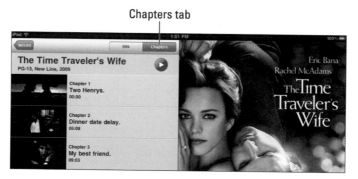

Figure 3-5: Click a chapter in this list to go to it.

5. **Tap a chapter to play it.**

You can also use the playback tools to go back one chapter or forward one chapter. See the "Playing movies, podcasts, or TV shows with Videos" section, earlier in this chapter, for more information.

Deleting an item from iPad

Media files can, as we all know, take up lots of space in a computing device. Even if you bought the iPad model with the largest amount of memory, its memory can fill up fast. When you've bought content on iTunes, you can always download it again, so if you're not planning on watching an item again soon, it's a good idea to delete it from your iPad and free up some space.

To delete items, start by tapping the Videos app icon on the Home screen. Locate the item you want to delete on the Movies, TV Shows, or Podcasts tab and then press and hold the item; a Delete button appears, as shown in Figure 3-6. Tap the Delete button, and the item is deleted.

Tap the Movies or TV Show tab

Figure 3-6: Click Delete, and your video is gone.

If you buy a video using iTunes, sync to download it to your iPad, and then delete it from iPad, you'll find it saved in your iTunes library. You can sync your computer and iPad again to download the video once more. However, rented movies, once deleted, are gone with the wind.

YouTube the iPad Way

How did we ever survive before YouTube? What would most of us do without all that free content, from new tech gadget demos by a 14-year-old kid or a CNET reviewer to TV show clips and dancing pets? Love it or not, YouTube, the popular video-sharing site, has become part of most of our lives.

So, you may be glad to hear that the preinstalled YouTube app on your iPad makes it easy to view, subscribe to, and save favorites from the site.

Finding videos on YouTube

Although you *can* go to YouTube and make use of all its features using iPad's Safari browser, there's an easier way: using the dedicated YouTube app that's included on the iPad. This version features buttons you can tap to display different content and features using the touchscreen.

Start by opening the app and finding videos you want to view:

1. **Tap the YouTube app icon on the Home screen to open it.**

2. **Tap the Featured button at the bottom of the screen (shown in Figure 3-7) if it's not already selected.**

Featured button

Figure 3-7: Buttons along the bottom help organize content.

3. **To find videos, tap in the Search field in the top-right corner of the screen.**

    The onscreen keyboard opens.

4. **Type a search term and tap the Search key on the keyboard.**

5. **Use your finger to scroll down the screen to see additional results.**

6. **To display the top-rated or most-viewed videos, tap the Top Rated or Most Viewed button at the bottom of the screen.**

7. **When you find a video you want to view, tap it to display it.**

    The video begins loading. See the next section for details on how to control the playback.

When you load a video, you can use the Related and More From tabs in the playback window to find additional content related to the topic, or more videos posted on YouTube by the same source. If you find a video you like, tap the More From tab and you can then tap the Subscribe button to subscribe to all movies from this source. View your subscriptions by tapping the Subscriptions button at the bottom of the YouTube screen.

Controlling video playback

The video playback controls in the YouTube app on your iPad sport all the familiar playback buttons you're used to, but just in case you haven't used a player in a few weeks, here's a quick rundown:

✔ The **Play button** is, logically enough, what you tap to get the video to play. (See Figure 3-8.)

Play/Pause button

Playback progress bar   Full Screen button

Figure 3-8: YouTube has the standard playback tools.

✔ The **Pause button** is used (quite logically) to pause playback. (If the button isn't visible, tap the screen once to display it.)

✔ You can move the **circular button on the Playback progress bar** (called a scrubber) right or left to move forward or backward in the video.

Was the video so good you have to watch it again? When the video is finished, you can replay it from the beginning by tapping the Play button once again.

Changing views

You know that there are times when you just have to switch from that smaller view to a full-screen view to get the most out of a video. By default, you watch a YouTube video on your iPad in the smallest of three available views for widescreen content. To change to another view, tap the Full Screen button (a two-headed arrow at the far right of the playback controls. (Refer to Figure 3-8.) The video displays in a full-screen version.

To return the movie to its smallest size, tap the button on the right side of the playback controls. Tap the button in the upper-right corner to return to the medium view.

You can use the double-tap method of enlarging the playback in either of the two larger screen formats. Double-tapping the smaller of the two moves you to the largest full-screen view. Double-tapping the largest full-screen view zooms out farther. But be forewarned: Depending on the quality of the video, the largest zoom factor can produce a rather grainy image.

Flagging content as inappropriate

If there's a chance your kids or younger siblings can get ahold of your iPad, you might appreciate the capability to flag inappropriate content on YouTube. First, you have to set a restriction in your YouTube account, and then set a flag using the iPad YouTube app. A flag requires that a passcode be entered in order to access that content.

Here are the steps involved in flagging content on the iPad, after you've set a restriction in YouTube:

1. **With a video open in the YouTube application in the smaller view, tap in the black area near the top of the screen to display tools, as shown in Figure 3-9.**

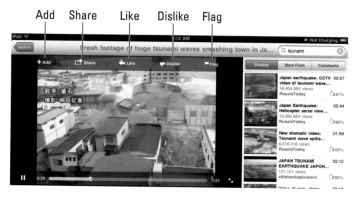

Figure 3-9: Displaying the toolbar in the YouTube app.

2. **Tap the Flag option.**
3. **Tap the Flag as Inappropriate button that appears.**

Rating videos

Part of the fun of YouTube is the fact that the masses can rate videos to express their opinions. This rating system also helps you find the best of the best videos, according to those who have recorded their opinion.

You can easily rate videos yourself using the YouTube app on your iPad. Follow these steps to rate a video:

1. **Display a video you want to rate in the smaller view.**

2. **Tap the Like or Dislike button (refer to Figure 3-9).**

   You're asked to sign into your YouTube account. After you're signed in, your Like or Dislike rating is accepted.

That's it! Your opinion has been noted and can help guide others to great content, or steer them away from the not so great.

You can view the highest-rated videos on YouTube by tapping the Top Rated button at the bottom of the screen.

Sharing videos

Found a video you like? Just as you can use your computer to share YouTube videos you like, you can share links to videos with others from your iPad using e-mail or Twitter. Here's how:

1. **Display a video you want to share in the smallest view.**

2. **Tap the Share button (refer to Figure 3-9).**

3. **Tap either Mail Link to this Video or Tweet.**

4. **In the e-mail form shown in Figure 3-10, type a recipient in the To field and add to the message if you like. If you chose to post a tweet, enter your message in the Tweet form.**

Figure 3-10: Fill out the simple e-mail form, which has the subject already filled in for you.

5. **Tap the Send button to send a link to the video or post your tweet.**

Connecting iPad to high-definition devices

iPad 2 added the capability to connect the device, using an Apple Digital AV Adapter cable (a $39 accessory), to another device that supports Thunderbolt and HDMI connections. At this writing, there aren't many of these devices actually out there, but many are being developed.

Thunderbolt is the latest and greatest high-speed input/out interface. Thunderbolt's major advantage is speed when working with high-resolution displays, and because of that speed, it may just become the new technology du jour.

Adding to video favorites

Have you discovered a video you want to play again and again? You can use the Favorites feature of the iPad YouTube app to save such videos to your Favorites folder for easy access.

Save a video to Favorites using these steps:

1. **Display a video you want to add to Favorites in the smallest view.**
2. **Tap the Add button (refer to Figure 3-9).**
3. **In the menu, tap Favorites.**
4. **To view your favorite movies, tap the Favorites button at the bottom of the YouTube screen.**

    Your Favorites folder containing all your favorite videos is displayed.

 To delete a favorite while in the Favorites screen, tap the Edit button. Delete buttons appear on each movie. Tap the movie-specific Delete button to remove that movie. Tap the Done button to leave Editing mode.

Chapter 4: Getting the Most Out of iPad Cameras and FaceTime

In This Chapter

✔ **Looking good in photos**

✔ **Taking videos**

✔ **Working with your videos in iMovie**

✔ **Making video calls with FaceTime**

*W*ith its gorgeous screen, the iPad is a natural for viewing photos and videos. It supports most common photo formats, such as JPEG, TIFF, and PNG. You can shoot your photos and videos by using the built-in cameras in iPad.

If you like to play around with photos, you'll enjoy the pre-installed app, Photo Booth, which provides some rather weird and wonderful effects that make your photos stand out.

If video is more up your alley, in this chapter you also discover how to use the video cameras in iPad and edit videos with the popular iMovie app. For those who want to share their video with others, I cover using the video cameras along with FaceTime to make video calls.

Working with Photos

With iPad 2 comes cameras — two, to be exact. These cameras allow you to capture video and photos. And because one camera is front-facing and the other is rear-facing, you can switch between them to capture images of yourself holding the iPad or images of what you're looking at. The front-facing camera captures VGA video and photos at 800 x 600 resolution; the rear-facing camera captures high-definition video and photos at 1280 x 720 resolution.

When you capture photos, they appear in the Photos app's Camera Roll, where you can view them, e-mail them, and so on. (See Book II, Chapter 6 for more about using the Photos app).

The cameras in the iPad 2 are just begging to be used, so let's get started!

Taking pictures with the iPad camera

When you use an iPad camera, you can switch it between a standard camera and a video camera, and choose whether to use the front or back camera. To work with the standard camera to take pictures, follow these steps:

1. **Tap the Camera app icon on the Home screen to open the app.**

   If the Camera/Video slider setting at the bottom-right corner of the screen (see Figure 4-1) is shifted to the right, slide it to the left to choose the still camera rather than video.

Switch between front and rear cameras

Options button

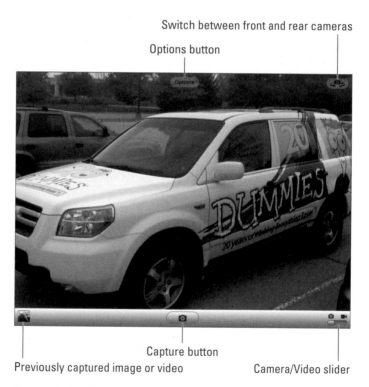

Capture button

Previously captured image or video

Camera/Video slider

Figure 4-1: The Camera app.

2. **Tap the Options button, tap the On/Off button for Grid, and then tap Done.**

   This turns on a grid that helps you position a subject within the grid and autofocus.

3. **Move the camera around until you find a pleasing image, and then you can do a couple of things at this point to help you take your photo:**

    - Tap the area of the grid where you want Camera to autofocus.

    - Pinch the screen to display a zoom control; drag the circle in the zoom bar to the right or left to crop the image to a smaller area.

4. **Tap the Capture button at the bottom center of the screen.**

    You've just taken a picture, and it has been stored in the Photos app automatically.

5. **Tap the icon in the top-right corner to switch between the front camera and rear camera.**

    You can now take pictures of yourself.

6. **Tap the Capture button and release it to take another picture.**

    (Remember to smile!)

7. **To view the last photo taken, swipe to the left or tap the thumbnail of the latest image in the bottom-left corner of the screen.**

    The Photos app opens and displays the photo.

8. **Tap the Menu button.**

    A menu appears, allowing you to e-mail, instant message, or Tweet the photo, assign it to a contact, use it as iPad wallpaper, print it, or copy it (as shown in Figure 4-2).

Delete button

Menu button

Slideshow button

Edit button

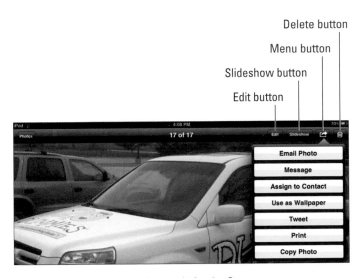

Figure 4-2: The simple set of controls for the Camera app.

9. **Tap the Delete button if you want to delete the photo.**

   The image is deleted.

10. **Tap the Home button to close Photos and return to the Home screen.**

Tap the screen in a particular area of an image before taking your photo to have the camera adjust focus on that area using the autofocus feature.

The iPad 2 cameras and the iPhone 4 and 4S cameras are similar, but they do have differences. If you want more useful tips on getting the most out of Photos on your iPad, check out *iPhone Photography and Video For Dummies,* by Angelo Micheletti (John Wiley & Sons).

Printing photos

If you have a wireless printer that's compatible with Apple AirPrint technology, you can print photos. As of this writing, only a handful of HP printers have this capability, but you can bet Apple's working with other manufacturers to provide more compatible choices. However, you can also use apps such as Printopia and AirPrint Activator 2 to provide this functionality to other wireless printers.

If you don't have access to this kind of wireless printer, when you plug iPad into your computer you can simply use Windows Explorer or, on a Mac, the Finder to open the DCIM folder on your iPad, and copy and paste photos into your computer for printing.

To print a photo, do this:

1. **With Photos open, maximize the photo you want to print.**

2. **Tap the Menu button (refer to Figure 4-2) and then tap Print.**

   The Printer Options dialog appears. (See Figure 4-3.)

Figure 4-3: The Printer Options dialog box.

3. **Tap Select Printer.**

   iPad searches for a compatible wireless printer.

4. **Tap the plus or minus symbols in the Copy field to set the number of copies to print.**

5. **Tap the Print button.**

   Your photo is on its way.

Playing around with Photo Booth

With each new iteration of its operating system, iPad tends to add an app or two that comes preinstalled. With iOS 4.3, Apple added Photo Booth, an app that goes hand in hand with the still camera built into the iPad 2 hardware. The app allows you to choose interesting effects such as Kaleidoscope and X-Ray to apply to the photos you take. You can then copy or e-mail photos from within Photo Booth.

Note that photos you take with Photo Booth open automatically and are saved to your Photos app Camera Roll.

Here's how to take photos using Photo Booth effects:

1. **Tap the Photo Booth icon on the Home screen.**

   The different possible effects that can be used in the current view of the camera appear. (See Figure 4-4.)

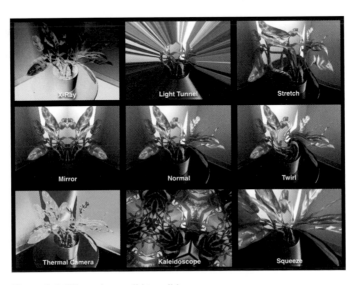

Figure 4-4: Effects from mild to wild.

   2. **Tap an effect.**

   3. **Tap the Capture button.**

   An image using that effect is captured. (See Figure 4-5.)

   To return to the various effects, tap the Effects button in the bottom-left corner of the screen.

   The image appears along with a filmstrip of all images you've captured using Photo Booth.

Figure 4-5: My calculator, twisted with a Photo Booth effect.

   4. **If you want to delete a photo, tap the Menu button, tap a photo, tap the X that appears, and then tap Delete.**

   5. **Tap the Home button.**

   You return to the Home screen, and your photos are now available in the Camera Roll folder of the Photos app.

Exploring the iPad Video Camera and iMovie

Perhaps you have a bit of Steven Spielberg in you — you long to make your own movies and edit them into masterpieces. If so, the iPad video camera turns this really cool device into your dream machine.

You can capture video with the iPad and then use iMovie software to edit and combine video clips any way you like. You can also edit videos taken with an iPhone or iPod touch you've synced through iTunes or iCloud. In this section, you discover the ins and outs of making movies with iPad.

Capturing your own videos with the built-in cameras

In iPad 2, two video cameras that can capture video from either the front or back of the device make it possible for you to take videos that you can then share with others or edit. (Find out more about video editing in the next section.)

To record a video, follow these steps:

Book II
Chapter 4

1. **Tap the Camera app on the Home screen.**

   The Camera app opens.

2. **Use the Camera/Video slider to switch from the still camera to the video camera (as shown in Figure 4-6).**

Getting the Most
Out of iPad Cameras
and FaceTime

Switch between front and rear cameras

Previously captured image or video

Record button   Camera/Video slider

Figure 4-6: It takes one tap to move between camera and video.

3. **If you want to switch between the front and back cameras, tap the icon in the top-right corner of the screen (as shown in Figure 4-6).**

4. **Tap the Record button to begin recording the video.**

   The Record button flashes when the camera is recording.

5. **To stop recording, tap the Record button again.**

   A thumbnail link to your new video is now displayed in the bottom-left corner of the screen.

Before you start recording, make sure you know where the camera lens is (in the top-center portion of the device on the front and top-right side of the back) — while holding the iPad and panning, you can easily put your fingers directly over the lens!

Editing movies with the iMovie app

The iMovie app has been supplied with Mac computers for several years, and now a less robust version is available for the iPad. After you capture a video, you can use iMovie to edit it. This task gives you a brief overview of what you can do with iMovie.

Now you should know, this one will cost you some cash. Start by purchasing iMovie from the App Store. (It costs $4.99.) For more about purchasing apps, see Book I, Chapter 5. After you've installed the app, you can edit movies by following these steps:

1. **Tap the iMovie app icon on the Home screen.**

   iMovie opens.

2. **On the screen that appears, tap the New button shown in Figure 4-7.**

   A new movie project opens. Any videos you've taken (see the previous section) are displayed as thumbnails in the top-left corner of the screen.

3. **Double-tap a video to open it (see Figure 4-8).**

4. **Tap the storyboard to scroll through your video frames.**

   Wherever the red line sits (refer to Figure 4-8) is where your next action, such as playing the video or adding a transition, begins.

5. **To add one video to the end of another, double-tap another clip in the list of media.**

   The clip appears to the right of the first one in the storyboard.

New button

Figure 4-7: Starting a new iMovie project.

Settings button
Undo button
Thumbnails of media   Toolbar   Media preview

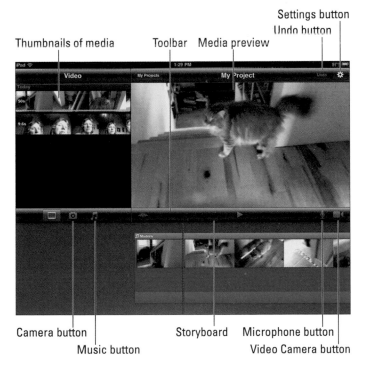

Camera button   Storyboard   Microphone button
        Music button   Video Camera button

Figure 4-8: Open a video on your iPad.

6. **If you want to add music to your videos, tap the Music button (refer to Figure 4-8).**

   The option of sound effects, music in your Music library, or theme music becomes available.

7. **Tap a music option to add it to the video, or drag the item to the time-line to make it a background track or associate it with a specific clip.**

   To undo any action, tap the Undo button. (Refer to Figure 4-8.)

8. **To record an audio narration, scroll to the point in the movie where you want it to be heard and tap the Microphone button (refer to Figure 4-8).**

   a. *Tap the Record button, wait for the countdown to complete, and then record.*

   b. *When you're done recording, tap Stop (as shown in Figure 4-9).*

Tap this button

Figure 4-9: Use the red button to start and stop recording.

9. **In the options shown in Figure 4-10, tap Review to hear your record-ing, Accept to save the recording, or Discard or Retake if you're not completely happy with it.**

   If you accept the recording, it appears below the storyboard at the point in the movie where it will play back.

Figure 4-10: Choose options for recording your video.

You can do more things with iMovie, such as add transitions between clips or rearrange and cut segments out of clips. Play around with iMovie to see the possibilities, or check out *iLife '11 For Dummies,* by Tony Bove, or *iPhone Photography & Video For Dummies*, by Angelo Micheletti.

If you want to create a slideshow with still photos rather than video, tap the Camera button (shown in Figure 4-8), and your stored photos are listed instead.

To quickly return from iMovie to your camera, perhaps to capture more footage, tap the Video Camera button shown in Figure 4-8.

You can tap the Settings button (refer to Figure 4-8) to open a menu that lets you make settings for playing theme music, looping the music to play continuously, and using a special effect to fade your movie in or out at the beginning and end.

Getting Face to Face with FaceTime

FaceTime is an excellent video calling app that's been available on the iPhone 4 since its release in mid-2010 and has now come to iPad 2. The app lets you call people who have FaceTime on their iOS 5 devices — whether iPhone 4/4S, iPad 2, or fourth-generation iPod touch — or Mac (running Mac OS X 10.6.6 or later) using either a phone number (iPhone 4 and 4S) or an e-mail address (Mac, iPod touch, or iPad 2). You and your friend or family member can see each other as you talk, which makes for a much more personal calling experience.

You can also show the person on the other end of the call your surroundings by using the rear iPad camera and panning around you. The possibilities are limitless: Show your husband the toy you're thinking of buying your son for his birthday, let your girlfriend see the new car you're thinking of buying while she's busy at work, or share your artwork or trip to wine country with friends.

You can use your Apple ID and e-mail address to access FaceTime, so once you install it, it works pretty much out of the box. See Book I, Chapter 5 for more about getting an Apple ID.

If you're having trouble using FaceTime, make sure the feature is turned on. Tap Settings on the Home screen and then tap FaceTime. Tap the On/Off button to turn it on, if necessary. You can also select the e-mail account that can be used to make phone calls to you on this Settings page.

Making a FaceTime call

You can make and receive calls with FaceTime using a phone number (iPhone 4/4S) or an e-mail account (iPad 2, iPod touch, or Mac) and show the person on the other end what's going on around you.

At the time of this writing, you can use FaceTime only over a Wi-Fi network, not over 3G, which limits the places from which you can make or receive video calls to your home wireless network or a public hotspot. On the other hand, you avoid costly data usage over a 3G network with this setup.

You have to use the appropriate method for placing a FaceTime call, depending on the kind of device the person you're calling has. If you're calling an iPhone 4/4S user, you should use a phone number the first time you call and thereafter you can use the phone number or e-mail address; if you're calling an iPad 2, an iPod touch, or a FaceTime for Mac user, you have to make the call using that person's e-mail address.

You can't adjust audio volume from within the app or record a video call. Nevertheless, on the positive side, though its features are limited, this app is very straightforward to use.

1. **Connect to a Wi-Fi network.**

   See Book I, Chapter 5 for details on connecting.

2. **If you know that the person you're calling has FaceTime on an iPhone 4/4S, an iPad 2, or a Mac, add the person to your iPad Contacts.**

   See Book V, Chapter 5 for how to do this if that person isn't already in Contacts.

3. **Tap the FaceTime app icon on the Home screen.**

   The FaceTime screen appears.

4. **Tap the Contacts button in the bottom-right corner of the screen.**

5. **Scroll to locate and tap a contact's name.**

   The contact's information is displayed (as shown in Figure 4-11).

6. **Tap the contact's stored phone number or e-mail address.**

   You've just placed a FaceTime call!

When you call somebody using an e-mail address, the person must be signed in to his Apple ID account and have verified that the address can be used for FaceTime calls. iPad 2 and iPod touch (fourth-generation) users can make this setting by tapping Settings and then FaceTime; FaceTime for Mac users make this setting by choosing FaceTime⇨Preferences.

When the person accepts the call, you see a large screen that displays the recipient's image alongside a small screen containing your image. (See Figure 4-12.)

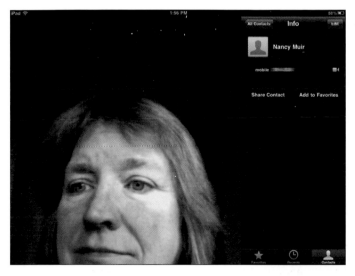

Figure 4-11: Information displayed in Contacts.

Figure 4-12: A FaceTime call in progress.

You can also simply go to the Contacts app, find a contact, and tap the FaceTime icon next to that person's phone number or e-mail address in the contact record to make a FaceTime call.

To view recent calls, tap the Recents button in Step 3. Tap a recent call, and iPad displays that person's information. You can tap the contact's phone number or e-mail to call the person back.

Accepting or ending a FaceTime call

If you're on the receiving end of a FaceTime call, accepting the call is about as easy as it gets. When the call comes in, follow these steps:

1. **Tap the Accept button to take the call or tap the Decline button to reject it (see Figure 4-13).**

   Chat away with your friend, swapping video images.

Figure 4-13: You're it; accept or decline the call.

2. **When you're done talking, tap the End button (shown in Figure 4-14).**

   The call ends.

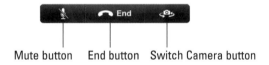

Mute button   End button   Switch Camera button

Figure 4-14: Ending a FaceTime call.

To mute sound during a call, tap the Mute button. (Refer to Figure 4-14.) Tap the button again to unmute your iPad or iPhone.

To add a caller to your Favorites list, with FaceTime open (refer to Figure 4-11), tap the Favorites button and then tap the plus sign and select the person's name from the contact list to add the person to Favorites. You can then locate the person to make a call to her by tapping Favorites rather than Contacts.

Switching views

When you're on a FaceTime call, you might want to use iPad's built-in camera to show the person you're talking to what's going on around you. Tap the Switch Camera button (refer to Figure 4-14) to switch from the front-facing camera that's displaying your image to the back-facing camera that captures whatever you're looking at (shown in Figure 4-15).

Figure 4-15: Show your friend what's in front of you.

Tap the Switch Camera button again. You switch back to the front camera, displaying your image.

Chapter 5: Getting Social with Twitter and iMessage

In This Chapter

✓ Using Twitter on iPad

✓ Creating an iMessage account

✓ Utilizing iMessage to address, create, and send messages

✓ Deleting a conversation

nless you've spent the last few years working in Antarctica without a radio, you know that Twitter is a social networking service referred to as a *microblog,* because it involves only short posted messages. Twitter has been incorporated into iOS 5, so you can tweet people from within the Safari, Photos, Camera, YouTube, and Maps apps. You can also download the free Twitter app and use it to post tweets whenever you like.

iMessage is another new feature in iOS 5 (available through the preinstalled Messages app) for instant messaging (IM). IM involves sending a text message to somebody's iPhone (using their phone number) or iPod touch or iPad (using their e-mail address) to carry on an instant conversation.

In this chapter, I introduce you to ways in which iPad makes use of Twitter and instant messaging to let you stay connected to the world.

Experiencing Twitter on iPad

Twitter is a social networking service for *micro-blogging,* which involves posting very short messages (tweets; limited to 140 characters) online so your friends can see what you're up to. Many readers already have a Twitter account and are hooked on tweeting. If you have never tweeted, you can go to www.twitter.com to sign up with the service; there is also a free Twitter app for iPad you can download and use to manage your Twitter account. Once you have an account, you can post tweets, have people follow your tweets, and follow the tweets that other people post.

With iOS 5 for iPad, the ability to tweet has been integrated into several apps. You can post tweets using the Menu button within Safari, Photos, Camera, YouTube, and Maps. First, sign up for an account, then download the free Twitter app to your iPad. (See Book I, Chapter 5 for more about downloading apps.) Go to iPad Settings and tap Twitter. Then add your account information.

Now, when you're using Safari, Photos, Camera, YouTube, or Maps, you can choose Tweet from a menu. You'll see a Tweet form like that shown in Figure 5-1. Just write your message in the form and then tap Send. Note that a number in the bottom-right corner lets you know how many characters you have left to use in your tweet.

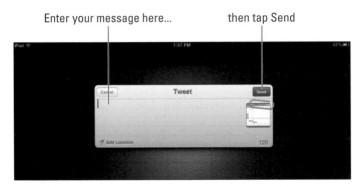

Enter your message here...   then tap Send

Figure 5-1: Tweeting is a simple menu choice in several apps.

See Book I, Chapter 6; Book II, Chapter 6; or Book II, Chapter 3 for more about tweeting in the Safari, Photos, or YouTube apps, respectively.

When you're filling out the Tweet form, you can tap Add Location to turn on Location Services, which allows Twitter to ascertain your location and share it with others. Be cautious about using this feature; if many people follow you on Twitter, they can use your location to track your movements and know where you live, where you go to school, where you socialize, and so on. This information can be used to commit a variety of online and offline crimes.

Setting Up an iMessage Account

iMessage is a new feature in iOS 5 (available through the preinstalled Messages app) that allows you to send and receive instant messages (IMs) to others using an Apple iOS device. Instant messaging differs from e-mail or tweeting in an important way. Whereas you might e-mail somebody and wait days or weeks before that person responds, or you might post a tweet that could sit there a while before anybody views it, instant messaging communication happens immediately. You send an IM, and it appears on somebody's iPhone, iPod touch, or iPad right away, and assuming the person wants to participate in a live conversation, it begins immediately, allowing a back-and-forth dialogue in real time.

To set up iMessage, follow these steps:

1. **Tap Settings on the Home screen.**

2. **Tap Messages.**

   The settings shown in Figure 5-2 are displayed.

Make sure this is set to On

Figure 5-2: Turn on iMessage in Settings.

3. **If iMessage isn't set to On, tap the On/Off button (shown in Figure 5-2) to turn it on.**

4. **Check to be sure the e-mail account associated with your iPad is correct.**

   (This should be set up automatically based on your Apple ID.)

5. **To allow a notice to be sent when you've read somebody's messages, tap the On/Off button for Send Read Receipts.**

6. **If you want to include a subject field in messages, tap the On/Off button for the Show Subject Field option.**

7. **Tap the Home button to leave the settings.**

To change the e-mail account used by iMessage, tap the name of the current e-mail account, then tap the Delete button that appears, and then follow the steps above to add another e-mail account.

Using iMessage to Address, Create, and Send Messages

Now you're ready to use iMessage. This is a remarkably simple process that involves typing and sending a message, and then waiting while the other person types and sends a message back. This can go on for hours, so prepare a quick exit message ahead of time, just in case. (I have to walk my dog, the cat just exploded, . . . you get the idea.)

1. **From the Home screen, tap the Messages icon.**

2. **If this is the first time you're using iMessage, on the screen that appears (see Figure 5-3), tap the New Message button to begin a conversation.**

3. **You can address a message in a couple of ways:**

   • Begin to type an address in the To field, and a list of matching contacts appears.

   • Tap the plus icon on the right of the address field, and the All Contacts list is displayed, as shown in Figure 5-4.

4. **Tap a contact on the list you chose to display in Step 3.**

   If the contact has both an e-mail address and phone number stored, the Info dialog appears, allowing you to tap on one or the other, which addresses the message.

5. **To create a message, simply tap in the message field near the bottom of the screen and type your message.**

6. **To send the message, tap the Send button (refer to Figure 5-3).**

   When your recipient(s) responds, you'll see the conversation displayed on the right side of the screen, as shown in Figure 5-5.

New Message button   Address field

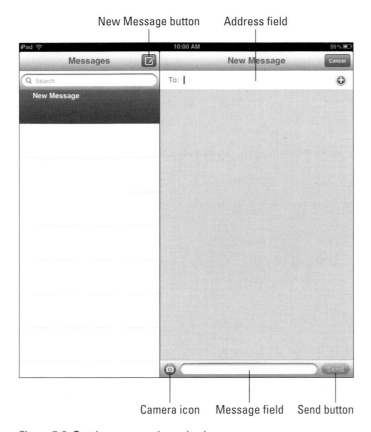

Camera icon   Message field   Send button

Figure 5-3: Get the conversation going here.

Note that you can modify your own profile with the Messages app. Just tap the tiny silhouette of a person in the upper-right corner, and an Info screen appears. Tap Edit, and a form is displayed where you can change your information, including your name, phone number, or e-mail, and add your photo to your messages.

If you want to include another photo or video with your message, tap the Camera icon to the left of the message field. (Refer to Figure 5-3.) Tap Take Photo or Video or Choose Existing and then Use, depending on whether you want to create a new photo/video or send one you've already taken. When you send your message, the photo or video will go along with your text.

Here are some additional tips for using iMessage:

✔ **Talking with multiple people:** You can address a message to more than one person by simply choosing more recipients in Step 4 in the preceding steps list.

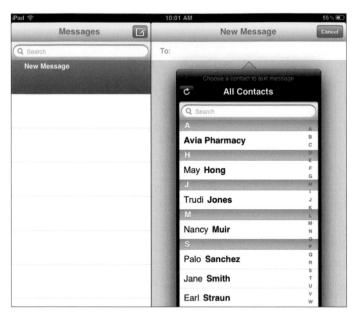

Figure 5-4: You can choose somebody to message from your Contacts list.

Menu button

The conversation is displayed here

Figure 5-5: Follow the conversation as you and your friend text back and forth.

✔ **Canceling a message:** If you begin a conversation and change your mind before sending your message, tap the Cancel button near the top of the screen.

✔ **Viewing a conversation:** Your conversations are listed in the left pane of the Messages app. Tap one, and the various comments in it are displayed, along with a note of the date and time of each comment.

Clearing a Conversation

When you're done chatting, you might want to clear a conversation to remove the clutter before you start a new one.

To clear a conversation, follow these steps:

1. **With Messages open, tap the Menu button (refer to Figure 5-5).**

2. **Tap the Clear All button (see Figure 5-6).**

Clear All button

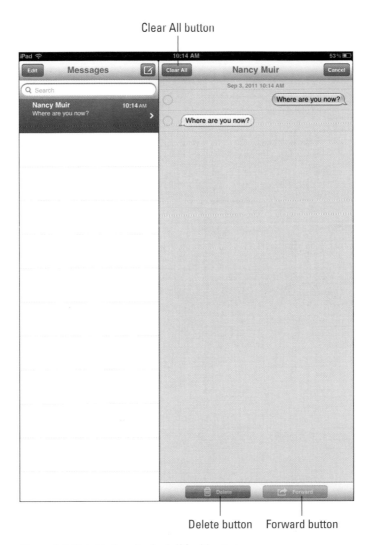

Book II
Chapter 5

Getting Social
with Twitter
and iMessage

Delete button   Forward button

Figure 5-6: Get rid of yesterday's IM with a tap.

3. Tap Clear Conversation.

You can also tap the Menu button, tap the text of a particular conversation, and then tap the Delete or Forward button on the bottom of the screen (refer to Figure 5-6) to delete that one conversation or forward its contents to somebody.

Chapter 6: Playing with the Photos App

In This Chapter

✏ **Importing photos from iPhone or a digital camera**

✏ **Viewing an album**

✏ **Viewing individual photos**

✏ **Editing photos**

✏ **Organizing photos in Camera Roll**

✏ **Sharing photos**

With its gorgeous screen, iPad is a natural for viewing photos. It supports most common photo formats, such as JPEG, TIFF, and PNG. With an iPad 2, you can shoot your own photos using the built-in cameras (see Book II, Chapter 4, for more about using them) or sync your photos from iCloud or your computer, iPhone, or digital camera. You can also save images you find online to your iPad or receive them by e-mail, iMessage, or tweet.

After you have photos to play with, the Photos app lets you organize photos from the Camera Roll (called Saved Photos on iPad 1), view them in albums, one by one, or in a slideshow. You can also e-mail, message, or tweet a photo to a friend, print it, or use your expensive gadget as an electronic picture frame, all of which you read about in this chapter.

Getting Photos into iPad

Before you can play around with photos, you have to take some with the iPad camera or get them into iPad from another source. There are a few different ways to get photos from elsewhere. You can buy an accessory to import them from your camera or iPhone, save a photo you find on the web or receive as an e-mail, message, or tweet attachment, or sync to iCloud or your computer to download photos you've saved there. The whole syncing process is discussed in Book I, Chapter 5. The two other methods are explained here.

Screenshots you take of your iPad screen are also saved to the Saved Photos/ Camera Roll album. To take a screenshot, display what you want to shoot, press and hold the Home button, tap the Sleep/Wake button, and then release. You'll find your screenshot in Photos' Camera Roll album on an iPad 2 or Saved Photos album on an original iPad.

Importing photos from an iPhone, iPod, or digital camera

Your iPad camera or a computer aren't the only source of photos. You can import photos from a digital camera and photos or videos from your iPhone/ iPod touch if you buy the iPad Camera Connection Kit from Apple, which will set you back about $29. The kit contains two adapters (see Figure 6-1): a USB Camera Connector to import photos from a digital camera or iPhone, and an SD Card Reader to import image files from an SD card.

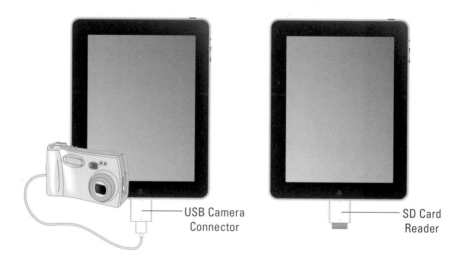

USB Camera Connector

SD Card Reader

Figure 6-1: These two adapters are included in the connector kit accessory.

 If you've got an iPhone 3G or earlier model, sad to say, it isn't supported by the connector kit.

 You can find information in Book I, Chapter 5 about syncing iCloud content or your computer with your iPad to port over photos. You can also find out how to take and use photos from iPad's built-in camera in Book II, Chapter 4.

Follow these steps to import photos, after you have the connector kit in hand:

1. **Start the import process by putting your iPad to sleep using the switch on the top right.**

2. **Insert the USB Camera Connector into the Dock connector slot of your iPad.**

3. **Connect the USB end of the cord that came with your digital camera or iPhone into the USB Camera Connector.**

4. **Connect the other end of the cord that came with your camera or iPhone into that device.**

5. **Wake your iPad.**

   The Photos app opens and displays the photos on the digital camera or iPhone.

6. **Tap Import All on your iPad; if you want to import only selected photos, tap individual photos, and then tap Import. Finally, tap Import rather than Import All.**

   The photos are saved to the Last Import album.

7. **Disconnect the cord and the adapter.**

   You're done!

Book II
Chapter 6

Playing with the
Photos App

 You can also import photos stored on an *SD* (secure digital) memory card often used by digital cameras as a storage medium. Simply put the iPad to sleep, connect the SD Card Reader to the iPad, insert the SD card containing the photos, and then follow Steps 5 through 7 in the preceding list.

 Though not promoted as a feature by Apple, people have discovered that you can also use the USB connector in the connector kit to connect audio devices such as speakers or headphones, and to hook up some USB-connected keyboards that have lower power consumption. Some media readers will also allow you to get photos off compact flash drives, memory sticks, and SD and xD cards.

Saving photos from the web

The web offers a wealth of images that you can download to your Photo library on the iPad. The built-in Safari browser makes it simple to save any image you come across to your iPad. (Of course, you should be careful not to violate copyrights when grabbing pictures online.)

Several search engines have advanced search features that allow you to search for only nonlicensed images, meaning, at least theoretically, you don't have to pay for the images. But it's always a good idea to get written permission to use an image, especially if you intend to use it to make money (as with a company brochure or online course).

Follow these steps to save images from the web:

1. **Open Safari and navigate to the web page containing the image you want.**

2. **Press and hold the image.**

   A menu appears, as shown in Figure 6-2.

Tap this option

Figure 6-2: Use this menu to save an image to your iPad.

3. **Tap Save Image.**

   The image is saved to your Camera Roll album in the Photos app, as shown in Figure 6-3. Note that this album is called Saved Photos on a first-generation iPad.

For more about how to use Safari to navigate to or search for web content, see Book I, Chapter 6.

Camera Roll album

Figure 6-3: Photos you save from the Internet go into the Saved Photos/Camera Roll album.

Looking at Photos

Pictures were made to be looked at, so knowing how to view the albums and individual photos you manage to get into your iPad is a way to tap into the key strength of the Photos app. In this section, you get some tips for taking your viewing experience to the max.

If you want to do more than look at photos, check out a few of these photo-editing apps that were designed to work with iPad: Photogene for iPad, PhotoForge for iPad, and the free PhotoPad by ZAGG. All three are available through the Apple App Store.

Viewing an album

The Photos app organizes your pictures into albums using such criteria as the folder on your computer from which you synced the photos or whether you captured your photo using the iPad 2 camera. You may also have albums for images you synced from devices such as your iPhone or digital camera.

To view your albums, start by tapping the Photos app icon in the Dock on the Home screen. If the Photos tab is selected when the Photos app opens, tap the Albums tab shown in Figure 6-4. Now you can tap an album, and the photos in it are displayed.

If you're a Mac user, try using iPhoto to create new albums for organizing your iPad content before you sync to your iPad. If you're on a Windows machine, check out two products for managing and syncing photos to iPad: Lightroom from Adobe (www.adobe.com) or Adobe's Photoshop Elements. You can also create picture subfolders in Windows Explorer and when you sync, each subfolder becomes an album on your iPad.

Tap this tab

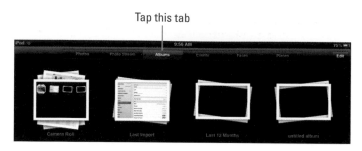

Figure 6-4: Switch between individual photos and albums using these tabs.

Viewing individual photos

After you figure out what album your images are in, you have several fun ways to interact with individual photos. The iPad touchscreen is the key to this very tactile experience.

Tap the Photos app icon in the Dock on the Home screen and then tap the Photos tab (shown in Figure 6-5).

Now try out these techniques:

Tap this tab

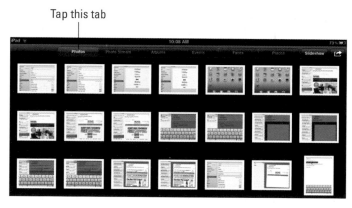

Figure 6-5: Viewing thumbnails of individual photos.

✔ **Full-screen view:** To view a photo, either tap the photo thumbnail or pinch your fingers together, place them on the photo, and then spread your fingers apart. The picture expands, as shown in Figure 6-6.

✔ **Browsing an album:** Flick your finger to the left or right to scroll through the individual photos in that album.

✏ **Multiple photos:** To reduce the display size of an individual photo and return to the multipicture view, place two fingers on the photo and then pinch them together. You can also tap the Albums button (which may display the currently open album's name) to view the album's entire contents.

✏ **Twirling:** Place two fingers on a photo and spin them to the left or right. This maneuver, known as *grab and spin,* twirls the photo on the screen (and it's lots of fun to do).

Do you like to associate a face with a name? Doing so can help you keep your clients or other contacts straight. You can place a photo on a person's information page in the Contacts app on your iPad. For more about how to do this, see Book V, Chapter 5.

Figure 6-6: An expanded photo.

You can use the Faces, Places, and Events buttons to view photos by faces included in them, by location, or by an event category, such as Wedding or Picnic. In fact, anything geotagged by a smart camera will include this type of data.

Editing Photos

A new feature in iOS 5 is the ability to edit photos. This feature allows you to rotate images, enhance image quality, get rid of that pesky red-eye, or crop to exactly the area of the image that you want to display.

To edit photos:

1. **Tap the Photos app on the Home screen to open it.**

2. **Using methods previously described in this chapter, locate a photo you want to edit.**

3. **Tap the Edit button.**

   The Edit Photo screen, shown in Figure 6-7, appears.

4. **At this point, you can take four possible actions:**

   - *Rotate:* Tap the Rotate button to rotate the image 90 degrees at a time. Continue to tap the button to move another 90 degrees.

   - *Enhance:* Tap Enhance to turn Auto-Enhance on or off. This feature optimizes the crispness of the image.

Figure 6-7: New with iOS 5 comes the ability to edit photos.

   - *Red-Eye:* Tap Red-Eye if a person in a photo has that dreaded red-eye effect. When you activate this feature, simply tap each eye that needs clearing up.

   - *Crop:* To crop the photo to a portion of its original area, tap the Crop button. You can then tap any corner of the image and drag inward or outward to remove areas of the photo.

In each of the four editing features you see Cancel and Revert to Original buttons. If you don't like the changes you made, use either of these to stop making changes or undo the changes you've already made. Choosing Cancel will end the editing session, while Revert to Original leaves you in editing mode.

Organizing Photos in Camera Roll

You can organize photos in albums so it's easier to locate them in the future. To do this, follow these steps:

1. **Display the Camera Roll album.**

   (If you have a first-generation iPad with no camera, this album is called Saved Photos.)

2. **Tap the Menu button in the top-right corner and then tap individual photos to select them.**

   Small check marks appear on the selected photos. (See Figure 6-8.)

Check marks indicate selected photos

Figure 6-8: Select the photos you want to work with here.

3. **Tap the Menu button and then tap Add to Existing Album or Add to New Album.**

4. **Tap an existing album or enter a name for a new album (depending on your previous selection) and tap Save.**

   If you created a new album, it now appears in the Photos main screen with the Albums displayed.

You can also choose the Share, Copy, or Delete button when you've selected photos in Step 2 of this task. This allows you to share, copy, or delete multiple photos at a time.

Sharing Photos

Part of the fun of taking photos is sharing those images with others. It's easy to share photos stored on your iPad by sending them as instant messages, tweets, or e-mail attachments. Follow these steps to do just that:

1. **Tap the Photos app icon in the Dock on the Home screen.**

2. **Tap the Photos tab and locate the photo you want to share.**

3. **Tap the photo to select it and then tap the Menu button (it looks like a box with an arrow jumping out of it).**

   The menu shown in Figure 6-9 appears.

Tap the Menu button...

then tap one of these options

Figure 6-9: The Menu offers different options.

4. **Tap the Email Photo, Message, or Tweet option.**

5. **In the message form that appears, make any modifications you want in the To, Cc/Bcc, or Subject fields for e-mail, or enter your iMessage or tweet text.**

6. **Tap the Send button.**

   The message and photo go on their way.

You can also copy and paste a photo into documents, such as those created in the Pages word processor app that you can purchase for about $9.99. To do this, press and hold a photo in Photos until the Copy Photo command appears. Tap Copy, and then in the destination app, press and hold the screen and tap Paste.

Running a Slideshow

You can run a slideshow of your images in Photos and even play music and choose transition effects for the show. This is a great way to give a presentation to a client on your easy-to-carry iPad, or show your friends a slideshow of your last adventure travel vacation.

To use the slideshow feature, follow these steps:

1. **Tap the Photos app icon to open the application.**

2. **Tap the Photos tab.**

3. **Tap the Slideshow button to see the Slideshow Options menu, shown in Figure 6-10.**

Tap this button

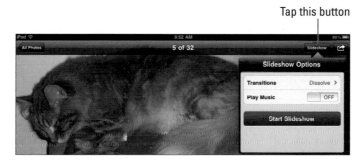

Figure 6-10: Use this menu to add transition effects and start the slideshow.

4. **If you want to play music along with the slideshow, tap the On/Off button in the Play Music field.**

5. **To choose music to play along with the slideshow, tap Music and, in the list that appears (see Figure 6-11), tap any selection from your Music library.**

6. **In the Slideshow Options dialog, tap the transition effect you want to use for your slideshow (refer to Figure 6-10).**

7. **Tap the Start Slideshow button.**

   The slideshow begins.

To run a slideshow that includes only the photos contained in a particular album, tap the Album tab, tap an album to open it, and then tap the Slideshow button to make settings and run a slideshow.

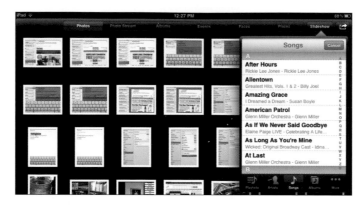

Figure 6-11: Pick a song that matches your slideshow's mood.

Displaying Picture Frame

You can use the slideshow settings you create in the previous section to run your slideshow while your iPad screen is locked so that you can view a continuous display of your pictures. This feature can help you make good use of the time when your iPad is recharging or subliminally flash images of your products again and again at your client while you make your sales pitch.

Here's how to use the Picture Frame feature:

1. **Tap the Sleep/Wake button to lock iPad and then tap the Home button to go to the Lock screen.**

   The bottom of this screen looks like Figure 6-12.

The Picture Frame button

Figure 6-12: Picture Frame is a great feature for showing off your product line — or cool new car.

2. **Tap the Picture Frame button (refer to Figure 6-12).**

   The slideshow begins. (See Figure 6-13.)

3. **To end the show, tap the Home button.**

If you don't like the effects used on the picture frame, go back to Photos and use the Slideshow button to change the slideshow's settings.

One iPad accessory you might look into is the iPad Frame Dock, which you can purchase at www.theipadframe.com. This item is a stand for your iPad that looks like a picture frame. You can even hang it and your iPad on a wall. That is, if you have nowhere else to place your several-hundred-dollar electronic device. Of course, the dock does allow you to charge your iPad while it's hanging around.

Figure 6-13: Use Picture Frame to show off several images at once.

Deleting Photos

You might find that it's time to get rid of some of those old photos of the family reunion or the last project you worked on. If a photo wasn't transferred from your computer but instead was downloaded or captured as a screenshot on the iPad, you can delete it using this procedure:

1. **Tap the Photos app icon in the Dock on the Home screen.**

2. **Tap the Albums or Photos tab and then tap an album to open it.**

3. **Tap the Menu button.**

4. **Tap each photo you want to get rid of (a blue check mark appears on each), and then tap Delete, as shown in Figure 6-14.**

Delete button   Check marks indicating selected photos

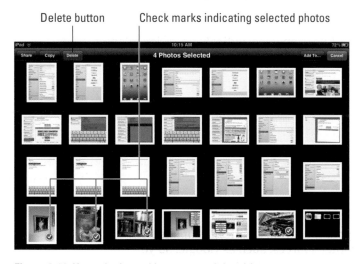

Figure 6-14: If you don't need it anymore, delete it!

5. **In the confirming dialog that appears, tap the Delete Photo/Selected Photos button to finish the deletion.**

Chapter 7: Using Your iPad as an E-reader

In This Chapter

- Discovering how iPad differs from other e-readers
- Finding books at iBooks
- Buying books
- Navigating a book
- Working with bookmarks, highlights, and the dictionary
- Organizing books in collections
- Experience periodicals with Newsstand

*A*pple has touted iPad as a great e-reader, so though it isn't a traditional dedicated e-reader device like the Barnes and Noble Nook, you won't want to miss out on this cool functionality.

Apple's free, downloadable application that turns your iPad into an e-reader is called *iBooks,* an application that enables you to buy and download books from Apple's iBookstore. You can also use several other free e-reader applications, such as Kindle, Stanza, or Nook, to download books to your iPad from a variety of online bookstores and other sources, such as Google, so you can read to your heart's content.

A new app that comes with iOS 5 is Newsstand, which has a similar look and feel to iBooks, but its focus is on subscribing to and reading magazines, newspapers, and other periodicals.

In this chapter, you discover the options available for reading material, and I tell you how to buy books and subscribe to periodicals. You also find out about the Newsstand and iBooks apps: how to navigate a book or periodical and adjust the brightness and type, as well as how to search books and organize your iBooks and Newsstand libraries.

Discovering How iPad Differs from Other E-readers

An *e-reader* is any electronic device that enables you to download and read books, magazines, or newspapers. These devices are portable and typically dedicated only to reading electronic content. Most use E Ink technology to create a paper-like reading experience.

The iPad is a bit different: As you know, it isn't used for only reading books, and you have to download an app to enable it as an e-reader (though just about every e-reader app I've found is free). Also, iPad doesn't offer the paper-like reading experience — you read from a computer screen (though you can adjust the brightness of the screen and change its background color).

When you buy a book or magazine online (or get one of many free publications), it downloads to your iPad in a few seconds using your Wi-Fi or 3G connection. After you've got your e-reader app and some content, iPad offers several navigation tools to move around a book, all of which you explore in this chapter.

Finding and Buying E-books

Before you can read books or other publications, you have to get your iPad's hands on them (so to speak). This involves downloading e-reader software, and then using it or online stores to buy publications. I start by introducing you to iBooks, a free e-reader that you can download from iTunes.

You can also buy content on your computer and sync your purchases to your iPad using iTunes or iCloud. See Book I, Chapter 5 for more about this topic.

Finding books at iBooks

In Book I, Chapter 5, I walk you through the process of downloading apps, so you should use those steps to download the iBooks app first, if you haven't already.

With iBooks downloaded, you can shop using iBooks by tapping the iBooks application icon to open it. (Note that it's probably on a secondary Home screen, so you may have to display another Home screen to locate it.)

If you become addicted to iBooks, consider placing it on the iPad Dock for quick access from any Home screen. To do this, press and hold the app till all apps jiggle, and then tap and drag the iBooks icon to the Dock. Tap the Home button, and the jiggling stops.

The iBooks library opens. (See Figure 7-1.) At this point, you see a bookshelf with no books on it. (If you don't see the bookshelf, tap the Library button to go there or, if no Library button is displayed on the screen, tap the Bookshelf button in the top-right corner of the screen — it sports four small squares.) Note that any PDF documents you download don't appear on this bookshelf; you have to tap the PDF Collection to view them (more about Collections later).

For a cool effect, tap the Store button, and the shelf pivots 180 degrees to display the iBookstore.

Figure 7-1: Your virtual iBooks bookshelf.

In the iBookstore shown in Figure 7-2, featured titles are shown by default, though you can tap Release Date to see titles chronologically by release date. Do any of the following to find a book:

✔ Tap the Search field and type a search word or phrase using the onscreen keyboard.

✔ Tap the Categories button to see a list of types of books, as shown in Figure 7-3. Tap a category to view those selections.

✔ Tap either the right or left arrow, halfway down the screen, to scroll to more suggested titles.

✔ Also in that same area, tap See All to view more titles.

✔ Tap the appropriate button at the bottom of the screen to view categories: Featured titles; the New York Times bestsellers list; books listed on Top Charts; browse-worthy lists of authors, categories, or only paid or free items; or Purchases to review the titles you've already purchased.

 If you go to an item by tapping a button at the bottom of the screen and you want to return to the original screen, just tap Featured again.

✔ Tap a suggested selection or featured book to display more information about it.

Categories button Featured button Search field
See All option Release Date button

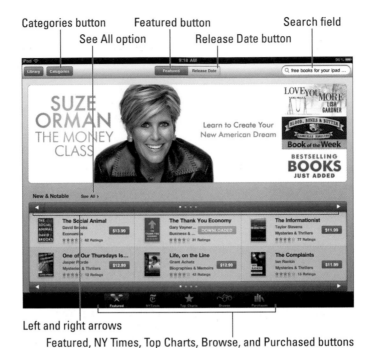

Left and right arrows
Featured, NY Times, Top Charts, Browse, and Purchased buttons

Figure 7-2: Use various links and tools to find the content you want.

Figure 7-3: Find your publication using the Categories feature.

To avoid buyer's remorse, you can download free samples before you buy. You get to read several pages of the book to see whether it appeals to you, and it doesn't cost you a dime! Look for the Get Sample button when you view details about a book to get your free preview.

Exploring other E-book sources

Your iPad is capable of using other e-reader apps to display book content from other bookstores, so you can get books from sources other than iBookstore. To do so, first download another e-reader application such as Kindle from Amazon or the Barnes & Noble Nook from the iPad App Store. (See Book I, Chapter 5 for how to download apps.) Then use that application's features to search for, purchase, and download content.

The Kindle e-reader application is shown in Figure 7-4. Any content you have already bought from Amazon for the Kindle is archived online and can be placed on your Kindle home page on your iPad for you to read any time you like. To delete a book from this e-reader, just press the title with your finger, and the Delete button appears.

Figure 7-4: Kindle was one of the first to offer a free e-reader for iPad.

You can also get content from a variety of other sources: Project Gutenberg, Google, some publishers like Baen, and so on. Get the content using your computer if you like and then just add it to Books in iTunes and sync to your iPad.

You can also sync books you've downloaded to your computer to your iPad by using the data connection cord and your iTunes account. Using this method, you can find lots of free books from various sources online, as long as they are in the ePub or PDF format, and drag them into your iTunes Books Library; then simply sync them to your iPad. See Book I, Chapter 5 for more about syncing. To convert e-books in other formats such as Mobi or RTF to ePub, use an application such as Calibre.

Buying iBooks

If you have set up an account with iTunes, you can buy books at the iBookstore easily. (See Book I, Chapter 5 for more about setting up an account.)

1. **When you find a book in the iBookstore that you want to buy, tap its price button.**

   The button changes to a Buy Book button, as shown in Figure 7-5. (If the book is free, these buttons are labeled Free and Get Book, respectively.)

   Tap a Price button...

   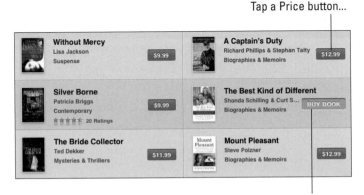

   and it changes to a Buy Book button

   Figure 7-5: Click the price to buy the book.

2. **Tap the Buy Book or Get Book button.**

   If you haven't already signed in, the iTunes Password dialog shown in Figure 7-6 appears.

   Figure 7-6: Enter your iTunes password to buy anything.

3. **Enter your password and tap OK.**

   The book appears on your bookshelf, and the cost is charged to whichever credit card you specified when you opened your iTunes account —
   or the cost is deducted from your store credit, if you have a balance.

If you have signed in, your purchase is accepted immediately — no returns
are allowed, so tap carefully!

Experiencing E-reading

Now that you have an e-book in your iBook, it's time to put on some music,
settle back in a comfortable chair, and read it. Luckily, reading an e-book
isn't much harder than reading a paperback. Here's how to do it.

Navigating an e-book

Here are the simple steps involved in making your way around an e-book
using the iBooks e-reader:

1. **Tap iBooks and if your Library (the bookshelf) isn't already displayed,
   tap the Library button.**

2. **Tap an e-book to open it.**

   The book opens, as shown in Figure 7-7. (If you hold your iPad in portrait orientation, it shows one page; if it's in landscape orientation, it will
   show two.)

3. **Take any of these actions to navigate the book:**

   • *To go to the book's table of contents:* Tap the Table of Contents button
     in the top-left corner of the page (it looks like a little bulleted list) to
     go to the book's Table of Contents (see Figure 7-8) and then tap the
     name of a chapter to go to it.

   • *To turn to the next page:* Place your finger anywhere on the right edge
     of a page and flick to the left.

   • *To turn to the preceding page:* Place your finger anywhere on the left
     edge of a page and flick to the right.

   • *To move to another page in the book:* Tap and drag the slider at the
     bottom of the page to the right or left.

To return to the Library to view another book at any time, tap the Library
button. If the button isn't visible, tap anywhere on the page, and the tools
appear.

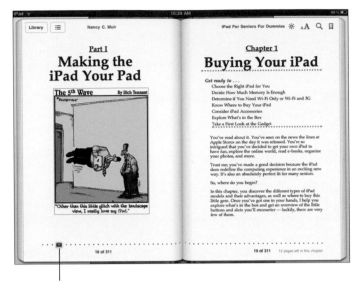

Slider to move to another page

Figure 7-7: Landscape orientation on iPad.

Tap any chapter to go to it.

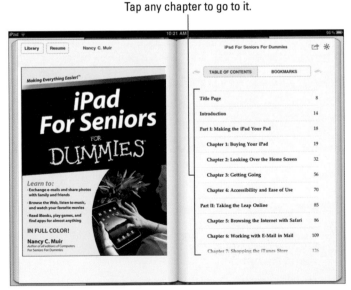

Figure 7-8: Use this virtual Table of Contents to go where you like in your e-book.

Adjusting brightness

iPad doesn't offer a simulated page surface as some dedicated e-readers such as Kindle do, so it's important that you make the reading experience as comfortable on your eyes as possible by adjusting the brightness.

iBooks offers an adjustable brightness setting that you can use to make your book pages comfortable for you to read. Follow these steps to make an adjustment:

1. **With a book open, tap the Brightness button shown in Figure 7-9.**

   The Brightness dialog appears.

Tap the Brightness button...

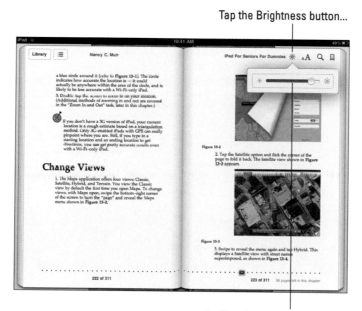

and adjust the screen brightness

Figure 7-9: Adjusting brightness can ease eyestrain.

2. **Tap and drag the slider to the right to make the screen brighter, or to the left to dim it.**

3. **Tap anywhere in the book to close the Brightness dialog.**

Experiment with the brightness that works for you. It's commonly thought that bright white computer screens are hard on the eyes, so setting the brightness to halfway (default) or below is probably a good idea.

Try using the Sepia setting located in the Fonts dialog, which is covered in the next task. This mutes the background to a soft beige color that may work better for some.

Changing the font size and type

If the type on your screen is a bit small for your taste, you can change to a larger font size or choose a different font for readability.

1. **With a book open, tap the Font button.**

   (It sports a small letter *a* and a large capital *A*, as shown in Figure 7-10.)

2. **In the Font dialog that appears (refer to Figure 7-10), tap the small letter *a* button on the left to use smaller text, or the button labeled with the capital *A* on the right to use larger text.**

Tap the Font button to change font size and type

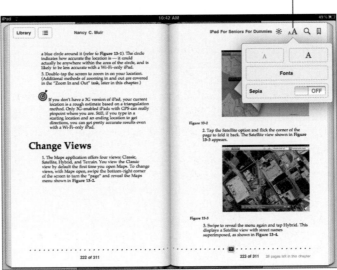

Figure 7-10: Need larger type? Set that up here.

3. **Tap the Fonts button.**

   The list of fonts, as shown in Figure 7-11, appears. This list may vary slightly if Apple adds more or you are using a language other than English on your iPad.

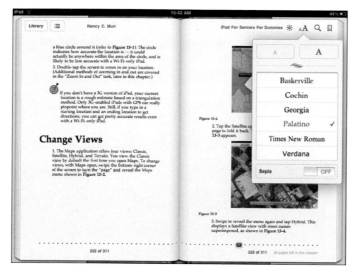

Figure 7-11: Though limited, a selection of fonts is available in iBooks.

4. **Tap a font name to select it.**

   The font changes on the book page.

5. **If you want a sepia tint on the pages, which can be easier on the eyes, tap the On/Off button to turn the setting on.**

6. **Tap outside the Fonts dialog to return to your book.**

Some fonts appear a bit larger on your screen than others because of their design. If you want the largest fonts, use Cochin or Verdana.

Searching in your book

You may want to find a certain sentence or reference in your book. To search for a word or phrase, follow these steps:

1. **With the book displayed, tap the Search button shown in Figure 7-12.**

   The onscreen keyboard appears.

2. **Enter a search term and then tap the Search key on the keyboard.**

   iBooks searches for any matching entries.

3. **Use your finger to scroll down the entries (see Figure 7-13).**

The Search button

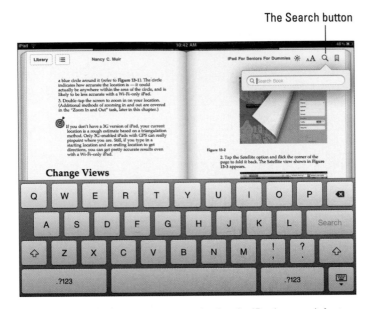

Figure 7-12: Find the content you need using the iBooks search feature.

Scroll through the entries

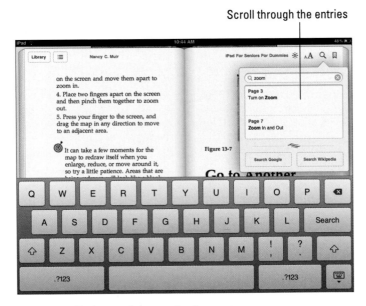

Figure 7-13: Find a spot in your e-book.

4. **You can use either the Search Google or Search Wikipedia buttons at the bottom of the Search dialog if you want to search for information about the search term online.**

You can also search for other instances of a particular word while in the book pages by pressing your finger on the word and tapping Search on the toolbar that appears.

Using bookmarks and highlights

Bookmarks and highlights in your e-books are like favorites you save in your web browser: They enable you to revisit a favorite page or refresh your memory about a character or plot point. Note that iBooks can retain these bookmarks and highlights across iDevices such as iPad and iPhone.

To add and use bookmarks and highlights, follow these steps:

1. **With a book open to a page you want to bookmark, tap the Bookmark button in the upper-right corner, as shown in Figure 7-14.**

   A colored bookmark is placed on the page.

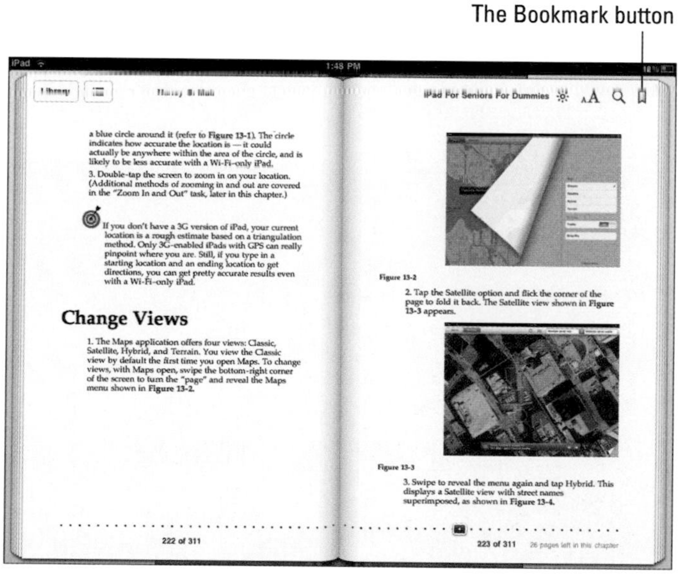

Book II
Chapter 7

Using Your iPad as
an E-reader

The Bookmark button

Figure 7-14: Assign a bookmark to a page.

2. **To highlight a word or phrase, press the text.**

   The toolbar shown in Figure 7-15 appears.

Tap this button

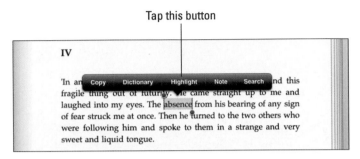

Figure 7-15: Use these tools to perform a variety of actions.

3. **Tap the Highlight button.**

   A colored highlight is placed on the word.

4. **To change the color of the highlighted word, remove the highlight, or add a note, tap the highlighted word.**

   The toolbar shown in Figure 7-16 appears. Note that a shortcut for removing a bookmark is to simply tap the bookmark symbol in the top-right corner of the page.

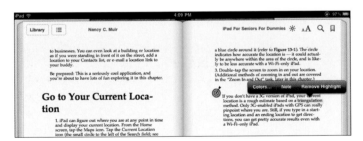

Figure 7-16: Choose the highlight color from this toolbar.

5. **Tap one of these three buttons:**

   • *Colors:* Displays a menu of colors you can tap to change the highlight color.

   • *Note:* Lets you add a note to the item.

   • *Remove Highlight:* Removes the highlight.

6. **Tap outside the highlighted word to close the toolbar.**

7. **To go to a list of bookmarks and highlights, tap the Table of Contents button on a book page.**

8. **In the Table of Contents, tap the Bookmarks tab.**

As shown in Figure 7-17, all bookmarks and highlights are displayed.

Bookmarks and Highlights are displayed here

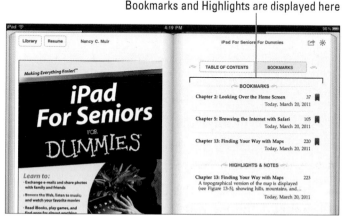

Book II
Chapter 7

Using Your iPad as
an E-reader

Figure 7-17: Tap the highlight or bookmark you want to display in this list.

9. **Tap a bookmark or highlight in this list to go there.**

iPad automatically bookmarks the page where you left off reading in a book so you don't have to do it manually.

You can also highlight illustrations in a book. Display the page and press the image until the Highlight button appears above it. Tap the button, and the illustration is highlighted in yellow. As with highlighted text, you can tap a highlighted illustration to change the color or remove the highlight.

Checking Words in the Dictionary

I know some people just skip over words they don't understand when reading, but being a writer, I like to know what every word means. If you do, too, you'll appreciate the iPad's built-in dictionary. As you read a book, if you come across unfamiliar words, don't skip over them — take the opportunity to learn a word! The built-in dictionary in iBooks even recognizes many proper names, such as historical figures and geographic locations.

1. **With a book open, press your finger on a word and hold it until the toolbar shown in Figure 7-18 appears.**

Tap this button

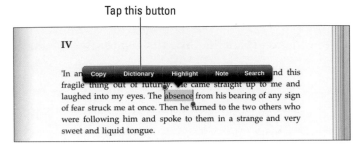

Figure 7-18: Check a selected word in the built-in dictionary.

2. **Tap the Dictionary button.**

   A definition dialog appears, as shown in Figure 7-19.

3. **Tap the definition and scroll down to view more.**

4. **When you finish reviewing the definition, tap anywhere on the page.**

   The definition disappears.

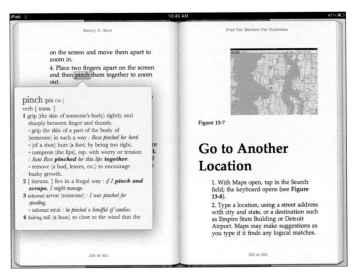

Figure 7-19: Find definitions for words fast using the dictionary.

Organizing Your Library

Your iBooks library looks like a bookshelf with all downloaded books stored on it, with the most recently downloaded title in the top-left corner. You can drag titles around on this bookshelf, and you can view your library in a few other ways.

1. **With the bookshelf version of the library displayed, tap the List button shown in Figure 7-20.**

   Your books appear in a list, as shown in Figure 7-21.

List button

Figure 7-20: Switch back and forth between Bookshelf and List view using these buttons.

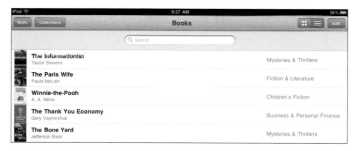

Figure 7-21: Organize your titles in various ways.

2. **To organize the list alphabetically by Titles, Authors, or Categories such as Series, tap the appropriate button on the bottom of the screen.**

   For example, if you tap Categories, your titles are divided by category titles such as Fiction, Mysteries & Thrillers, or Literary.

3. **To return to Bookshelf view at any time, tap the Bookshelf view button.**

Tap the Bookshelf button at the bottom of the List view to remove categories and list the most recently added book first.

Use the Edit button in List view to display small circles to the left of all books in the list. Tap in any of the circles and tap the Delete button at the top of the page to delete books, and then tap the Done button to exit the Edit function.

Organizing Books in Collections

After you've downloaded lots of books (I know one woman who has 600), you may become organizationally challenged. iBooks lets you create collections of books to help you organize them by your own logic, such as Astronomy, Work-related, and Cooking. You can place a book in only one collection, however.

Here are the steps for creating and working with collections:

1. **To create a collection from the Library bookshelf, tap Collections.**

2. **In the dialog that appears, tap New.**

3. **On the blank line that appears, type a name (see Figure 7-22) and tap Done.**

Enter a name for the collection...

then tap Done

Figure 7-22: Name your collection.

4. **Tap Books.**

   The dialog closes, and you return to the Library.

5. **To add a book to a collection from the Library, tap Edit.**

6. **Tap one or more books and then tap the Move button that appears in the top-left corner of the screen.**

   A dialog appears. (See Figure 7-23.)

Figure 7-23: Move books into collections one by one or several at a time.

Book II
Chapter 7

Using Your iPad as
an E-reader

7. **Tap a collection to move the book to.**

8. **When you've finished a book, with the collection displayed, tap Edit, tap the selection circle for the book, and then tap Delete.**

   The book is deleted from iPad.

To delete a collection, with the Collections dialog displayed, tap Edit. Tap the minus sign to the left of any collection and then tap Delete to get rid of it. A message appears, asking you to tap Remove to remove the contents of the collection from your iPad or Don't Remove. Note that if you choose Don't Remove, all titles within a deleted collection are returned to their original collections in your library.

Browsing the Newsstand

Newsstand is a new app that focuses on subscribing to and reading magazines, newspapers and other periodicals rather than books. The app has a similar look and feel to iBooks.

Download magazines apps to Newsstand

Newsstand is a new app that focuses on subscribing to and reading magazines, newspapers, and other periodicals rather than books. The app has a similar look and feel to iBooks. When you download a free publication you're actually downloading an app to Newsstand. You can then tap that app to buy individual issues, as covered in the next section. To download magazine apps to Newsstand, follow these steps:

1. **Tap the Newsstand icon on the Home screen to open Newsstand (see Figure 7-24).**

Figure 7-24: View all your subscriptions and publication issues in one place.

2. **Tap the Store button.**

   The store opens, offering Featured periodicals, Genius recommendations, Top Charts, and Categories for your shopping pleasure (see Figure 7-25).

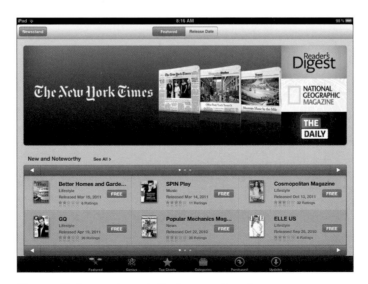

Figure 7-25: Browse for periodicals to your heart's content.

3. **Tap any of the items displayed, tap the arrow buttons to move to other choices, or tap in the Search field at the top and enter a search term to locate a publication you're interested in.**

If you tap other icons at the bottom of the screen, such as Top Charts or Categories, you're taken to other types of content than periodicals. Also, if you tap Featured again after tapping one of these icons, you're taken to other kinds of apps than periodicals. Your best bet: Stay on the Store screen that displays when you tap the Store button in Newsstand.

4. **When you find an item, tap it to view a detailed description (see Figure 7-26).**

5. **Tap the Free button and then tap Install App.**

The app downloads to Newsstand.

Book II
Chapter 7

Using Your iPad as an E-reader

Figure 7-26: Get the lowdown on a particular publication by viewing details.

Buy issues

To purchase issues of periodicals and magazines within the Newsstand app, follow these steps:

1. **Tap a periodical app.**

The message shown in Figure 7-27 appears, asking if you'd like to be informed of new issues.

2. **Tap OK if you would.**

3. **Tap the Preview Issue button to take a look at a description of its content, or tap the Buy button.**

4. **In the purchase confirmation dialog that appears, tap Buy.**

The issue is charged to your iTunes account.

Figure 7-27: If you want to know about upcoming editions, let iPad know here.

Read periodicals

To read issues of periodicals and magazines within the Newsstand app, follow these steps:

1. **If you buy a periodical or you have downloaded a free subscription preview, such as The New York Times Update shown in Figure 7-28, you can tap the publication in Newsstand to view it.**

Figure 7-28: Open any publication with a tap.

2. **In the publication that appears, use your finger to swipe left, right, or up and down to view more of the pages.**

For many publications, you can tap the Sections button shown in Figure 7-29 to navigate to different sections of the publication.

3. **To subscribe to a publication when viewing a free sample, tap the Subscribe Now button (refer to Figure 10-29).**

Note that different stores offer different options for subscribing, buying issues, and organizing issues. Think of Newsstand as a central collection point for apps that allow you to preview and buy content in each publication's store.

Figure 7-29: Moving around publications may vary from one to the other.

Chapter 8: Playing Games

In This Chapter

✓ **Appreciating iPad's gaming strengths**

✓ **Finding games of all kinds**

✓ **Exploring iTunes Game Center**

*i*Pad is, after all, a close relative of the iPhone, and no matter who tells you that they use their iPhone to get work done, they're probably spending most of their time gaming. iPad outstrips iPhone as the ultimate portable gaming machine because of its beautiful screen and unique features.

In this chapter, you discover why iPad is such a great mobile gaming device, what kinds of games are out there, how to create a Game Center account and purchase and download games, how to play games against yourself and others, and what cool accessories you must get to be a completely awesome iPad gamer.

Let the games begin!

Appreciating iPad's Gaming Strengths

The iPhone is a fun gaming device, but the screen is too small. Your computer is a good gaming device, but it may lack some of the tactile input of a touchscreen. iPad may be just right as the ultimate gaming device for many reasons, including these:

✓ **iPad's fantastic screen:** You've got a few things going for you here. First, the high-resolution, 9.7-inch screen has a backlit LED display. As Apple describes it, it's "remarkably crisp and vivid." They're not lying. The in-plane switching or IPS technology means you can hold it at almost any angle (it has a 178-degree viewing angle) and still get good color and contrast.

✓ **Faster processor:** The dual-core A5 chip in your iPad is a super-fast processor that can run rings around your iPhone, making it a great device for gaming.

✔ **A built-in accelerometer and three-axis gyroscope:** Gamers will find these elements useful to shift around in a more versatile manner as they virtually move through games that involve motion. The built-in accelerometer and three-axis gyroscope let you grab your iPad and use it as a steering wheel or other game feature, so you really feel in the action. With iPad 2, the gyroscope, accelerometer, and compass were added to help apps like Maps pinpoint your location and movements as you stroll around town.

✔ **Playing games in full screen:** Rather than playing on a small iPhone screen, you can play most games designed for the iPad in full-screen mode on your iPad. Having a full screen brings the gaming experience to you in an even more engaging way than a small screen ever could.

✔ **Dragging elements around the screen:** The Multi-Touch screen in iPad may be based on the same technology as the iPhone, but it's been redone from the ground up for iPad. The iPad screen is responsive — and if you're about to be zapped by aliens in a fight-to-the-death computer game, that responsiveness counts.

✔ **The ten-hour battery life of an iPad:** This long battery life means you can suck energy out of it playing games into the wee hours of the night.

✔ **Specialized game-playing features:** Some games are coming out with features that take advantage of iPad's capabilities. For example, Gameloft came out with a version of its N.O.V.A. game that includes a feature called *multiple-target acquisition,* which lets you target multiple bad guys in a single move to blow them out of the water with one shot. The Need for Speed racing games allow you to look in your rearview mirror to see what's coming up behind you, a feature made possible by iPad's larger screen.

✔ **Great sound:** The built-in speaker is a powerful little thing, but if you want things even more up-close and personal, you can plug in a headphone, some speaker systems, or a microphone using the built-in jack.

Understanding the Accelerometer

iPad has a built-in motion sensor called an *accelerometer,* as well as a three-axis gyroscope. These allow those developing apps for iPad to have lots of fun as they use the automatically rotating screen to become part of the gaming experience. For example, they can build in a compass device that reorients itself automatically if you switch your iPad from landscape to portrait mode. Some racing games allow you to grab the iPad as if it were a steering wheel and rotate the device to simulate the driving experience.

Check out Firemint's Real Racing 2 HD app ($6.99) to try out the cool motion sensor feature. As you can see in Figures 8-1 and 8-2, this is a very fun gaming environment.

Figure 8-1: Move the iPad around to steer left or right.

Figure 8-2: Size up your competitors in this cool racing game that takes advantage of iPad's accelerometer.

Finding Some Very Cool Games

Now it's time to tell you about some of my favorite iPad games (the part of the book where you wonder why I get paid for what I do, 'cause reviewing games is so fun).

Check out some sites such as iPadgames.org and TCGeeks.com for cool downloadable, free iPad games.

Looking at what's out there

First, take a look at the gaming landscape. Several types of games are available (some ported over from iPhone and some customized for iPad), for example:

- **Arcade games** include apps such as Arcade Bowling Lite, Arcade SpinBall Lite, Foosball HD, and The Simpsons Arcade.

- **Kids' games** are sometimes educational, but almost always entertaining. These include Ace Kids Math Games, Addition UnderSea Adventures, and Word Monkey.

- **Card and board games,** such as Astraware Solitaire – 12 Games in 1 by Handmark, Inc., Mahjong Epic HD, and Payday Roulette.

- **Adventure games** like Plants vs. Zombies (see Figure 8-3), Everest: Hidden Expedition, AirAttack, Amazon: Hidden Expedition, and Carnivores: Dinosaur Hunter.

- **Sports games,** such as X Games SnoCross, Stick Golf, and Pool Bar – Online Hustle.

Figure 8-3: Plants vs. Zombies: May the best man (thing?) win!

Exploring a half-dozen games

Narrowing down choices to just a few must-have games is hard because we all like different kinds of fun. To add to the choices, there are both iPhone- and iPad-engineered games you can use on your iPad, and more are coming out all the time.

Still, the following list is a sampling of six recommended games for you to try that won't break the bank:

- **SCRABBLE for iPad ($9.99):** You remember SCRABBLE, that favorite old board game that can let you shine or put you to shame for your spelling and vocabulary skills? SCRABBLE is now available on iPad and it's hot. (See Figure 8-4.) Shake your iPad to shuffle tiles. Use the drag-and-drop motion to play your letters. Want to share the fun? Reach out to your Facebook friends to take the game to the multi-player level.

- **Broken Sword: Director's Cut HD ($6.99):** This classic adventure game lets you virtually become the main character to experience all the game has to offer. Great art and animation distinguish this game, and the iPad version (see Figure 8-5) has a handy hint system you'll appreciate.

- **Civilization Revolution for iPad ($12.99):** If you like a world-building type of game, you'll find Civilization Revolution right up your alley. It's been fine-tuned for iPad to be even better than the iPhone version. The game also offers a feature called Scenario Creator, which lets you create your own unique challenges, essentially allowing for unlimited variety in the game.

- **Flight Control HD ($4.99):** Ever wanted to be an airline pilot? This game gives you a taste of the experience. Create flight paths that ensure your plane lands safely. A favorite with iPhone gamers, this one translates well to iPad. This game has lots of multiplayer options, including the option of using a split screen to keep both players in the action.

- **Monkey Island 2 Special Edition: LeChuck's Revenge for iPad ($9.99):** A point-and-click adventure game classic on iPhone, in its iPad incarnation Monkey Island (see Figure 8-6) has great graphics and sound, and an engaging story at its heart. If you like adventure games, don't miss this one.

- **Angry Birds HD ($4.99):** This game has become a cult — you can even buy Angry Birds stuffed animals. Use little birds to attack pigs and smash them in a variety of intriguing and oddly satisfying ways. You have lots of levels to work your way through, but don't worry; if you get stuck, the Mighty Eagle is there to help you out!

Book II Chapter 8

Playing Games

Figure 8-4: SCRABBLE is awesome on iPad.

✔ **tChess Pro ($7.99):** This game is another app designed for iPhone that works just great on iPad. (See Figure 8-7.) You can play against the computer or another player. You can modify the appearance of the chess pieces. It even sports features that help chess beginners learn the game painlessly, but more advanced players will enjoy it as well.

As well as costing money, games take up a lot of memory, so choose the games you buy wisely. If you no longer want to play a game, delete it from your iPad to save space, keeping a backup on iCloud or via iTunes on your Mac or PC in case you change your mind at a later date.

Figure 8-5: Broken Sword is a classic game updated from its iPhone version for iPad.

Figure 8-6: Monkey Island is a very fun adventure game.

Special mention: ComicBookLover isn't a game, but it's a blast of an app that most gamers can appreciate. The iPad screen is perfect for those bright, crisp graphics, and iPad's navigation tools let you swipe your way through the panes in several interesting ways.

Figure 8-7: If you love chess, this is one of the better apps for your iPad.

Getting Gaming Accessories

Some interesting accessories are coming out for iPad. No doubt more will appear over time, and Apple itself may add features in a next-edition device. For example, a new iPad might sport control buttons so you don't have to cover up your onscreen game to use onscreen control mechanisms, and they might add rumble to simulate gaming sounds.

For now, here are a few iPad gaming accessories in the works that caught my attention:

✔ **Incipio iPad Hive Honeycomb dermaShot Silicone Case** ($19.99) is a rugged case for serious gamers. The back sports molded grips that help you keep a good hold on your iPad while playing those action-packed games.

✔ **JoyStick-It** from ThinkGeek is an arcade-style stick you attach to your iPad screen. The joystick won't harm your screen, and you can move it around at any time. It gives you that real arcade game feel for controlling games and will run you about $20. It won't work with every game but does claim to work with thousands of them.

iTunes Game Center

The Game Center is an app that comes preinstalled with iPad (iOS 4.2 and later). If you're into gaming, you may enjoy the features it offers that allow you to invite friends to play games, buy games, and keep track of your games, friends, and achievements.

Of course, you can also download games from the App Store and play them on your iPad without having to use Game Center. What Game Center provides is a place where you can create a gaming profile, add a list of gaming friends, keep track of your scores and perks, and shop for games (and only games) in the App Store, along with listings of top-rated games and game categories to choose from.

Think of the Game Center as a kind of social networking site for gamers, where you can compare your scores and find players to go a few rounds with. The app can automatically match you with other players who have a similar ability. Say you need three other people to play a certain game; Game Center can find them for you. And the Achievements listing shows you your score history for all the games you play. Finally, Leaderboards allow you to compare your performance with your gaming friends.

Figure 8-8 shows you the Game Center interface with the following four choices along the bottom:

✔ **Me:** Contains your profile and summary of number of friends, games, and achievements.

✔ **Friends:** Tap to invite friends to play.

✔ **Games:** Takes you to iTunes to shop for games.

✔ **Requests:** Shows you any requests from your friends for a game.

Figure 8-8: Game Center's opening screen shows an overview of your friends, games, and achievements.

Opening an account in Game Center

Using the Game Center app, you can search for and buy games, add friends with whom you can play those games, and keep records of your scores for posterity. In order to do this, however, you must first open a Game Center account by following these steps:

1. **From the Home screen, tap the Game Center icon.**

   If you've never used Game Center, you're asked whether to allow *push notifications:* If you want to receive these notices alerting you that your friends want to play a game with you, tap OK. You should, however, be aware that push notifications can drain your iPad's battery.

2. **On the Game Center opening screen (refer to Figure 8-8), tap Create New Account.**

3. **If the correct country isn't listed in the New Account dialog, tap the Location field and select another location; if the correct location is already showing, tap Next to confirm it.**

4. **In the next dialog you see, tap the Month, Day, and Year fields, enter your date of birth, and then tap Next.**

5. **In the Game Center Terms & Conditions dialog, swipe to scroll down (and read) the conditions, and then tap Agree if you want to continue creating your account.**

6. **In the confirmation dialog that appears, tap Agree once more to accept for real!**

7. **In the next dialog that opens, tap each field or the Next button above the onscreen keyboard and enter your name, e-mail address, and password information.**

Tap the Question field to select a security question to identify yourself, and tap the Answer field and type in an answer to the question. Be sure to scroll to the bottom of this dialog and choose to turn off the e-mail notification subscription if you don't want to have Game Center send you messages.

8. **Tap Next to proceed.**

See the next section to find out how you can create your Game Center profile in subsequent dialogs.

When you first register for Game Center, if you use an e-mail address other than the one associated with your Apple ID, you may have to create a new Apple ID and verify it using an e-mail message that's sent to the e-mail address associated with your Apple ID. See Book I, Chapter 5 for more about creating an Apple ID when opening an iTunes account.

Creating a Game Center profile

When you reach the last dialog in Step 8 of the preceding section, you're ready to create your profile and specify some account settings. You can also make most of these settings after you've created your account, by tapping your Account name on the Game Center Home screen. To create your Game Center profile, follow these steps:

1. **In the Create Profile dialog that appears (see Figure 8-9), in the Nickname field, enter the "handle" you want to be known by when playing games.**

2. **If you don't want other players to be able to invite you to play games when Game Center is open, tap the Game Invites On/Off slider to turn off the feature.**

3. **If you don't want other players to be able to see your real name, tap the Public Profile On/Off slider to turn this feature off.**

Figure 8-9: When you're playing games with others, your handle will identify you.

4. **If you want your friends to be able to send you requests for playing games via e-mail, check to see if the e-mail address listed in this dialog is the one you want them to use. If not, tap Add Another Email and enter another e-mail address.**

5. **To use your contacts saved in the iPad Contacts app to get friend recommendations, tap the Use My Contacts On/Off slider to turn this feature on.**

   Game Center can now recommend friends from that list.

   If you leave this feature on, be sure to scroll down and verify the e-mail address you want others to be able to use.

6. **Tap Done when you're finished with the settings.**

   You return to the Game Center Home screen, already signed in to your account with information displayed about friends, games, and gaming achievements (all at zero initially).

7. **To add a picture to your profile, tap Change Photo.**

   You see a message that your photo will be shared with all other Game Center players. Tap OK. The two options of Take Photo (on iPad 2 only) or Choose Photo appear (or on an iPad 1 which lacks a camera, only the Choose Photo option appears).

8. **Tap Choose Photo to select a photo from your Camera Roll or a photo album.**

9. **Tap the album you want to use and scroll to locate the photo.**

10. **Tap the photo.**

    It appears in a Choose Photo dialog. You can use your finger to move the photo around or scale it, and then tap Use. The photo now appears on your Game Center home screen.

After you create an account and a profile, whenever you go to the Game Center, you log in by entering your e-mail address and password and then tapping Sign In.

You can change account settings from the Game Center Home screen: Tap your account name and then tap View Account, make changes to your settings, and then tap Done.

Adding friends

If you want to play Game Center games with others who have an Apple ID and an iPhone, iPod touch, or iPad, follow these steps to add them as friends so you can invite them to play:

1. **From the Game Center Home screen, tap the Friends button at the bottom of the screen.**

2. **On the Friends page, tap Add Friends.**

3. **Enter an e-mail address in the To field and edit the invitation, if you like.**

4. **Tap the Send button.**

   A confirmation message tells you that your invitation has been sent.

5. **In the confirmation message, tap OK.**

   After your friend accepts your invitation, his name is listed on the Friends screen.

With iOS 5, Game Center gained a friend Recommendation feature. Tap the Friends tab, and then tap the A-Z button in the top-left corner. A Recommendations section appears above the list of your current friends. These are people who play the same or similar games, so if you like, try adding one or two as friends.

You will probably also receive requests from friends who know you're on Game Center. When you get these e-mail invitations, be sure that you know the person sending it before you accept it — especially if you've allowed e-mail access in your account settings — otherwise, you could be putting a stranger in communication with you.

Book II
Chapter 8

Playing Games

Purchasing and downloading games

Time to get some games to play! And here's how you do just that:

1. **Open Game Center and sign in to your account.**

2. **Tap the Games button at the bottom of the screen, and then tap Find Game Center Games (see Figure 8-10).**

Tap here to find more games

Figure 8-10: Game Center takes you right to a great world of games apps.

3. **In the list of games that appears, scroll through the list of featured games.**

   To view different games, tap either the Top Charts or Categories button at the bottom of the screen.

   Accessing apps from the Game Center displays only game apps, as opposed to accessing apps from the App Store, which shows you all categories of apps.

4. **To search for a particular title, tap the Search field and enter the name by using the onscreen keyboard.**

5. **Tap a game title to view information about it.**

6. **To buy a game, tap the button labeled with either the word** *Free* **or the price, such as $1.99; tap the button again, which is now labeled Install App.**

7. **Enter your Apple ID and password in the dialog that appears and tap OK.**

   Another verification dialog appears, asking you to sign in. Follow the instructions on the next couple of screens to enter your password and verify your payment information if this is the first time you've signed in to your account from this device.

8. **When the verification dialog appears, tap Buy.**

   The game downloads.

 You may see buttons labeled Buy It Now or Available at the App Store while you're exploring game recommendations in the Games section of Game Center. Tapping such a button takes you from Game Center directly to the App Store to buy the game.

 If you've added friends to your account (see the previous section), you can go to the Friends page and view games your friends have downloaded. To purchase one of these games, just tap it in your friend's list.

Playing against yourself

Many games allow you to play all on your own. Each game has different rules and goals, so you'll have to study a game's instructions and learn how to play it, but here's some general information about these types of games:

- Often a game can be played in two modes: with others or in a *solitaire* version, where you play yourself or the computer.

- Many games you may be familiar with in the offline world, such as Carcassonne or SCRABBLE, have online versions. For these, you already know the rules of play, so you simply need to figure out the execution. For example, in the online Carcassone solitaire game, you tap to place a tile on the board, tap the placed tile to rotate it, and tap the check mark to complete your turn and reveal another tile.

- All the games you play on your own record your scores in Game Center so you can see how you're progressing in building your skills.

Playing games with friends in Game Center

After you have added a friend and both of you have downloaded the same game, you're ready to play. The rules of play are different for each game, but here are the basic steps for getting a game going:

1. **Tap the Game Center app icon on the Home screen and sign in, if necessary.**

2. **Tap the Friends button on the bottom of the screen.**

   The Friends page shown in Figure 8-11 appears.

Figure 8-11: Keep adding friends to widen your gaming universe.

3. **Tap the name of the friend you want to play and then tap the name of a game you have in common.**

   At this point, some games offer you an invitation to send to the friend — if so, wait for your friend to respond, which they do by tapping Accept or Decline on their device.

4. **The game should appear on your screen, and you can tap Play to start playing according to whatever rules the game has and your scores mount up as you play.**

5. **When you're done playing, tap either Friend or Game in Game Center to see your score and your friend's score listed.**

   Game Center tracks your achievements, including points and perks that you've earned along the way. You can also compare your gaming achievements to those of top-ranking players across the Internet — and check your friends' scores by displaying the Friends page with the Points portion showing. (Refer to Figure 8-11.)

 If your friends aren't available, you can play a game by tapping its title on the Games page and then tapping Play. You can then compare your scores with others around the world who have also played the game recently.

Book III
iPad on the Go

The 5th Wave   By Rich Tennant

iPad

"In fact it does come with a compass."

*1*t's lightweight, portable, and packed with features, so why shouldn't iPad be your go-to device when you're going on the road? In this part, you get all set up with your Wi-Fi and 3G settings for connecting to the Internet from just about anywhere. You get to play with the Maps app, a very cool way to swipe and flick your way to just about any place on the planet. Finally, in this part I address you road warriors out there — you know who you are. You are the iPad users who need to find the best hotels, airfares, travel guides, and restaurants in the next city or next country. You want to track expenses and keep in touch with the office. That's just what you learn in the last chapter of this part.

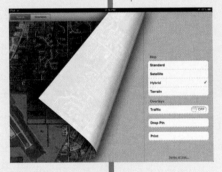

Chapter 1: Configuring iPad to Connect Everywhere

In This Chapter

✓ Making Wi-Fi settings

✓ Making 3G settings

✓ Tethering your iPad to your smartphone

✓ Setting up a Microsoft Exchange account

This chapter is all about connecting, whether you're connecting to the Internet via Wi-Fi or 3G or connecting to your company network. Apple has made an effort over the years with iPhone to support enterprises, meaning that you can use the phone to connect with your company network and vital work data. The iPad continues that tradition with support for Microsoft Exchange Server, virtual private networks (VPNs), and Lightweight Directory Access Protocol (LDAP) accounts.

Your best ally in setting up the more technical of these is your network administrator. In this chapter, I give you an overview of the capabilities of iPad to connect and some guidance in making the settings you need to make.

Making Wi-Fi and 3G Settings

The way people with iPads can connect to the Internet, the grandmother of all networks, is via its Wi-Fi or 3G capabilities (assuming they have a 3G model). In this section, I go into the settings you can make to manage your Wi-Fi or 3G connection.

Making Wi-Fi settings

Book I, Chapter 5 gives you the information you need to connect to a Wi-Fi network, a matter of simply signing in to the network, with a password if necessary. Now it's time to go over some of the finer points of your Wi-Fi connection.

A basic Wi-Fi setting is the one that tells iPad to automatically search for and join networks that are in range. If several networks are in range, using this setting, iPad will join the one that it used most recently.

After iPad has joined a network, a little Wi-Fi icon appears in the Status bar. The number of bars indicates the strength of the signal, just as you're used to on your cellphone.

To get to Wi-Fi settings, tap Settings on your Home screen and then tap Wi-Fi. (See Figure 1-1.) Here's a rundown of the items you can work with in Settings for your Wi-Fi configuration:

✓ **Wi-Fi On/Off:** Simply tap this to On to turn Wi-Fi on. If you want it off, perhaps to save battery drain or because you're on an airplane and the pilot tells you to, set this to Off. (Note that iPads also have an Airplane Mode setting, which I discuss in the next section.)

Figure 1-1: Wi-Fi settings.

✓ **Other:** If you want to join a network that doesn't show up on the list, tap Other under the Choose A Network section of these settings. In the dialog that appears, enter the network name and choose a type of security, such as WEP or WPA. When you choose a form of security and return to the dialog shown in Figure 1-2, a Password field appears. Some networks might need other information, such as a username or static IP address, to complete this dialog. Check with your administrator for any information you can't provide.

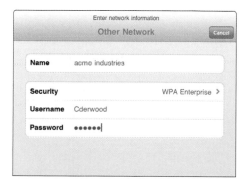

Figure 1-2: Accessing a closed network.

✔ **Ask to Join Networks:** iPad automatically connects to the previously joined network but does not go looking for other networks unless this setting is on. Tap this to the On position, and iPad displays all possible network connections in this dialog. If a network requires a password, it will sport a little padlock symbol. If no known networks are available, you're asked if you want to join unknown networks. To forget a network so iPad doesn't join it automatically, tap the arrow on the right of the network name and then tap Forget This Network.

To adjust settings for individual Wi-Fi networks, tap the arrow icon at the right of a listed network.

After you set up your Wi-Fi and sign into your home network, you can set up Home Sharing to share music and video content from your PC or Mac with your iPad. See Book V, Chapter 1 for more about Home Sharing.

Making 3G settings

When you own a Wi-Fi/3G model of iPad, in addition to modifying Wi-Fi settings as covered in the previous section, you can make changes to your cellular data in Settings. Cellular data settings enable you to manage data roaming and your account information. (See Figure 1-3.)

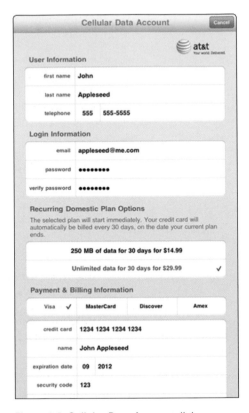

Figure 1-3: Cellular Data Account dialog.

You can find the following items under the Cellular Data category in Settings:

- ✔ **Cellular Data Network:** Turn 3G on or off here.

- ✔ **Data Roaming:** Data roaming is a feature of cellular networks that takes advantage of other carriers' networks if you're out of range of your primary carrier's network. Using data roaming can result in additional charges, so you may want to turn it off here at times.

- ✔ **View Account:** Tap this setting to view account information.

- ✔ **Add a SIM PIN:** If you want to protect the data on your SIM card from prying eyes, you can assign it a PIN number here. Don't forget your PIN, though, or you won't be able to unlock your SIM card.

 If you change your cellular data carrier, you might need to remove the SIM card and replace it with another. To do this, you need to use a SIM eject tool to press and open the SIM tray located on the left side of 3G-enabled iPads.

(Don't have a SIM eject tool? Don't worry; Apple recommends using a very high-tech instrument — a paper clip.) Replace the SIM card and push the tray back in. That's it!

With a Wi-Fi and 3G model iPad with iOS 4.2 or later, you also have access to the Airplane Mode setting. This setting allows you to disable wireless features of your device as required by airline regulations when you're flying. With Airplane Mode turned on in Settings, you won't be able to browse, e-mail, sync, buy stuff online, or stream videos (which you would only be able to do with a 3G model a mile in the sky). Also, the GPS locator of Maps won't work, but you can play content you've downloaded, play games, and create documents in apps like Pages and Numbers. Just don't forget to turn the Airplane Mode setting off when you land!

Connecting with Personal Hotspot or iPhone 3G Tethering

If you want to connect iPad to your smartphone to go online when out of range of a Wi-Fi network, you can tether it using Verizon's Personal Hotspot or AT&T's iPhone 3G Tethering. *Tethering* with either service allows your iPad's Wi-Fi capability to tap into your phone's data connection to go online. You can get a connection anywhere your phone gets a connection — even if you have a Wi-Fi-only iPad model.

Tethering involves a few challenges. You don't go online instantly, because you have to complete a few steps to do so, the connection speed might be a tad slow, and it can drain your phone battery faster.

Once you're comfortable with the tethering option, you need to do two things:

1. **Add the tethering option for your carrier on the carrier's website by logging in to your account and adding the feature.**

   There is a cost; for example, AT&T offers two levels of tethering support at $45 and $60 at the time of this writing.

2. **Make the setting on your iPad to turn on the tethering service feature.**

   a. *Tap the Settings icon.*

   b. *Tap Wi-Fi.*

   c. *Tap the tethering service in the Choose a Network section and make settings specific to your carrier.*

Sprint, AT&T, and Verizon pricing and features are still in flux, and you need both a basic data plan and a tethering feature plan, which can add up. Still, if you often wander into areas that have no Wi-Fi and you don't have a 3G iPad, it may — or may not — be more cost effective to use this feature.

Consider using the new FaceTime app to make Wi-Fi calls. Using this app, you can make video calls to others who have FaceTime on their devices. See Book II, Chapter 4 for more about using FaceTime.

Connecting to an Enterprise Remotely

When previewed in early 2010, iPad had no support for Microsoft Exchange. Between that time and its release in April 2010, somebody got smart and added Exchange support. That opened up possibilities for connecting with an enterprise network and its data remotely. If you work at a company using Microsoft Exchange and use an iPad, this is very good news.

Thanks to these enterprise features, here are some of the things you can do to connect to your organization's network and data.

Setting up a Microsoft Exchange account

Microsoft Exchange is a messaging standard that allows exchange of information between networks. Many companies use Microsoft Exchange and a feature called ActiveSync to exchange their e-mail, contacts, and calendar information with devices. iPhone has supported Microsoft Exchange for a while now, and iPad carries on the tradition. You can use Microsoft Exchange to wirelessly sync that information to your iPad from your corporate network.

One benefit of a connection with Microsoft Exchange is that you can wipe the data and settings off a device remotely by using a command in Exchange if it's lost or stolen, keeping those confidential business contacts private. Another option for this is to use iCloud's Find My iPad feature, covered in more detail in Book I, Chapter 9.

With a configuration profile in place, you can set up a Microsoft Exchange account on your iPad. To do so, follow these steps:

1. **Tap Settings.**

2. **Tap Mail, Contacts, Calendars.**

3. **Tap Add Account.**

4. **Tap Microsoft Exchange.**

5. **Enter your account information in the dialog shown in Figure 1-4 (e-mail address, domain such as IT or Marketing, username, password, and a description) and then tap Next.**

    iPad then uses Microsoft's Autodiscover feature to verify your Exchange server.

Figure 1-4: The Exchange dialog box.

6. **If it can verify your information, tap Save, and you're all set.**

If it can't, you may have to enter additional information yourself. Check with your network administrator to get what you need.

 When you're setting up a Microsoft Exchange account, you can choose which items you want to sync with, including e-mail, contacts, or calendar. You get choices for how existing data on your iPad will be handled (merged, kept in a separate account, or overwritten).

Setting up a configuration profile

A configuration profile is a way for the network administrator at your enterprise to set up your iPad to use the systems in your company, via Microsoft Exchange or a VPN which control access to corporate e-mail or contacts.

Your administrator should check out the Enterprise Deployment Guide and iPad Configuration Utility from Apple (`www.apple.com/support/ipad/enterprise`) to get a configuration profile set up. After a configuration profile is in place, it can be e-mailed to you or placed on a secure web page. Also, your company's network administrator can install a configuration profile on your iPad.

If you receive a configuration profile, you can install it yourself by opening the message and tapping the file. Tap Install and enter any information that's requested, such as your password.

 You can't change the settings in a configuration profile. To set up a different configuration profile, first remove the existing configuration profile, have the new profile sent to you, and then install it. To remove a profile, in Settings, choose General, then Profiles, and then select the configuration profile you want to get rid of and tap Remove.

Setting up an LDAP account

You can also set up an LDAP (Lightweight Directory Access Protocol) account. LDAP accounts allow you to search for contacts on an LDAP server, which many organizations use to store data, and access them through iPad Contacts.

Here's how to set up an LDAP account on your iPad:

1. **In Settings, tap Mail, Contacts, Calendars.**

2. **Tap Add Account.**

3. **Tap Other.**

4. **Tap Add LDAP Account.**

5. **Enter your LDAP account information (see Figure 1-5) and then tap Next to verify the account.**

6. **Tap Save.**

Figure 1-5: The LDAP dialog.

When you have set up this type of account, contacts imported from the account appear as a group in the iPad Contacts app. To see these contacts, your iPad has to be connected to the Internet because they aren't stored locally on it. If necessary, check with your company's network administrator for information about your network and LDAP requirements.

Setting up a virtual private network

If you want to be able to connect to your organization's network, you may be able to use a virtual private network, or VPN. VPN works over both Wi-Fi and 3G cellular data connections. A VPN allows you to access data securely, even if you're on a public Wi-Fi connection. After a VPN is set up at your company, you can use Network Settings on your iPad to modify your VPN settings and connect to your network.

You might need to ask your network administrator for information on making settings for accessing a VPN. If you've set up VPN on your computer, you should be able to use the same VPN settings on your iPad. You might want to let your admin know that iPad can connect to VPNs that use the L2TP, PPTP, or Cisco IPSec protocol.

To add a new VPN configuration, go to iPad Settings. Tap General, tap Network, tap VPN and, if necessary, tap to turn on VPN. The dialog shown in Figure 1-6 appears. Fill in the information requested and tap Save.

Figure 1-6: The Add Configuration dialog.

To delete a VPN configuration, tap the blue arrow to the right of the configuration name in the Network settings and then tap Delete VPN.

Have your administrator check out third-party tools that help to enable the use of the corporate network by remote iPad users. Good for Enterprise helps a user manage and update smartphone-like standards if that person's company has no single standard. Array Networks provides the iPad app Desktop Direct – My Desktops that, along with Citrix Receiver software, helps users access their desktop from afar.

Status icons

In case you're wondering what the icons in the Status bar on top of the iPad screen mean relative to your connections, here's a rundown:

Icon	*Meaning*
✈	Airplane mode is on, and your Wi-Fi and 3G connection capabilities are turned off.
3G	A 3G network is available.
E	A carrier's EDGE network is available.
o	A GPRS network is available.
📶	Your iPad has a Wi-Fi Internet connection. The more bars you see, the stronger your connection.
✳	Network or another type of activity involving a third-party app is detected.
VPN	You're connected to a VPN network.

Chapter 2: Finding Your Way with Maps

In This Chapter

- ✔ **Going to your current location**
- ✔ **Knowing where you've been**
- ✔ **Finding directions, info, and more**
- ✔ **Conveying location information beyond maps**

*I*f you own an iPhone or iPod touch, the Maps app on iPad will be very familiar. The big difference with iPad is the large screen on which you can view all the beautiful map visuals and terrain and street views as long as you have an Internet connection.

You can find lots of great functions in the Maps app, including getting directions with suggested alternate routes from one location to another by foot, car, or public transportation. You can bookmark locations to return to them again. And the Maps app makes it possible to get information about locations, such as the phone numbers and web links to businesses. You can even look at a building or location as if you were standing in front of it on the street, add a location to your Contacts list, or e-mail a location link to your buddy.

Be prepared: This app is seriously cool, and you're about to have lots of fun exploring it in this chapter.

Getting Where You're Going

The first duty of a map is to get you where you want to go. The Maps app can go directly to wherever you are or to any other location you wish to visit. You can also use tools that help you find different views of locales by displaying streets, terrain, or aerial views, or zooming in and out for various levels of detail. In this section, you find out how to use Maps to get around.

Going to your current location

iPad is pretty smart; it can figure out where you are at any point in time and display your current location using GPS technology (or a triangulation method if you have a Wi-Fi model). You must have an Internet connection; your location can be pinpointed more exactly if you have a 3G iPad, but even Wi-Fi models do a pretty good job, and do even better when you're surrounded by hotspots.

To display your current location in Maps, follow these steps:

1. **From the Home screen, tap the Maps icon.**

2. **Tap the Current Location icon (the gray arrow to the left of the Search field; see Figure 2-1).**

   Your current location is displayed with a blue pin and a blue circle around it. (See Figure 2-1.) The circle indicates how accurate the location is — it could actually be anywhere within the area of the circle.

Current Location icon

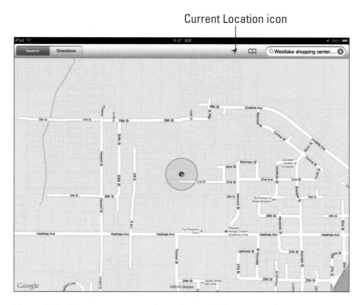

Figure 2-1: Go to your current location quickly to see where you are.

3. **Double-tap the screen to zoom in on your location.**

   (Additional methods of zooming in and out are covered in the "Zooming in and out" section, later in this chapter.)

If you don't have a 3G version of iPad, your current location is a rough estimate based on a triangulation method. Only 3G-enabled iPads with GPS can really pinpoint your location. Still, if you type a starting location and an ending location to get directions, you can get pretty accurate results even with a Wi-Fi–only iPad.

Changing views

The Maps app offers four views: Standard, Satellite, Hybrid, and Terrain. You view the Standard view by default the first time you open Maps. Here's what these views offer:

- ✔ **Standard:** Your basic street map you might find in any road atlas
- ✔ **Satellite:** An aerial view
- ✔ **Hybrid:** A satellite view with street names included
- ✔ **Terrain:** A topographical map showing mountains and other variations in the landscape

Another cool app for those who like their maps of the topographical variety is Topo Maps for iPad from Phil Endecott ($7.99). This app taps into the United States Geological Society (USGS) and Canadian topographical maps and is great for planning that next trek into the wilderness.

Follow these steps to switch among the views in Maps:

1. **To change views, with Maps open, swipe the bottom-right corner of the screen to turn the "page" and reveal the Maps menu shown in Figure 2-2.**

2. **Tap the Satellite option.**

   The Satellite view shown in Figure 2-3 appears.

3. **Swipe to reveal the menu again and tap Hybrid, as shown in Figure 2-4.**

   Doing this displays a Satellite view with street names superimposed.

4. **Swipe to reveal the menu one more time and tap Terrain.**

   A topographical version of the map is displayed (see Figure 2-5), showing hills, mountains, and valleys. (Seeing this is very helpful if you want to walk around San Francisco and avoid those steep streets!)

Having trouble getting Maps to work? That could be because if you turn Location Services off in iPad Settings, Maps can't find you. Go to Settings and make check that Location Services is set to On.

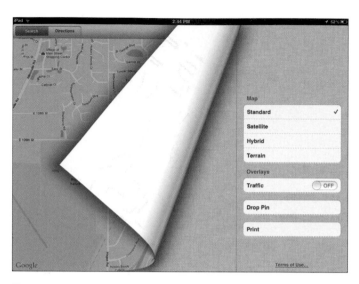

Figure 2-2: The controls for Maps are tucked underneath the map display page.

Figure 2-3: Using Satellite view, you look at a location from the sky.

You can drop a pin to mark a location on a map that you can return to. See the "Dropping a pin," section later in this chapter, for more about this feature.

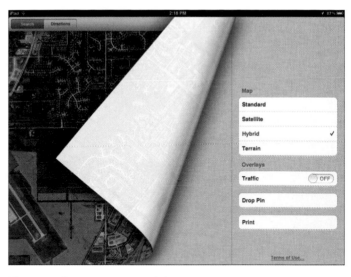

Figure 2-4: Street names and highway numbers appear in Hybrid view.

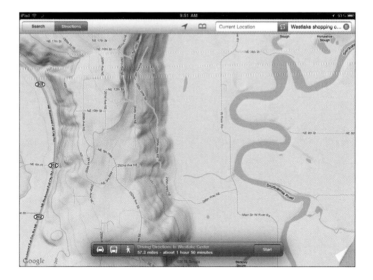

Figure 2-5: Terrain is a great view for hikers — if you get reception out in the woods!

You can also turn on a feature that displays an overlay on the Standard map to show current traffic conditions. (The setting for this feature is shown earlier in Figure 2-2.) This feature shows works best in major metropolitan areas and displays roads in red, yellow, or green to indicate any obstructions (red for serious, yellow for caution) or roads on which cars are moving right along (green).

To print a displayed map to an AirPrint-compatible wireless printer, tap the Print button on the Maps menu.

Zooming in and out

If you've used an online mapping program, you know that you frequently have to move to more or less detailed views of the map to find what you're looking for: The street detail doesn't show the nearest highway, and the region level doesn't let you see that all-important next turn. You'll appreciate the feature in the Maps app that allows you to zoom in and out to see more or less detailed maps and to move around a displayed map.

You can use the following methods on a displayed map to zoom in and out and move around a map:

✔ **Double-tap with a single finger** to zoom in (and reveal more detail), as shown in Figure 2-6.

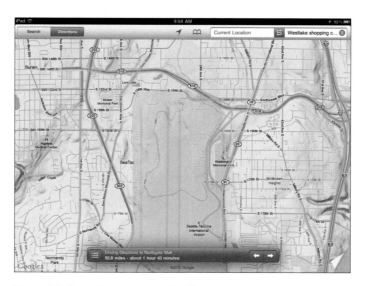

Figure 2-6: Zoom in to see more detail.

✔ **Double-tap with two fingers** to zoom out (and reveal less detail), as shown in Figure 2-7.

✔ **Place two fingers together on the screen and move them apart** to zoom in.

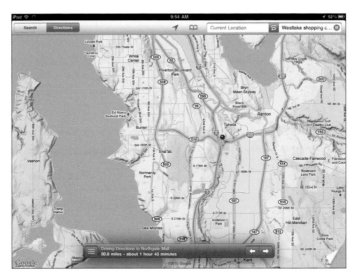

Figure 2-7: Zoom out to get a larger view of the region — with less detail.

- ✏ **Place two fingers apart on the screen and pinch them together** to zoom out.

- ✏ **Press your finger to the screen and drag the map in any direction** to move to an adjacent area.

It can take a few moments for the map to redraw itself when you enlarge, reduce, or move around it, so have a little patience. Areas that are being redrawn will look like a blank grid but will fill in, in time. Also, if you're in Satellite view, zooming in may take some time; wait it out because the blurred image will resolve itself.

Going to another location

If you're at Point A and want to get to Point B, Calcutta, Des Moines, or wherever, you need to know how to find any location other than your current location using Maps. Doing this involves entering as much information as you have about the location's address in the Search field.

Try going to another location using these steps:

1. **With Maps open, tap in the Search field.**

   The keyboard opens (as shown in Figure 2-8).

Tap in the Search field...

then type a location

Figure 2-8: You can use the onscreen keyboard to enter location information.

2. **Type a location, using a street address with city and state, or a destination, such as *Empire State Building* or *Detroit airport*.**

   Maps may make suggestions as you type if it finds any logical matches.

3. **Tap the Search button.**

   The location appears with a red pin inserted in it and a label with the location, an Information icon, and in some cases a Street View icon (shown in Figure 2-9). Note that if several locations match your search term, you may see several pins on the map.

4. **You can also tap the screen and drag in any direction to move to a nearby location.**

   See the upcoming "Dropping a pin" section to find out how to zero in on the location and get the label with links to additional information, like you see in Figure 2-9.

5. **Tap the Bookmark icon (the little book symbol to the left of the Search field; refer to Figure 2-9) and then tap the Recent tab to reveal recently visited sites.**

6. **Tap a bookmark to go there.**

The information bar   Bookmark icon   Search field

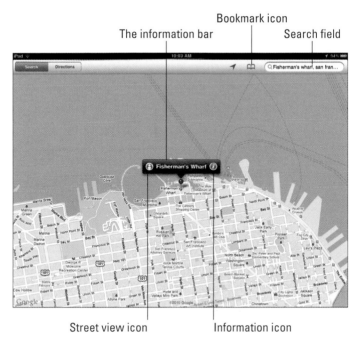

Street view icon   Information icon

Figure 2-9: The more specific the address information you enter, the more likely you are to find just the right location.

As you discover later in this chapter in the "Adding and viewing a bookmark" section, you can also quickly go to any location you've previously visited and saved using the Bookmarks feature.

Add the city and state, if you know them, whenever you enter a destination. A search for *Bronx Zoo* landed me in the Woodland Park Zoo in Tacoma, Washington, because the search uses the individual words and the closest geographical location for a *Zoo* match to find results!

Remembering Where You've Been

Why reinvent the (mapping) wheel? One of the great capabilities of a mapping program is the ability to store locations you like to go to for future reference. In Maps, you can do this in a few different ways. You can drop a pin on a map, which marks a beginning point for getting directions from one site to another. Or you can place a bookmark for a site you want to revisit often.

Dropping a pin

With iPad, pins act like the pins you might place on a paper map to note routes or favorite locations. With iPad, pins are also markers; a green pin marks a start location, red pins mark search results, a pin you drop yourself appears in a lovely purple, and a blue pin (referred to as the *blue marker*) marks your iPad's current location.

Use these steps to try out the pin feature of iPad:

1. **Display a map that contains a spot where you'd like to drop a pin to help you get directions to or from that site.**

   If you need to, you can zoom in to a more detailed map to get a better view of the location you'd like to pin using the techniques I cover in the earlier "Zooming in and out" section.

2. **Press and hold your finger on the screen at the location where you want to place the pin.**

   The pin appears, together with an information bar (shown in Figure 2-10).

The information bar

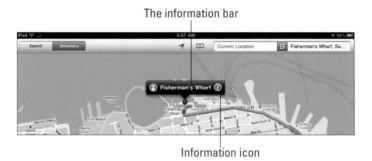

Information icon

Figure 2-10: The information bar provides access to yet more Maps tools.

3. **Tap the Information icon (refer to Figure 2-10) on the information bar to display details about the pin location (shown in Figure 2-11).**

To delete a pin you've dropped, tap the pin to display the information bar and then tap the Information icon. In the Information dialog that opens, tap Remove Pin. This only works with pinned sites that aren't bookmarked.

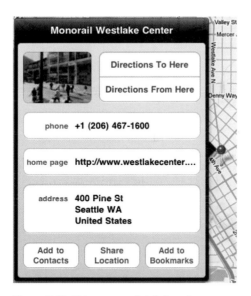

Monorail Westlake Center

Directions To Here

Directions From Here

phone **+1 (206) 467-1600**

home page **http://www.westlakecenter....**

address **400 Pine St
Seattle WA
United States**

Add to
Contacts

Share
Location

Add to
Bookmarks

Figure 2-11: This very useful dialog gives you
information and lets you share what you know.

Adding and viewing a bookmark

Bookmarks are a tried-and-true way to save a destination so that you can
display a map or directions to that spot quickly. You've probably used a
bookmark feature in a web browser that works similarly. With Maps, you can
save bookmarks and access those locations from a drop-down list.

Here's how to add a bookmark in Maps:

1. **Place a pin on a location, as described in the preceding section.**

2. **Tap the Information icon to display the Information dialog.**

3. **Tap the Add to Bookmarks button (shown in Figure 2-12).**

   The Add Bookmark dialog and keyboard appear (as shown in Figure 2-13).
   If you like, you can modify the name of the bookmark.

4. **Tap Save.**

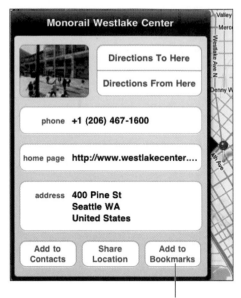

Tap the Add to Bookmarks button

Figure 2-12: Grab a destination you like and add it to your bookmarks.

Figure 2-13: Name the bookmark.

5. **To view your bookmarks, tap the Bookmark icon (it looks like a little open book; refer to Figure 2-9) at the top of the Maps screen.**

   Be sure the Bookmarks tab is selected; a list of bookmarks is displayed, as shown in Figure 2-14.

Figure 2-14: The list of saved bookmarks.

6. **Tap a bookmark to go to the location.**

You can also view recently viewed locations even if you haven't bookmarked them. Tap the Bookmark icon, and then, on the bottom of the Bookmarks dialog that appears, tap Recents. Locations you've visited recently are listed there. Tap a location to return to it.

Deleting a bookmark

Eventually, a site you used to visit gets crossed off your A list. At that point, you might want to delete a bookmark, which you can easily do by following these steps:

1. **Tap the Bookmark icon and then tap the Bookmarks tab at the bottom of the dialog that appears.**

2. **Tap the Edit button.**

   A red minus icon appears to the left of your bookmarks, as shown in Figure 2-15.

Red minus icons

Figure 2-15: Tap a bookmark's red icon to select it for deletion.

3. **Tap a red minus icon.**

4. **Tap Delete.**

The bookmark is removed.

You can also use a touchscreen shortcut after you've displayed the bookmarks in Step 1 above. Simply swipe across a bookmark and then tap the Delete button that appears.

You can also clear out all recent locations stored by Maps to give yourself a clean slate. Tap the Bookmark icon and then tap the Recents tab. Tap Clear and then confirm by tapping Clear All Recents.

Getting Directions, Information, and More

Maps can provide all kinds of information, from directions from one location to another to the street address and phone number for a particular business or landmark or the compass direction you're headed in. There's even a street-level view provided for some locations so you can see what the Empire State Building or your favorite downtown spot looks like (though be aware that only some locations offer this feature, and the images may have been taken a few years ago and therefore may not be totally accurate).

Getting directions

You can get directions by using pins that you drop on a map for the starting and ending locations, or by entering an address or name of a place, such as an airport or shopping mall. The directions are shown in a blue line leading from one place to another. You can even choose directions by car, bus, or foot. Directions also give you an idea of the miles and hours it will take you to get to your destination. (It will take you 15 hours and 43 minutes, for example, to walk from the Bronx Zoo to the Empire State Building — in case you wondered.) Here are the steps to get directions to two different locations in Maps using pins:

1. **With at least one pin on your map (at your destination) in addition to your current location, tap the Directions tab.**

   A line appears, showing the route between your current location and the closest pin. (See Figure 2-16.)

The line indicating your route

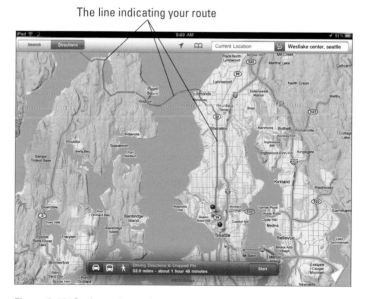

Figure 2-16: Go from pin to pin on your map to get directions.

2. **To show directions from your current location to another pin, tap the other pin.**

   The route is redrawn.

   You can also enter two locations in the boxes at the top of the page to get directions from one to the other.

Here are the steps to get directions in maps by typing the addresses in the Search fields:

1. **With the Directions tab selected in Maps, tap in the field labeled Current Location.**

   The keyboard appears. (See Figure 2-17.)

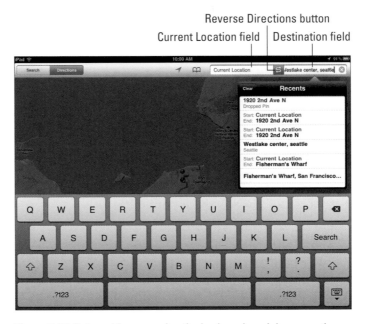

Figure 2-17: Enter addresses using the keyboard or pick a recently visited location from this list.

2. **Enter a different starting location.**

3. **Tap in the Destination field, enter a destination location, and then tap the Search button on the keyboard.**

   The route between the two locations is displayed.

You can also tap the Information icon on the information bar that appears above any selected pin and use the Directions To Here or Directions From Here button (shown in Figure 2-18) to generate directions.

With a route displayed, a blue bar appears along the bottom of the Maps screen, with information about the distance and time it takes to travel between the two locations. Here's what you can do with this informational display:

Tap either of these buttons
to generate directions

Figure 2-18: Use these buttons to go to or from a location.

✔ **Transportation mode:** Tap the car, bus, or pedestrian logo to get driving, public transportation, or walking directions when available. (See Figure 2-19.)

✔ **Turn-by-turn directions:** Tap Start to change the tools offered. The Start button changes to back and forward arrows. Tap the forward arrow, and the first step of your journey is displayed. At any time, if you prefer to see the directions in a larger display, tap the icon on the left showing several lines of text as if in a small document. That takes you to step-by-step directions shown in Figure 2-20. Tap the icon in the top-left portion of the display to return to the arrow keys that take you through the directions one step at a time.

✔ **Alternative route:** Maps notes, along the top of the informational display, the number of alternative routes it finds and adds the routes to the map. Tap a route number to make it the active route, which displays in a darker blue than the alternates, as shown in Figure 2-21.

In the Directions view of Maps, notice the Reverse Directions button (the zigzag line between the Current Location and Destination fields; refer to Figure 2-17). After you generate directions from one location to another, tap this button to generate reverse directions. Believe me, they aren't always the same — especially when one-way streets are involved!

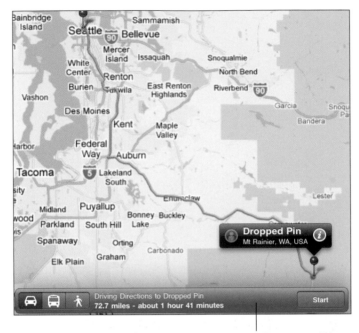

Use this bar to get travel distance and time

Figure 2-19: Find out how long a trip you're in for.

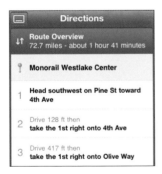

Figure 2-20: Get a blow-by-blow
description of your route.

Getting information about a location

You've displayed the Information dialog for locations to add a bookmark or
get directions in previous sections of this chapter. It's time to focus on the
other useful information displayed there. Using the Information button for
any location, you can get the street address, phone number, and even the
URL for some businesses or landmarks.

Tap a route number to select it

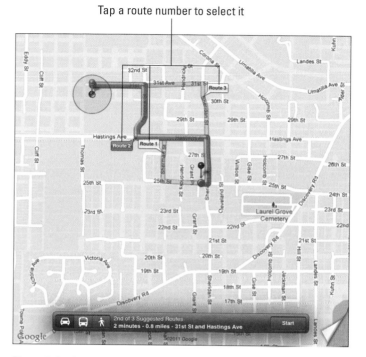

Figure 2-21: Select the active route or an alternative

To get to the Information dialog, go to a location and tap the pin. In the information bar that appears above the pinned location, tap the Information icon (shown in Figure 2-22).

Tap this icon

Figure 2-22: Display the Information dialog.

In the Information dialog, you can tap the web address listed in the Home Page field (see Figure 2-23) to be taken to the location's web page, if it has one associated with it.

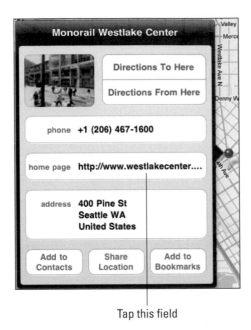

Tap this field

Figure 2-23: Going to a business's website with a tap.

You can also press and hold the Phone or Address fields and use the Copy button to copy the phone number, for example, so you can place it in a Notes document for future reference. When you've got all the information you need, tap anywhere outside the Information dialog to close it.

Rather than copy and paste information, you can easily save all the information about a location in your Contacts address book. See the "Adding a location to Contacts" section, later in this chapter, to find out how that's done.

Viewing a location from street level

Street view is seriously cool. You can not only get a picture of what the location looks like from the street, but also pan all around it to look up at tall skyscrapers, around to get a feel for the neighborhood, or down to see the actual street. You can view only certain locations from street level (indicated by the presence or absence of the Street View icon shown in Figure 2-24), so you'll have to explore to try this out.

Street view is available for this location

Figure 2-24: The red icon with a little person in it indicates that Street view is available.

If you want to give it a try, follow these steps to explore one location at street level:

1. **In the Search tab of Maps, shown in Figure 2-17, tap the Search field and enter a location, such as your favorite local shopping mall.**

   (Enter *Monorail Westlake Center, Seattle, WA* if you have trouble finding a location that offers a street-level view, indicated by a little red icon on the information bar for the location.)

2. **When the location appears, tap the Street View icon on its information bar.**

   The Street view appears.

3. **When you're in Street view (see Figure 2-25), you can tap and drag the screen to look around you in all directions.**

4. **Tap the small circular map in the bottom-right corner (refer to Figure 2-25) to return to the standard map view.**

You can also drag the screen down to get a better look at tall skyscrapers or up to view the street and manhole covers. The small circular map in the bottom-right corner highlights what you're looking at in the specific moment. In addition, street names are displayed down the center of streets.

Using the Compass

Sometimes it helps you to find your way if you know the direction that you're headed in. The Compass feature of Maps displays a small compass that helps you figure out if you're going north, south, east, west, or any combination, such as southeast.

**Book III
Chapter 2**

**Finding Your Way
with Maps**

Tap here to return to the standard map view

Figure 2-25: The monorail station in downtown Seattle.

Note that the Compass feature works from only your current location, so start by tapping the Current Location icon (shown earlier in Figure 2-17) at the top of the Maps screen. Tap the icon again to turn the Compass on. A small compass appears in the top-right corner of the screen. (See Figure 2-26.)

Now move your iPad around in different directions and note that the compass symbol moves as well, indicating which direction you're facing. To turn the Compass off, tap the Current Location icon one more time.

Compass

Figure 2-26: The little Compass icon shows you where you are relative to the rest of the world.

You may get a message that there's interference and the Compass needs resetting. You can deal with this by moving away from any electronic equipment that might be causing interference, and moving the iPad around in what Apple describes as a figure-eight motion.

Location Services has to be turned on in iPad Settings for the Compass feature to be available.

Sending Location Info beyond Maps

When you find a location you want to come back to or tell others about, you can use features of Maps that help you out. You can save a location to the Contacts app, which also saves the address, phone number, and URL, if any. You can also share a link to locations with friends via e-mail or Twitter. They can then access the location information by using Maps.

Adding a location to Contacts

The beauty of this feature is that not only can you store valuable information such as phone numbers and street addresses in Contacts quickly and easily, but you can also use stored contacts to quickly find locations in Maps.

Here's how this works:

1. **Tap a pin to display the information bar.**

2. **Tap the Information icon.**

3. **In the Information dialog that appears (see Figure 2-27), tap Add to Contacts.**

   A dialog appears.

Tap this button

Figure 2-27: Use handy buttons in the Information dialog to add a location to Contacts.

4. **Tap Create New Contact.**

   The New Contact dialog appears (as shown in Figure 2-28). Whatever information was available about the location has been entered.

5. **Enter any additional information you need, such as name, phone, or e-mail.**

6. **Tap Done.**

   The information is stored in your Contacts address book.

You can choose a distinct ringtone or text tone for a new contact. Just tap the Ringtone or Text Tone field in the New Contact form to see a list of options. When that person calls via FaceTime or texts you via iMessage, you will recognize him or her from the type of tone that plays.

After you store information in Contacts, you can also share it with friends from there by tapping the Share button in the address record. See Book V, Chapter 5 for more about using Contacts.

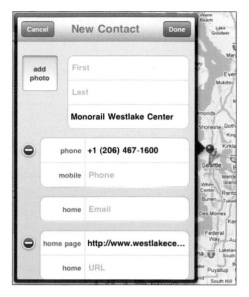

Figure 2-28: Any available information can be stored to Contacts.

Sharing location information

Have you found a fantastic restaurant or movie theater you absolutely have to share with a friend? From within Maps, you can use a simple procedure to e-mail a link to your friend. When your friend, who is connected to the Internet, taps the link, it opens the map to the location in Maps (a free service).

After you've saved a location in Contacts, take these steps to share a location:

1. **Tap a pin to display the information bar.**

2. **Tap the Information icon.**

3. **In the Information dialog that appears, tap Share Location.**

   In the dialog that appears, you can choose to share via text message, tweet, or e-mail.

4. **Tap Email to see how this option works.**

5. **In the e-mail form that appears (see Figure 2-29), use the onscreen keyboard to enter a recipient's e-mail address, any Cc/Bcc addresses, and add or change the subject or message as you like.**

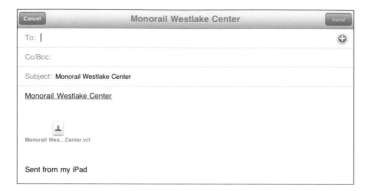

Figure 2-29: Your basic e-mail form, ready for you to fill in pertinent information.

6. **Tap Send.**

   A link to the location information in Maps is sent to your designated recipient(s).

 If you choose Tweet in Step 4, you have to have installed the Twitter app and have a Twitter account set up using iPad Settings. Tapping Message in Step 4 displays a new message form; just enter an e-mail address or phone number in the To field, enter your text message, and then tap Send.

 Use this feature to share your current location so a friend or emergency service can find you. However, beware of sharing your current information with strangers!

Chapter 3: Apps for Road Warriors

In This Chapter

- ✔ **Arranging travel**
- ✔ **Finding the best hotels**
- ✔ **Locating restaurants**
- ✔ **Staying connected**

*i*Pad is practically perfect for people who have to travel a lot for business or who love to travel for pleasure. It's lightweight, slender, and stays powered up for about 10 hours at a time. Depending on the model, you can connect around the world using 3G or Wi-Fi (or both) to stay in touch or browse the Internet for whatever you need. You have an onscreen keyboard, so you don't have to tote around a physical keyboard. Robust business apps such as those in the iWork suite let you get work done as you travel. You may never drag a laptop on a trip again!

That's why, in this chapter, the focus is on how people on the road can use iPad. I start by pointing out the pre-installed apps that work for travelers and then provide some general advice and specific app suggestions for making travel arrangements, finding great hotels and restaurants, getting maps and travel guides, and keeping track of what you spend as you travel. I also cover use of Personal Hotspot to make phone calls where no Wi-Fi connection exists, and FaceTime, a great way to connect with others who are remote, face to face.

Starting with What You Have

Before I get into the marvelous world of apps for travelers, you should consider the tools that come with the iPad out of the box. You could find your way around the world quite nicely with these little gems, including:

- ✔ **Maps:** This app allows to you locate worldwide locations and get detailed street maps, view some buildings from street level, show directions from one point to another, and bookmark favorite locations. You can navigate as you drive, take public transportation, or walk around using an onscreen compass (see Figure 3-1), and share location information with others by e-mail. (See Book III, Chapter 2 for details about how to use Maps.)

Compass

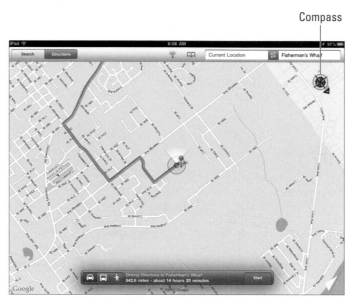

Figure 3-1: If your rental car doesn't have a navigation feature, use iPad instead!

✓ **Contacts:** If you're going on the road to visit clients or friends and have their address information in Contacts, you can tap the address and be taken to it instantly in the Maps app. Keep phone numbers handy to get in touch when you hit town, and even use the Notes field in a Contacts entry to keep track of your business activities with that person or company. Remember that you can add fields to contact records, including job title, related people, department, and birthday using editing tools in Contacts. (See Book V, Chapter 5 for more about Contacts features.)

✓ **Safari browser:** Don't forget that if you have an Internet connection, you can use the Safari browser to get online and tap into all the travel-related information and sites on the web. Use sites such as Expedia.com, shown in Figure 3-2, or KAYAK.com to book travel, check flight information at airline websites, go to sites such as MapQuest to get directions and maps, and so on. (For more about using Safari, go to Book I, Chapter 6.)

✓ **Mail:** This built-in e-mail client lets you keep in touch through any accounts you set up in iPad as long as you have an Internet connection. Find out more about setting up e-mail accounts in Book I, Chapter 7.

Figure 3-2: Expedia offers travel booking services for flights, hotel, car rental, and more.

✓ **Notes:** Although there isn't a travel expense tracker in iPad, you can always use Notes to keep a record of what you spend or any other information about your trip you need to recall after you get home. You can even e-mail a note to yourself or your accountant so it's on your office computer when you get back.

Travel can get tedious with long waits in line or terminals. Don't forget that you have a built-in music player in Music and a built-in video player in the Videos app to keep you entertained.

Making Travel Arrangements

Now I'll move on to apps that don't reside on your iPad when you buy it. This chapter features just a few of the available apps — more are covered in Book VI, Chapter 2. Some are actually iPhone apps that work on iPad (so be sure to check out the iPhone apps category), and some were built specifically for iPad.

Start at the beginning, when you are planning your trip. You need to book flights or other modes of travel and check to see that your flight is on time. You may need a rental car when you arrive and perhaps maps of public transit to help you plan your route. All these are covered in this section.

Getting there by air

This list is a mixed bag of travel booking tools and apps that help you check on your seat assignment or flight status. Try these:

✔ **Travelocity:** This free, nicely designed app shown in Figure 3-3 lets you book travel online, save itineraries, and get flight information. My favorite feature is the ability to explore destinations by great deals, upcoming events, or available travel guides. You can even check out hotels and sort the results by distance, price, or rating.

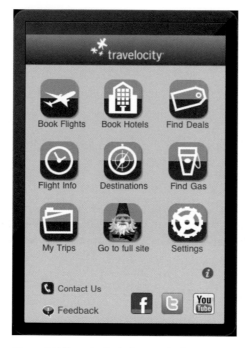

Figure 3-3: Travelocity is free and offers lots of travel booking options.

✔ **Airline Seat Guide:** You know how you always get on the plane thinking your seat will be fine only to find out you're three miles from the restroom or stuck in the middle of a seven-seat row on an international flight? By using Airline Seat Guide, which has data from over 100 airlines and 1,200 plane models, you get the advice you need to choose the best seat to make your travel more enjoyable. This one costs $1.99 but may be well worth it in terms of in-flight comfort.

✔ **AirportStatusFree:** Get information about flight status and delays all around the United States and parts of Canada with this free app. (See Figure 3-4.) You even get information about the cause of delays, such as weather and airport closures. And, as the name implies, it's absolutely free.

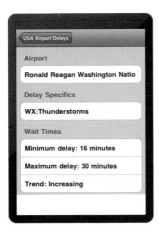

Figure 3-4: Check about delays before you leave home using AirportStatusFree.

Several airlines have their own mobile apps for booking or checking flight status (see Figure 3-5 for an example) and, in some cases, features for checking your standby status, checking in, and generating a boarding pass. These include:

Figure 3-5: Enter information about your flight and get information back.

- American Airlines HD
- Southwest Airlines
- Alaska Airlines/Horizon Air Mobile
- British Airways
- Virgin Atlantic Flight Tracker
- United Airlines

If you're a frequent flier, check out the Air Milage Calculator app. (Make sure you exclude the *e* in *mileage* when searching iTunes for this app.) For $1.99, you can get the mileage for travel between airports worldwide with up to three legs for each trip. You can also have the app calculate bonuses based on your frequent flyer status and the class of travel.

If packing is a challenge for you and you don't have a valet to help you out, try Packing Pro. Keep track of lists of what you need by trip, including your passport, clothing, and vital accessories such as an umbrella for that trip to Seattle. It costs you $2.99, but if you're organizationally challenged, it might save your neck as you prepare for business or family trips.

Renting a car

If you want to deal with your car rentals from your iPad, you'll be glad to hear that there are apps that help you do just that. Consider sites such as these that help you find the right rental deal:

- **Priceline Hotel & Car Negotiator:** Helps you find the best deal on airport car rentals, as you can see in Figure 3-6. If you're in a rush, you can book up to 30 minutes before you need your car using this app. And Priceline lets you bid on the best price to save you the most money on your rental car.

- **Car Rentals – CarRentals.com:** Lets you search among 15,000 national and international car rental options. You can sort your options by their distance from you and book the car of your choice from major car rental companies.

You can also get individual apps for your favorite car rental companies, such as Avis Reservation App or Hertz Car Rental.

Road Trip Lite is a free utility that helps you track your mileage and fuel economy, which may help you estimate your costs if your rental car doesn't include unlimited miles. It sports a nice visual graph of fuel economy, and if you use your own car on the road, the feature that lets you track mileage and fuel cost by trip could be a neat way to sum up your travel expenses every month.

Figure 3-6: Priceline helps you get the best deal on your rental car.

Finding your way around town

Before you set off on your trip to cities such as New York, San Francisco, or Chicago, you might want to download one of these apps to get local transit system maps, schedules, and more.

Transit Maps is free and comes with one transit map, but enables you to download transit maps as graphics files from the Internet using its own browser feature.

iTransitBuddy is a series of 99-cent apps for various metro areas designed for iPhone but usable on iPad. If you want lots of transit maps, you can subscribe to iTransitBuddy and get access to all their map apps. This app has a helpful feature for looking up free transfers and schedule updates. Maps are downloaded to your device, so you don't have to have an Internet connection to use them. This one is handy for commuters as well as those who travel to metro areas on business or for pleasure.

As you're exploring a new town, make sure you're dressed right for the weather. SHSH PocketWeather lets you get weather reports on the go.

Finding Just the Right Hotels

Though airlines are jumping on the iPad app bandwagon, individual hotel chains don't seem to have gotten the app memo. Some, such as Holiday Inn and Best Western, do offer apps. Others only offer apps for individual hotels. Therefore, you may not find a Marriott app (as of this writing); instead, you can find apps for Annapolis, Maryland, San Francisco, and Dallas/Plano for single hotels in the chain, for example. Another option for finding hotels around the country or world is to depend on hotel booking apps for your hotel travel.

Here are a few free hotel booking apps (be sure to check out Book VI, Chapter 2 for a few more) that can get you started on your iPad hotel search/booking experience. Most (including the Hotels for iPad app, shown in Figure 3-7) allow you to search for hotels and check ratings, price, and availability. You can also book your reservation and, in some cases, check local attractions.

Figure 3-7: Details about hotels include a description, map, list of facilities, policies, and more.

- Hotels for iPad
- Hotels HD
- Booking.com
- Choice Hotels Locator
- Hotelpal – Hotels & Hotel Room Reservations
- HotelsByMe – Hotels & Hotel Room Reservations

Some general travel sites, such as KAYAK.com and Travelocity.com, also have hotel searching and booking features. Check out Book VI, Chapter 2 for more about these.

Locating the Perfect Restaurant

What's a road warrior without his or her lunch? Hungry, that's what. So, why not use your iPad to find food? Here's a selection of some intriguing restaurant-listing apps for you to explore:

✔ **Vegetarian Restaurants:** Do you avoid meat in your diet? If so, check out the free Vegetarian Restaurants (shown in Figure 3-8). Look for vegetarian restaurants worldwide as well as vegetarian recipes and information about the vegetarian lifestyle.

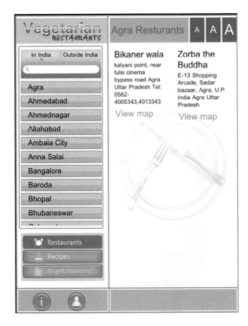

Figure 3-8: Vegetarian Restaurants helps you locate food without meat around the world.

✔ **ZAGAT TO GO:** This one is a bit pricey at $9.99 but provides a wealth of information and ratings from a reliable source. You also get maps and menus from major restaurants and chains around the world.

✓ **Michelin Guide Restaurants:** For anywhere from $9.99 to $18.99 you can get the latest Michelin guide by country. Michelin is kind of the gold standard in restaurant rating systems, so if you are a serious world traveler and gourmand, you can appreciate its insights into the quality of food, specialties of the house, hours, and even the name of the chef.

✓ **Where to Eat? HD:** A poor man's Michelin can be found in Where to Eat? HD, a $2.99 app that has been reworked for iPads. Search for the closest restaurants anywhere you are in the world, find the cuisine you're looking for, and customize searches.

If you want to find a restaurant with available Wi-Fi, you can find such locations using WiFi Get HD. This very handy app helps you spot hotspots even if you're not connected at the moment. This one costs $2.99.

If you're concerned about your waistline, here are a few more free and helpful food-oriented apps:

✓ **CrazyMenu:** Allows you to view restaurant menus and get and give recommendations to Facebook friends.

✓ **Fast Food Calories Hunter:** Can help you control how many calories you ingest along with your fast food meal.

✓ **Restaurant Nutrition:** Shows you carbohydrates, calories, and fat for more than 80 chain restaurants, such as TGI Friday's and The Cheesecake Factory. (Well, forget what I said about watching your waist!)

Note that in the Maps app you can enter the term "restaurants" in the search field, search, and pins are dropped on the map indicating restaurants near your location.

Using Maps and Travel Guides

One important part of the road warrior experience is finding your way around and connecting with the local culture. For that, you can explore some mapping apps and travel guides. These will get you started:

✓ **World Atlas w/Factbook & Travel for iPad:** With this 99-cent app you get high-definition country maps you can browse using your finger and touchscreen. There's also a link to the CIA's World Fact book for different countries and a cool graphical compass that gives a direction in both analog and digital form.

✔ **cityscouter.com guides:** These handy little guides run about $3.99 per city and can be used offline. That's useful if you're on a plane, wandering around a foreign city nowhere near a hotspot, or out of range of your 3G provider's services. Find out about top attractions, take advantage of a currency converter, or find a wiki article, photos, or maps. (See Figure 3-9.) Many include up-to-date information about local public transportation as well.

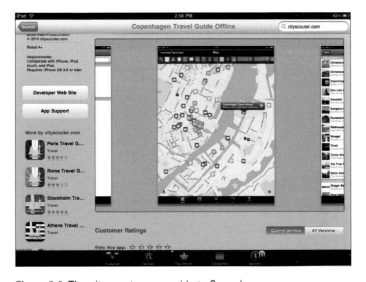

Figure 3-9: The cityscouter.com guide to Copenhagen.

✔ **World Travel Guide Offline:** This guide costs $2.99 and gives you lots of information on about 23,000 destinations. Again, after you download it, you don't need an Internet connection to read all about your travel locations. Suggested itineraries and even a phrasebook to help you with the local lingo are included. This app supports full-screen iPad display, unlike some iPhone clone apps.

✔ **World Customs & Cultures:** Do you know whether it's appropriate to tip in Turkey? Or whether you should bring a gift to a dinner host in Japan? It's important to understand local customs to shine at international business interactions or just appear polite. This free app covers more than 165 countries, giving you tips on common greetings, eye contact, acceptable (and unacceptable) gestures, and local laws, among other things.

In addition to the preceding apps, check out popular travel guides and tools with an iPad presence, including:

- ✔ Lonely Planet Travel Guides
- ✔ Frommer's Travel Tools
- ✔ Footprint Travel Guide

Tracking Your Expenses

My favorite part of any business trip is when I get that expense reimbursement check. Of course, to get that check I have to go through my receipt collection trying to figure out what I spent where and itemize it for my client.

To make your iPad travel experience easier, try out these great apps that help you keep all your trip expenses in order:

- ✔ **JetSet Expenses and JetSet Expenses Lite:** These are identical, except that the Lite version is free and supported by advertising and the advertisement-free version costs $4.99. They allow you to track expenses in 15 expense categories and more than 100 subcategories. Use either app to track mileage, calculate business expense percentages, and generate a daily summary of expenses.

- ✔ **myExpenses:** Also with a regular ($7.99) and free lite version, this app designed for the iPhone is easy to use for tracking expenses and has some very nice tools for analyzing your expenditures as well. Plus, you can export the data to use it with Excel, Numbers, or Quicken.

- ✔ **Expenses Mobile:** For 99 cents, you can get this handy iPhone app that stores data locally to prevent having account information snatched over an Internet connection. You can generate graphs of your expense habits, e-mail comma-separated-value (CSV) reports, and use the app in English, Spanish, French, and Italian.

If you frequently travel out of the country, you might want to check out Book VI, Chapter 5 for apps that help you juggle currency exchange rates.

Staying Connected

When you're on the road, staying connected with your office or family is important. That's why you should be sure to take advantage of two features that were introduced with iPad 2, FaceTime and Personal Hotspot. Here's what you can do with these two:

✔ **FaceTime:** This video calling app (covered in detail in Book II, Chapter 4) allows you to take advantage of iPad 2's video camera to call others who have the FaceTime feature on their iPad, Mac, iPhone, or iPod touch. You can use the front camera to show the person you called your own bright smile, or switch to the back camera to let that person see what you're looking at right now. Great way to make others jealous when you snagged that sales account in Hawaii!

✔ **Personal Hotspot:** Gives you the ability to use your iPhone's 3G connection (for a fee to your service provider) to take your Wi-Fi model iPad online when Wi-Fi is out of reach. Personal Hotspot can, in fact, perform this service for up to five Wi-Fi devices on the Verizon, Sprint, and AT&T versions of iPhone. This is a very useful feature for driving road warriors who can't sit in an airport or hotel lobby to get online or make calls. (I cover Personal Hotspot in more detail in Book III, Chapter 1.)

Don't forget that by using the iCloud storage and sharing service, you can have all the content you buy on other Apple devices automatically synced to your iPad. If your spouse downloads some new music or a movie to her iPhone and you both use the same AppleID, for example, you can access that movie on your iPad wherever you are!

Book III
Chapter 3

Apps for Road Warriors

Book IV
Getting Productive with iWork

The 5th Wave   By Rich Tennant

"Other than this little glitch with the landscape view, I really love my iPad."

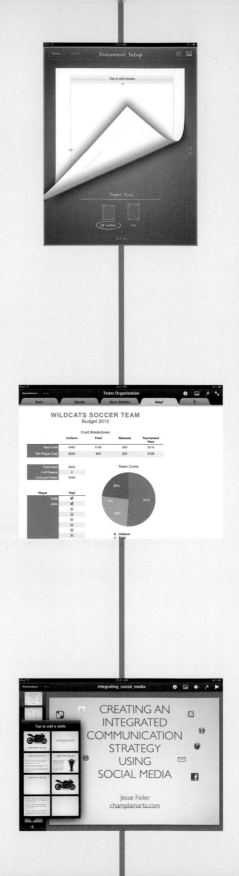

You may not think of your iPad as a productivity tool (it's way too fun for that!), but it can be. One good place to start is to learn all about iWork, Apple's productivity suite of apps. The first chapter in this part gives you an overview of some of the common features of this suite of products. Then I dive into chapters about each of the three software products in the suite: Words, Numbers, and Keynote. These word processing, spreadsheet, and presentation software programs provide some pretty robust tools and features that let you get your work done on your favorite new device, your iPad.

Chapter 1: Introducing the iWork for iOS Apps for iPad

In This Chapter

✐ Getting familiar with the iWork for iOS apps

✐ Discovering the basics of the iWork apps

✐ Improving documents by adding photos and images

✐ Managing your iWork documents

*W*ord processing and spreadsheet applications are among the most widely used software products on personal computers; presentation software is a not far behind, along with programs such as graphics and database editors. Having started from scratch on the hardware side and then the operating system side, Apple employees started dreaming about what they could do if they were to start from scratch to write modern versions of word processing, spreadsheet, and presentation programs. They knew they'd have to follow one of their advertising campaign themes: *Think Different.*

The result was the iWork suite of applications (a collection of applications that can work together) for the Mac — Keynote, Pages, and Numbers — that were developed one by one over a period of several years.

Today, iWork is a terrific suite of programs that have become a trio of dynamite apps for iOS and the Mac.

In this chapter, you'll find an introduction to the three iWork for iOS apps, including how to use the common interface elements. You'll also find a summary of differences between iWork for iPad and iWork for Mac in those cases where it matters.

Apple's development tools now allow developers to easily develop a single app that runs on all of the iOS devices — iPhone, iPod touch, and, of course, iPad. There are no longer separate versions because the code automatically adjusts to the device on which it is running (these apps are called *universal* for this reason). So do not look for Pages for iPhone or Numbers for iPad: look instead for Pages, Numbers, and Keynote for iOS. They are separate programs, each of which runs on all the iOS devices.

Presenting the iWork for iOS Apps

iWork is an *office suite,* like Microsoft Office. Office suites provide applications that are, well, office-oriented. The iWork office suite includes three applications that are similar to Microsoft Office applications (but way cooler, I think):

- **Pages:** A word processing application (similar to Microsoft Word)
- **Numbers:** A spreadsheet application (similar to Microsoft Excel)
- **Keynote:** A presentation application (similar to Microsoft PowerPoint)

On Mac OS X, all three programs are sold at the Mac App Store. They also come preinstalled on some Macs and can be configured as part of a build-to-order Mac. On iOS, each program is sold on its own for about $10 apiece, but each app runs on all your iOS devices. You can purchase the iWork for iOS apps from the App Store. (See Book I, Chapter 5, for more information.) Their features and integration are almost the same on both platforms.

In the following sections, you take a quick look at these three iWork for iOS apps. Although they also run on iPhone and iPod touch, this minibook focuses exclusively on iPad.

Pages

For many people, word processing is the core of an office suite. In fact, many people don't get beyond it. Pages for Mac adds a big desktop publishing plus to word processing in that it also allows you to create page layout documents. These have the type of structure you see in newspapers and magazines — articles don't just flow one after the other. Instead, an article on Page 1 may be continued on Page 4, and another article on the first page may be continued on Page 8. Also, objects such as photos are often placed in specific positions on a page, and they don't move as text is added or deleted.

iWork provides you with a variety of sophisticated tools to create your Pages documents. These include advanced font handling, color, tables, and charts, as well as the ability to place QuickTime movies and hypertext links in your Pages documents. iWork applications also provide a variety of template options for your documents. Figure 1-1 shows some of the templates available with Pages for iOS.

For more on the Pages app, see Book IV, Chapter 2.

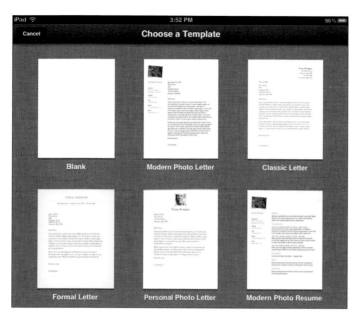

Figure 1-1: Choose a Pages template as a starting point.

Numbers

Like all spreadsheet programs, Numbers enables you to enter data in rows and columns. One of the most useful features of spreadsheets is that they perform calculations by means of formulas. For example, if you have a column listing your grocery expenditures by week, the addition of another grocery bill will cause the program to recalculate the column's total. Spreadsheets are about data (usually numbers) and fast calculation updates, but they can also help you organize data such as address lists and even generate charts to show data trends.

Spreadsheets can go beyond the common grid interface, and Numbers excels at this approach. Take a look at the Numbers document shown in Figure 1-2, a Numbers document based on the Travel Planner template. A single document can have a number of *sheets* (like sheets in a Microsoft Excel workbook). On iPad, sheets appear as tabs, as shown in the figure.

A Numbers sheet can contain a variety of objects such as tables and charts, but it can also contain other iWork objects, such as graphics, text boxes, movies, and audio. In Figure 1-2, the sheet is shown with a table and five pictures above it.

**Book IV
Chapter 1**

Introducing
the iWork for iOS
Apps for iPad

For more on the Numbers app, see Book IV, Chapter 3.

Sheets in a Numbers document

Figure 1-2: A typical Numbers document.

Keynote

Call them lectures, classes, sermons, or sales pitches, but presentations are all much the same: Someone stands in front of a large or small group of people and explains, teaches, entertains, or informs them. Today, a presentation often includes multimedia elements: slides of buildings in an architecture class, slides with music in a presentation about your community theater's latest musical production, and movies of good times on the beach in a talk about Uncle Charlie's summer vacation.

Keynote was the original iWork application. Built by Apple engineers for MacWorld and Worldwide Developers Conference keynote speeches delivered by Steve Jobs, Keynote has been refined over the years to become the powerful tool it is today. (See Figure 1-3.)

For more on the Keynote app, see Book IV, Chapter 4.

Figure 1-3: Editing a Keynote document.

Starting Out with an iWork App and iCloud

If you're running iOS 5 (or later), you can use an iWork app with iCloud. The first time you run an iWork app, you're greeted by a welcome screen. (As you've probably noticed by now, you see few of these "splash" screens on iPad: you normally open an app and find yourself exactly where you were the last time you left it.) This screen appears only the first time. Each iWork app has its own graphic; the first-time Welcome screen for Keynote is shown in Figure 1-4.

Click Continue, and you're given the option to use iCloud, as shown in Figure 1-5.

If you choose Later, you can turn iCloud on or off with Settings. All your apps that have settings are listed together at the bottom of the Settings list. Just tap your iWork app and turn iCloud on or off as you wish.

The next screen looks like Figure 1-6, although the details vary by the specific iWork app. You can choose a tutorial or just get started creating your own iWork document.

After the first time, your iWork app reopens to the screen where you left it.

Book IV
Chapter 1

Introducing
the iWork for iOS
Apps for iPad

Figure 1-4: Keynote is launched for the first time on an iCloud-enabled iPad.

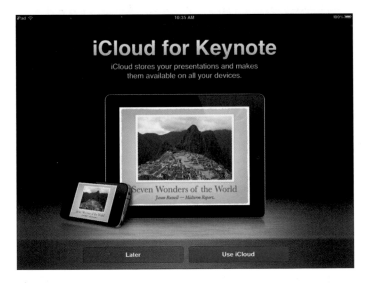

Figure 1-5: You can use iCloud . . . or not.

Figure 1-6: Get started or find out more.

Getting Familiar with the iWork Interface

You'll find that each of the iWork apps has a similar look and feel. One of the coolest advantages of iWork is that major features — not just small operations such as changing a font or selecting a color — are available using the same method in all its apps. You have only one app you must understand when you're using iWork, so I give you an overview of all that common functionality to get you started.

The iWork apps are updated periodically. If an update is available, you see the App Store on your iPad Home screen with a number indicating that downloads are available. It's generally a good idea to update your iWork apps when updates are available so that their interfaces remain in sync. You don't have to worry about massive changes: The apps are quite stable, and updates are few and far between.

Creating a new document

You create a new document in the same way for each iWork app. Follow these steps:

1. **Tap any of the iWork app icons to launch the application.**

   The documents screen appears. This screen is titled Documents in the Pages app (see Figure 1-7), Spreadsheets in Numbers, and Presentations in Keynote.

Book IV
Chapter 1

Introducing
the iWork for iOS
Apps for iPad

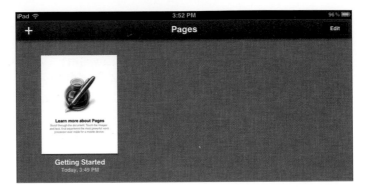

Figure 1-7: Create a new document from the Documents screen.

Note that when you first open an iWork app, you see a single document that contains basic information and instructions for that app.

If you see Documents on the button in the top-left corner, you're not on the documents screen; you're on the screen for working with an individual document, and tapping Documents (or Spreadsheets or Presentations) brings you to the documents screen.

2. **Tap the plus sign (+) in the top-left corner of the Documents screen.**

   The popover shown in Figure 1-8 appears. You can create a new document with Create Document, or you can make a copy of a document from iTunes, iDisk, or a WebDAV server. The three copy options are described later in this chapter, in the section "Managing Your iWork Documents."

Tap this button

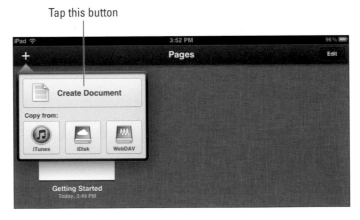

Figure 1-8: Select a template.

3. **Tap the Create Document button (refer to Figure 1-8).**

   The Choose a Template screen appears.

4. **Tap the template you want to use as a starting point, or tap Blank to start working with a completely clean document.**

   If you change your mind, you can tap Cancel (which replaces +) and you return to the Documents screen.

   The templates are different for each of the iWork apps, so I discuss them in the appropriate chapters in this minibook.

5. **Your new document opens on the screen.**

Locating a document

Before long, you'll have created several documents, and chances are good that you'll want to go back and work on some of them or print them, email them, or share them on iWork.com. As with creating new documents, locating a document is done the same way in each of the iWork apps.

To locate a document, follow these steps:

1. **Tap any of the iWork app icons to launch the application.**

   The documents screen appears. After you have created several documents, that screen will look like Figure 1-9,

Figure 1-9: Gradually, your documents screen fills up.

2. **View the documents and find the one you want to work with.**

   Below each document, you see its title and the date you last worked on it.

3. **Tap the document you want to work with.**

   The document opens, and you can begin working in it.

Book IV
Chapter 1

Introducing
the iWork for iOS
Apps for iPad

Identifying other common iWork features

You've already seen the major iWork controls. Now it's time to look at them more closely.

Using popovers

An important interface element in the Pages document shown in Figure 1-8 is the popover. Common to all iWork apps, the *popover* resembles the dialog in Mac OS X and other operating systems but is redesigned for iPad. This list describes three actions you can take with a popover:

- **Recognize the purpose of the popover:** Each popover includes an arrow that points to the object that opened it.

- **Dismiss the popover:** If you want to dismiss the popover (the equivalent of the Close or Cancel button on your Mac), tap anywhere outside the popover.

- **Make a selection on the popover:** When you tap a choice in a popover, it's carried out and the popover closes automatically.

Working with the Documents toolbar

Also visible in Figure 1-8 and most other figures in this chapter is the toolbar, which runs along the top of the screen. There are two types of toolbars. On a documents screen, it has the name of the app in the center and the Edit button at the right along with the + at the left.

Tap Edit, and your document icons start to jiggle — just as on the Home screen of your iPad. (And, just as on the Home screen, tap and hold a document icon and you enter Edit mode automatically.) While the icons are jiggling, you can drag one onto another to create a folder — just as on your iPhone and iPad.

Tap a folder to open it, as shown in Figure 1-10. From there, you can tap any document to open it.

Tap in the folder name, and the keyboard slides up so that you can rename the folder.

You can drag a document out of the folder and back to the documents screen. When you remove the last document from a folder, the folder disappears.

On the left side of the toolbar, three icons let you manage your documents. You can find out more about them later in this chapter, in the section "Managing Your iWork Documents."

When you're finished organizing your documents, tap Done to make them stop jiggling.

Figure 1-10: Name your folders.

If you choose an action such as copying a document, the iWork app automatically ends the jiggle-editing without your having to tap Done.

Working with a toolbar for a single document

When you're working on a single document, you have a different toolbar, as you can see in Figure 1-11. (This is from Keynote rather than Pages, you soon see the reason.)

On the far-left side of the toolbar, the Documents button lets you see all your Pages documents. Next to Documents is the Undo button. (It's the same as the Edit⇨Undo command you may have on Mac OS X for iWork and most other apps.) In the center of the window is the document's name.

At the right of the iWork toolbar are four or five buttons:

- ✔ **Info:** Provides information and choices about the current selection in the document. From here, you may choose a style, a list format, or a layout (alignment, columns, and line spacing) for a selected paragraph. If nothing is selected, this button is dimmed.

- ✔ **Insert:** Lets you insert images from your photo albums on iPad. If you want to insert a photo into your iWork document, add it to your album by taking the photo or synchronizing it in iTunes. (I tell you more about this button later in this chapter, in the "Working with Photos and Images" section.)

- ✔ **Animation:** Used to add an animation to slide transitions. This double-diamond button (refer to Figure 1-11) appears only in Keynote.

**Book IV
Chapter 1**

Introducing
the iWork for iOS
Apps for iPad

Info   Automate
Animation
Insert   Tools

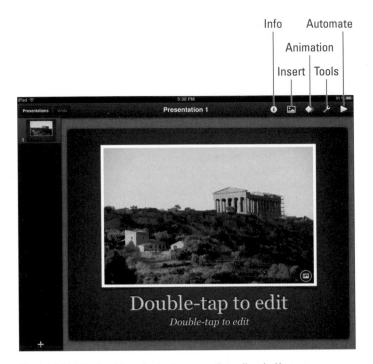

Figure 1-11: Work with a single document's toolbar in Keynote.

✔ **Tools:** The wrench opens a popover containing tools that are based on the document as a whole rather than on the current selection within the document. Figure 1-12 shows the tools for a Pages document.

Full-screen
Insert
Info   Tools

Figure 1-12: Tools for a Pages document.

Both Share and Print as well as Settings have disclosure triangles that let you drill down one more level. Figure 1-13 shows the Share and Print options. The Print settings are described in Book V, Chapter 1.

Figure 1-13: Sharing documents.

You can use the left-pointing arrow in the popover to return to the tools.

The Settings are shown in Figure 1-14. Note that Word Count has been turned on; it appears at the bottom of the document.

✓ **Full-screen:** The double arrows expand the document to fill your iPad screen, hiding the toolbar and other features. Tap in the full-screen document to return to the editable view with the toolbar.

Keynote also has an Automate button to the right of the Tools button. (Refer to Figure 1-11.) Tapping the Automate button begins playing your presentation.

The ruler that you may have seen in Pages is used by its word processing features. Similar tools at the top of the screen are used in Numbers and Keynote depending on what you're trying to do. I discuss them in the relevant chapters in this minibook.

Another interface element that you encounter from time to time is known as a *Modal view*. Think of it as a dialog that appears on top of the screen (sometimes covering all of it) with the background appearing to be slightly dimmed. Often, a button in the upper-right corner (usually with a blue background) lets you accept the information in the view. Sometimes, a modal view presents you with a choice — buttons appear in both the upper-right and upper-left corner (they may be labeled Cancel, Edit, or Done in most cases). In these instances, tap the button that represents the action you want to take.

**Book IV
Chapter 1**

Introducing
the iWork for iOS
Apps for iPad

Word Count is displayed here

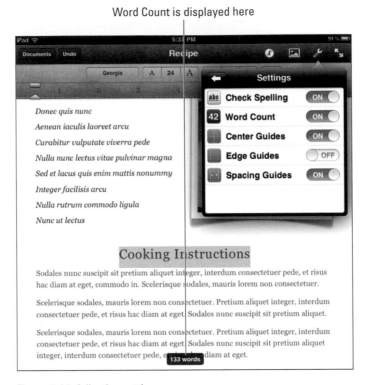

Figure 1-14: Adjusting settings.

Working with Photos and Images

One important feature that distinguishes Apple software from many other products is how easily you can use graphics and video in the documents you create. It's probably not surprising for you to see Pages templates with photo placeholders in them, and it certainly makes sense that Keynote templates often include photos. In today's world, you expect images in word processing documents and presentations. But spreadsheets? Take a look at the Numbers templates to see how the people at Apple are suggesting you rethink your understanding of spreadsheets.

Photos, images, and video can be added — easily and productively — to any iWork for iPad document. You have two ways to do this:

- Use the Insert button at the right end of the toolbar.
- Use a template that includes a placeholder image.

Using a template with a placeholder image requires one more step than using the Insert button. Here's how this process works:

1. **Create a document based on a template that includes a placeholder image.**

   Some templates contain several placeholder images. Figure 1-15 shows the Photo Portfolio template in Keynote, for example.

   Notice in the lower-right corner of the image a button that matches the Insert button at the right end of the toolbar at the top of the Keynote window. This indicates that the image is a placeholder.

Indicates a placeholder figure

Figure 1-15: Create a document with placeholder images.

2. **Tap the placeholder button to open a list of your photo albums, as shown in Figure 1-16.**

   You can browse photos on your iPad as well as albums you have created in iPhoto or other programs such as Photoshop Elements and synchronized to your iPad.

3. **Select the image you want to use instead of the placeholder.**

4. **Double-tap the image to show the masking control (see Figure 1-17), which lets you adjust the size of the image.**

Book IV
Chapter 1

Introducing
the iWork for iOS
Apps for iPad

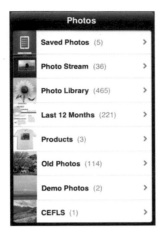

Figure 1-16: Choose a photo.

Masking control

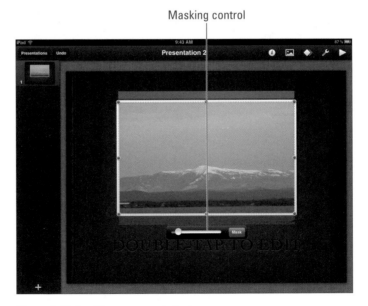

Figure 1-17: Double-tap to mask the image.

5. Adjust the slider to change the image mask.

The slider adjusts the size of the image. It starts with the image the same size as the frame, but if you move the slider all the way to the right, as you see in Figure 1-18, the image is shown dimly filling the entire screen. You can drag the image around so that the part you want is inside the frame. You can also use the eight handles on the frame to change its size and shape. This is a hands-on way to handle tasks such as cropping images. Rest assured that the original image file is unchanged by these steps: you're only changing the image's appearance within the document.

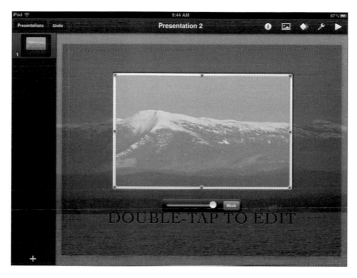

Figure 1-18: Adjust the mask.

Managing Your iWork Documents

The data for your iWork documents is stored in files on your iPad, possibly on your Mac or PC, and also sometimes on shared WebDAV (Web-based Distributed Authoring and Versioning, used for collaboration and managing of files on the web) servers, your iDisk, and, as you will see, on iWork.com, if you choose.

You can store iWork files on a PC, but iWork runs on only iOS and Mac OS X. As you'll see, you can easily convert your iWork files to the comparable Microsoft Office file types so that you can work on them on a PC in that format.

One feature that makes iWork for iOS successful is that the iWork team has made it easy for you to move documents around and work on them in whatever environment you want, from your desktop to a mobile device such as your iPad.

Book IV
Chapter 1

Introducing
the iWork for iOS
Apps for iPad

What matters is that you can get to your documents, read and write them, and share them with people. It's also critical that you can get to documents that other people share with you without either one of you having to jump through hoops.

Deep down inside the iPad operating system (iOS) are files and folders, but most of the time you manipulate them indirectly through apps. When it comes to apps, the files and folders are in a special area reserved only for that app (it's called a *sandbox*). Some apps such as the iWork apps can read files from servers such as iDisk and WebDAV; if you select one of those files, as you can see later in this section, it's copied into the appropriate place on your iPad for you to work on it.

The storage areas for files on your iPad are kept separate for each app. If you install Pages and then remove it from your iPad, your Pages documents disappear along with the Pages app. Before uninstalling any app from your iPad, make certain that you have backed up any files you have created.

Copying a file into an iWork for iPad app

If you have a file on your Mac or on a server (an iDisk or WebDAV server), you can copy it into an iWork app to work on it there. Of course, the document needs to be saved as one of these compatible file types:

- ✔ **Numbers:** .numbers, .xls, .xlsx
- ✔ **Keynote:** .key, .ppt, .pptx
- ✔ **Pages:** .pages, .doc, .docx

These are the primary document types. You can import other files such as JPEG image files by adding them to your iPhoto library, music files in iTunes, and so forth.

1. **From your documents page (Documents, Spreadsheets, or Presentations), tap + at the left end of the toolbar, as described previously in the section "Creating a new document."**

2. **For iDisk or a WebDAV server, log in with your password.**

   You have no login for iTunes because your account ID is stored and your iPad is paired with only one computer.

3. **Select the file you want.**

   As you can see in Figure 1-19, you can navigate folders. Files that are dimmed out aren't compatible with the app you're running. In Figure 1-19, the only file that can be copied is a Keynote presentation because it's the Keynote for iOS app. The file will be copied into your documents (Presentations, Spreadsheets, or Documents).

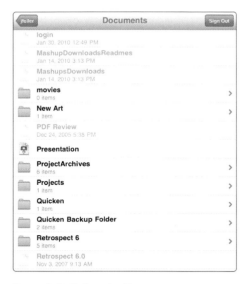

Figure 1-19: Select the file to copy.

4. **You're warned if any errors occurs, as you can see in Figure 1-20.**

The most common errors are caused by opening a document created in another application or an earlier version of an app; these errors can include missing fonts, resizing of slides in Keynote, and the use of unsupported features. Wherever possible (almost always), the app works around these issues.

5. **Correct any errors and then get to work.**

Figure 1-20: Review any errors.

Copying a file from an iWork for iOS app

You've copied a file from another place onto your iPad, and now it's time to reverse the process. To share a file you've created in iWork on your iPad, follow these steps:

Book IV
Chapter 1

Introducing
the iWork for iOS
Apps for iPad

1. **You can export your documents from the documents screen. Begin by tapping Edit at the right end of the toolbar.**

2. **Tap the document you want to copy.**

   As you see in Figure 1-21, the three buttons at the left of the toolbar are now enabled.

   The one on the right lets you move the selected document to the trash. The one in the middle lets you make a duplicate of the document. The one at the far left is the one you want: it lets you copy the document to a new location.

   These buttons are now enabled

   Figure 1-21: Copy a document.

3. **Tap the Export button.**

   The popover shown in Figure 1-22 opens.

   You see that in addition to moving files to iTunes, iDisk, and WebDAV, you can e-mail a file and share it on iWork.com. (iWork.com is described in the "iWork.com: Playing well together" section, later in this chapter.)

   When you e-mail a file, the recipient can work on the file or place it on an iDisk or WebDAV server. Anyone with proper access (including you) can then copy it back into your or someone else's iWork for iPad app.

Figure 1-22: Export a file.

4. **Whenever you're exporting, you're asked to choose the export format.**

   In the case of an iDisk or WebDAV server, you may be prompted to log in. Figure 1-23 shows the export formats for Pages documents.

   Your document is on its way.

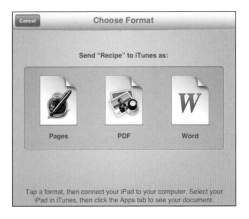

Figure 1-23: Choose a format.

Moving files with iTunes

You can move files to and from iTunes on your computer with a cable or, in iOS 5, with a Wi-Fi connection.

Book IV
Chapter 1

Introducing
the iWork for iOS
Apps for iPad

Moving files to your computer from your iPad

Each iWork app has its own storage area for your files. You move files from your iPad to your computer using iTunes and these steps:

1. **Connect your iPad to the computer where you want to move the files.**

    Your computer can be a Mac or PC. It must have iTunes installed. If iTunes isn't installed, see Book I, Chapter 4 and then come back here.

    In iOS 5, you can sync between your iPad and your computer using a Wi-Fi connection rather than a cable. On the iTunes Summary screen select Sync with This iPad over Wi-Fi under Options. If you have that option turned off or do not want to use it, you can connect your iPad to your computer with a cable.

2. **When iTunes launches, find your iPad in the Devices section of the Source List (see Figure 1-24), and select it by clicking once.**

    If you look carefully, you notice the menus such as File, Edit, and View at the top of the window shown in Figure 1-24. This is iTunes running on Windows and connecting to an iPad to be able to transfer iWork files back and forth.

3. **Select the Apps tab from the group of tabs running across the top of the pane.**

Locate your iPad here

Figure 1-24: Connecting your iPad to iTunes on your Mac or PC.

4. **Scroll down to the bottom of the pane and select the iWork app you're interested in.**

   The documents on your iPad for that app are shown.

5. **Select the document you want and click Save To.**

6. **Choose the folder and the name you want to use for the saved file.**

   The file is moved to your computer.

Moving files to your iPad from your computer

The process for moving files from your computer to your iPad is similar to the process described in the previous section. To copy files from your computer to your iPad, follow these steps:

1. **Connect your iPad to the computer from which the files are to be moved.**

   You can use a cable, or a Wi-Fi connection if you have selected that option.

   You can use a Mac or PC, but you must have installed iTunes on it.

2. **Find your iPad under the Devices section of the Source List (refer to Figure 1-24), and click it.**

3. **Select the Apps tab from the group of tabs running across the top of the pane.**

4. **Scroll down to the bottom of the pane and select the iWork app you're interested in.**

   The documents on your iPad for that app are listed.

5. **Click Add in the lower-right portion of the window.**

6. **When prompted, select the file on your computer's disk.**

   When you select a file, it is moved to the list of files in iTunes and usually moves immediately to your iPad. If it doesn't move immediately, click Sync.

In Step 5 in the preceding list, you can also simply drag the document icon from the Finder or Windows Explorer window into the file list area.

iWork.com: Playing well together

iWork.com lets you work together with other people and lets devices such as iPads, iPhones, Macs, PCs, and iWork.com work together. (You can even throw other, browser-equipped smartphones into the mix. Some rumors indicate that iPhone is not the only smartphone in existence.) Want to work

Book IV
Chapter 1

Introducing
the iWork for iOS
Apps for iPad

with two colleagues on a presentation? No problem: Start by uploading your Keynote document to iWork.com on the Internet. Then a friend can download the document and make changes in it as a Microsoft PowerPoint document. Back it goes to iWork.com, and someone else can download it in another different format. This is an example of the *cloud computing* process. When working in the cloud, people can work together on their own terms. They don't have to get together and decide which presentation (or spreadsheet or word processing) application they'll all use.

Sharing starts from the assumption that although there may be one basic document, comments and changes are tracked separately for each user. (You can be several different users in a sharing environment.) Rather than use the automated synchronization, iWork.com collects changes and comments and lets you decide which to use. It is deliberately a less automated process because its goal is to handle multiple users rather than a single user on multiple devices.

You can post an iWork document to your iWork.com area, where it's visible to you and the people you invite to view it. Those people can then add notes and comments to the documents on the web.

Recognizing the difference between iCloud and iWork.com

iCloud and iWork.com both let you work on the same document in several environments, but they implement two different types of functionality. As you may have seen, iCloud synrhconizes your documents among your devices. After it's set up, your documents are available on all your devices. The key word here is *you:* Your documents are on all your devices without your having to worry about moving them around. This process (which has long been implemented for Address Book and iCal) is called *syncing,* or *synchronization.*

iWork.com implements *sharing.* Your documents are available for various people on their own devices so that they can work together on the same document.

With synchronization, the assumption is that your actions on a document on any device should be reflected almost immediately on every one of your iCloud-enabled computers and mobile devices. Although a lot of sophisticated work is going on behind the scenes, the intention is to make you feel as though there's just one document. In fact, the only time you may be aware that anything is going on behind the scenes is the occasional message alerting you to a document having been deleted on another device. In a case such as that, the seamless processing is interrupted to make certain that you can jump in to make an executive decision about which copy to use. For the most part, it appears that you're working on one document that is everywhere.

You can share your iWork documents with people using other cloud services, such as Google Docs.

You can download documents from iWork.com in a variety of formats. This makes it possible for you to take two types of actions:

- **Add comments and notes to iWork documents:** You can add comments to specific parts of iWork documents (a section of text, for example); you can also add notes to the document as a whole (rather than to a specific part of it). As a result, a number of people can work together on a document.

- **Track multiple revisions to iWork documents:** You can download the documents to your own computer in a variety of formats. Many of these formats preserve the comments that you and others have added. After you've downloaded a document, you can modify it and add more comments describing your modifications.

All these actions are made possible by the iWork.com site; the actual sharing of documents is handled by your web browser and iWork software. Here's the division of labor:

- **Upload to iWork.com:** This is done from your iWork software: the Share menu on Mac OS X and from your documents screen (refer to Figure 1-22).

- **Download from iWork.com:** You do this by connecting to iWork.com with your browser and logging in with your iWork ID and password. This process works with a browser that can run on Mac OS X, your iPad, your iPhone or iPod touch, and Windows (among other operating systems). If you can run a browser, and if your device and its operating system support downloading via browsers, you can receive a shared file. You can find a list of supported browsers at `www.apple.com/iwork/iwork-dot-com`.

  After you have downloaded an iWork file, you can get to work. Even if iWork doesn't run on your computer, you may have another application that does run and can read the standard formats (including the Microsoft Office formats). That means you can edit downloaded iWork documents using Microsoft Office on Windows or Mac OS X, or by using Google Docs on any platform it runs on.

iWork.com is designed to be the bridge across various platforms and formats so that you can share your iWork documents. You may want to share your documents with yourself as you switch from your iPad to your Mac or to Windows. For that reason, the following sections show how to log on to iWork.com from iWork on Mac OS X as well as iPad.

**Book IV
Chapter 1**

**Introducing
the iWork for iOS
Apps for iPad**

Sharing a document on iWork.com

You need an Apple ID to log on to iWork.com. If you've used MobileMe or you now use iCloud, you have an Apple ID. If you've purchased items from iTunes or an App Store, you have an Apple ID. If you use iChat, you have an Apple ID. And if you've activated an iPhone or iPad, you also have an Apple ID. If you're not certain whether you have an Apple ID (or if you want to create a new one), log on to `https://appleid.apple.com/cgi-bin/WebObjects/MyAppleId.woa`.

You log in to iWork.com to upload (share) documents and retrieve documents. In this section, I tell you about sharing documents. In the next section, I tell you how to log in to retrieve documents.

1. **Open the document you want to share in the appropriate iWork for iPad app.**

2. **On your documents screen, share it via iWork.com (refer to Figure 1-22).**

3. **If prompted, log in as shown in Figure 1-25.**

Figure 1-25: Log in to iWork.com.

4. **Address the e-mail to the person (or several people) you want to be notified of the file.**

   You can type in a message, if you want. (See Figure 1-26.)

5. **If you want, tap Sharing Options at the right to change default sharing settings, as you see in Figure 1-27.**

   You're done. The file is uploaded, and your e-mail is sent.

Figure 1-26: Let people know that the document is ready to be shared.

Figure 1-27: Change the Sharing options, if you want.

Accessing shared documents on iWork.com

Your message, together with a download link, is delivered to all the address-ees you have listed. People only have to click the link in the e-mail. A recipi-ent who has an iWork.com account has more options. If you have an iWork.com account, you can access shared documents by following these steps:

1. **You're notified of the newly shared file; you also have an option to view all of your shared files, as shown in Figure 1-28.**

**Book IV
Chapter 1**

Introducing
the iWork for iOS
Apps for iPad

Figure 1-28: Download the file.

2. **If the Sharing Options permit, the blue Download button lets people download the file in various formats. (See Figure 1-29.)**

Tap here to download a file

Figure 1-29: Download the file.

 To find out more about iWork.com (such as how to download and modify iWork.com documents), check out *iWork For Dummies,* by Jesse Feiler (John Wiley & Sons).

Knowing the Differences: iWork on the iPad versus iWork on a Mac

You can work happily and productively using only your iWork for iPad apps, but you may want to use your Mac for some additional work that iWork for Mac supports.

On iPad, you have a subset of the templates available on Mac OS X. For example, the project proposal template on Mac OS X has half a dozen sample pages (budget, schedule, and executive summary, for example); on iPad, there are only a couple. You can certainly add more if you want. Also, some of the large document features (track changes and automatic table of contents creation) are available only on Mac OS X.

The range of document features available on iPad is amazing: spell-checking, fonts and styles, the ability to add and manipulate images, charts and tables (not just in Numbers!), columns and pagination, and much, much more. However, some features that tend to be used by large and complex documents aren't supported.

Don't make the mistake of thinking that iWork documents on iPad are small documents. Because of the way in which the iPad apps are designed, there are essentially no practical limits to document size except for the memory in your device. There's no reason to think that you can't write your 1,000-page novel on the Pages iPad app (but you'd better get busy).

**Book IV
Chapter 1**

Introducing
the iWork for iOS
Apps for iPad

Chapter 2: Pages Has a Way with Words

In This Chapter

✔ **Making changes to a Pages document**

✔ **Toiling with text**

✔ **Focusing on formatting with the ruler**

✔ **Setting advanced formatting options with the Info button**

✔ **Formatting the document**

This chapter delves into the *Pages* app, which is the word processing tool in the iWork suite of apps. Pages gives you powerful tools for creating documents of all kinds.

In this chapter, I tell you how to work with text and text boxes, format a document, and use the simplified Pages for iOS interface.

To find basic instructions for managing documents and sharing them via WebDAV or iWork.com, e-mail, or iTunes, see Book IV, Chapter 1.

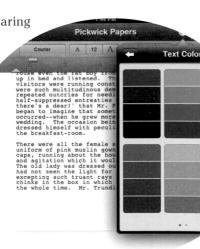

Editing a Pages Document

After you open a Pages document, you edit it in Document Editing view, shown in Figure 2-1.

To find out how to create a new Pages document, see Book IV, Chapter 1.

When you're editing a document, Document Editing view remains open until you move to another document, return to the Documents screen, or leave Pages. When you leave an iWork for iOS app and then return to it, remember that you return to the same location you left.

When you're in Document Editing view, the Documents button is visible to the left of the toolbar, at the top of the screen. When you're in Documents view, the button is labeled with the plus sign (+).

Full-screen

Insert

Info Tools

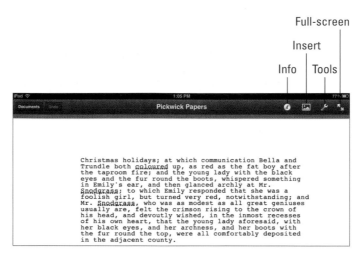

Figure 2-1: Document Editing view.

When working on a multipage document in the Document Editing view, you can quickly move through the document by swiping or flicking up or down.

In Pages, you can touch and hold your finger anywhere at the right side of a page to bring up the *navigator* (shown in Figure 2-2), which shows a thumbnail of a page; you can move very quickly through the document by dragging up or down on the screen. When you're on the page you want, just lift your finger off the screen. If you don't want to leave the page you started from, swipe to the right to make navigator disappear.

Figure 2-2: Using the navigator.

Working with Text in Pages

You can get a leg up on creating a document if you start from an iWork template (a template other than the Blank template, which is, well, blank). Even though you may see only a text placeholder in the template, the basic structure helps you get started.

After you open a document, entering the text is simple. You have three ways to start entering text:

- ✔ **Type text:** Tap the spot in the document where you want to enter text, and start typing. You can use the onscreen keyboard, a wireless keyboard, or the iPad Keyboard Dock.

- ✔ **Copy, cut, or paste text (or a combination):** Use the cut, copy, and paste tools to copy text in your Pages document and move it to another location, or to copy text in any iPad app (for example, from a website accessed by the Safari browser) and paste it into your Pages document.

- ✔ **Import text:** You can use iWork.com or iTunes to move existing documents to your iPad. You can create the documents on your Mac or PC by using tools such as iWork, Microsoft Office, or Google Apps. When a large chunk of the document is ready, move it to your iPad as described in Book IV, Chapter 1 and continue working with the document on your iPad.

After you have text in your Pages document, you can start to manage it.

Setting Basic Formatting by Using the Ruler

As is the case in most word processing programs, a ruler at the top of a page in Document Editing view lets you set basic formatting. The ruler can be partially hidden (refer to Figure 2-1), but tapping the small, visible portion of it enlarges it, as shown in Figure 2-3. The small X-in-a-circle to the right of the ruler lets you hide the ruler when you no longer need it.

Figure 2-3: Displaying the ruler in Pages.

The ruler shows you the settings for whatever is selected in the document. If nothing is selected, the ruler is disabled: All you see is the ruler measurements; no margin controls or tabs or other elements are shown. Tap in the document, and the ruler is immediately enabled and reflects the settings for the selection (in this case, the location of the insertion point). Tapping in the document may also bring up selection buttons, as shown in Figure 2-4. You can use them to use features such as cut, copy, and paste.

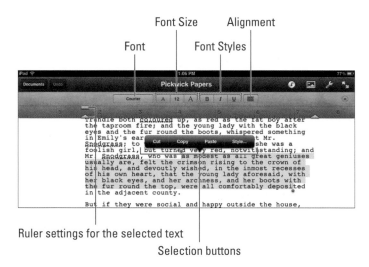

Figure 2-4: The ruler indicates settings for the current selection.

 To display the magnifying glass, touch and hold at the right side of the page until it appears, and then drag to position it. This tool lets you position the insertion point accurately. A single tap brings up the selection buttons, a double-tap selects the word at the insertion point, and a triple-tap selects the paragraph.

The ruler also provides basic formatting for the current selection. The tools on the ruler that can be used on the selection (from left to right in Figure 2-4) are described in this list:

✔ **Font:** In Figure 2-4, the font is Courier. Tap the font name to open a pop-over with a list of fonts to select from.

✔ **Font Size:** Tap the large *A* on the right to enlarge selected text by one point; tap the smaller *A* on the left to decrease the text size. In the middle, the font size can be set to an exact number.

✓ **Font Styles:** You can choose bold, italic, or underlining.

✓ **Alignment:** The selected paragraph can be aligned to the left, center, or right, or justified so that both margins are straight with no ragged edges. You don't have to select the paragraph with a triple-tap for alignment to work. If you have selected a word or an insertion point, the paragraph containing either item is the selected paragraph.

Feel free to experiment with the formatting within your Pages documents, and remember that the Undo button in the upper-left corner is there to help you out.

Most buttons on the ruler require you to simply tap them, but some (for example, the Fonts and Font Size buttons) open their own popovers for further selections; Figure 2-5 shows the Fonts popover.

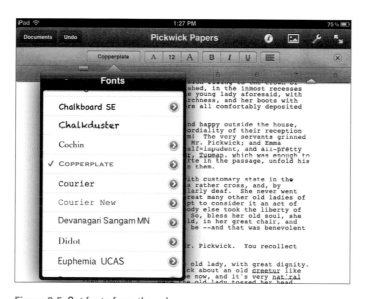

Figure 2-5: Set fonts from the ruler.

Book IV
Chapter 2

Pages Has a Way with Words

You can also use the ruler to set the margins for paragraphs. Just slide the indicators along the ruler, as shown in Figure 2-6. Note that the top indicator for the left margin reflects the margin of the first line in a paragraph; the lower indicator is the left margin of all other lines in the paragraph. You can indent the first line of a paragraph, but you can also outdent it (or provide a hanging first line); an outdent works well in a list.

Figure 2-6: Set margins from the ruler.

Getting and Setting Info about the Selection

The Info button to the right of the ruler opens a popover that provides settings in addition to those shown on the ruler. (See the preceding section, "Setting Basic Formatting by Using the Ruler.") When you select text and tap the Info button, you see a popover with three buttons along the top: Style, List, and Layout. Click a button to access various formatting options, as I describe in the following three sections.

Setting character style: Font, size, and color

One setting you can adjust by using the Info button is Style. Tap the Info button, and the popover shown in Figure 2-7 opens. (The Style button in the top-left corner of the popover is selected by default.)

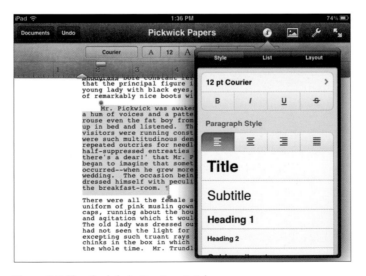

Figure 2-7: Use the Info button to set styles.

The powerful Style popover has a wide range of functionality. The topmost section lets you set the character style for the selected text. The *character style* is simply the style applied to characters. The second section of the pop-over lets you set the paragraph style — the style for the entire paragraph in which the selection is set.

After selecting the characters you want to style, tap Info and then the current setting in the popover. (It's 12-point Courier in Figure 2-7.) The popover shown in Figure 2-8 opens, and you can select another font, font size, or color for the font.

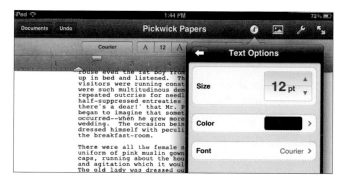

Figure 2-8: Adjust character styles.

Tap the color well (the swatch of color next to the word *Color*), and you can select a new color, as shown in Figure 2-9.

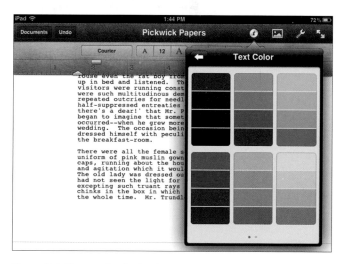

Figure 2-9: Change the font color.

Creating indents and list styles

After you select a paragraph, tap the Info button and then, in the popover, tap the List button to experiment with indentation and lists. The arrows at the top of the view shown in Figure 2-10 let you move the left margin in *(indent)* or out *(outdent)*. You also can choose to make automatic numbering available by choosing a list format.

Figure 2-10: Handle indents and lists.

 When you add an element to the list or delete an element from it, Pages automatically renumbers the list for you.

Establishing alignment, columns, and line spacing

The Layout button in the top-right corner of the Info popover lets you set layout options, as shown in Figure 2-11. These include the options for creating columns and adjusting line spacing.

Figure 2-11: Adjust layout settings.

Formatting a Document

You can format the text in your document, but you should attend to one other type of formatting: formatting the document itself. It includes page headers and footers, page numbers, and backgrounds that appear on all pages. Here's how to proceed:

1. **Open a Pages document, and tap Tools.**

   The Tools popover appears, as shown in Figure 2-12.

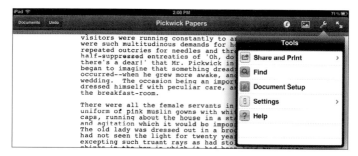

Figure 2-12: Set up your document.

2. **Tap the Document Setup option.**

   You see a blueprint-like section that's markedly different from the view you see when you edit an individual page.

3. **Tap a header or footer to customize it.**

   You can use the three sections to insert the author's name, a title, the version number, or the page number, for example. Just type some text in the section you want to customize.

4. **If you want to add page numbers to your document, tap in the header or footer section you want to use for the page number. Then tap the pound sign symbol (#) in the top-right corner of the screen.**

   (The # is only shown when you have selected a header or footer.)

   You can choose the format of the page numbers, as shown in Figure 2-13. Simply tap the style you prefer.

Figure 2-13: Insert page numbers.

5. **Set the outer limits of the area for the page content (as well as for header and footer) by dragging the lines, as shown in Figure 2-14.**

   These settings determine the printable area of your document on the page. Margins you set using the ruler define this area.

6. **Tap the bottom-right corner of the page (the corner that appears slightly curled) in the blueprint to select a predefined paper size, as shown in Figure 2-15.**

   Tap US Letter to print on 8½-x-11-inch paper or A4 to print on standard international letter paper.

After your page is set up, you're ready to finish entering text in your document and print it when it's done.

Figure 2-14: Set the print margins.

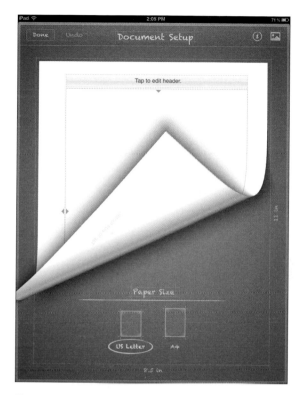

Figure 2-15: Select a paper size.

Working with Selection Buttons

When you read this chapter from start to finish, you see various sets of selection buttons shown on the black bar that appears whenever you double-tap in a document — and often shown with selected text. The command that's shown on a selection button varies depending on which element is selected. Some selection buttons may look familiar to you from other apps you may have used on the iPad and the Mac (as well as on other types of computers), including the Cut, Copy, and Paste commands.

When you select a chunk of text, you may also see these clickable options:

- **Replace:** Look up words you might want to use in place of the selected word, such as synonyms or simple typing mistakes.
- **Define:** View the definition of a word.
- **Style:** Use special Copy and Paste commands. You can copy and paste a style so that it picks up the formatting from a word and applies it to other text that's selected elsewhere in the document.

Chapter 3: Counting on Numbers

*N*umbers is a different approach to the concept of spreadsheets. It brings to spreadsheets not only structure, but also data formats you may never have seen. In addition to being able to use numbers and text in your spreadsheets, you can use on-off check boxes and star ratings as part of your data. Think of an inventory spreadsheet with check boxes for in-stock items and star ratings based on reviews or user feedback. Before long, what you may have thought of as just a bunch of numbers can provide true meaning and context to users.

First launched as part of iWork '08, Numbers joins the other iWork apps on iPad. Tables and charts are built into Keynote and Pages, but Numbers is the main number-crunching tool on iPad.

In this chapter, you discover how Numbers helps organize data into manageable units. When you can manage your data, you can display it in charts and graphs.

Introducing Numbers

When you create a Numbers document, you work with these three items:

✓ **A Numbers document:** A container for all elements, including worksheets (sheets) and their data; similar to a Microsoft Excel workbook.

✓ **One or more sheets:** One or more spreadsheets called simply *sheets*.

	Schedule		Budget	

WILDCATS SOCCER TEAM
Budget 2010

Cost Breakdown

	Uniform	Field	Referees	Tou
Team cost	$480	$180	$60	
Per Player Cost	$240	$90	$30	

			Team Costs
Total Cost	$936		
# of Players	2		
Per Player	$468		

23%

6%

Paid
✓

✔ **Zero or more tables:** The subspreadsheets or tables, created in other spreadsheet programs, that exist in Numbers as formal, structured tables rather than as a range of cells within a spreadsheet. Numbers gives them a specific name: *tables.* (And yes, a Numbers document can have no tables but must have at least one sheet.)

The simple idea of making tables into an actual part of the Numbers application rather than letting people create them any which way leads to a major change in the way you can use Numbers when compared to other spreadsheet programs. Because a table is an entity of its own and not a range of cells, you don't break the tables you've organized in a spreadsheet when you reformat another part of the spreadsheet. You can work within any table, and you can reorganize tables within a sheet, but you can't break tables by simply adding a row or column to your spreadsheet.

Figure 3-1 shows a Numbers for Mac template (Team Organization).

Figure 3-1: The Team Organization template in Numbers for Mac.

Figure 3-1 is a single document with six sheets visible at the left in the *Sheets pane:*

✔ Roster

✔ Stats

✔ Schedule

✔ Field and Positions

✔ Playoff Bracket

✔ Budget

Some sheets contain tables or charts, and you see them listed in the Sheets pane under their corresponding documents. For example, the Roster sheet contains the Team Roster and Admin. Info tables. At the bottom, the Budget sheet contains two tables (Cost Breakdown and Cost per Player) as well as a chart (Team Costs). The idea that a single sheet can contain defined charts and tables that don't depend on ranges of cells is the biggest difference between Numbers and almost every other spreadsheet program.

As you can see in Figure 3-1, sheets can also contain images and other graphics; they aren't parts of the structure of charts and tables. You simply insert these elements the same way you insert any other objects in iWork documents.

In Figure 3-1, the Team Roster table on the Roster sheet is selected. You can select it with a mouse click in the Sheets pane at the left or by clicking in the table itself. Notice in Figure 3-1 that a selected table has a frame with its column and row titles as well as other controls. Note also that each table within a sheet has its own row and column numbers (you can also name them, if you want) and that each table you deal with starts with cell A1. (The first row is 1, and the first column is A.)

Apple's iWork team moved the Numbers concepts elegantly to iPad. Figure 3-2 shows the comparable template on iPad. Each sheet is a tab. When you tap a table on iPad, you see a frame that lets you manipulate the table just as on Numbers for Mac. (See the section "Using Tables," later in this chapter, for more information.)

Numbers for iOS lets you insert charts along with tables on your sheets, as you see in Figure 3-3. (Remember that you can also insert graphics and other objects on your sheet.)

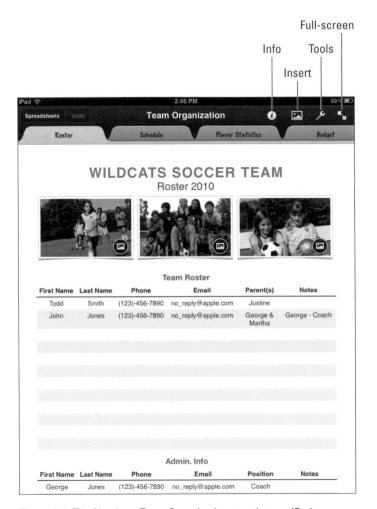

Figure 3-2: The Numbers Team Organization template on iPad.

Numbers for iOS also includes the ability to create *forms,* which simplify data entry. When you create a form, you select a table and you're taken to a tab that displays each column heading with a text entry box next to it. You can then focus on entering data for one row at a time and eliminate the possibility of accidentally tapping and entering data in the wrong row. You can find more about forms in the "Using Forms" section, later in this chapter.

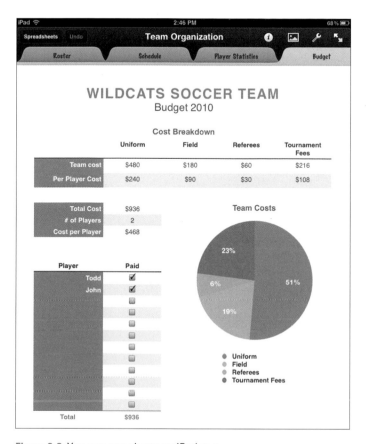

Figure 3-3: You can use charts on iPad, too.

Using the Team Organization Template

This chapter uses the Numbers Team Organization template to demonstrate Numbers features. You can create your own copy of the template so that you can follow along on your iPad, if you want. Sample data is part of the template, so you have data to work with, but you can add any other data you want. After you have experimented with Team Organization, you can pick another template and customize it for your own data.

To find out how to create a new Numbers spreadsheet that isn't based on a Numbers template, see Book IV, Chapter 1.

To create your own copy of the Team Organization template, follow these steps:

1. **Launch Numbers on iPad.**

2. **Go to Spreadsheets.**

   If you had a spreadsheet open when you were last using Numbers, you return to that spreadsheet. Simply tap Spreadsheets at the top left to go to Spreadsheets, and then tap the plus sign (+). If you need a refresher on creating a new spreadsheet, see Book IV, Chapter 1.

3. **Tap Create Spreadsheet.**

4. **Tap Team Organization.**

   Your new spreadsheet opens.

Working with Tabs and Sheets

Every tab displays a sheet, which can have one or more tables or charts (or both) on it. Tabs help you organize your Numbers documents. In this section, I tell you what you need to know about setting up tabs in a document.

Adding a new tab

As with all iWork apps, starting a new Numbers document involves choosing a template. Each template has its own, predefined tabs. (The Blank template has only one tab, cleverly titled Sheet 1.) You can add more tabs by using the + tab on the rightmost end of the tabs. (See Figure 3-4.)

Tap here to add a new tab

Figure 3-4: The + tab always appears to the right.

Tap the + tab, and Numbers asks whether you want to add a new sheet or form. (Refer to Figure 3-5.) Tap New Sheet, and Numbers creates for the sheet a new tab that contains one table. The sheet is labeled Sheet #, where # is the next number in the internal list of sheets you have created. See "Changing a tab's name," later in this section, if you want to rename the tab. (If you're interested in forms, I tell you about that topic later in this chapter, in the "Using Forms Efficiently" section.)

Figure 3-5: Add a new sheet or form.

Deleting or duplicating a tab

If you add a tab by mistake, Numbers allows you to remove it. Also, if you want to reuse a tab for a new tab, Numbers allows you to duplicate it. To perform either of these actions, tap the tab you want to delete or duplicate, and selection buttons appear above it. (See Figure 3-6.) All you have to do now is tap the option (Duplicate or Delete) for the action you want to take.

Figure 3-6: Duplicate or delete a tab.

Remember that a double-tap starts editing. A single-tap brings up the selection buttons, if they're available for the object you've tapped.

Rearranging tabs

If you don't like the order of your tabs, tap and hold a tab to rearrange the tab order. You simply drag the tab to the right or left in the row of tabs and then remove your finger when the tab is in the position you want. (See Figure 3-7.)

Figure 3-7: Rearrange tabs.

Navigating tabs

If you have more tabs than can be shown on the screen, just flick right or left to slide along the tabs. Remember to flick in the row of tabs. Flicking the body of the sheet scrolls over to the right or left of the content on that sheet.

If you're holding iPad in portrait orientation, turn it to landscape orientation to allow more tabs to display on the screen.

Changing a tab's name

Double-tapping text anywhere on iPad allows you to edit the text. The same statement applies to tabs, too. Double-tap the name of a tab to begin editing it; you see standard editing commands, such as Select, Select All, and Paste in the selection buttons above the tab. (See Figure 3-8.)

Figure 3-8: Edit a tab's name.

Using Tables

Tables are at the heart of Numbers — they're where you enter your data. This section shows you how to work with a table as a whole; the later section "Working with Cells" shows you how to work with individual cells within a table.

Selecting a table

To be able to work on a table, you need to select it. To select a table in Numbers, tap it. If the table isn't visible in the current tab, just tap the tab it's in first.

If you need to find an entry within a table, it's easy to do. Tap the wrench in the top-right corner to open the Tools popover. Tap Find to search the entire Numbers document for a word or phrase that may be in the table you're looking for.

When a table is selected, its appearance changes. (See Figure 3-9.) A selected table is framed with gray bars above (the column frame) and to its left (the row frame). To the left of the column frame, a button with concentric circles lets you move the table. To the right of the column frame as well as beneath the row frame are two other buttons, each with four small squares (looking a bit like table cells). These Cells buttons let you add rows, columns, or cells and manipulate the cells in the table. (See the later section "Working with Cells.")

Select a table by tapping it once; the location of your tap is important:

Row frame   Column frame

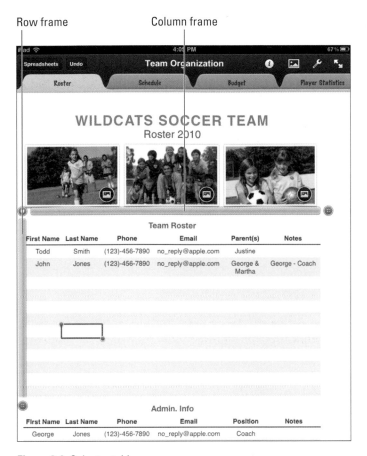

Figure 3-9: Select a table.

- ✓ **If you tap in a cell, the table and that cell are selected.**
- ✓ **If you tap inside the table bounds but outside the cells, the table itself is selected.** For example, if you tap the table's title or the blank space to the left or right of the title, the table itself is selected. (Refer to Figure 3-9.)

Moving a table

You can move a table around on its sheet. Select the table and tap the round button to the left of the column frame. Then drag the table where you want it. As you can see in Figure 3-10, Numbers shows you the absolute coordinates of the location you're drtagging to. Light-colored lines help you align the table to other objects on the sheet. These lines appear and disappear as the table is aligned with the edges or centers of other objects.

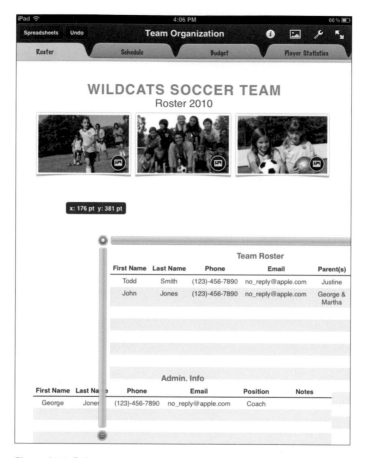

Figure 3-10: Relocate the table.

 You can select several objects at the same time. Tap the first object to select it, and then, while still holding your finger down, tap with another finger the other objects you want to add to the selection. After that, they move or resize together. (You may need two hands for this task.)

Cutting and pasting a table

You can select a table and then drag it around on a sheet by using the round button at the top left of the column frame; you can resize the table as described in the "Resizing a table" section, later in this chapter. But what if you want to place the table on a different sheet? To copy and paste a table onto a different sheet, follow these steps:

1. **Select the table by tapping the round button at the top left.**

   You see the Cut, Copy, and Delete buttons, as shown in Figure 3-11.

Tap here to select the table

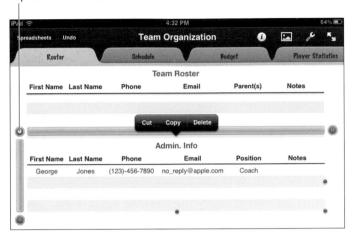

Figure 3-11: Select an entire table.

2. **Tap Cut from the selection buttons that appear above the table.**

3. **Tap the tab of the sheet you want to add the table to.**

4. **Tap in the sheet (but not in an existing table).**

   This step brings up new selection buttons.

5. **Tap Paste.**

   Now move and resize the table as you want.

Adjusting columns or rows

If you've ever used a spreadsheet program, you know that data you enter doesn't always fit into columns and rows. In Numbers, you can select the columns or rows you want to work on and then rearrange or resize them.

Selecting a row or column

Tap in the row frame to select the corresponding row, as shown in Figure 3-12.

Tap in the column frame to select the corresponding column.

Tap in this bar to select a row

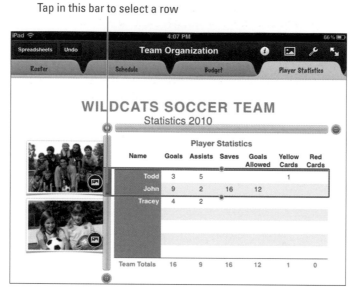

Figure 3-12: Select a row.

After you've selected a row or column, you can adjust the selection by dragging the handles (the round buttons) at the top and bottom (or left and right for columns), as shown in Figure 3-13.

Use the handles to adjust the selection

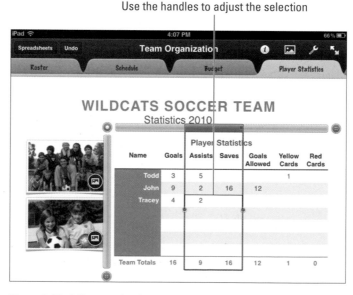

Figure 3-13: Adjust a selection.

The selection buttons (Cut, Copy, Paste, Delete, Insert, and Sort) appear above a selected column or row. Select an object. In Figure 3-14, the image on the left shows an entire column selected; note that the selection border extends into the column or row frame and that the section within the column or row frame is broader than the other three borders. The image on the right shows several cells selected within a column. When cells within a row or column are selected, all four borders of the selection are the same width.

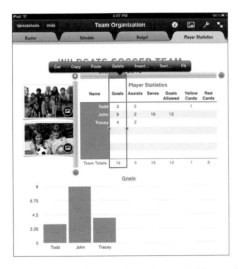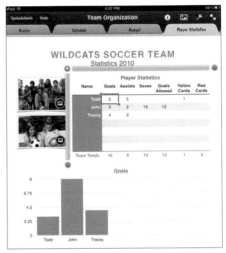

Figure 3-14: Select a column (on the left) or a single cell in a column (on the right).

The selection button you tap affects the selected column or cell.

You can also use the selection button to sort a column (or row). Tap Sort in the selection button and then choose ascending or descending sort order.

Resizing a row or column

The two vertical lines (known as the Cells button) in the top-right corner of the column frame (refer to the left image in Figure 3-14) and the bottom-left corner of the row frame (refer to Figure 3-12) let you resize the selected columns or rows. You always resize a column to its right and a row to its bottom, whether you're making it larger or smaller. The contents are automatically adjusted, and the adjoining rows or columns are moved aside.

Moving a row or column

Sometimes, you want to rearrange the rows or columns in a sheet. With one or more rows or columns selected, drag it (or them) to a new position. All selected rows or columns move as a unit, and the other rows or columns move aside.

Resizing a table

You can resize a table in two ways: Add or remove rows or columns to or from the table, or leave the number of rows and columns the same and change the overall size of the table. You may even want to do both.

Adding or removing rows and columns at the right or bottom

Tap the Cells button in the top-right corner of the column frame to add a new column at the right of the table. To add a new row at the bottom, tap the Cells button in the bottom-left corner of the row frame, and a new row is added to the bottom of the table.

To remove a blank column or row at the right side or bottom of a table, drag the appropriate Cells button to the left or to the top of the frame — the extra rows or columns disappear.

Adding or removing rows and columns inside the table

Select the row or column below or to the right of the new row or column. From the selection buttons, tap Insert to add a new row above the selected row or a new column to the left of the selected column.

Changing a table's size

Select the table so that the handles (small blue dots) are visible at the right side and bottom. These handles work like any other resizing handles in Numbers: Simply drag them horizontally or vertically to change the table's size. The content of the table automatically resizes to fit the new table size. The numbers of rows and columns remain unchanged, but their sizes may be adjusted.

You can select the table by tapping the round button at the top left of a table. (Refer to Figure 3-11.)

Read more information on formatting tables in the "Working with New Tables" section, later in this chapter.

Working with Cells

You tap or double-tap a cell to work with it. If you want to add or edit data, double-tap a cell. A blue outline appears around the cell, and the keyboard appears so that you can begin entering data. Single-tap if you want to select a cell. The cell is outlined, and the table-selection elements (the column and row frames, the Cells button, the round button to the left of the column frame, and the button to the right of the column frame as well as beneath the row frame) appear.

A double-tap always makes the cell available for editing. Figure 3-15 shows how, after a double-tap in a cell, the keyboard appears.

After you have set up your spreadsheet, most of your work consists of entering and editing data of all types. That's what you find out about in this section.

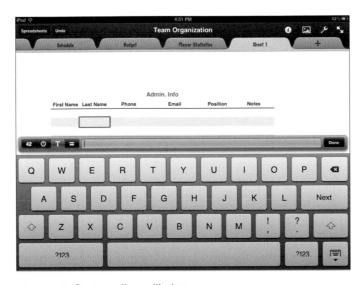

Figure 3-15: Start to edit a cell's data.

Entering and editing data

The keyboard for entering data into a Numbers cell is a powerful and flexible tool — it's four keyboards in one. Above the keyboard, the Formula bar lets you quickly and easily enter formulas. (Refer to Figure 3-15.) At the left of the Formula bar are four buttons that let you switch from one keyboard to another. You can choose these keyboards, starting from the left:

- **42:** The first button, labeled 42, lets you use the numeric keyboard.
- **Clock:** The second button, showing the image of a clock, lets you enter dates and times.
- **Text:** The letter *T* displays the standard text keyboard.
- **Formulas:** The equal sign (=) opens the formula-editing keyboard.

Whichever keyboard you're using, you see the characters you're typing in the Formula bar above the keyboard. To the right of the oblong area is a button labeled Done (or OK, depending on which keyboard you're using) that moves your typing into the selected cell and then hides the keyboard.

You can bring up the keyboard only when you double-tap a cell or another text field (such as a tab name). That means it's selected and that the keyboard knows where the data should go when you tap OK or Done.

To the right of the keyboard area are three large buttons:

- **Delete:** This is the standard keyboard delete button.

- **Next (adjacent):** The Next button with the right-pointing arrow inserts the typed data into the selected cell and moves to the next cell to the right.

- **Next (next line):** The Next button with the hooked arrow pointing left inserts the typed data and moves to the next line and to the leftmost cell in the section of cells you're entering. For example, if you start in the third column of the fourth row, the Next (next line) button moves you to the third column of the fifth row, not the first column.

The two Next buttons are available only on the numeric keyboard.

Entering numeric data

The numeric keyboard (accessed by tapping the 42 button) has a typical numeric keypad along with four large buttons on the left. (Refer to Figure 3-15.) These four buttons let you choose the formatting for the cell you're editing. If you need a symbol (such as stars for ratings or a currency symbol), it's added before or after the numeric value as is appropriate. Your formatting options, from top to bottom, are described in this list:

- **Currency:** This option adds the appropriate currency symbol, such as $ or €.

- **Percentage:** The percent symbol follows the value.

- **Stars (rating):** This option lets you display a number from 1 to 45 as a star rating. Numbers greater than 5 are displayed with five stars. Figure 3-16 shows how to edit stars. To change the number of stars, type a new number or tap the star display in the cell or in the display above the keyboard. You can use stars in a spreadsheet and then sort the column of stars so that the ratings are ordered from highest to lowest, or vice versa.

- **Check box:** A check box is either selected or not. Check boxes are selected and deselected by a user or as the result of a calculation.

Figure 3-16: Stars can be used for ratings.

Customizing check boxes

A check box can indicate, for example, that an item is in stock or out of stock (yes/no or true/false). However, you can also use it to represent numeric data. Computers and programs often represent yes/no or true/false values. That's one way you can use check boxes to track inventory. If you have the number of in-stock items in a cell, you can use a check box to indicate that none is in stock (a deselected check box) or items are in stock (a selected check box). Numbers handles the conversion for you.

Here's how check box customization can work:

1. **Double-tap a cell to start editing it, and tap the Checkbox button as soon as the keyboard opens.**

   You see a check box in the selected cell; in the area above the keyboard, you see the word *false* in a green outline, as shown in Figure 3-17. The green outline distinguishes the word *false* from text you type in. It has the value *false* because, before you type anything, its numeric value is zero.

Figure 3-17: A check box starts as off and false.

2. **Type a nonzero value.**

   This value can represent the number of items in stock, for example.

3. **Tap the Checkbox button again.**

   You see that the value you typed changes to *true* (see Figure 3-18) and that the check box is selected in the table.

   Because the formatting is separate from the data value, you can sometimes display the in-stock inventory count as a number and sometimes as the check box. Customers are likely to care only about the check box, but the inventory manager cares about the number.

Figure 3-18: A nonzero value is on and true.

Everything in Numbers is linked, so you don't have to worry about a sequence for doing most things. If you've followed these steps, you've seen how to enter a number and have it control a check box, but that's only one of at least three ways of working with a check box.

With a cell selected and the Checkbox formatting button selected, you see the true/false value above the keyboard and the check box itself in the table cell. Tap the check box in the table cell: The true/false value is reversed, as is the check box itself.

Likewise, if you tap the word *true* or *false* in the display above the keyboard, the check box flips its value and true/false reverses.

When you tap a formatting button, it turns blue and formats the number in the selected cell (or cells). You can tap another formatting button to switch to another format (from stars to a percentage, for example). Tapping a high-lighted formatting button turns it off without selecting another.

Entering date/time data

Tap the clock to enter date/time or duration data, as shown in Figure 3-19. The Date & Time button lets you specify a specific moment, and the Duration button lets you specify (or calculate) a length of time.

Figure 3-19: Enter date or duration data.

Above the keyboard, the units of a date or duration are displayed. To enter or edit a date or time (both), tap Month in the Formula bar and use the key-pad to select the month. (The keys have both the month name abbreviations and the month numbers on them.) Similarly, tap any other component and enter a value. As you do so, the display changes to show the value. (Tapping AM or PM toggles the value — you don't need to type anything.)

If you select a cell containing Date & Time or Duration data, you can use the Info button to choose the formatting to use. The Duration popover has a par-ticularly interesting user interface for formatting, as shown in Figure 3-20. The possible components of duration are shown at the top of the view (week, day, hour, minute, second, and millisecond). Above them, a display lets you know which ones are selected. Drag the left or right border to dis-play the units you want displayed. The units are always in sequence, so you can display hours, minutes, and seconds, but not hours and seconds.

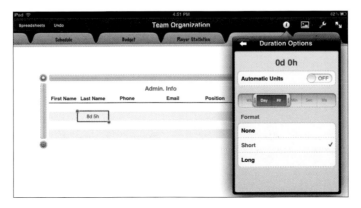

Figure 3-20: Customize the duration format.

Entering text data

When you tap T to enter text data, the QWERTY keyboard appears, as shown in Figure 3-21.

Figure 3-21: Enter text.

As with most onscreen keyboards, you can switch among letters, numbers, and special characters. (If you need a refresher on how to do it, see Book I, Chapter 2.) Everything you type is inserted into the selected cell until you tap the Done button, to the right of the display above the keyboard. If you enter a Return character, it's part of the text in the cell. The cell automatically expands vertically to accommodate the text you type, and you can resize the column so that the cell is the appropriate size.

Entering formulas

Tapping the equal-sign (=) button lets you enter a formula, which automatically computes values based on the data you type. The result of the formula can be displayed in a cell in any of the usual formats, and that value can be used in a chart.

When you're entering a formula, the four buttons controlling the date-and-time, text, and numeric keyboards disappear. In their place, a button with three dots appears. Tapping this button returns you to the display that includes the other three keyboards. It's just a matter of Numbers saving space.

Formulas are accompanied by good news and bad news. The good news is that you don't have to type many common formulas: Almost all spreadsheets have the same built-in list of formulas. The bad news is that the list of formulas is quite long.

Formulas can consist of numbers, text, dates, durations, and true/false values. They can also include the results of formulas and the values of individual cells.

The example in this section, which presents the basics of creating a simple formula in Numbers, adds a number to the value of an existing cell and then displays the result in the cell that contains the formula. In this example, I'm using the Team Organization template that you see in the figures throughout this chapter.

The formula adds 2½ hours to the starting time of a game and displays the estimated completion time in a new column. Follow these steps:

1. **Rename the Title column** Start.

2. **Add a column to its right and name it** End.

3. **Select the cell in which you want to insert the formula by double-tapping it.**

   I selected the End column cell next to Start, as you can see in Figure 3-22.

4. **Tap the equal-sign (=) button at the top-left side of the keyboard.**

Figure 3-22: Select the cell that will contain the formula.

The keyboard changes to the formula keyboard, as shown in Figure 3-23.

Figure 3-23: Begin to create a formula.

The tables' column and row frames now contain row and column identifiers. The columns are labeled A, B, C, and on; the rows are labeled 1, 2, 3, and so on. Every cell can be identified by its coordinates (such as A1 for the top-left cell).

Also note that, at the right of the keyboard, is a different set of buttons than in the text, date, and number keyboards. To the immediate right of the keypad, you'll find four buttons that represent the following:

- *Functions:* Brings up a list of functions. (Refer to Step 3.)

- *abc:* Displays the text keyboard. You can type text and tap Done, and the text is added to the formula you're constructing. You return to the formula keyboard.

- *Date/Time:* Takes you to the date keyboard. The date or duration you enter uses the same interface shown in Figure 3-18. When you tap Done, the date or duration is added to the formula, and you return to the formula keyboard.

- *True/False:* Uses the same interface as check boxes; the result is added to the formula you're constructing, and you return to the formula keyboard.

5. **Add the game starting time to the formula.**

   Just tap the cell containing the game start time. The formula reflects the name of the table and the referenced cell. In this case, that reference is

   C2

   This references column C, row 2 in the Game Schedule table. You don't have to type a thing — just tap, and the correct cell is referenced.

   You now need the formula to add 2½ hours to the starting time.

6. **Tap + from the operators on the left side of the keyboard.**

7. **Tap the Date/Time button to the right of the keyboard and then tap the Duration button at the left.**

8. **On the formula bar, tap Hours and enter** 2.

9. **Tap Minutes and enter** 30.

   Figure 3-24 shows what the screen should look like now.

Figure 3-24: Enter the formula.

10. **Tap Done.**

    You're done entering the duration. You return to the formula keyboard.

11. **Finish the formula by tapping the button with a check mark on it.**

    Figure 3-25 shows the formula as it is now. Note that rather than see the Done button, as with other keyboards, you see a button with a check mark and a button with an X at the right. The X cancels the formula, and the check mark completes it. If you want to modify the formula with the keys (including Delete) on the keyboard, feel free.

Figure 3-25: Tap the check mark to accept the formula.

Changing a cell's formatting

Your end time may include the date, which is probably not what you want. Here's how to change the formatting of a cell:

1. **Select the cell by making a single tap.**

   You can also select a cell and drag the highlighted selection to include more than one cell. Your reformatting affects all selected cells.

2. **Tap the Info button at the top of the screen.**

3. **In the Info popover, tap Format.**

4. **Tap the format you want to use in the selected cell or cells, or tap the arrow at the right of the format name to customize the format.**

   Not all formats have customizations.

To properly format the end time cell, you may want to remove the date. Tap Date & Time Options and set the date option for None and the time option for the hour, as shown in Figure 3-26.

Figure 3-26: Format the result.

Using Forms Efficiently

A *form* is a user-friendly way to provide input to a single row of a spreadsheet. A simple form, such as one you fill out on a clipboard at your doctor's office, is much easier for many people to deal with. Because a form interacts with a table, you must create a table in your spreadsheet before you can create an associated form.

To create a form, tap the + tab on the rightmost end of the row of tabs. You're asked whether you want to create a new sheet or a form. (Refer to Figure 3-5.) Choose New Form, and you see a screen similar to the one shown in Figure 3-27; I'm using my Team Organization template for the example.

Figure 3-27: Start to create a form.

You'll see a list of all the sheets and all the tables on them. Choose the one that the form will be used with. In this case, I'm using my Admin. Info table.

TIP

Every form is associated with only one table, and every table can be associated with only one form (though it doesn't have to be associated with any forms).

The form is then created automatically, as shown in Figure 3-28.

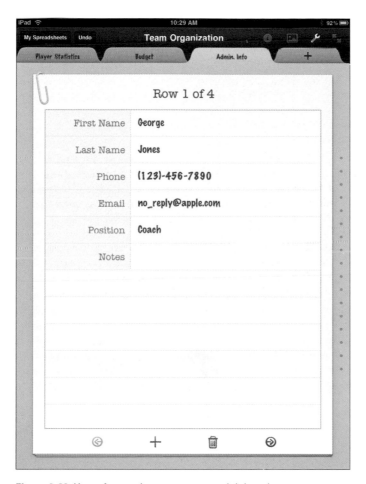

Figure 3-28: Use a form to browse, enter, and delete data.

The labels for the columns on the form are drawn from the labels of the columns on the tables. You don't have to label the columns on your tables, but it makes creating forms and calculations much easier if you do so.

You can use the tab to go to the form and enter data or browse it. The four buttons at the bottom of a form let you (from left to right) go to the previous record (row), add a new row, delete the current row, or go to the next row.

You can delete a form by tapping the form's tab and then tapping Delete, but you can't duplicate a form as you can duplicate a sheet tab.

Working with New Tables

Tables contain the data for your spreadsheets and charts, so it may be a bit surprising if you have reached the end of the chapter without creating a single table. That's because you have numerous templates to work with. You don't have to start from the beginning; instead, you can start from farther along in the development process.

Tables can be relatively small and focused. You can use formulas to link them, and that's a much better strategy than putting every single piece of data into an enormous spreadsheet.

Tables aren't simply repositories of data; they also drive charts. When you're organizing data in a table, you may want to consider how to transform it to create the kind of charts you want.

As you're planning the structure of your tables and sheets, pay attention to the moments when you realize you have to add more data to a table. Ask whether you truly need more data in that table or need a table that can be linked to the first table by a calculation.

A table often has a *header row* above its data rows; the header row usually contains titles but may also contain calculations such as sums or averages. Numbers tables can have several header rows. A column to the left of the table also has the same functionality — it's a *header column*. People often believe that a header appears only at the top, but in this usage, it appears on whichever side is appropriate.

Creating a new table

Follow these basic steps to create a new table:

1. **Go to the sheet you want the table on.**

   It can be an existing sheet from a template or a new sheet you create just for the table. Remember that tables can be cut and pasted, so you have a second (and third and fourth . . .) chance to determine the sheet for your table.

2. **Tap the Insert button (the one with the mountain view) on the right side of the toolbar at the top of the window.**

The Insert popover opens.

3. **Select Tables from the top row of the popover.**

4. **Swipe from one page to another to find the table layout you like.**

   Though you can change any element in the table layout, start with one close to what you want.

   There are six pages of templates — each of the six pages has the same layouts but with different color schemes. This list describes them from the upper-left corner, as shown in Figure 3-29:

   - *Header row and a header column at the left:* This is one of the most common table layouts.

   - *Header row at the top:* This one works well for a list such as students in a class.

   - *No header row or header column:* Before choosing this blank spreadsheet, reconsider. Headers and titles for the tables make your spreadsheet more usable. You can add (or delete) them later and change them, but take a few moments to identify the table along with its rows and columns as soon as you create it.

   - *Header and footer rows and a label column:* This one works well for titles at the top and left and for sums or other calculations at the bottom.

   - *Check boxes in the left column:* This option makes a great list of things to do.

5. **Tap the table layout you like.**

   It's placed on the sheet you have open.

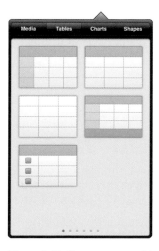

Figure 3-29: Create a new table.

Formatting a table's look

Whether you recently created a new table or created it long ago, you might want to change its appearance. Here's how:

1. **Select the table you want to format (to select the table, tap inside the table bounds but outside the cells) and tap the Info button in the toolbar.**

   The Info popover opens, as shown in Figure 3-30. You can change the basic color scheme and layout by tapping the design you want to use.

2. **Tap Table Options to fine-tune the table (see Figure 3-31).**

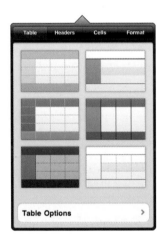

Figure 3-30: Use Info to reformat a table.

Figure 3-31: Set table options.

Every table has a name. (It starts as Table #, with the next sequence number for all your tables.) The Table option simply controls whether the title is shown. Change the name to something meaningful that you can use in referencing it in formulas. Likewise, each table is a certain size. The Table Border option determines whether a thin line is applied as the table's border. In the Alternating Rows option, every other row is shaded with a contrasting color.

For large tables, alternating the shading of the rows can make it easier for users to follow the data.

3. **Tap Grid Options to show or hide the cell dividers.**

   Many people think that showing the lines in the main table and hiding them in the headers looks best. Experiment. As you tap Yes or No, the display changes so that you can see the effect.

4. **Tap Text Size and Table Font to format the text in the table.**

5. **Tap Headers to modify headers for rows and columns.**

   You can set the number of header rows or columns. (You have either zero footer rows or one footer row.) These elements are created using the existing color scheme. To change the scheme, tap Table in the popover and choose a new one.

   Freezing rows and columns keeps the header rows and columns on each page. As you scroll the data, the data itself moves, but the headers never scroll out of sight. This option is often the best one unless the table's content is self-explanatory.

6. **When you're finished, tap anywhere outside the popover to close it.**

Chapter 4: Presenting Keynote

In This Chapter

- ✏ **Issues to consider before you create a presentation**
- ✏ **Working with Keynote**
- ✏ **Animating a presentation with transitions and builds**
- ✏ **Preparing to present**
- ✏ **Playing a presentation**

*K*eynote, the first component created for iWork, was originally written for Steve Jobs to use in presentations at conferences and trade shows, including Apple's Worldwide Developers Conference and Macworld conferences. After these "trials by fire," Keynote was joined by Pages to became the first two components of iWork.

Presentation software is a different type of product, compared to other iWork applications. It typically consists of content presented by a speaker (whether in person or in absentia) to an audience.

Now, with the Keynote for iOS app in hand, you have new presentation possibilities. Small-group or one-on-one presentations using iPad are made possible in a new way because you can easily present short but impressive presentations almost anywhere. In addition, you can connect the iPad Dock Connector to a VGA adapter or connect using the Apple Digital AV Adapter and present to larger groups from a smaller machine. On iPad 2, you can also use the video mirroring feature.

In this chapter, you find out how to prepare and stage a presentation using Keynote. After adding text to slides and using animated transitions, you'll soon have a sophisticated and useful presentation.

Concepts to Consider Before You Create a Presentation

A presentation is meant to be viewed. A person (usually you but sometimes the viewer) controls the pace of the presentation. Follow these tips when building a presentation:

✏ **Weigh small-group versus large-group presentations.** You have new options on iPad in addition to the traditional model of presenting to a group. This model offers an opportunity for one-on-one presentations that you can give in almost any setting, such as a sales call in a client's office. If you're working on a small-group or one-on-one presentation, the text and graphics don't have to reach across a ballroom to the viewer's eye, so size elements on the slide accordingly.

✏ **Make use of existing content.** Keynote for iOS helps you easily transfer presentations between your iPad and your Mac. Sometimes, that's the right thing to do. You can reuse the slides and rearrange them (possibly splitting a large presentation into many). Restructuring and rearranging an existing Keynote presentation that's going to be presented to a small group rather than to a larger audience can be a good idea.

✏ **Consider your canvas.** When working on a presentation, you're using a small canvas. A slide has much less space to hold information than does a piece of paper (or a spreadsheet page). No matter how large your audience, never overcrowd your slides.

✏ **Avoid too much variety.** Using too many graphical object styles (such as illustrations, photos, and line drawings) or too many font styles (such as bold and underline) can make for a choppy-looking presentation. Luckily, Keynote themes help you provide a cohesive and clean look for your presentation. Even though you may make small changes to text and add graphics, try to maintain an overall look and feel.

✏ **Adding movement to slides.** You have options for movement (see the "Using Transitions and Builds" section, later in this chapter) that you don't have with printed documents. You can add effects to transition from one slide to another. Experiment with the Keynote transitions, and use them to help people understand your progress in the presentation. For example, you can use a transition to introduce a new topic.

Getting Started with Keynote for iOS on iPad

You get started with the Keynote app the same way you do with Numbers or Pages: Create a new document, or open an existing one. The basic windows are the same, but Keynote has some minor differences. This section is your guide.

Navigating the Keynote screen

When you open (or create) a Keynote document, the basic Keynote screen appears, as shown in Figure 4-1. The name of the document is centered on the toolbar at the top. At the left, the Presentations button functions exactly like the Spreadsheets button does in Numbers and the Documents button in Pages — small images represent the first page of each of your saved files. And, for good measure, the Undo button behaves the same as it does in the other apps — it lets you undo your last action.

Figure 4-1: The basic Keynote screen.

On the right side of the toolbar (refer to Figure 4-1) are the usual buttons, with two additions. The buttons, from left to right, are described in this list:

Book IV
Chapter 4

- ✔ **Info:** As always, lets you modify the selected object or objects. Your choices depend on which type of object is selected. (If nothing on the slide is selected, the button is grayed-out.)

- ✔ **Insert:** Looks like a landscape and lets you insert media such as photos, tables, charts, and shapes, as shown in Figure 4-2.

Presenting Keynote

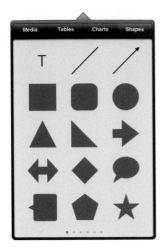

Figure 4-2: Insert objects into slides.

✔ **Transitions on a single slide:** Effects such as slide and zoom and a number of other transitions you probably have never seen. These elements are described later in this chapter, in the "Working with transitions" section.

✔ **Tools:** Shows you the popover you see in Figure 4-3. You can select Find to search the Keynote document, go to Help for assistance with using the application, type presenter notes (even if they're directed to yourself), and get help.

Figure 4-3: Use the Keynote tools.

Use Advanced for even more tools:

- *Advanced:* These tools let you turn slide numbers on and off, set the presentation type, and use guides and remotes, as shown in Figure 4-4.

- *Presentation Type:* Set a presentation here to loop or to autoplay, as shown in Figure 4-5.

Figure 4-4: Use the advanced tools in Keynote.

Guides for alignment are guidelines that can appear as you move an object toward the center of the slide or other objects, at the edges of the slide, or in 10 percent increments horizontally and vertically along the slide. You can turn automatic slide numbering on and off. Just as with pages of a Pages document, you should let the app handle the numbering so that the slide (or page) numbers are correct even if you move elements around, delete slides, or add slides. You don't need a special check-spelling option because it's now built into iOS.

Figure 4-5: Set the presentation type.

- *Remote Settings* lets you enable a remote device to control the presentation. The remote device (such as an iPhone) communicates wirelessly with your iPad, which then plays your presentation as though you were tapping the screen. This setting means that you can put your iPad next to a projector and avoid a tangle of wires while you speak from the front of a room.

  ✔ **Play:** Starts playing the presentation; if you have an external display adapter, the slides appear on the display while the iPad screen shows the controls.

One difference between Keynote and the other iWork apps is that it always appears in landscape (horizontal) orientation; as you rotate the iPad, the image doesn't rotate, because the slides are all designed to be shown horizontally. It isn't a Keynote limitation as much as a nod to the realities of projectors and displays.

On the left side of the screen, in the *navigator,* are thumbnail views of the slides in your presentation. To go to any slide in your presentation, just tap its thumbnail.

Creating your first Keynote slide and adding text

The templates in all iWork apps provide you with useful starting points. In Keynote, you're almost certain to find prebuilt slides you can use, so it's only a matter of organizing your own data.

1. **To begin a new presentation, tap Keynote on the Home screen.**

2. **On the Presentations screen, tap the plus sign (+) and create your new presentation from a template or from another presentation, as described in Book IV, Chapter 1.**

3. **On the Choose a Theme screen, tap a theme for your presentation.**

   (Note that the themes determine the background color and font to be used.) The presentation appears with one slide in it.

4. **Double-tap a text placeholder on the slide to edit it.**

   The text placeholder opens for editing, and the onscreen keyboard appears.

5. **Enter any text you want and then tap the slide itself to close the keyboard when you're done.**

Formatting text

With Keynote — perhaps more than with the other iWork apps — it's more fill-in-the-blanks than fuss around with formatting. You can get right to work. The font is determined by the theme you choose, but you can modify its size and add effects such as bold and italic. Here's how:

1. **Double-tap text to select the type you want to change.**

2. **Tap the Info button, choose a text style option (Title or Subtitle, for example), and tap any of the formatting choices (Bold, Italic, Underline, or Strikethrough) to apply them to the selected text.**

3. **Tap anywhere else on the screen to hide the Info popover.**

Adding a new slide

To add a new slide, tap + in the lower-left corner (see Figure 4-6) and choose the style of slide from the gallery that appears. Want to add a bulleted list? Just choose a slide style with a bulleted list already on it.

Figure 4-6: Add a new slide.

You can choose the layout for the slide you're adding from the thumbnails shown in the popover. As Figure 4-7 demonstrates, the layouts for new slides vary from template to template.

Figure 4-7: Slides vary by template.

Adding media

Themes provide some slide layouts with image placeholders in them. To change a placeholder image, simply double-tap it. A dialog opens, showing media sources, such as your Photo Albums. Locate an item and tap to insert it.

If you want to add an image outside a placeholder, make sure no placeholder is selected and then tap the Insert button. Tap any of the four tabs: Media, Tables, Charts, or Shapes. Choose the item you want to insert, and it appears on your slide.

You can now move the object around with your finger. You select an object on a slide with a single tap (the same as in Numbers and Pages). You can drag the object around; Keynote provides the coordinates for precise positioning and also provides you guidelines as you align the object with the center of the screen or the edge of other objects. To resize an object, drag a corner handle until it's the size you want and then let it go.

Managing slides

Tap a slide in the navigator to select it. Then tap the slide again to bring up the selection buttons shown in Figure 4-8. You can now take an action; for example, tap Delete, and the slide is gone. (Remember, if it's a mistake, just tap Undo at the top left of the screen.)

Figure 4-8: Delete a slide.

You can also use the selection buttons to cut, copy, and paste slides. After you have cut or copied a slide (tap it and tap Cut or Copy), tap the slide after which you want it to appear, and then tap Paste. (You always paste the contents of the clipboard after the slide you select.)

A new option appears in the selection buttons: Skip. It collapses the selected slide in the navigator into a thin line. When you play the presentation, the slide is skipped over. The thin line in the navigator is big enough for you to tap it to bring up its selection buttons: It now has a Don't Skip button, which lets you bring it back to full size and include it in the presentation as it plays.

Select the slide from the navigator. If you tap the slide itself, the selection buttons act on the selected object within the slide.

Using Transitions and Builds

You can enliven a presentation and make it a better communication tool by using Keynote animations to animate the transition from one slide to another. You can also use animations to build a slide. *Building* refers to the process of animating the appearance of each bullet or another object within a single slide. The process of creating transitions and builds is much the same, and I cover them in this section.

TIP

A little animation is a good thing. Feel free to try out all the options, but then decide which one — or maybe two — you want for your presentation. Too many animations are distracting and replace the content you're presenting, unintentionally becoming the focus of your presentation.

Working with transitions

Use the Transitions button (refer to Figure 4-1) at the right end of the toolbar, at the top of the Keynote screen, to begin setting a transition. When you tap the button, you move to the transition editor. Notice the Done button in the top-right corner of the screen — until you tap the Done button, you're working on a transition.

Transitions can work on slides as a whole or work on parts of slides; when they work on parts of slides, they're often called *builds.* Note that a transition consists of two parts:

 ✔ **Effect:** This is the visual effect that's displayed.

 ✔ **Options:** Options include the direction in which the animation moves as well as whether it starts in response to a tap or after a previous transition is finished. Options also include the duration of the transition.

Though a transition may appear to happen *between* two slides, it happens *after* you tap a slide to go to the next one. The transition is attached to the from, or first, slide in the sequence of two adjacent slides.

Here's how to build a transition:

1. **Tap the Transitions button to enter the transition editor.**

    The screen now looks similar to the one shown in Figure 4-9.

Figure 4-9: Begin building a transition.

2. **In the navigator on the left side of the screen, tap the slide for which you want to build a transition.**

   The list of transition effects appears in a popover, as shown in Figure 4-10. A number of transition effects are available; swipe up and down to see them all. (The list of transitions is controlled by the Effects button at the bottom-left corner of the popover.)

Figure 4-10: Choose an effect.

3. **When you find a transition effect that interests you, tap the name to select it and see a preview.**

4. **You can tap the triangle in the top-right corner of the popover to repeat the preview.**

   After you apply a transition effect to a slide, it appears whenever you select that slide in the navigator while using Transitions, as shown in Figure 4-11.

5. **Tap the Options button in the bottom-right corner of the popover (refer to Figure 4-10) to set the effect options, as shown in Figure 4-12.**

   You can set the duration and when the effect starts.

Book IV
Chapter 4

Presenting Keynote

Figure 4-11: The effect is shown on the slide in the navigator.

Figure 4-12: Set the duration and start.

6. Continue to change the effects and options until you're satisfied.

You'll probably want to try out the combinations with the triangle in the upper-right side of the popover several times.

Working with builds

Builds are much like transitions except that they work within a single slide and control how elements such as bullets are displayed. Here's how to set a build:

1. Tap the Transitions button.

Until you tap the Done button, you're creating a transition. Because builds are done within a slide, you work on the slide itself (not on the navigator).

2. In the display portion of the screen, tap the object you want to build, as shown in Figure 4-13.

Each object can have two sets of builds: effects to build it *into* the slide (when the slide is shown) and effects to build it *out* of the slide (when the slide is closed).

Figure 4-13: Set builds for an object.

3. Tap the appropriate button for the type of build you want to apply — either a build-in or a build-out.

4. Select the build effect you want to use, as shown in Figure 4-14.

As with slide-to-slide transitions, as soon as you select an effect, it's previewed for you. You can repeat the preview with the triangle in the upper-right corner.

Figure 4-14: Select the build effect.

5. **As soon as you select a build effect, you can set options, as shown in Figure 4-15.**

   Note that a number in a yellow circle is created on the object you're applying the build to; you can tap the number later to go back and change the effect or options.

Figure 4-15: Choose an option.

6. **Tap the Delivery button at the bottom of the popover to select whether the build happens all at one time or with the addition of each component, as shown in Figure 4-16.**

   Depending on what the selected object is, this step can build each item in a bulleted list separately or each wedge in a pie chart in sequence. (Delivery options may not be available if they don't apply.)

Figure 4-16: Set the delivery options.

Managing multiple builds on a single slide

As you create builds, each one is numbered. The numbers appear in small, yellow circles as soon as you have chosen an effect. You can manage the sequence of these builds. To do so, follow these steps:

1. **Select the appropriate slide and tap the Transitions button.**

   You see the yellow circles around the numbers of the builds on that slide.

2. **Tap any build to edit it using the techniques you used to create the build.**

   (See the earlier section "Working with builds.")

   The yellow circle for a build is shown in Figure 4-17. You can see two transitions for the selected object. In this case, transition 2 is the build-in, and transition 1 is the build-out. (That happens to be the order they were created in, but they don't have to be in that order.) Thus, you can separately tap either transition number to change its settings or even delete it if you've gone transition-crazy.

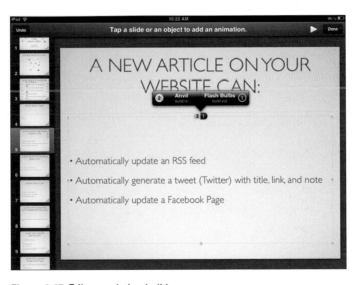

Figure 4-17: Edit an existing build.

3. **To reorder the builds, tap the Order button in the bottom-right corner of the popover.**

   Using the horizontal bars at the right of each build (see Figure 4-18), drag them to the order you want them to be executed. The numbers automatically change. Keynote picks up identifying text, such as the title, so that you can keep them straight.

Figure 4-18: Set the build order.

4. **When you're finished, tap Options again to review the reordered builds.**

   You can use the arrow in the top-right corner of the popover to test the builds.

5. **When you're satisfied, click Done.**

Preparing to Present

After you've dotted every *i* and crossed every *t* in your presentation, added all the great ideas you've been storing in your brain, and tweaked the animations, you're happy with what you have. Now you need to prepare for a captivating presentation.

Using a projector

The cable known as the Apple iPad Dock Connector to VGA Adapter ($29 from the Apple Store at the time of this writing) connects your iPad to any VGA device, such as a projector. With it, you can use Keynote to give your presentation.

The Digital AV Adapter cable accessory is available for $39. You can use it to connect to devices enabled with Thunderbolt high-definition media technology or to devices such as HDTVs that have HDMI connectors.

When you connect a projector (or any other type of display) to your iPad with the iPad Dock Connector to VGA Adapter, the Keynote app can sense that it has a second display. It uses this display when you start a slideshow in the Keynote app. (See the "Playing Your Presentation" section, later in this chapter.) While it's sending the presentation to the external display, it lets you control it from your iPad. Figure 4-19 shows what you see on the iPad as it plays a presentation on an external display.

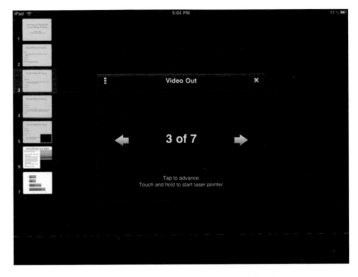

Figure 4-19: Control a presentation on an external display.

The slides are displayed on the external display, but you can control the presentation using your iPad. On the left side of the screen, a navigator shows thumbnail images of your slides. Being able to see the next slide helps you transition to it elegantly without shuffling papers and distracting your audience and yourself. You can tap the arrows in the center of the iPad screen to move forward and backward among slides.

Using nanopresentations

iPad is a game-changer in many ways. Its size (and therefore its portability) and its remarkably clear screen are only two of its features that open great new opportunities. Keynote for iPad can help you take advantage of a new opportunity — *nanopresentations* (presentations you make to a small group of people).

Whether you're used to presentations as a presenter or an audience member, you'll probably be pleasantly surprised at how well presentations to small groups can work. Perhaps the most interesting difference is the simplest one: Because the speaker can sit down and join the audience around a table or in a circle or in a group of chairs, the speaker/audience or teacher/student paradigm of many presentations is immediately broken — and can be a breath of fresh air. It certainly seems to make discussions and audience questions more lively.

For presentations to large (or even medium-size) groups, your iPad and a projector work well. But for a smaller group, a projector is often a bit of overkill. You can use your iPad for a presentation to a few people seated around a table or — to be more iPad-like — seated or standing anywhere they want. This characteristic isn't one that most people have considered much because the mechanics of a presentation have been bulky; you wouldn't normally think of offering short presentations of a few minutes to informal groups who may not even be seated for a formal presentation.

Think about the possibilities. If you're selling something that's not easy to carry around, a photo album on your iPad is a helpful way to show prospective customers what you're talking about. But a Keynote presentation — even a handful of slides — can be much more effective and impressive than a photo album.

Are you canvassing door to door for a politician or a cause? Again, a Keynote presentation of perhaps half a dozen slides can present the issue with pictures, text, and diagrams. You can fill in the gaps and answer questions, but it's certainly more effective than knocking on a door and asking if you can come in and set up a computer and a projector.

 One great advantage of nanopresentations is that you don't talk to a large group that's sitting in the dark when you're presenting to a few people around a table or sitting on a sofa with you. People generally don't have enough time to doze off or become distracted.

Here are a few final presentation pointers:

- **Avoid the dark.** If you're using a projector, use the least possible amount of room-darkening for your presentation. Make certain you can see your audience.

- **Use question-and-answer sections.** Use frequent, short Q&A sections in your presentations to involve your audience as much as possible.

- **Use a road map.** Let people know where they're going in your presentation and where they are at any moment. When you're reading a book, the heft of the unread pages gives you an idea of how far you've come. With a presentation, one slide after another can come out of the dark with no clue to how each one fits into the presentation.

✔ **Use big font sizes.** Have you ever looked closely at the presentations given by Steve Jobs and others at Apple? Consider using 60 points for the font size. Whether you're creating your Keynote presentation on a Mac or an iPad, you're probably close to the screen. Your audience will be far away (even if you're just sitting across a table from them). In addition, you may have become accustomed to using font sizes that print well. Those font sizes are smaller than sizes that appear well on a screen. Go big.

✔ **Buy a dock or cover for your iPad that acts as a stand.** Several iPad cover options let you prop up your iPad display so that somebody sitting across from you can get a good view of its screen. Check out the Apple iPad accessories section in the online store, or search for *iPad covers* at a search engine and find one that appeals to you.

Playing Your Presentation

After you've prepared all the elements in your presentation, little remains to do when you want to play it. Tap the Play button at the right side of the toolbar to begin playing. The transitions and builds happen automatically.

Tap to advance to the next slide. If you're using an external monitor, tap the Next and Previous buttons. (Refer to Figure 4-19.)

If your presentation contains hyperlinks, simply tap to open them in Safari on iPad. (Keynote automatically detects hyperlinks by the presence of an Internet schema, such as http://.)

The Keynote app has a built-in laser pointer, so to speak: Tap and hold the iPad screen, and a red pointer appears on the display. (If you're using an external display or projector, it appears on that display as well.) You can then emphasize parts of the slide to the audience. One advantage of this method is that you can continue to face your audience while pointing out details on the slides. The alternative is to walk over to the slide, turn your back on the audience, and point — not an outstanding idea. (Audience members sometimes sneak out the moment you turn your back.)

Book V
Using iPad to Get Organized

The 5th Wave   By Rich Tennant

"What I'm doing should clear your sinuses, take away your headache, and charge your iPad."

This is one of my favorite parts of this book because it's where you use so many wonderful built-in apps to keep your life in line. You discover how to manage files on iPad and print out those hard copies we all — let's face it — still need now and then. You explore the Notes app, a simple note-taking feature you can use for anything from writing to-do lists to creating the outline of your next novel. In addition to Notes, in this part I teach you all the wonderful features of the Calendar and Contacts apps. These are the apps that will keep you on schedule and in touch with all those important people in your life. You also discover how the new Reminder app and Notifications allow you to stay on track and alert to everything coming at you.

Chapter 1: Managing Files and Printing

In This Chapter

✔ **Understanding how iPad stores files**

✔ **Sharing files by e-mailing**

✔ **Sharing files in the cloud**

✔ **Setting up Home Sharing**

✔ **Printing wirelessly from iPad**

✔ **Using third-party printing services**

Okay, I'm going to be very upfront about this: Apple has not used a traditional paradigm for moving files to and from your iPad or managing files on the device. In essence, this is partially a chapter about what iPad does differently from how traditional file management is handled by OS interfaces such as Mac OS's Finder or Windows Explorer and how you can get things in and out of the device without a USB port or DVD drive. One exciting development that arrived with iOS 5 is *iCloud,* which allows you to backup and store content online, and I discuss that in this chapter as well as in Book I, Chapter 5.

The other topic in this chapter is printing, and there are two options here: Use iPad's native printing capability with a compatible wireless printer, or use a third-party printing app.

In this chapter, I provide you with some ways to manage files in your iPad and take advantage of its wireless printing capabilities.

Finding Your Files

iPad stores files locally by app, or if you use iCloud, iPad will automatically store and share files among iOS devices. Here's how this works.

How iPad stores files

Though there's no Windows Explorer or Mac Finder on iPad where you can view all your stored files in one place, iPad does store files. Open up the Photos app, for example, and you see lots of photos, each one contained in a separate file. The Music app contains audio files, Videos contains movie files, iBooks contains e-book files, and if you own Pages, it contains word processing documents (as shown in Figure 1-1), and so on.

Though there's no Windows Explorer feature on iPad, when you connect iPad to a PC, you can use the Windows Explorer feature on your computer to move files around on iPad.

Figure 1-1: Documents stored by Pages.

How did those files get there? You may have created them in iPad (as with the Notes or Numbers apps); you may have downloaded them from the Internet, as with music or video purchases from iTunes; or you may have synced them from your computer or had them pushed to all your iOS devices from iCloud, as with music files or photos. Perhaps you grabbed a document from a website, or from an online storage service such as Dropbox.

Depending on the app you open, you may see a My Documents button to display thumbnails of documents, as shown in Figure 1-1, libraries of photos as in Photos, albums of music or individual song files as in Music (see Figure 1-2), or bookshelves or lists of e-books as in iBooks. Each app offers a slightly different way to find whatever you've created on, downloaded to, or synced to your iPad.

If you go to iTunes on your computer with your iPad connected, you can see your iPad file structure organized by app. But however the files got in there and however you find them when you open an app, getting them out of your iPad is the focus of this chapter.

Figure 1-2: Music shows you files by album, song, composer, or artist.

See Book II, Chapter 1 for information about buying and downloading content, and Book I, Chapter 5 for information about syncing to your computer and buying apps. Book IV, Chapter 1 gives some details about moving files around for use with iWork products.

Going with iCloud

iCloud isn't so much a place as it is a storage service. If you choose to back up or share files by using iCloud, you can't go to a website and organize those files. Rather, they're automatically backed up from your devices, and new files created or downloaded to one device are automatically pushed to your other devices. In essence, this process is invisible to you. You still access these files by opening the associated app.

The one thing you can do at iCloud (at www.icloud.com) is use the Find My iPad feature, which allows you to send a sound or message to your lost device, remotely lock it, or wipe data from it.

Sharing Files

As mentioned in the previous section, iPad doesn't let you get at files the way your computer does with a series of folders and files. You open files in individual apps, such as Photos and Videos. You can't save files to a storage medium, such as a flash drive that you can remove and place in another computing device. Therefore, managing and sharing your files with other devices or other people works a bit differently on your iPad.

You have a few options for getting files out of your iPad: Sync them via iCloud, which automatically pushes them to other iOS devices; e-mail them; sync with a computer to share things like calendar events, contact records, music, or photos, which is covered in Book I, Chapter 4; share them over a network; or use the Safari browser and a third-party service, such as Dropbox, to upload and view files *in the cloud* (collectively, the places on the Internet where data or apps can be stored and accessed using a browser).

Relying on good old e-mail

You can use tools in individual applications to e-mail files to yourself or others. E-mailing files to yourself can be useful if you've worked on a document on your iPad and then want to get a copy of it on your computer. You can't exactly save a copy because (remember) there is no removable storage medium on your iPad, so you e-mail the file and save the e-mail attachment to your computer hard drive or other storage.

Here's an example of e-mailing from an app, in this case, Photos:

1. **Open Photos and locate a picture you'd like to e-mail.**

2. **Tap the picture to open it and then tap the Menu button shown in Figure 1-3.**

Tap the Menu button

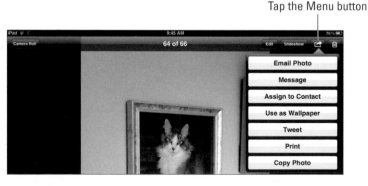

Figure 1-3: Tap the Menu button.

3. **Tap Email Photo.**

The e-mail form shown in Figure 1-4 appears.

Figure 1-4: The e-mail form and onscreen keyboard appear together.

4. **Fill out the e-mail form and tap Send to get the e-mail on its way to yourself or somebody else.**

Going through the cloud

iCloud is a new storage and sharing service from Apple that allows you 5GB of free storage or additional purchased storage for your content. This storage allowance doesn't include apps, contents shared via Photo Stream, any content shared via iTunes Match, and content you've purchased from the iTunes Store. Book I, Chapter 5 provides details on setting up an iCloud account and making settings to choose what to back up and share via iCloud.

You have, in addition to iCloud, other cloud-based options for sharing files. Apps such as iDisk (through MobileMe, which will be discontinued in June 2012), Dropbox, DropCopy Lite, and FileFly – Easy WiFi Sharing and Viewing (a wireless file-sharing app) allow you to upload files to an online site and, using an app you download to your iPad, access and view those files.

I explain how this works with Dropbox, which is a good, free file-sharing app that provides one of the easiest ways to get any and all files to and from your iPad to any and all other computers and devices.

Dropbox is a cloud-based service that allows you to store your files on their servers and access them on any device that's connected to the Internet. (Figure 1-5 shows you what the Dropbox interface looks like if you surf there on your computer.) It directly supports (in the form of dedicated software) Windows, Mac OS X, Linux, Android, BlackBerry, and of course iOS.

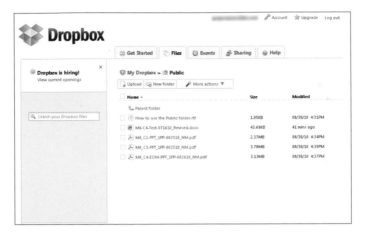

Figure 1-5: Dropbox with files stored in its Public folder.

When you're on a computer, Dropbox works like any other folder on your hard drive. When you open it with your browser, you have instant access to all your files. When you drop something into your folder, it's copied to the company's servers, and then pushed out to anywhere you've set up with your Dropbox account, including your iPad.

After you download the Dropbox app, you can open a file on iPad and view but not edit it, unless you choose the option of opening the document with an app you have on your iPad that would be a logical fit. For example, Figure 1-6 shows the Sharing button, and iPad suggests opening this Word document in Pages, where you can edit it, or PrintCentral, a printing app I cover in the later section "Printing with third-party apps."

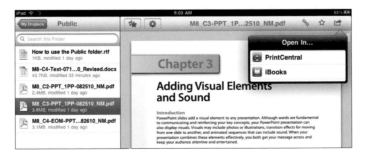

Figure 1-6: Choosing an app to open your document in.

Dropbox folders can be selectively shared with other Dropbox users, making it a great tool for any sort of collaborative project.

In addition to the Dropbox app, iOS app developers can add Dropbox functionality directly to their apps, just as the Quickoffice folks did. This functionality makes working with your files in those apps easier.

iWork provides a Share via iWork.com option for sharing documents you create in those apps (Pages, Numbers, and Keynotes). Tap the Menu icon to choose this option from the menu.

Setting Up Home Sharing

With Home Sharing, you have the ability to stream content from any PC or Mac to your iPad directly. You simply set up Home Sharing on your iPad, turn the feature on in iTunes on your computer, and you're good to go.

Here are the steps for setting up Home Sharing:

1. **On your computer, open iTunes.**

2. **Click the Advanced menu and choose Turn On Home Sharing.**

    The Home Sharing dialog appears.

3. **Enter your Apple ID and password and then click Create Home Share.**

    A message appears, telling you to use the same account you just signed in to on devices you want to share with.

4. **Click Done.**

5. **On your iPad, tap Settings and then tap Music.**

6. **In the Home Sharing section, shown in Figure 1-7, enter your Apple ID and password for the same account you used in iTunes on your computer.**

7. **Tap the Home button and then tap Music.**

    Music opens, displaying a Library button.

8. **Tap the Library button to see a list of shared libraries and then tap the one you want to display a catalog of what's available in it.**

    You can now play any content in that folder from your iPad. To view shared videos, open the Videos app.

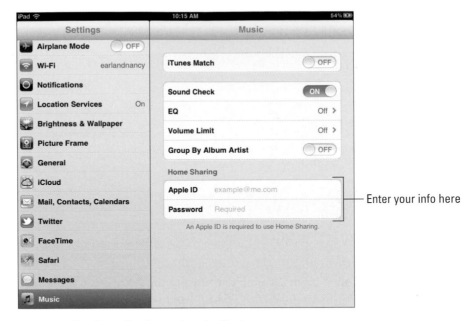

Figure 1-7: The Home Sharing settings for Music.

Printing from iPad

If you need to print from your iPad, you can use its built-in wireless printing capability or a third-party app, which is likely to give you a few more printing controls.

Native printing from iPad

As of iOS version 4.2, native printing capability is part of iPad's bag of tricks. This capability requires a wireless-enabled printer that supports the AirPrint protocol (and as of this writing, they're few and far between) or an app such as Printopia or AirPrint Activator 2, and the only control you have over your printing is to set the number of copies to be printed (though no doubt Apple will add more robust features to this in future iOS releases).

You can print photos, e-mail messages, web pages, and documents from iWork apps such as Pages. Tap the little Menu button with an arrow on it (available in the Safari, Mail, and Photos apps) to find the Print command. When you tap that command, you see the Print dialog. Follow these steps to print:

1. **In the Printer Options dialog, shown in Figure 1-8 (if you haven't yet used this feature with your printer), tap Select Printer.**

   iPad searches for any available wireless printers; tap your printer to select it.

Figure 1-8: Choose your printer and the number of copies and print away!

2. **Tap Printer Options to return to the Printer Options dialog and use the + or – buttons in the Copies field to adjust the number of copies.**

3. **Tap Print.**

   Your print job goes on its way.

When you have print jobs going to your printer, you can access a Print Summary dialog that shows the name of the document that's printing, the printer it's printing to, the number of copies, when the print job started, and its status (for example, Printing 1 of 3). You access this summary by double-tapping the Home button and scrolling in the list of apps to locate the Print Center app. Tap it, and the summary displays.

Printing with third-party apps

There are several third-party apps to choose from: PrintCentral, Print n Share for Advanced Printing, and PrintBureau, to name a few.

One of the best of these is PrintCentral Pro for iPad, available for $8.99. This app has a file browser and an e-mail reader that allows you to access anything on your iPad, and it also allows you to print to a network printer across your Wi-Fi network. If you install a free printer server called WePrint, provided by EuroSmartz, on your Mac or PC, you can even print to your printer remotely through a 3G connection on the iPad model that includes Wi-Fi and 3G. (I recommend installing the print server anyway because it gives you more printing options.)

The apps Printopia and AirPrint Activator 2 make any shared or network printer on your home network visible to your iPad. Printopia has more features but is more expensive, while AirPrint Activator is free.

After purchasing and downloading PrintCentral to your iPad, in order to use the app you need to follow these steps:

1. **Download WePrint to your computer.**

   Both Mac and Windows versions are available at `http://mobile.eurosmartz.com/print/download.html`.

2. **Plug your connector cable into your iPad and one of your computer's USB ports.**

3. **Open WePrint.**

   You see your server address, as shown in Figure 1-9.

Figure 1-9: The WePrint app on your computer.

4. **Now open PrintCentral on iPad.**

5. **Tap the Getting Started file listed there to test your printer.**

6. **Tap the Print icon in the top-right corner.**

   The Print dialog shown in Figure 1-10 appears.

7. **Tap the Choose button and enter the server address you found in WePrint into the dialog that appears.**

   PrintCentral connects and displays all possible printers (see Figure 1-11).

Figure 1-10: PrintCentral's Print dialog.

Figure 1-11: PrintCentral's possible printers dialog.

8. **Tap the printer you want to use and then tap the Print button in the Print dialog.**

   The test document prints.

After you have PrintCentral working, you can use the Menu button from within apps to open a document in PrintCentral and print it. In other apps, you can make a copy of a file that places the copy on your Clipboard and then open the Clip archive in PrintCentral (see Figure 1-12), choose the file you want to print, and print the file.

Figure 1-12: PrintCentral's Clip archive dialog.

Chapter 2: Making Notes

*N*otes is a preinstalled application you can use to do everything from jotting down notes at meetings to maintaining to-do lists. It isn't a robust word processor like Apple Pages or Microsoft Word by any means, but for taking notes on the fly or writing a few pages of your novel-in-progress while you sit and sip a cup of tea on your deck, it's a great option.

In this chapter, you discover how to enter and edit text in Notes and manage notes by navigating among them, searching for content, or e-mailing or deleting them.

Making Notes

Notes are pretty simple to create — kind of like grabbing a sticky notepad, jotting your thoughts down, pulling off the note and sticking it somewhere, and starting to write the next one. You can use the included editing tools to select, cut, copy, and paste. Notes are saved for you in a list of notes so you can easily find the one you need (covered in the next section).

Opening a blank note

If you have no stored notes, Notes opens with a new, blank note displayed. (If you have used Notes before, it opens to the last note you were working on. If that's the case, you might want to jump to the next section to create a new blank note.)

If you have no stored notes and open Notes to a blank document, follow these steps:

1. **Tap the Notes app icon on the Home screen.**

   Depending on how you have your iPad oriented, you see the view in Figure 2-1 (portrait) or Figure 2-2 (landscape).

2. **Tap the blank page.**

   The onscreen keyboard, shown in Figure 2-3, appears.

Figure 2-1: This yellow-lined pad format should look familiar.

Figure 2-2: Landscape orientation shows you the current note and a list of saved notes on the left.

Figure 2-3: Use the onscreen keyboard or your keyboard dock, if you have one.

3. Tap keys on the keyboard to enter text.

.?123

If you want to enter numbers or symbols, tap either of the keys labeled .?123 on the keyboard. The numeric keyboard, shown in Figure 2-4, appears. When you want to return to the regular keyboard, tap either of the keys labeled ABC.

Figure 2-4: Use this alternative keyboard for numbers and many common symbols.

4. **To capitalize a letter, tap the Shift key at the same time that you tap the letter.**

   If you enable the Enable Caps Lock feature in Settings, you can also turn on Caps Lock by double-tapping the Shift key; tap the Shift key once to turn off the feature.

5. **When you want to start a new paragraph or the next item in a list, tap the Return key.**

6. **To edit text, tap the text you want to edit and use the Delete key to delete text to the left of the cursor or type new text.**

When you have the numbers keyboard displayed (refer to Figure 2-4), you can tap either of the keys labeled #+= to access more symbols, such as the percentage sign, the euro symbol, and additional bracket styles. Pressing and holding some of these keys displays alternative characters. This also works on some keys on the alphabetic and numeric keyboards. (For example, pressing and holding N gives you foreign language options such as the Spanish ñ, and pressing and holding the exclamation key on the numeric keyboard offers the upside-down exclamation point used in some languages.)

No need to save a note — it's automatically kept until you delete it.

Creating a new note

If you have stored notes, when you open Notes the most recently used note is displayed. If you then want to create a new note, it's a simple procedure. To create a new note, tap the New Note button (the one with the + symbol on it) in the top-right corner. A new, blank note appears (refer to Figure 2-1). Enter and edit text as described in the previous section.

If your iPad is in portrait orientation and you want to see the list of saved notes beside the current note, switch to landscape orientation on your iPad or tap the Notes button at the top left.

Using copy and paste

After you enter content into a note, you may want to modify it. The Notes app includes essential editing tools you're familiar with from other word processors: select, copy, and paste. You can use these to duplicate content, or to cut and paste it from one part of a note to another.

To use the copy and paste tools, follow these steps:

1. **With a note displayed, press and hold your finger on a word.**

   The selection toolbar, shown in Figure 2-5, appears.

Press and hold on a word to display this toolbar

Figure 2-5: This toolbar provides selection and pasting tools.

2. **Tap the Select button.**

   The toolbar shown in Figure 2-6 appears.

Figure 2-6: After you select text, you can access the Copy command.

3. **If you want to modify the selection, you can tap either blue endpoint dot and drag it to the left or right.**

4. **Tap the Copy button.**

5. **Press and hold your finger in the document where you want to place the copied text.**

6. **In the toolbar that appears (see Figure 2-7), tap the Paste button.**

   The copied text appears.

Tap this button

Figure 2-7: Use the press-and-hold method again to display the editing toolbar.

If you want to select all text in a note to either delete or copy it, tap the Select All button in the toolbar shown in Figure 2-5. When the Cut/Copy/ Paste/Suggest toolbar appears, you can use it to deal with the selected text. To extend a selection to adjacent words, press one of the little handles that extends from the selection and drag to the left or right. To get an alternative spelling suggestion, you can tap Suggest.

To delete text, you can use the Select or Select All command and then press the Delete key on the onscreen keyboard.

Finding Notes

After you've created notes, you're likely to want to find one to open again. You can scan the Notes List to find a note or use a search tool. You can also use the Next and Previous buttons on the Notes pad to move among notes. The following sections help you find and move among notes you've created.

Displaying the Notes List

The Notes List contains all your notes listed chronologically by the last date/ time you modified the note. This list isn't always available in every orientation, but it's the list you need in order to see the notes you have stored. If you're using landscape orientation, a list of notes appears by default on the left side of the screen. (Refer to Figure 2-2.)

If you're using portrait orientation, you can display this list by tapping the Notes button in the top-left corner of the screen; the Notes List appears, as shown in Figure 2-8. Tap any note on the list to display it.

Tap this button...

to display the list of notes

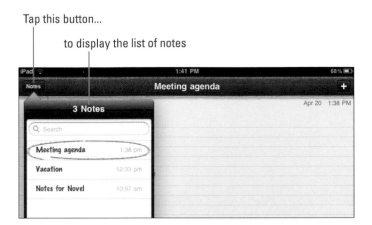

Figure 2-8: Tap the Notes button to display a list of saved notes.

Notes names your note using the first line of text that you enter. If you want to change the name of a note, display that note, tap at the beginning of the first line of text, enter a new title, and tap Return. The newly added text becomes the name of your note in the Notes List.

Moving among notes

You have a couple of ways to move among notes you've created, and they're both simple:

1. **Tap the Notes app icon on the Home screen to open it.**

2. **With the Notes List displayed, tap a note to open it.**

   You can display the Notes List by either turning iPad to landscape orientation or tapping the Notes button in portrait orientation; see the previous section for more on viewing the Notes List.

3. **Tap the Next button (the right-facing arrow) or Previous button (the left-facing arrow) on the bottom of the Notes pad, shown in Figure 2-9, to move among notes.**

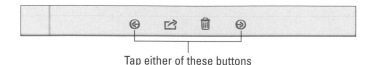

Tap either of these buttons

Figure 2-9: The familiar Next and Previous buttons you've used in browsers make navigation easy.

Notes isn't a file-management pro; it allows you to enter multiple notes with the same title, which can cause confusion. Be advised, and name your notes uniquely!

Notes names your note using the first line of text. If you want to rename a note, first display the note, tap at the end of the first line of text, and then tap the Delete key on your onscreen keyboard to delete the old title. Enter a new title; it's reflected as the name of your note in the Notes List.

Searching notes

If you're not sure which note contains that very important item, you can search to locate a note that contains certain text. The Search feature lists only notes that contain your search criteria, however; it doesn't highlight and show you every instance of the word or words that you enter in a note.

The Spotlight search feature in iPad also locates notes that match any search term you enter there, along with many other types of content.

Follow this procedure to use the Notes search feature:

1. **Tap the Notes app icon on the Home screen to open it.**

2. **Either hold the iPad in landscape orientation or tap the Notes button in portrait orientation to display the Notes List, as shown in Figure 2-10.**

Tap this button...

to display the list of notes

Figure 2-10: The Search feature is located on the Notes List.

3. **Tap in the Search field at the top of the Notes List (see Figure 2-11).**

   The onscreen keyboard appears.

   Tap here to display the onscreen keyboard

   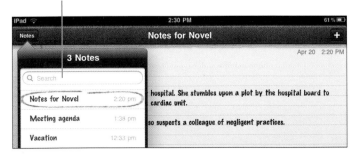

   Figure 2-11: Enter search terms using the onscreen keyboard or keyboard dock.

4. **Begin to enter the search term.**

   All notes that contain matching words appear on the list, as shown in Figure 2-12.

   Figure 2-12: The search feature narrows the results by words that match your entry.

5. **Tap a note to display it and then locate the instance of the matching word the old-fashioned way — by scanning through it.**

If you want to look for a note based on how long ago you created or last modified it, it might help you to know that notes are stored with the most recently created or modified notes at the top of the Notes List. Older notes fall toward the bottom of the list. The day you last modified a note is also listed in the Notes List to help you out.

E-mailing a Note

Today, it's all about sharing content. If you want to share what you wrote with a friend or colleague, or even access your note on your main computer to move it over into a word processing program and flesh it out, you can easily e-mail the contents of a note by following these steps:

1. **With a note displayed, tap the Menu button on the bottom of the screen (see Figure 2-13).**

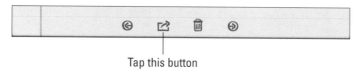

Tap this button

Figure 2-13: Share your scribblings with others by e-mail.

2. **In the pop-up menu that appears, tap Email.**

3. **In the e-mail form that appears (see Figure 2-14), type one or more e-mail addresses in the appropriate fields.**

   At least one e-mail address must appear in the To field.

Enter e-mail addresses here

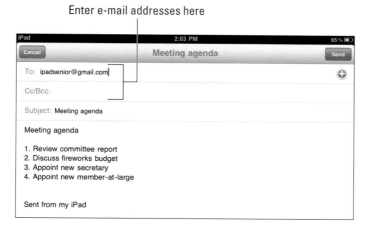

Figure 2-14: You can't save iPad contents to a storage medium, so e-mail may be your best bet!

4. **If you need to make changes to the subject or message, tap in either area and make the changes.**

5. **Tap the Send button.**

   Your e-mail is on its way.

 You can tap the button with a plus sign (+) on it in the top-right corner of the e-mail message form to display your contacts list and choose recipients from there. This tip works only with contacts for which you've entered e-mail addresses. See Book V, Chapter 5 for more about using the Contacts app.

 If you want to print a note in Step 3, choose Print rather than Email. Complete the Printer Options dialog by designating an AirPrint-enabled wireless printer (or shared printer on a printer on a network that you can access using AirPrint) and how many copies to print and then tap Print.

 To cancel an e-mail message and return to Notes without sending it, tap the Cancel button in the e-mail form and then tap Don't Save on the menu that appears. To leave a message but save a draft so that you can finish and send it later, tap Cancel and then tap Save. The next time you tap the E-Mail button with the same note displayed in Notes, your draft appears.

Deleting Notes

Over time, notes can accumulate, making it harder to find the note you need in the long list that's displayed. There's no sense in letting your Notes List get cluttered, or leaving old content around to confuse you. When you're done with a note, it's time to delete it:

1. **Tap the Notes app icon on the Home screen to open it.**

2. **With the iPad in landscape orientation, tap a note in the Notes List to open it.**

3. **Tap the Trash Can button, shown in Figure 2-15.**

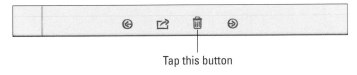

Tap this button

Figure 2-15: With a note displayed, tap the Trash Can button to delete it.

4. **Tap the Delete Note button that appears (see Figure 2-16).**

The note is deleted.

Tap this button

Figure 2-16: Go ahead; delete whatever you don't need with a tap of this button.

Notes is a nice little application, but it's limited. It offers no formatting tools, although you can change among three font options in Settings, Notes. You can't paste pictures into it. (Actually, you can, but what appears is the file-name, not the image.) So if you've made some notes and want to graduate to building a more robust document in a word processor, you have a couple of options. One way is to buy the Pages word processor application for iPad, which costs $9.99, and copy your note (using the copy and paste feature discussed earlier in this chapter). Alternatively, you can send the note to yourself in an e-mail. Open the e-mail and copy and paste the text into a full-fledged word processor, and you're good to go.

If you want to move beyond Notes and use a note-taking app that lets you write with a stylus, check out PaperDesk for iPad ($2.99) or Penultimate ($1.99) in the App Store. Both make drawing and writing handwritten notes easy and fun. Pogo Sketch and Pogo Stylus are two good stylus tools to check out (at www.tenonedesign.com).

Chapter 3: Keeping On Schedule with Calendar

In This Chapter

✏ Viewing your calendar

✏ Adding calendar events

✏ Creating repeating events

✏ Deleting events

✏ Sharing calendars with other devices

Most of us have busy lives full of activities that aren't always easy to keep straight. You may need a way to keep on top of all those work-related and personal activities and appointments. The Calendar app on the iPad is a simple, elegant, electronic daybook that helps you do just that.

In addition to being able to enter events and view them by the day, week, month, or year, you can set up Calendar to provide alerts to remind you of your obligations, and you can search for events by keyword. You can also set up repeating events, such as the weekly staff meeting, a regular social get-together, or monthly flea treatments for your cat. And, given that you probably have calendars on your computer and mobile phone, you'll be happy to hear that you can sync your iPad calendar with them using iTunes or iCloud.

In this chapter, I show you how to master simple procedures for getting around in your calendar, entering and editing events, setting up alerts, syncing, and searching.

Taking a Look at Your Calendar

You've probably used calendar apps in a slew of settings — in your e-mail client, on your cellphone, and even in robust contact management programs. The Calendar app on iPad is more robust than some and less robust than others, but it's quite a nicely designed and simple-to-use program that saves you the cost of buying one more app. Calendar offers several ways to view your schedule, so the first step in mastering Calendar is to understand how to navigate those various views.

You get started by tapping the Calendar app icon on the Home screen to open it. Then tap one of the top buttons to change the view. The choices are described in this list:

✔ **Day:** This view, shown in Figure 3-1, displays your daily appointments with times listed on the left page, along with a calendar for the month and an hourly breakdown of the day on the right page.

Calendar for the month

List of the day's appointments

Hourly breakdown of the day

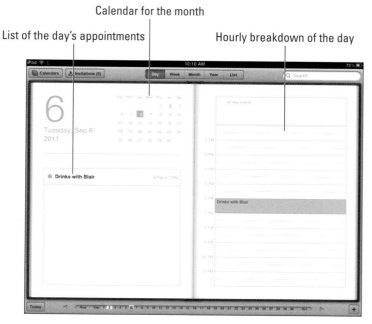

Figure 3-1: Calendar in landscape orientation. In portrait orientation, the two pages are narrower.

✓ **Week:** Use Week view to see all your events for the current week, as shown in Figure 3-2. In this view, appointments appear in their scheduled time slots on the grid.

Week button

Figure 3-2: Tap another week in the row beneath the weekly calendar to jump there.

✓ **Month:** See one month at a time and switch among months in Month view. (See Figure 3-3.) In this view, you don't see the timing of events, but you can spot your busiest days and determine which days have room for another event.

✓ **Year:** Tap the Year button to see an entire year of commitments, as shown in Figure 3-4. In this view, days that have scheduled events display the color of the calendar associated with the event.

Month button

Figure 3-3: Tap a month name along the bottom of the screen to jump to another month.

Year button

Figure 3-4: If you want an overview of your year, this is the view for you.

✔ **List:** List view displays your daily calendar with a list of all commitments for the month to the left of it, as shown in Figure 3-5.

Figure 3-5: List view shows today and all the days containing events in the month ahead.

To move from one day, week, month, or year to another, use the *Timeline,* displayed along the bottom of every view. Tap a day to move to it, or tap the

Forward or Backward button to move forward or backward one increment at a time: a day at a time in Day view, a week at a time in Week view, to the next scheduled event in List view, and so on.

To jump back to today, tap the Today button in the bottom-left corner of Calendar. And now you know the basics about views in Calendar!

For the feel of a paper calendar book, rotate the screen to landscape orientation in the Calendar app. This orientation provides a nice, book-like experience, especially in Day view.

If you're looking for a more robust scheduling app, consider buying Pocket Informant HD for $14.99. This app is easy to use and has helpful scheduling tools for your tasks. You can also sync information you save in the app by using Google Calendar, making almost superfluous a paid-for service, such as MobileMe, that coordinates all your device calendars. Also, if you want to use a calendar program for business, check out Shifty, a workshift management app that has tools that can be quite useful to managers and supervisors.

Adding Calendar Events

Events in your life might range from business meetings to karaoke dates, but whatever the nature of your appointments, Calendar can help you keep them all straight. You can enter single events or repeating events and include alerts to remind you that they're coming up.

Adding one event at a time

If you've used other calendar programs, you know that adding events is usually a simple procedure. You can easily add events using iPad's Calendar app, but if you haven't used a touchscreen computer or smartphone, it's worth a walk-through.

Follow these steps to add an event to your calendar:

1. **With Calendar open in any view, tap the Add button to add an event.**

   The Add Event dialog, shown in Figure 3-6, appears.

2. **Enter a title for the event and, if you want, a location.**

3. **Tap the Starts/Ends field.**

   The Start & End dialog, shown in Figure 3-7, is displayed.

Figure 3-6: Add your event details in this dialog.

Figure 3-7: Use this cool slot–machine–like interface to set up event timing details.

4. **Place your finger on the date, hour, minute, or AM/PM column, and flick your finger to scroll up or down.**

   If you want to change the time zone, tap that field, begin to enter a new location, and then tap the location in the suggestions that appear.

5. **After all items are set correctly, tap Done.**

   (Note that, if the event lasts all day, you can simply tap the All-day On-Off button and forget setting starting and ending times.)

6. **If you want to add notes, use your finger to scroll down in the Add Event dialog and tap in the Notes field.**

7. **Type your note and then tap the Done button to save the event.**

Note that you can edit any event at any time by simply tapping it in any view of your calendar. The Edit Event dialog appears, offering the same settings as the Add Event dialog (refer to Figure 3-6). Just tap the Done button in this dialog to save your changes after you've made them.

Creating repeating events

Many events in our lives happen regularly: that Tuesday evening book club, the monthly sales meeting, or your company's yearly audit, for example. You can use the repeating events feature of the Calendar app to set repeating events.

Follow these steps to create a repeating event:

1. **With any view displayed in the Calendar app, tap the Add button to add an event.**

   The Add Event dialog (refer to Figure 3-6) appears.

2. **Enter a title and location for the event, and set the start and end dates and times as shown in the previous section.**

3. **Tap the Repeat field.**

   The Repeat Event dialog, shown in Figure 3-8, appears.

Figure 3-8: You have to use preset intervals, but you can choose from several.

4. **Tap a preset time interval: Every Day, Week, 2 Weeks, Month, or Year.**

5. **Tap Done.**

   You return to the Add Event dialog.

6. **Tap Done again to save your repeating event.**

Other calendar programs may seem to give you more control over repeating events; for example, you might be able to make a setting to repeat an event every Tuesday. If you want a more robust calendar feature, consider setting up your appointments in iCal or Outlook and syncing them to iPad. But, if you want to create a repeating event in iPad's Calendar app, simply add the first event on a Tuesday and make it repeat every week.

If you have an iCloud or Gmail account, your iPad recognizes and supports all calendars you've compiled there as well as those you've synced and the iPad calendar.

Adding alerts

Once upon a time, helpful assistants placed printed paper schedules of the day's activities in front of their bosses to remind them of scheduled commitments. Today, I'm not sure anybody but the highest-paid CEOs get this type of service. Instead, we all get to set up alerts in calendar programs to remind ourselves where to be, and when.

Luckily, in the iPad Calendar app, you can easily set up alerts by following these steps:

1. **Tap the Settings icon on the Home screen and choose General, and then choose Sounds.**

2. **Tap Calendar Alerts and then tap any alert tone, which plays the tone for you.**

3. **After you've chosen one, tap Sounds to return to the Sounds settings.**

4. **Tap the Home button and then tap Calendar.**

5. **Create an event in your calendar or open an existing one for editing (see the preceding sections).**

6. **In the Add Event dialog or Edit dialog for an existing event (refer to Figure 3-6), tap the Alert field.**

   The Event Alert dialog appears, as shown in Figure 3-9. Note that if you want two alerts — say, one a day before and one an hour before — you can repeat this procedure using Second Alert instead.

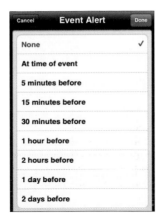

Figure 3-9: Use these preset intervals to set up alerts.

7. **Tap any preset interval, from 5 Minutes Before to 2 Days Before or at the time of an event.**

   (Remember that you can scroll down in the dialog to see more options.)

8. **Tap Done to save the alert and then tap Done in the Add Event dialog to save all settings.**

9. **Tap the Day button to display the date of your event in Day view.**

   Note that the alert and time frame are listed under the event in that view, as shown in Figure 3-10.

If you're on the road and change time zones, iPad may not recognize the local time, which can cause your alerts to become useless. To avoid this problem, you can adjust the time of your iPad manually by using the Date & Time feature in the General category in Settings.

If you work for an organization that uses a Microsoft Exchange account, you can set up your iPad to receive and respond to invitations from colleagues. When somebody sends an invitation that you accept, it appears on your calendar. Check with your company network administrator (who will jump at the chance to get her hands on your iPad) or the *iPad User Guide* to set up this feature if having this capability sounds useful to you. Alternatively, you can check into iCloud, which does much the same thing, minus the IT person.

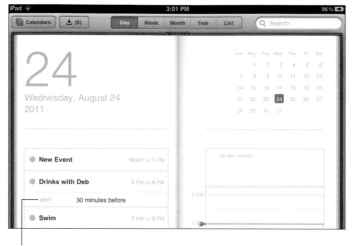

An event's alert and timeframe

Figure 3-10: An alert is noted along with the appointment in your calendar.

Working with Your Events

After you have entered some events in Calendar, you can use features to search for events, sync your events with other calendars on other devices, or delete events that have been canceled.

In this section, you work with the various events on your calendar to keep things up to date and organized.

Searching calendars

Displaying events by day or week and scrolling the pages is one way to look for appointments, but if you need to view a particular event and can't remember its time frame, you can use the Calendar search feature to find it.

Follow these steps to search for events in Calendar:

1. **With Calendar open in any view, tap the Search field (refer to Figure 3-5) in the top-right corner.**

   The onscreen keyboard appears.

2. **Type a word or words to search by and then tap the Search key on the onscreen keyboard.**

   As you type, the Results dialog appears, as shown in Figure 3-11.

Figure 3-11: Every instance of an event that includes your search term is displayed.

3. **Tap any result to display it in the view you were in when you started the search.**

   The Edit dialog appears, and you can edit the event, if you want.

Working with multiple calendars

You can choose a calendar — for example, Business, Personal, Parties, Classes, and Volunteering — for every event. If you're synchronizing your calendars with your Mac or PC or by using iCloud, Google, Microsoft Outlook, or AOL, each source can have its own calendars. On your iPad, tap Calendars at the top-left of the screen in the Calendar app. Every calendar's events are shown in a different color.

You can choose to display the events from several calendars at one time, including your iPad calendar and calendars you sync with from your PC, only your PC calendars, or only your iPad calendar. With the Calendar app open, click the Calendars button, and in the Calendars dialog, tap to select or deselect the calendars you want to display: All from My <Account>, Birthday Calendar, My Calendar, or US Holidays. If you have synced to calendars from other sources, you can choose them by tapping them to select or deselect them; for example, tap All iCloud to show all your iCloud-synced calendars. Tap Done, and your chosen calendar displays. When you add a new event, use the Calendar field to choose the calendar you want to add the event to.

If you have created lots of events, you might want to tap Hide All Calendars in the Calendar app and then tap the one or two calendars you need to see now so that you can quickly find their events.

Subscribing To and Sharing Calendars

If you use a calendar available from an online service such as Yahoo! or Google, you can subscribe to that calendar to read events that are saved in it on your iPad. Note that you can only read, not edit, these events. To subscribe, follow these steps:

1. **Tap the Settings icon on the Home screen to get started.**

2. **Tap the Mail, Contacts, Calendars option on the left.**

3. **Tap Add Account.**

   The Add Account options, shown in Figure 3-12, appear.

Figure 3-12: Choose accounts with calendars to copy to iPad.

4. **Tap an e-mail choice, such as Gmail or Yahoo! Mail.**

5. **In the dialog that appears (see Figure 3-13), enter your name, e-mail address, and e-mail account password.**

6. **Tap Save.**

   iPad verifies your address.

Figure 3-13: Enter your calendar account information.

7. **Your iPad retrieves data from your calendar at the interval you have specified. To review these settings, tap the Fetch New Data option in the Mail, Contacts, Calendars dialog.**

8. **In the Fetch New Data dialog that appears (see Figure 3-14), be sure that the Push option's On-Off button reads *On* and then choose the frequency option you prefer for pushing data to your iPad.**

Make sure this is set to On

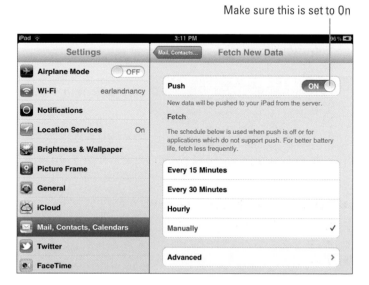

Figure 3-14: More frequent pushing of data can use battery power and data charges on a 3G connection.

If you use the Windows version of Microsoft Outlook calendar or iCal on your main computer, you can sync the calendar to your iPad calendar to avoid having to reenter event information. To do this, use iCloud settings to sync automatically (see Book I, Chapter 5) or connect your iPad to your computer with the Dock Connector to USB Cable (or sync wirelessly) and use settings in your iTunes account to sync the calendars. Click the Sync button and your calendar settings are shared between your computer and iPad (in both directions). Read more in Book I, Chapter 5 about working with iTunes to manage your iPad content.

If you store the birthday of someone listed in your Contacts app, the Calendar app displays it when the day arrives so that you don't forget to pass on your congratulations!

You can also have calendar events shared with your iPad if you use a push service such as iCloud. The service can sync calendars from multiple e-mail accounts with your iPad calendar. However, keep in mind that if you choose to have data pushed to your iPad, your battery may drain faster.

Deleting Events

Let's face it: Things change. When that scheduled luncheon or meeting is canceled, you need to delete the appointment in Calendar. Here's how:

1. **With Calendar open, tap an event.**

   The information bar appears. (See Figure 3-15.)

Tap this button

Figure 3-15: Tap an event, and use the Edit button to make changes to it.

2. **Tap the Edit button.**

3. **In the Edit dialog, tap the Delete Event button, shown in Figure 3-16.**

   Confirming options appear.

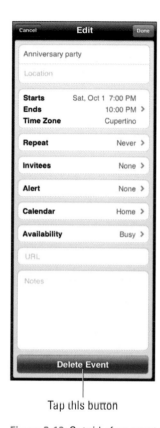

Tap this button

Figure 3-16: Get rid of an event you no longer need by tapping Delete Event.

4. **If this is a repeating event, you can delete either this instance of the event or this and all future instances of the event (see Figure 3-17). Tap the button of the option you prefer.**

   The event is deleted, and you return to Calendar view.

If an event is moved but not canceled, you don't have to delete the existing one and create a new one; simply edit the event to change the date and time in the Edit Event dialog.

Figure 3-17: Choose whether to delete one instance or all instances of a repeating event.

Syncing with Calendars on Other Devices

Many people now have several computing devices they use to keep track of events. Now that you have an iPad as well, you don't want to have to enter and edit events one by one on it, your mobile phone, desktop computer, and laptop computer, right? That's where syncing comes in handy.

If you use a calendar, such as Microsoft Outlook or Apple iCal, on your main computer, you can sync that calendar to your iPad calendar via iCloud or iTunes. To use iTunes, change the iPad settings in iTunes to manage sync settings when your iPad is connected via the Dock Connector to USB Cable or wirelessly using the iTunes Wi-Fi Sync setting.

To make calendars in your other accounts available to your iPad, you subscribe to and share the calendars first. If you haven't done this, see the "Subscribing To and Sharing Calendars" section, earlier in this chapter, before proceeding.

Now it's time to sync your calendars. Follow these steps to sync Calendar information using iTunes:

1. **Open iTunes and sign in.**

2. **Connect your iPad using the Dock Connector to USB Cable, or choose Settings, General, iTunes Wi-Fi Sync, and tap Sync.**

3. **When your iPad appears in the Source List on the left side of the screen, click it.**

4. **Click the Info tab, shown in Figure 3-18, and select the Sync iCal Calendars check box.**

Select this check box

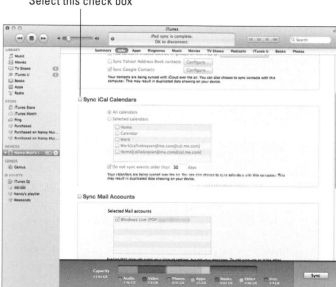

Figure 3-18: The iTunes Info tab.

5. **To sync all calendars, click the All Calendars option.**

   If you don't want older appointments synced, select the Do Not Sync Events Older Than check box and set the number of days. (It's 30 days by default.)

6. **To sync only selected calendars, click the Selected Calendars option and choose the calendars with which you want to sync.**

7. **Click Apply.**

8. **Click the Sync button.**

   Your Calendar settings are shared between your computer and iPad (in both directions).

Find out more about working with iTunes to manage your iPad content in Book I, Chapter 5.

iCloud syncs your calendars automatically on all your devices without your having to place the devices in docks and sync them using a computer. For more about iCloud, see Book I, Chapter 5.

Chapter 4: Working with Reminders and Notifications

In This Chapter

✓ Adding a new task in Reminders

✓ Editing a task

✓ Scheduling a reminder

✓ Displaying reminders in a list or by date

✓ Making a new list

✓ Syncing with other devices and calendars

✓ Completing or deleting a reminder

✓ Setting Notification types

✓ Reviewing and alerts reminders in Notification Center

✓ Jumping from Notification Center to an app

✓ Getting rid of old notifications

With the arrival of iOS 5, the Reminders app and the Notification Center feature appeared, warming the hearts of iPad owners who need help remembering the details of their lives.

Reminders is a kind of to-do list that lets you create tasks and set reminders so that you don't forget them. Notifications let you review all elements you should be aware of in one place, such as mail messages, text messages, calendar appointments, and alerts.

In this chapter, I tell you how to set up and view tasks in Reminders, and I explain how the new Notification Center can centralize all your alerts in one easy-to-find place.

Creating a Task in Reminders

Reminders help you stay on schedule, avoid embarrassing missed appointments, and stay on track of your hundreds of errands each and every day. Creating a task in Reminders is pretty darn simple.

To create a reminder, follow these steps:

1. **Tap Reminders on the Home screen.**

2. **On the screen that appears (see Figure 4-1), tap the plus sign (+) to add a task.**

   The onscreen keyboard appears.

Tap here to create a new task

Figure 4-1: Tap to add reminder tasks.

3. **Enter a task name or description using the onscreen keyboard and tap the Return button.**

   The new task is added to the Reminders list.

You can't add details about a task when you create it, only a descriptive name. To add details about timing and so forth, see the next task.

Editing Task Details

What's a task without the details? For example, try to remember the task *Pick up Grammy Award* without having a few notes to specify when and where and what you should wear. Reminder tasks get you where you need to be when you need to be there.

To edit a task and add details, follow these steps:

1. **Tap a task to open the Details dialog.**

2. **To see all available options, tap Show More to display the choices shown in Figure 4-2.**

   (I describe reminder settings in the next section.)

Figure 4-2: Add the information you need about a particular event in this dialog.

3. **Tap Priority.**

4. **Choose None, Low, Medium, or High from the choices that appear.**

5. **Tap Done.**

6. **Tap List and then, from the options that are displayed (see Figure 4-3), choose My Calendar or Reminders to choose whether to display the task in Calendar or in the Reminder app.**

Choose where to display the task

Figure 4-3: Your event can be viewed in either Calendar or the Reminder app.

7. **Tap Done.**

8. **Tap Notes.**

9. **Using the onscreen keyboard, enter a note about the task.**

10. **Tap Done when you're finished entering details.**

 As of this writing, the Notes app, priority settings don't do much of anything, such as set a flag of any kind on a task in a list or reorder tasks to show priority tasks first. You can see the priority of a task only by displaying its details.

Scheduling a Reminder

A major feature of Reminders, given its name, is to remind you of upcoming tasks. After you've saved a task, you can set a reminder for it.

To set a reminder, follow these steps:

1. **Tap a task.**

2. **In the dialog that appears, tap Remind Me.**

   Another dialog appears.

3. **Tap the On/Off field for the On a Day field to turn it on.**

4. **Tap the Date field to display the settings shown in Figure 4-4.**

5. **Tap and flick the Day, Hour, and Minutes fields to scroll to the date and time for the reminder.**

Make date settings here

Figure 4-4: Scroll to set the date and the time of your event.

6. **Tap the Done button.**

   The settings for the reminder are saved.

If you want a task to repeat with associated reminders, tap the Repeat field, and from the dialog that appears, tap Every Day, Week, 2 Weeks, Month, or Year (for annual meetings or fun-filled holiday get-togethers with the gang). Tap Done twice to save the setting.

Displaying Tasks as a List or by Date

You can display various lists of reminders (which also include tasks originating from My Calendar, completed tasks, and lists you create yourself, as explained later in this chapter), or display reminders by date alongside a panel display of monthly calendars, which is truly helpful in planning your schedule.

To display reminders, follow these steps:

1. **Tap Reminders and then tap the List button.**

   A list of reminders appears, as shown in Figure 4-5.

Figure 4-5: All your reminders are listed here.

2. **Tap the Date tab.**

   You see the tasks for the current date.

   A set of calendars is displayed, as shown in Figure 4-6.

You can scroll the monthly calendar display to show past or future months, and you can tap any date to show its tasks in the daily list on the right.

Set of calendars   Current date   Tasks for current date

Figure 4-6: Get an instant overview of all your events.

Creating a List

You can create your own lists of tasks to help you organize different parts of your life. To do so, follow these steps:

1. **Tap Reminders on the Home screen.**

   Reminders opens.

2. **Tap the List tab to display List view, if it isn't already selected.**

3. **Tap the Edit button.**

4. **Tap Create New List (see Figure 4-7) and enter the name of the list using the onscreen keyboard.**

5. **Tap Done.**

   You return to the Edit dialog.

If you tap the list in List view now, a new, blank sheet appears on the right with the title you entered in Step 4. Tap the plus sign (+) to add new tasks to the list, as shown in Figure 4-8.

Tap this option

Figure 4-7: Lists might include reminders for personal or work-related events.

Tap this button to add a new task to the list

Figure 4-8: Keep creating tasks using the plus sign button.

Syncing with Other Devices and Calendars

You can determine which tasks are transferred or pushed to your device from other devices or calendars such as Outlook or iCal. To make all the settings in this task work correctly, first set up your default calendar in the Calendar settings, and set up your iCloud account under Accounts in the Mail, Contacts, Calendar settings.

After you've made these settings, follow these steps to sync with other devices and calendars:

1. **Tap the Settings button on the Home screen.**

2. **Tap iCloud.**

3. **Be sure that in the right pane Reminders is set to On.**

4. **Make sure that Calendars is also set to On in the right pane (see Figure 4-9).**

5. **Tap Mail, Contacts, Calendars and scroll down to the Reminders category.**

Make sure these are set to On

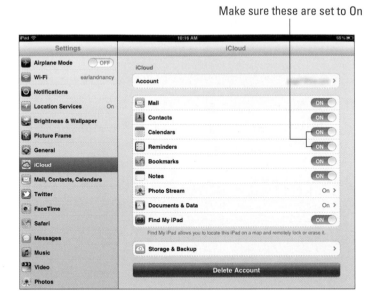

Figure 4-9: Make settings to control what information is shared with your iPad via iCloud.

6. **Tap the Sync field and then choose how far back to sync reminders (see Figure 4-10).**

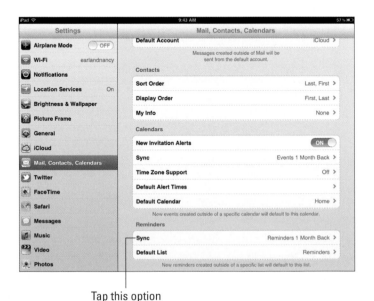

Tap this option

Figure 4-10: If you don't need all reminders, sync to a specific period.

Marking as Complete or Deleting a Reminder

Are you making progress in checking tasks off your list? You may want to mark a task as completed, or delete it entirely, to give yourself a feeling of accomplishment. Here's how:

1. **With Reminders open, tap a task.**

   The Details dialog, shown in Figure 4-11, displays.

Figure 4-11: The Details dialog contains a handy Delete button to get rid of a reminder.

2. **Tap Delete.**

   You're asked to confirm the deletion.

3. **Tap Delete again.**

4. **To mark a task as complete, tap in the check box to the left of the task in List view and then tap the Completed category.**

   The task moves to that category and is removed from the My Calendar category.

Setting Notification Types

Notification Center is on by default, but you can change certain settings to control which types of notifications are included in it.

Follow these steps to set notification types:

1. **Tap Settings.**

2. **Tap Notifications.**

   In the settings that appear (see Figure 4-12), note that there is a list of items included in Notification Center and a list of items not included. For example, Messages and Reminders may be included, but alerts in game apps may not.

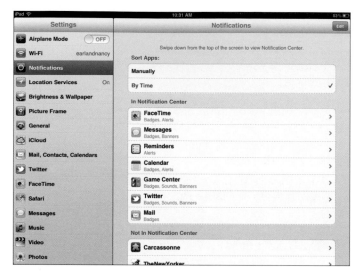

Figure 4-12: Choose your Notification Center options here.

3. **Tap any item.**

   Notification settings appear, as shown in Figure 4-13.

4. **Tap the On-Off button to include or exclude that item from Notification Center.**

5. **Tap an Alert Style to have no alert appear or to have a banner across the top of the screen or a boxed alert appear.**

Include or exclude from Notification Center

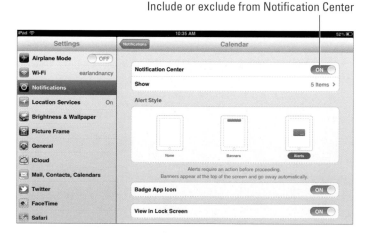

Figure 4-13: Control each item you want to include in Notification Center in this dialog.

If you choose Banner, a banner appears and then disappears automatically. If you choose Alert, you have to take an action to dismiss the alert when it appears.

6. **To turn off the feature, tap the On-Off button in the Badge App Icon field.**

   The Badge App Icons feature places a red circle and a number on icons on your Home screens to represent alerts associated with those apps.

7. **Turn on the View in Lock Screen setting.**

   Turn on this setting if you want to be able to view alerts when the Lock Screen is displayed.

8. **When you've finished making settings for an individual app, tap the Notifications button to return to the Notifications settings.**

Viewing Notification Center

After you've specified which alerts and reminders should appear in Notification Center, you can review them regularly to keep yourself on track.

To view notifications, follow these steps:

1. **From any screen, tap the black status bar on top and drag down to display Notification Center (see Figure 4-14).**

   Note that items are divided into lists by type, such as reminders, Calendar items, and Mail.

2. **To close Notification Center, tap the three lines in the bottom-middle of the Notification Center and drag up, toward the Status bar.**

Notification Center

Figure 4-14: Notification Center is a convenient one-stop location for all your commitments and reminders.

To determine which alerts and reminders are displayed in Notification Center, see the previous task.

Going to an App from Notification Center

To jump easily from Notification Center to any app that causes an alert or reminder to be displayed, follow these steps:

1. Tap the Status bar and drag down.

The Notification Center is displayed.

2. Tap any item.

The item opens in its originating app.

If you've tapped an e-mail message, you can reply to the message by using the procedures described in Book I, Chapter 7.

Clearing Notifications

Who needs notifications of past events? To get rid of old notifications for an app, follow these steps:

1. Tap the Status bar and drag down to display Notification Center.

2. Tap the pale gray X to the right of a category of notifications, such as Mail.

The button changes to read *Clear* (see Figure 4-15).

3. Tap the Clear button.

All items for that category are removed.

If you change your mind about clearing all items in a group after you tap the Clear button, just close Notification Center.

Tap this option

Figure 4-15: Wipe your notification slate clean periodically!

Chapter 5: Managing Contacts

In This Chapter

✔ **Adding contacts**

✔ **Syncing contacts using iTunes or iCloud**

✔ **Specifying related people**

✔ **Assigning a photo to a contact**

✔ **Addressing e-mails using Contacts**

✔ **Sharing contacts**

*C*ontacts is the iPad equivalent of the address book on your cellphone. In fact, if you own an iPhone, it's similar to your Contacts app. The Contacts app on iPad is simple to set up and use, and it has some powerful little features beyond simply storing names, addresses, and phone numbers.

For example, you can pinpoint a contact's address in the iPad Maps application. You can use your contacts to quickly address e-mails, messages, and tweets. If you store a contact record that includes a website, you can use a link in Contacts to view that website instantly. And, of course, you can easily search for a contact by a variety of criteria, including people related to you by family ties or mutual friends.

In this chapter, you discover the various features of Contacts, including how to save yourself time entering their information by syncing your e-mail contacts list to your iPad.

Populating Your Contacts with Information

The Contacts app's sole purpose is to store contact information and make it available to you, but first you have to make that information available to it. You can do it by manually adding records one at a time or by syncing via iTunes or iCloud to transfer your contacts instantly.

Adding contacts

You can, of course, enter your contacts the old-fashioned way, by typing their names, addresses, phone numbers, and other information in a contact form. Follow these steps to create a new contact record:

1. **Tap the Contacts app icon on the Home screen to open the application.**

   If you haven't yet entered a contact, you see a blank address book with the Add button at the bottom, as shown in Figure 5-1.

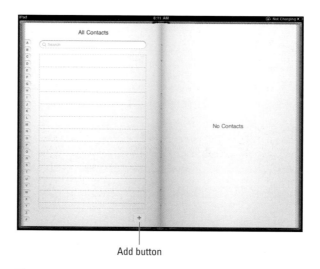

Add button

Figure 5-1: Tap to add a new contact.

2. **Tap the Add button (the button with a small plus sign on it).**

   A blank Info page opens, and the onscreen keyboard is displayed, as you can see in Figure 5-2.

3. **Enter some contact information.**

   Enter a name in the First field, for example.

4. **To scroll down the contact page and see more fields, flick up on the page with your finger.**

5. **If you want to add a mailing or street address, tap Add New Address, which opens additional entry fields.**

6. **To add an information field such as Nickname or Job Title, tap Add Field. In the Add Field dialog that appears (see Figure 5-3), choose a field to add.**

   (You may have to flick your finger upward to view all available fields.)

Figure 5-2: Enter as much information about your contact as you want.

Figure 5-3: Round out a contact's information by adding information fields.

7. Tap the Done button when you finish making entries.

The new contact appears in your address book. Figure 5-4 shows an address book with several entries added.

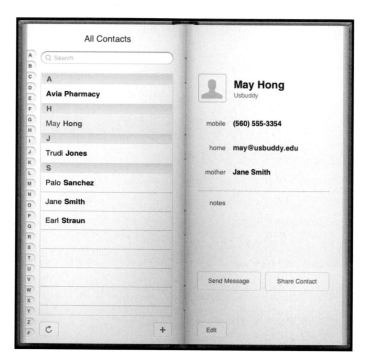

Figure 5-4: A list of contacts, arranged alphabetically.

 If you're entering a contact record and the phone number requires a pause, such as when you access an outside line from your workplace, simply insert a comma into the number at the spot where the pause must occur. If you sync this contact information to your phone via iTunes, it's then set up to dial correctly.

 If your contact's name is difficult for you to pronounce, add the Phonetic First Name (or Phonetic Last Name) field to that person's record. (Refer to Step 6, earlier in this section.)

 If you have set up an LDAP account on iPad to connect with your organization's directory service, you may able to access its directories via Contacts. See Book III, Chapter 1, for more about setting up an LDAP account.

Syncing contacts by using iTunes

You can use your iTunes account, accessed from your computer, to sync contacts between an e-mail account (such as the one shown in Figure 5-5) and the iPad Contacts application. This sync works in both directions: Contacts from iPad are sent to your e-mail account and contacts from your e-mail account are sent to iPad.

Figure 5-5: A Gmail account with contacts displayed.

Make sure that you have the most recent version of iTunes before syncing with iPad. If you use a PC, open iTunes and choose Help➪Check for Updates. On a Mac, choose iTunes➪Check for Updates.

Follow these steps to sync contacts between your e-mail and iPad:

1. **Connect your iPad to your computer with the Dock Connector to USB Cable, or use the iTunes Wi-Fi Sync setting in General Settings to perform a wireless sync.**

2. **In the iTunes window that opens on your computer, double-click the name of your iPad (such as Nancy's iPad), which is now listed in the iTunes Source List.**

3. **Click the Info tab, shown in Figure 5-6.**

4. **Click to select the Sync Contacts check box and then select your e-mail provider.**

   You may be required to agree to share your contacts and provide your username and password for the e-mail account.

5. **Enter your account information in the dialog that appears and then click Apply.**

6. **Click the Sync button.**

   The iPad screen changes to show that syncing is in progress.

Click this tab...

then select this option

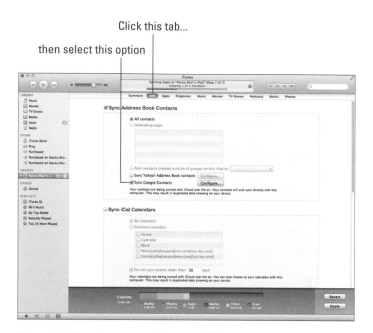

Figure 5-6: Choosing to sync Contacts in iTunes.

7. **When the sync is complete, open Contacts on your iPad.**

   All contacts have been brought over to it.

8. **Unplug the Dock Connector to USB Cable.**

You can use iCloud to automatically sync contacts among all your Apple devices. See Book I, Chapter 5 for more about making iCloud settings to specify whether your contacts are synced in the cloud.

Assigning a photo to a contact

It's always helpful to associate a face with a name. In Contacts, you can do just that by adding a person's photo to his contact record. You can add photos from various sources, such as:

✔ The Photos app albums you have saved from websites

✔ Digital cameras

✔ E-mail attachments

✔ iPad's camera

✔ Photo collections stored on your computer or in iCloud (see Book II, Chapter 6, for more about working with the Photos app)

Follow these steps to add a stored photo to a contact record:

1. **With Contacts open, tap the contact to whose record you want to add a photo.**

2. **Tap the Edit button.**

3. **On the Info page that appears (see Figure 5-7), tap Add Photo.**

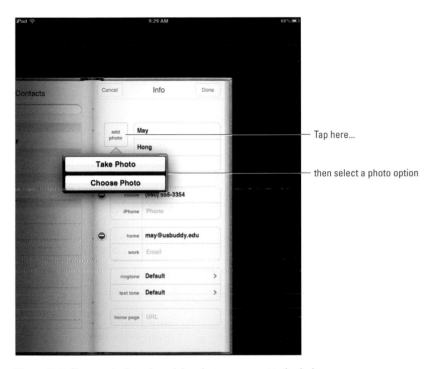

Figure 5-7: Choose the location of the photo you want to include.

4. **Tap Choose Photo.**

5. **In the Photo Albums dialog that appears, tap Camera Roll (named Saved Photos on the first-generation iPad), Photo Library, or any photo album you might have created yourself, depending on where the photo is stored.**

    You can also choose Take Photo to take that contact's photo on the spot, if you have iPad 2.

    A *saved* photo is one that you've downloaded to your iPad or taken using the screen capture feature or an iPad 2 camera; the Photo Library contains photos synced from your computer.

6. **In the photo album that appears, tap a photo to select it.**

   The Choose Photo dialog, shown in Figure 5-8, appears. If you want to modify the photo, move the image around in the frame with your finger, or shrink or expand it by pinching your fingers inward or outward, respectively.

Figure 5-8: Select or edit the photo you want to include.

7. **Tap the Use button to use the photo for this contact.**

   The photo appears on the contact's Info page, as shown in Figure 5-9.

8. **Tap Done to save changes to the contact.**

To edit a photo you've added to a contact record, simply display the contact information and tap it. Choose Edit Photo from the menu that appears, and then, in the dialog shown earlier, in Figure 5-8, use the described gestures for moving and scaling the image. Click Use when you're done to save the changed figure.

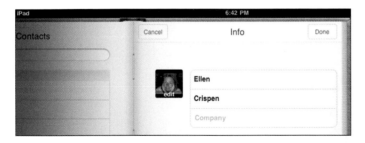

Figure 5-9: A photo displayed with a contact in iPad.

If you want a more powerful contact-management app, check out Contacts Journal – iPad Edition. It syncs with your Contacts app content and can also sync with a computer contact-management program such as Outlook. The most helpful aspect of Contact Journals for road warriors is that it maintains a record of who you've visited and when you've e-mailed them.

Adding Twitter or Facebook Information

New with iOS 5, you can add Twitter information so you can quickly *tweet* (send a short message) to others using Twitter or post a message to your contact's Facebook account.

To specify Facebook or Twitter account information for a contact:

1. **With Contacts open, tap a contact.**
2. **Tap the Edit button.**
3. **Scroll down and tap Add Fields.**
4. **In the list that appears (refer to Figure 5-10), tap Twitter.**

    Both Twitter and Facebook fields open (see Figure 5-10).

5. **Tap Done.**

    The information is saved.

    The account is now displayed whenever you select the contact. You can send a tweet or a Facebook message by simply tapping the username and choosing the appropriate command (such as Tweet, as shown in Figure 5-11).

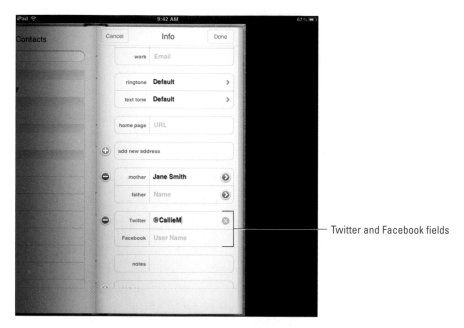

Twitter and Facebook fields

Figure 5-10: Choose Twitter to begin composing a tweet.

Figure 5-11: Your contact is now associated with the appropriate social network.

Designating Related People

You can quickly designate a relation — such as your mother, assistant, friend, or manager — in a contact record if the person is saved to Contacts. To save a contact, follow these steps:

1. **Tap a contact and then tap Edit.**

2. **Scroll down the record and tap Add Field.**

3. **Tap Related People (see Figure 5-12).**

   A new field, labeled Mother, now appears.

4. **Tap the word *mother* and a list of other possible relations appears.**

5. **Tap one to change the label, if you want.**

6. **Tap the blue arrow in the field.**

   Your contacts list appears.

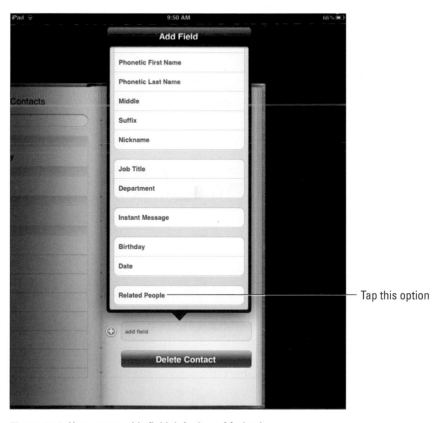

Tap this option

Figure 5-12: How sweet; this field defaults to Mother!

7. **Tap the person's name.**

It appears in the field.

A new, blank field also appears (see Figure 5-13).

Figure 5-13: You can make someone a friend, an assistant, and a spouse, if you want!

 After you add a relation to a contact record, whenever you select the person on the Contacts main screen, all related people for that contact are listed.

Setting Ringtones

If you want to hear a unique tone whenever you receive a FaceTime call from a particular contact, you can set up one in Contacts. For example, if you want to be sure that you know instantly when your spouse, a sick friend, or your boss is calling, set a unique tone for that person by following these steps:

1. **Tap to add a new contact or select a contact from the list of contacts, and tap Edit.**

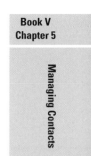

2. **Tap the Ringtone field.**

    A list of tones appears (see Figure 5-14).

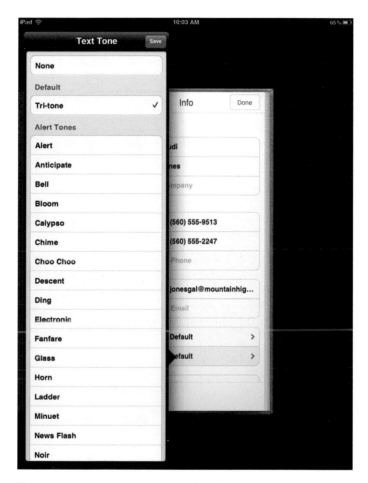

Figure 5-14: Choose from these available ringtones.

3. **Tap a tone to preview it.**

4. **When you hear a tone you like, tap Save.**

5. **Tap Done to save the new tone setting.**

If your Apple devices are synced via iCloud, setting a unique ringtone for an iPad contact also sets it for your iPhone. See Book I, Chapter 5 for more about iCloud.

Finding Contacts

You can use the Spotlight Search feature to find a contact in the Contacts app by looking for that person's first or last name or a company name. This feature on the iPad is much like every search feature you've ever used. It's somewhat simple in comparison to others because you can search only for names and because no advanced search techniques are available.

You can also use the Spotlight Search feature to locate contacts that match specified search criteria. The Spotlight screen is the leftmost Home screen when you scroll the screens.

Follow these steps to search for a contact:

1. **With Contacts open, tap in the Search field at the top of the left page (see Figure 5-15).**

   The onscreen keyboard opens.

   Tap in the Search field

Figure 5-15: Easily search for contacts.

2. **Type the first letter of either the first or last name or company name.**

   All matching results appear, as shown in Figure 5-16. In the example, typing **N** displays `Nancy Boysen`, `Nellie Dillon`, and `Space Needle` in the results, which all have *N* as the first letter in either their first or last name.

3. **Tap a contact's name in the results to display that person's information on the page on the right (refer to Figure 5-16).**

You can't search by address, phone number, or website in Contacts (at the time this book was written), though you can search by these criteria using Spotlight Search.

Search results

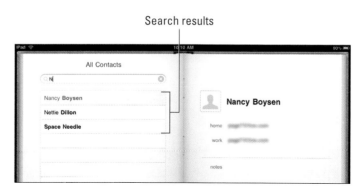

Figure 5-16: Search results narrow as you type.

You can use the alphabetical listing to locate a contact: Tap and drag to scroll the list of contacts on the All Contacts page on the left. You can also tap any tabbed letter along the left side of the page to scroll quickly to entries starting with that letter (refer to Figure 5-15).

Using Contacts Beyond Your iPad

Contacts isn't simply a static database of names and addresses. After you've entered contact information into the app, you can use the information to reach out to people in several useful ways. You can jump to a contact's website to see what she, or her company, is up to online; use a contact's e-mail information to quickly send an e-mail message; share the contact information with somebody else; or find the physical address of the contact by using the iPad Maps app.

Visiting a contact's website

Everybody (well, almost everybody) now has a website, so whether your contact is a person or an international conglomerate, you're likely to find an associated website that you might want to access now and then. You can access it from your iPad by using the Contacts app.

If you entered information in the Home Page field of a contact, the text you entered automatically becomes a link in the contact's record. With Contacts open, tap a contact to display the person's contact information on the page at the right and then tap the link in the Home Page field, as shown in Figure 5-17.

The Safari browser opens with the web page displayed, as shown in Figure 5-18.

Tap this link

Figure 5-17: Tap to go to a web page related to a contact.

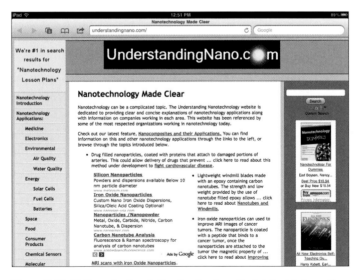

Figure 5-18: Visit contact websites to check on their latest information.

You cannot return directly to Contacts after you follow a link to a website. You have to tap the Home button and then tap the Contacts app icon again to reenter the application. Or, you can use the multitasking feature to get back to Contacts by double-tapping the Home button and choosing Contacts from the icons that appear along the bottom of the screen.

Addressing e-mails using contacts

If you've entered an e-mail address for a contact, the address automatically converts to a link in the record that allows you to open an e-mail form and send a message. This shortcut is handy for getting in touch.

First, be sure that you've entered an e-mail address in the contact's record and then follow these steps:

1. **Tap the Contacts app icon on the Home screen to open Contacts.**

2. **Tap a contact to display her contact information on the page on the right, and then tap the e-mail address link labeled Home, as shown in Figure 5-19.**

   The New Message dialog appears, as shown in Figure 5-20. The title bar of this dialog initially reads *New Message* but changes, as you type on the Subject line, to the specific title, as shown in the figure.

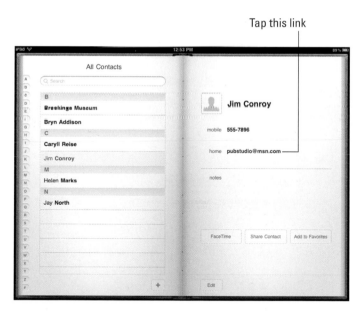

Figure 5-19: Tap to open a new e-mail message.

3. **Use the onscreen keyboard to enter a subject and a message.**

4. **Tap the Send button.**

   The message goes on its way!

Figure 5-20: A new e-mail message form.

Sharing contacts

After you've entered contact information, you can share it with others in an e-mail message. Sharing is especially handy when you store locations in Contacts, such as your favorite restaurant or movie theater.

Here's how to share your contacts' information:

1. **With Contacts open, tap a contact name to display its information.**

2. **On the Information page, tap the Share Contact button, as shown in Figure 5-21.**

3. **In the dialog that appears, tap either Email or Message.**

   The New Message form appears.

Tap this button

Figure 5-21: Easily share contact information with others.

4. **On the New Message form, shown in Figure 5-22, use the onscreen keyboard to enter the recipient's e-mail address.**

| Cancel | New Message | Send |

To: eb@buildinggadgets.com

Cc/Bcc:

Subject: |

Space Needle.vcf

Sent from my iPad

Figure 5-22: If you like, enter a subject and a message.

5. **Enter information in the Subject field.**

6. **If you like, enter a message and then tap the Send button.**

   The message goes to your recipient with the contact information attached as a .vcf file (in the *vCard* format, commonly used to transmit contact information).

Someone who receives a vCard containing contact information simply clicks the attached file to open it. At that point, the recipient can perform various actions (depending on the e-mail or contact-management program she's using) to save the content. Other iPhone or iPad users can easily import .vcf records into their own Contacts apps.

Viewing a Contact's Location in Maps

If you've entered a person's street address in Contacts, you have a shortcut for viewing that person's location in the Maps app. Once again, this is useful for places you need to visit for the first time, such as several clients' offices on that next business trip.

Follow these steps to pinpoint your contacts in the iPad Maps app:

1. **To open the Contacts app, click its icon on the Home screen.**

2. **Tap the contact you want to view to display his information.**

3. **Tap the address.**

   Maps opens and displays a map of the address, as shown in Figure 5-23.

Figure 5-23: Click the information bar to view more details in the Maps app.

 You can use information stored in Contacts to access more than your friends' addresses: You can also save information about your favorite restaurant or movie theater or any other location and then use Contacts to jump to the associated website in the Safari browser or to the address in Maps.

 After you jump to a contact's location in Maps, you may want to use the features of Maps to display different views, determine the condition of traffic on that route, or calculate the route between two locations. For more about using the Maps application, see Book III, Chapter 2.

Deleting Contacts

Remember that iPad's memory is limited compared to your standard computer. Though a contact record is tiny compared to a TV show, there's no sense keeping lots of old records around when you no longer need them. When you need to remove a name or two from your Contacts, doing so is easy.

 To make a wholesale update of your contacts, sync with iTunes, where you can choose to sync your Google, Outlook, Windows, Mac Address Book, or Yahoo! contacts to your iPad or coordinate contacts across devices using the MobileMe subscription service.

Follow these steps to delete contacts on iPad:

1. **With Contacts open, tap the contact you want to delete.**

2. **On the information page on the right, tap the Edit button.**

3. **On the Info page that displays, drag your finger upward to scroll down (if necessary) and then tap the Delete Contact button at the bottom, as shown in Figure 5-24.**

   The confirmation dialog shown in Figure 5-25 appears.

4. **Tap the Delete button to confirm the deletion.**

Tap this button

Figure 5-24: Tap this red bar and your contact record is gone forever.

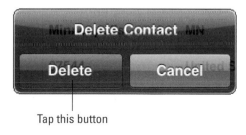

Tap this button

Figure 5-25: Tap the Delete button to confirm.

 During this process, if you change your mind before you tap Delete, tap the Cancel button in Step 4. But be careful because after you tap Delete, the only way to put it back is to resync with your computer, assuming you haven't deleted it there!

Book VI

Must-Have iPad Apps

The 5th Wave   By Rich Tennant

"Hold on Barbara. I'm pretty sure there's an app for this."

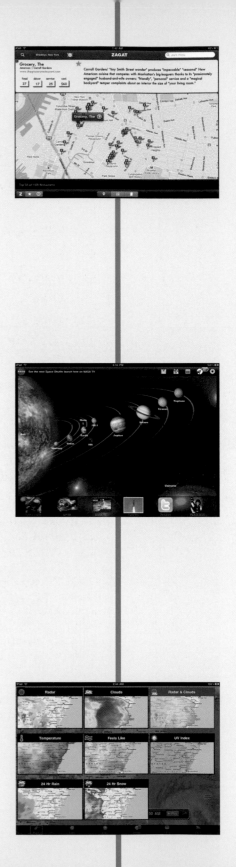

*O*kay, you probably roamed around earlier parts of this book and picked up some useful information and advice. Now it's time to just play around with the wonderful world of apps out there, and let's face it, there's an app for just about everything. The first two chapters in this part cover apps that help you conduct business or arrange your next trip. Chapter 3 gets you thinking about the possibilities of social web apps to stay in touch with all your online friends through Facebook, Twitter, blogs, and more. Chapter 4 covers news and weather, so you'll always be in the know and dry. Chapter 5 provides information on apps that help with your finances, while Chapter 6 is pure entertainment.

Chapter 1: Business Apps

In This Chapter

- ✓ iWork
- ✓ Quickoffice Connect Mobile Suite
- ✓ Dropbox
- ✓ Dragon Dictation
- ✓ OmniGraffle
- ✓ iThoughtsHD
- ✓ iAnnotate PDF
- ✓ PowerME
- ✓ Prompster and Teleprompt+ for iPad

One compelling strength of all Apple iOS devices is the App Store — and its thousands of apps you can download and then use to do just about anything you might want to do. (*iOS* is the name of the operating system that runs the iPad, iPhone, and iPod touch.) In this chapter, I show you some of the best apps for business, including some useful productivity apps. I tell you the qualities that make the app stand out and describe things you can do with it so that you can decide whether you need it on your iPad.

Some of the apps I describe in this chapter were written specifically for the iPad; others, however, were written by their developers to run as native apps on both the iPad and iPhone (or iPod touch) — the plus-sign (+) symbol appears next to the prices of these *hybrid* apps. You can buy a hybrid app and then use it on whatever iOS devices you own.

For the latest iPad updates, be sure to check out my website at www.ipadmadeclear.com.

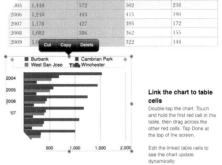

iWork

by Apple, Inc.

$9.99 per application

What you can do with it: *Pages:* Write letters and reports. *Numbers:* Create and manage spreadsheets. *Keynote:* Make gorgeous, professional-looking presentations.

iWork is Apple's productivity suite, made up of Pages, Numbers, and Keynote. Book IV covers the basics of using these apps. This chapter helps you decide whether they're right for you.

 Pages is Apple's advanced word processor and page layout program for the Mac, and now for the iPad. It's one of the best apps available to demonstrate on the iPad how the touchscreen interface can be used to get things done.

Pages for iPad was built from the ground up to create letters, résumés, thank-you notes and cards, newsletters, proposals, reports, term papers, and even posters and flyers. It's a pretty darn good layout app, as well.

Everything in the iWork app was designed to be accomplished by making gestures (pinch, zoom, tap, and swipe) and using the onscreen keyboard, including layout and formatting and placing graphics such as photos, charts, and graphs. The app comes supplied with 16 templates and a library of tables, customizable charts, and shapes. You can also add photos from your photo libraries, as I did in Figure 1-1, including any images you may have created in another iPad app and saved to your photo library.

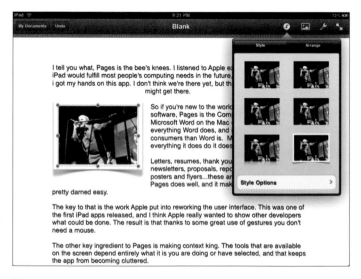

Figure 1-1: Picking a style for the inserted photo.

One cool characteristic of Pages is the way objects work. After you drop, say, a photo into your document, you can move the photo, resize it, change its presentation style, or even rotate it — and the text simply autoflows around it in real time. The app makes layout and design so easy on your iPad that you may have to try it to truly appreciate it.

Pages works with Apple's free `www.iwork.com` site, so you can share your Pages documents directly on the web.

For more on the Pages app, see Book IV, Chapter 2.

The Numbers spreadsheet app is useful for working with small-business and home-office spreadsheets, maintaining budgets and logs, and organizing teams and other group competitions. It's an even better app for turning your spreadsheets and data into gorgeous charts and graphs that you can use to make your reports, presentations, and other documents look great.

As in Pages, all tasks in Numbers were designed to be done by making gestures. Filling in data in a spreadsheet, changing colors, adding a chart or graph, resizing documents — all these tasks can be completed quickly and easily on your iPad. You can see a sample chart and data set in Figure 1-2. Some tasks are even easier and faster to complete using this app on the iPad than performing them on your desktop computer using a full-blown spreadsheet application.

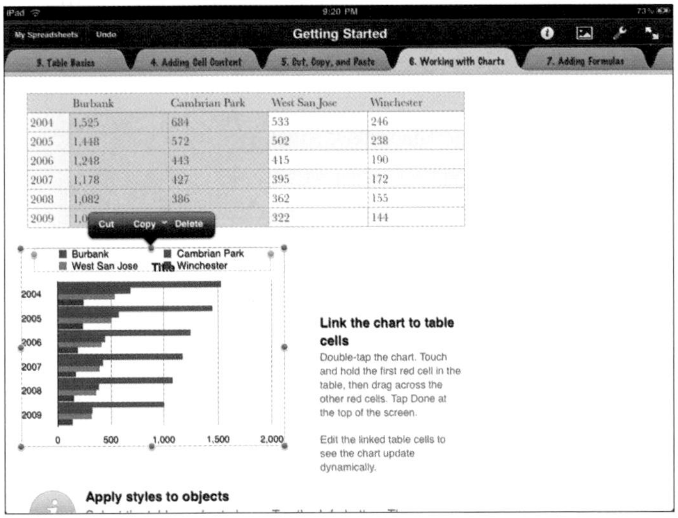

Figure 1-2: Double-tap an element in your spreadsheet to pull up resizing handles and the Cut/Copy/Delete menu.

Numbers comes supplied with 16 templates (checklists, budgets, invoices, schedules, and rosters, for example), and the library of charts and graphs contains nine different varieties for you to use. All nine types feature several different color palette choices that can then be further edited. The same statement applies to the included shapes: You can edit the color, style, and other attributes in just a few taps.

For more on the Numbers app, see Book IV, Chapter 3.

Keynote on the iPad makes great-looking presentations and is just about as feature rich as Keynote on a Mac, which makes it better than PowerPoint for Mac or Windows. Keynote is perfect for anyone wanting to work on a presentation on the go.

All 16 terrific-looking Keynote templates include several premade slides that comport to a different theme (such as Modern Portfolio, Showroom, Chalkboard, or Photo Portfolio, which you can see in Figure 1-3). You can create your own presentation without a template, of course, but if you want to start with a style all laid out for you, try using a template.

Figure 1-3: Choosing a transition in a Keynote presentation.

Most of the time, a presentation is displayed on a projector or another type of large display; if you have a small group, however (say, a couple of customers or your boss), you can simply create a presentation in Keynote and display it directly on your iPad!

After you're working on a presentation, you have access to awesome transitions and effects, each of which has options and controls that are a breeze to understand and use. You can add photos and images from your photo library, and the app has the same charts, graphs, and shapes that come with Pages and Numbers. Creating new slides is easy, and editing them is even easier.

For more on the Keynote app, see Book IV, Chapter 4.

Quickoffice Connect Mobile Suite

by Quickoffice, Inc.

$14.99

What you can do with it: Create and edit word processing and spreadsheet documents in the Microsoft Word and Excel formats. You can also view PowerPoint files, but you can't edit them.

This app is intended for people who are more comfortable using Microsoft Word and Excel than Apple's iWork approach. Quickoffice Connect Mobile Suite for iPad is built on the same paradigms as Word and Excel — in fact, its *raison d'être* is to view, create, and edit files in Microsoft Office file formats. You can switch among your Mac, PC, and iPad with Word and Excel files (you can view PowerPoint files only with Quickoffice, as of this writing), as long as you use DOC, DOCX, TXT, XLS, XLSX, XLT, and XLTX file formats. Unless and until Microsoft brings the real deal to iOS, Quickoffice is the best way to work on your Office files on the iPad in an Office-y kind of way.

Another useful aspect of Quickoffice is that it has Dropbox support built into it. The excellent Dropbox utility gives you access to files on a variety of devices, including iPad. (I talk about Dropbox in more detail in the next section.) With Dropbox support in Quickoffice, you can create a Word document on your PC at work and put it in your Dropbox. Then, when you're at the coffee shop that afternoon and you need to edit it, simply open it from your Dropbox in Quickoffice on your iPad. When you get home to your Mac, you can open the file from Dropbox there, too! If for some bizarre reason Dropbox doesn't float your boat, Quickoffice also supports Google Docs, MobileMe, and Box (www.box.net).

The Quickoffice Connect Mobile Suite app offers a nifty navigation tool, too: Press and hold the right margin in a multipage document to see the thumbnail view of all pages in your document, as shown in Figure 1-4. Just slide your finger down the page until you see the thumbnail of the page you want to jump to, and you're there. It's a nifty feature.

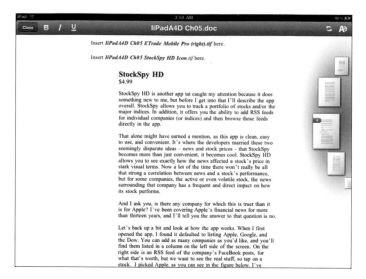

Figure 1-4: Using the cool thumbnail-navigation feature to go to another page.

Quickoffice doesn't have a lot of fancy formatting tricks, like Pages and Numbers do, but it's the best app to use if you have to, or are accustomed to, working with Microsoft Office, OpenOffice, or another Office-like productivity suite.

Dropbox

by Dropbox

Free — Hybrid

What you can do with it: Access important files on your iPad anywhere you have an Internet connection.

 If you're doing serious work on your iPad, whether it's for business or another type of task, Dropbox is the easiest and best way to move files from your iPad to any other computer or device, or from another device to your iPad.

Let me back up a bit. The Dropbox *cloud-based service* lets you store your files on the provider's servers and access those files from any device that's connected to the Internet. Dropbox directly supports (in the form of dedicated software) Windows, Mac OS X, Linux, Android, BlackBerry — and, of course, iOS. Even if you're using another operating system (such as webOS, Windows Mobile, or Sun Solaris), or if you don't have Dropbox installed on the device you're using now, you can access your files by using a web browser.

When you're using a computer, Dropbox works like any other folder on your hard drive. You open Dropbox and see all your files, for instantaneous access. An item you drop into a folder is copied to the company's servers and then pushed out to any location where you've set up a Dropbox account, including on the iPad.

A Dropbox folder can be selectively shared with other Dropbox users, making it a helpful tool for any sort of collaborative project.

Apple has provided us with iCloud to share documents among Apple devices, and you might use apps that support Apple iTunes File Sharing. Still, as a power user, you need a solution like Dropbox to share all your content among Apple and non-Apple devices.

Dropbox works on your iPad in two ways. First, you download this free app from the App Store and find all your Dropbox files and folders. Second, using the iOS Open With feature, you can tap a file to select it and then tap the Sharing icon in the upper-right corner, as shown in Figure 1-5, to choose which supporting app to send your file to for editing or another task.

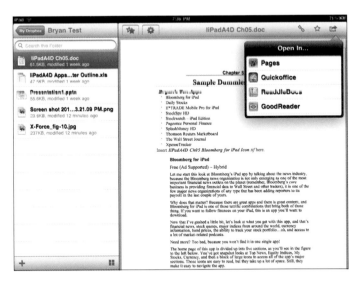

Figure 1-5: Using the Open With feature in iOS to open a Pages document in My Dropbox with the Pages app.

The Dropbox file preview feature shows you the contents of the file you have highlighted (refer to Figure 1-5). The file preview, which supports many major file formats, lets you easily pick the app you want to work with on your iPad.

iOS app developers can add Dropbox functionality directly to their apps, like the Quickoffice folks did in the Quickoffice Connect Mobile Suite app (discussed in the preceding section). You can work with your files even more easily in these apps. I hope to see more apps take advantage of the services that Dropbox can provide.

If you want to easily move files on and off your iPad, Dropbox is currently the best way to do so.

Dragon Dictation

by Dragon Naturally Speaking

Free — Hybrid

What you can do with it: Input words by speaking them instead of keying them. Edit and share text.

If you prefer to speak to your iPad rather than tap it, consider getting Dragon Dictation. The mobile version of Dragon Naturally Speaking speech recognition software is darn simple for anyone to use, but if you're a busy professional who breaks a wrist playing handball or suffers another mishap that limits your typing ability, it might even save your hide.

With Dragon, you speak and the app turns your speech into text typed on the screen. To be honest, recognition is the name of the game for any speech recognition program, and none of these apps is perfect. After you record yourself speaking, you will find that certain words don't sound quite right. (The word *darling* somehow worked its way into a paragraph from a review at the Macworld site — and I don't even know the author of the article.)

Don't worry: Part of the tool set in Dragon includes the ability to easily edit text to make corrections. (See Figure 1-6.) When the text matches exactly what you said, you can then easily cut or copy the text and paste it into a word processor or send it by e-mail. You can even find tools for posting the text you speak on your Twitter or Facebook account.

Settings allow you to choose which language to use, including the usual language suspects English, French, German, Italian, and Spanish. Dragon is quite handy for taking trips abroad when you can speak in English and your waiter can read what you say in his own language. (Just hope that no *darling* glitches work their way in.)

One interesting feature of Dragon is its ability to import all your contacts into its database to help it recognize the names you speak.

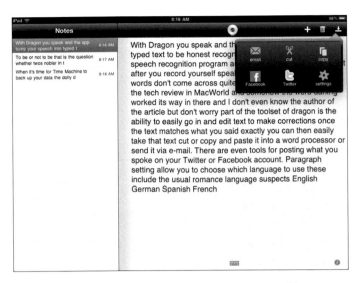

Figure 1-6: Tools allow you to work with the text generated from your speech.

Dragon is free, so why not install it and give it a whirl? It's fun to watch what you say being preserved in print!

Quick Hits

This section describes several apps you should check out.

OmniGraffle

by The Omni Group

$49.99

OmniGraffle is a somewhat expensive iPad app, but it's worth the cost if you need to make flowcharts or diagrams. The app is as intuitive as the apps in Apple's iWork suite, and it's a breeze to work with. OmniGraffle comes supplied with a wide array of customizable tools that let you make anything from basic flowcharts to complex drawings, such as the full espresso machine that The Omni Group includes in a sample chart in the app. Anyone who considers flowcharts, process charts, floor plans, diagrams, and other types of charts important will find that OmniGraffle on the iPad makes them rethink what they can do on a tablet device.

You can open on your iPad any OmniGraffle apps that were created in the Mac version of the software — or vice versa!

iThoughtsHD
by Craig Scott

$9.99

When you engage in *mind mapping,* you use a diagram to show the structure of an idea or plan and highlight the relationships between different aspects of that idea or plan. Many mind-mapping apps are available for Mac and Windows, but only a few (so far) are on the iPad. The dedicated iThoughtsHD mind-mapping app is the best one I've found, and it has easy-to-use tools for quickly developing your own maps. This area is one that's ideally suited to the tablet-in-your-lap form factor.

iAnnotate PDF
by Aji, LLC

$9.99

If you simply want to be able to view PDF files on your iPad, check out GoodReader for iPad. This useful app costs only 99 cents. If you need to be able to annotate or mark up PDF files on your iPad, check out iAnnotate PDF instead. It lets you quickly and easily highlight text, add notes, draw lines, strike out or underline text, or even doodle in the margins, if that's your thing. Workers in certain professions need to be able to annotate PDF files, and this app makes doing so on your iPad so easy that you might want to move all those tasks from your computer to your iPad.

PowerME HD
by AppTime, LLC

$29.99

If you manage projects, consider buying PowerME HD. This handy (though not cheap) app helps you organize your workflow, collaborate with team members, and sync all your plans in the cloud. If you're a mobile professional, these tools come in handy for keeping track of your work and your team's activities. Create and manage projects, juggle deadlines, and organize tasks in your PowerME inbox. Check out the Drawing feature, which can quickly change the old way of creating preliminary plans, by jotting them down on napkins in hotel coffee shops.

Prompster and Teleprompt+ for iPad
by Dante Varnado Moore and Gene Whitaker (respectively)

$9.99 and $9.99

In addition to all the other things your iPad can do, it can serve as a portable teleprompter, useful for giving speeches and other presentations. I recommend Prompster and Teleprompt+ for iPad. Prompster lets you record your speech right there on your iPad as you're giving it, and it has great onscreen controls. Teleprompt+ for iPad has more and better options for controlling your speech, though it has no recorder function, as of this writing. For more control over timing, display colors, and other factors, though, Teleprompt+ for iPad is the better pick.

Chapter 2: Travel Apps

In This Chapter

I love to travel, but I'll be the first to tell you that I'm not very organized before or during (or after!) my outings. Fortunately, there are a lot of iPad apps that can help me — and you — with that. There are apps for booking travel and accommodations, apps to show you where to go, apps for tracking flights, and even apps for helping you find local services and other information. In this chapter, I show you some of these apps so you can use your iPad to make your trips more fun, more efficient, and maybe even hassle-free. (But don't hold me to that last one!)

Many of the apps I talk about in this chapter are apps that were written for the iPad. Some apps, however, have been written by the developer to run as native apps on both the iPad and iPhone (or iPod touch). These are called *hybrid* apps, and you'll find a little + sign next to the price for those apps. Hybrid apps have the advantage of allowing you to buy once and use on whatever iOS device you have.

KAYAK HD — Flights, Hotels, Explore

by KAYAK Software Group

Free

> **What you can do with it:** Find flights, rental cars, and hotels, or use the Explore feature to find destinations you might not even realize you want to visit.

 You may be familiar with KAYAK as an online travel service. Or you may have used the company's iPhone apps, but either way, you should check out KAYAK HD — Flights, Hotels, Explore. This free app offers the standard flight search features, but it also has some cool features like Explore that may help you have a little fun, too.

KAYAK claims to offer the fastest flight search in the world. I can't speak to the claim of fast*est,* but it's definitely fast. The interface is straightforward and easy to use and understand. Plug in your From and To airports, your Departure and Return dates, number of passengers, class of flight (Economy, Business, First), and whether you prefer nonstop flights, and then tap Search. On the left side of Figure 2-1, you can see that I was looking for some flights from San Francisco to New York City in September, and in the Search History pane, you can see past searches. That's very handy if you're comparing prices between different date ranges and/or locations. You'll also see a map of my route. (In landscape mode, you also get a separate pane for recommended hotel deals.)

Figure 2-1: Search results for a cross-country flight (left) and the Explore interface for finding flights to destinations around the world (right).

There's also a pane called Hot Searches from *Your Departure City* that shows some great deals to random cities from the departure city you entered. These are deals that other KAYAK users found, and you never know when you might see a destination or killer price that strikes your fancy.

When you perform a search, you get a list of all the flights from the major airlines that service that route. A progress bar lets you know the status of your search. You can order the search results by Price, Airline, Stops, Duration, and Class. (Some search results may include a mix of classes, even though you specified a particular class.) You can also toggle any particular airline (or other factors) on or off from a list on the right side of the screen.

Under the Filter pane, tap the Price tab to get a slider that limits your search results from the cheapest flight in the list to a maximum price. This can limit the amount of scrolling you need to do.

I like this interface for searching and filtering my results, and I bet you will, too. You can also search for cars and hotels, and there's a Deals section that includes various vacation packages and other travel deals to and from different cities around the world. The Deals section is really a web page being served up through an in-app browser, and these pages include sponsored links to vacation packages and flights. Those sponsored links were not generated by the KAYAK engine, so be careful about what you tap in the Deals page if you want to limit yourself to KAYAK-searched results.

But let's talk about that fun feature I mentioned. It's called Explore, and with it you can choose your departure city and quickly get flight destinations to cities all over the world. It works like this: Set your city, and you'll get a map of the planet with orange dots all over it, as shown on the right side of Figure 2-1. Each of those dots represents a flight. Pinch and zoom in far enough, and those dots become red rectangles with prices in them. Tap a rectangle (or a dot), and you get a little pop-up window with the name of the destination city and a date range that the price represents. Tap that square, and you're taken to the Flights search page so you can see all flights to that city.

But it gets even cooler because there are three tabs at the bottom of the screen, as you can see on the right side of the figure. The When tab lets you specify a date range; the What tab lets you specify activities (Golf, Beach, Gambling, Skiing) and a temperature range (how cool is that?); and the Flight tab lets you specify whether you want nonstop flights and a maximum travel time. Tweak these as you want, and the dots (or rectangles) are filtered accordingly!

I realize that this isn't a great feature for planning a business trip, but how about for planning a vacation or a get-away-from-it-all trip? I think it's just great for finding a place to visit that you might not otherwise have considered.

Under the Settings menu, you can specify the currency you want to see your prices in. It defaults to U.S. dollars, but there are a dozen currencies to choose from.

You can sign in with your KAYAK account login, but you don't have to do so to use the flight search and other features of the app.

There are lots of travel sites and services, but KAYAK is one of the best apps on the iPad for finding a flight. It's also one of the only apps that will help you if you don't know where you want to go!

Wikihood Plus for iPad

by Dr. Stephan Gillmeier

$6.99

What you can do with it: Find nearby sights, landmarks, buildings, and shopping destinations, all with links to their Wikipedia entries for in-depth information.

I'm not that great a tourist. No, seriously, when I travel I want to hang out with local friends in local (nonchain) restaurants and coffee shops. If there's sidewalk seating, all the better! I don't want to rush around ogling every tourist trap and monument that I could squeeze into the four hours I allotted to this city or that village. I don't rush around, and I don't get up early, unless there's a very compelling reason to do so. On the one hand, I enjoy traveling this way. On the other, there's a lot of stuff I don't get around to seeing even when I do want to take the time to sightsee, in part because I often don't even know it's there. Wikihood Plus for iPad is the kind of app that might solve this issue for me, and it might even change the way I travel.

Wikihood Plus for iPad is an app that taps into that vast reservoir of (mostly accurate) information known as Wikipedia. Using either your current location or a location you pick, Wikihood Plus tells you what's nearby, based on the millions of entries in Wikipedia. The creator said his app "intelligently organizes Wikipedia information for any place in the world using advanced semantic data mining." In other words, the app digs into Wikipedia for you and uses algorithms to sift through that data to show you what's near you, what's significant, and how to get there. Building further on the wiki theme, there are thousands of in-app user ratings, too.

A *wiki* is a website that can be edited by its users, which usually means anyone and everyone. Some wikis have no oversight, while others have professional editors or moderators. Wikipedia is an encyclopedia that is comprised of information supplied by its users, and there are hundreds of thousands of contributors around the world! It's far more often than not accurate info, though that's certainly not always the case. In recent years, however, the organization behind the project has increased the amount of oversight that entries and edits are given. But if you have any questions, you should probably check with another source just to be sure.

Let's say I am visiting New York City and am ready to leave from hanging out in Central Park. If I open Wikihood Plus and let it use my current location (you'll need an Internet connection for that!), it shows me that the Museum of Natural History's subway stop is right next to me (and the museum itself is close, too), and a really cool apartment building (if you like looking at architecture) and the Hayden Planetarium are nearby, as you can see on the left side of Figure 2-2. If I scroll farther down, there are more museums, galleries, theaters, historical societies, and schools than I could shake a stick at, even if I had a really big stick!

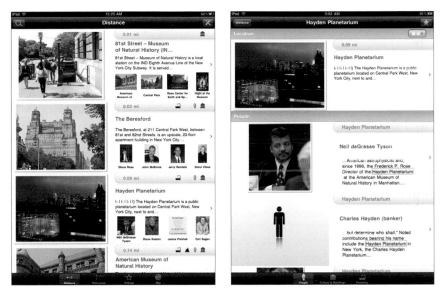

Figure 2-2: Search results for locations near me (left) and info on the Hayden Planetarium, including other Wikipedia entries relating to it (right).

If I tap the Hayden Planetarium entry, I'm taken to a new page, as you can see on the right side of the figure. That page has more entries that relate to the planetarium, and I can drill down for more information. For instance, when I tap the top entry for the planetarium, I get the full Wikipedia entry for the page, all laid out nice and pretty for my iPad.

In the image on the right in Figure 2-2, you'll see a star icon at the top of the screen. Tap the star to rate the main place described in the main entry — in this case, the Hayden Planetarium.

There are additional tabs on the bottom of the screen, too, that allow you to filter the entries you see relating to a particular location. When you have drilled down to the entry on a specific location, those icons include a link to directions (which takes you to the iPad's Maps app).

I love this app, and while I intend to use it for traveling, I've even learned things about my neighborhood and city that I hadn't known before. If you're the type of traveler who is curious about what's near, you need this app.

Urbanspoon for iPad

by Wanderspot, LLC

Free

What you can do with it: Find nearby restaurants based on your location, or based on the city or neighborhood you choose. The app has a great random search feature that gives you as much, or as little, control over your results as you want.

I think a lot of people consider Urbanspoon an app that solves the "I don't know; where do you want to eat?" eternal quandary, but to me, it has a lot of value as a travel companion, especially when you're visiting an unfamiliar place where you don't have any friends (or a good concierge) to give you advice.

The basic premise of the app is to let you find restaurants by randomly choosing from various cuisines, price points, and different neighborhoods on three slot machine reels. Shake your iPad (or tap the Shake button) and you get a random suggestion for where to eat. If you don't like the result, shake it again. If you want to limit your options, say to a particular neighborhood or a type of food, you can lock one, two, or even all three reels to try to find a particular kind of restaurant.

When you get a restaurant you like, just tap its name and you'll see a screen with its address, phone number, kind of restaurant, Urbanspoon user rating, cost rating (connoted by one, two, or three dollar signs), and reviews of the place (where applicable).

Tap various items on the screen to reveal details such as hours, a menu (sometimes), more about the restaurant's user rating (such as how many people voted), the opportunity to submit your own rating, suggestions of other restaurants you might like, an advertisement (it's an ad-supported app), and directions in Google Maps, as you can see on the right side of Figure 2-3.

Figure 2-3: All about Joe The Art of Coffee (left) and locking in my search for a coffee shop in the West Village, in the $10 or less range (right).

If you really like (or hate) a place, take the time to contribute to the user ratings, and make sure you leave a written review. More importantly, think about the kinds of reviews that you find helpful and include similar information in yours. ("This place rocks" isn't any more helpful than "This place stinks.")

Since I'm talking about Urbanspoon as a travel app, I should also note that Google Maps is embedded right in the app. When you are viewing the app in Map mode, all of the results come up on the map that dominates two-thirds of your screen, as shown on the right side of the figure. When you Shake for a restaurant, the map zooms to that location's neighborhood, with the selected restaurant and other restaurants nearby represented by pins in the map. This makes it easy to quickly look at what other options you have in that neighborhood.

The more popular a restaurant is with Urbanspoon's users, the darker its pin will be. If you tap the Show Popular button in the upper-left corner of the map, all the light blue pins go away. Also, the restaurant that is currently selected is denoted by a bright red pin, as you can see on the right side of Figure 2-3.

Using the map to display the results this way cuts a couple of steps out of the process of using Urbanspoon for iPad, and being a visual learner, I really like it. There's a list mode, as well, but it shows only the most popular restaurants in the city you're looking at.

This is some of my favorite advice to give to people who have even an ounce of adventure in them: Instead of spinning and spinning until you get a result that's familiar to you, try limiting yourself to one shake and sticking to whatever comes up. Oh yeah, it could be awful, but it might also be great! This is a must-have app if you're going to be traveling and don't have every second of every day already planned. With Urbanspoon, finding a restaurant is only a shake away.

Yelp is another great app for this sort of crowd-sourced finding of nearby restaurants, and I recommend both it and Urbanspoon for the traveler.

ZAGAT TO GO

by Handmark, Inc.

$9.99 — Hybrid

What you can do with it: Find nearby restaurants that have been reviewed and rated by ZAGAT. You can get directions, hours of operation, features of the restaurant, contact information and the menu, and many restaurants have links to their websites.

While I'm talking about finding good restaurants whilst traveling, I should mention ZAGAT TO GO, which represents a different approach for a restaurant guide. There's a time and place for crowd sourcing, but ZAGAT TO GO offers reviews compiled by professional editors based on customer surveys, and in an age where budget-constrained newspapers are cutting back on local coverage like restaurant reviews, ZAGAT is the kind of resource that will only become more valuable as time goes on, especially with iOS devices.

ZAGAT is one of the most comprehensive restaurant guides on the planet, and this hybrid iPhone, iPod touch, and iPad app gives you access to thousands of restaurant reviews, a GPS-enabled restaurant locator, the ability to search for restaurants according to multiple criteria, and more. This is definitely a must-have app for foodies, and unlike the print version (once you buy it), the app is constantly updated with new reviews.

Because ZAGAT is not a crowd-sourced guide, its reviews are limited to major metropolitan areas. That means you should check to make sure the areas where you're intending to use it are actually covered.

ZAGAT TO GO allows you to pick a city or use your iPad's Location Services to determine your current location. The interface itself is almost entirely dominated by a Google Maps display of the area, with ZAGAT-reviewed restaurants highlighted with Z pins. Tap a pin, and you'll get a pane at the top of the screen with basic information about the place, including its name; its food, décor, and service ratings on a scale of 0-30; along with the average cost of a meal (including one drink and a tip). You'll also find the beginning of the ZAGAT review, which will often be enough to let you know if you want to eat there.

In Figure 2-4, I'm looking at restaurants in Brooklyn, where I found The Grocery, which has a stunning 27 rating for its food, though it's what I'd call pricey, at $60 per meal.

**Book VI
Chapter 2**

Travel Apps

Figure 2-4: The Grocery is a very highly rated restaurant in Brooklyn.

If that isn't enough information for me, however, I can tap the pane to get a full-screen workup on the restaurant. This includes the hours of operation, features of the restaurant, address and phone number, an e-mail link, and the ability to drop the contact information directly to your iPad's Address Book! I really like that feature, and I hope to see it make its way to more apps in the future.

What's with all those quotes in a ZAGAT review? The company's editors compile their reviews from customer surveys, and they use (very) short quotes from those surveys throughout their reviews.

There's also a Star icon for adding the restaurant to your Favorites, and a little *i* (for *information*) icon you can tap to see an explanation of ZAGAT's review system. ZAGAT uses a 30-point scale, and if you're not familiar with just what those numbers mean, this is a very handy explanation that's just a tap away.

If you don't want to browse restaurants from a map, tap the icon that looks like six little boxes at the bottom of the screen to browse local restaurants in list form. You can sort by food, décor, and service ratings, by cost, or alphabetically. Just swipe the screen to go to the next page, and tap any of the eight listings on each page to get the full-screen workup I mentioned previously.

Note that you'll need a connection to the Internet to make the most use of this app, as it pulls reviews from the company's servers. This will ensure you have the very latest information and most up-to-date reviews. You can, however, view reviews in your History and Favorites without a connection.

ZAGAT TO GO is the app for foodies or anyone who is interested in getting a more formal, organized, and edited approach in a restaurant guide. Whether you're traveling for business or pleasure, if you care about where you eat, take ZAGAT TO GO with you.

FlightTrack Pro – Live Flight Status Tracker by Mobiata

by Ben Kazez

$9.99 — Hybrid

What you can do with it: Track flights all over the globe. With integrated TripIt support, entering your flight information is super easy.

Ignore the long name and call this app what everyone else calls it, FlightTrack Pro. This app is great for when you're traveling, but it's also a good app to have when you're expecting friends, family, or business associates who are traveling to you! With it, you can track flights all over the world on a map, and you can do it in real time, too. In addition, it has integrated support for TripIt, which makes tracking those flights super easy.

I don't have any upcoming flights to show you of my own, but FlightTrack Pro has a fun little feature that allows you to shake your iPad to find a random flight. To be honest, this fun feature is easier to use on the iPhone, but it's still a great way to show off the app to your friends. You can also add flights by hand if you know the flight number, or search for them by route if you don't.

You can also make an in-app purchase for $3.99 to add the ability to search for flights according to the departing airport. Except for those who live in metro areas with two or three airports servicing travelers, most users aren't likely to need that ability, but if you're a flight junkie — and there are flight junkies out there, let me tell you — you won't want to miss it.

On the left side of Figure 2-5, I've picked several random flights in the United States. The pop-up window lists all the flights I am tracking, and I can remove any individual flight by tapping the little eyeball icon underneath the date. You can see take-off and landing times, status (the top flight is en route), and I can delete a flight by tapping the Edit button.

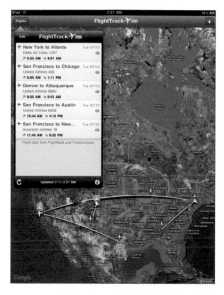

Figure 2-5: Monitoring several flights in the continental United States (left) and a push notification about a flight I was monitoring (right).

Now, on the map you'll see green and red squares, and an airplane icon and line representing each of the routes. The red squares are destinations, and the green ones are departure cities. If you tap those squares, you'll get a pop-up window with information and any warnings regarding that specific airport.

Tap a jet, and you'll find additional information about that flight. The pop-up window includes take-off and landing times, and on-time status, and if I scroll down, I get total air time, elapsed time, the remaining time for the flight, a weather forecast, and other information.

The mapping service is provided by Google, and it includes an overlay of live weather information, as you can see on both sides of the figure.

Most people aren't going to fire up this app just to watch random flights. Its main use is to monitor flights you actually care about. There are two key features that make this app very convenient for this use. The first is support for TripIt, a third-party service that monitors your flights for you. You can use TripIt to get e-mail notifications of status updates for your flight, and with support for the service in this app, you can use it to make entering your flight information easy. TripIt, which is free (there's a paid Pro level that FlightTrack Pro currently doesn't support), allows you to simply forward your itinerary to the company, and then they automagically grab all your flight (and other data) for you. When you enter your TripIt account information in FlightTrack Pro, it automatically looks to TripIt for any flights you are taking and presents them to you on a silver platter. No muss, no fuss!

The other key feature is the way the app uses Push Notification Service to send you any updates on the flights you are tracking. On the right side of Figure 2-5, you see a Push notification for a new arrival time for one of my flights. These Push notifications show up even if you don't have the app open, meaning you get those status updates without having to go look for them! And since this app is a hybrid app that works on your iPhone, iPod touch, and iPad, you're a lot more likely to find out when your wife is landing early or when your boss's flight has been canceled. Believe you me, this is a great feature, especially if you have to travel frequently or work with people who do.

You can e-mail flight information directly from the app, too. You'll appreciate this when you get a Push update that a flight has been delayed and need to send it to your co-worker or family member who is picking someone up.

FlightTrack Pro is gorgeous, and tracking a flight is fun (to me) even if I'm not involved with it. To me, it's a must-have app for anyone involved with any sort of semi-regular travel. It's more convenient on your iPhone when you're in the car, but it looks so great and is so much easier to use on your iPad that you'll use it there whenever you can.

Quick Hits

In addition to the apps discussed up to this point, here are some quick reviews of other apps worthy of your inspection.

INRIX Traffic! and INRIX Traffic! Pro

by INRIX, Inc.

Free; $9.99 per year or $24.99 for life

When you're traveling to another city, one thing you're not likely to have much knowledge of is local traffic. Of course, if you have to commute for 45 minutes each way just to get to work, you might consider that "travel," too. Whatever the case, INRIX Traffic! and its Pro counterpart can provide you with the kind of real-time traffic data that could be the difference in getting to that wedding, business meeting, dinner reservation, or maybe just your job, on time. The free version works well enough for most people, and it displays real-time conditions in Google Maps in a straightforward and easy-to-follow way. (It shows green lines for normal traffic, orange for slow, and red for heavy traffic.) The Pro version, which costs $9.99 per year or $24.99 for a lifetime subscription, offers you fastest-route information, expected travel time (and ETA), directions, the best time to leave, traffic cameras, and the ability to save frequent destinations. Try out the free one, and if you like it, you'll probably want the Pro version.

World Customs & Cultures

by Hooked In Motion, LLC

Free

Pay attention, because this is the only iPhone app that hasn't been updated for the iPad that I am recommending in this entire book within a book! World Customs & Cultures is a fantastic guide for local customs, attitudes, and other things (like taboos) that you'll need to know when traveling to another country. Greetings, Communication Style, Personal Space & Touching, Eye Contact, Views of Time, Gender Issues, Gestures, Taboos, and Law & Order information is offered for 165 countries! I wish I had this when I first went overseas, let me tell you! This app might also help you when dealing with foreign nationals visiting you. Sure, they should be learning your customs just like you're learning theirs, but understanding something like the fact that direct eye contact, in some cultures, is considered threatening can make a world of difference (Get it? *World?*) in helping to understand your foreign friends.

The World Clock

by Orlin Kolev

$1.99

Have you ever been traveling and picked up your phone to call your wife, husband, friend, or co-worker without realizing it was midnight where they are? Or maybe you've been on the other side of that, and someone who is important to you is traveling — and you just can't for the life of you remember what time it is in Japan? There are several apps for that, but my favorite is The World Clock. It shows up to 12 clocks at a time (they scale according to how many you choose), and you have lots of options for what is displayed. You can have the faces of the clocks indicate daylight/nighttime or business hours, and each clock can provide additional information, including local date, sunrise/sunset times, and more. It also features a beautiful map of the planet with real-time daylight and nighttime markings. Lastly, you can choose from two analog clock styles and one digital clock.

World Atlas HD

by The National Geographic Society

$1.99

Admittedly, this app will probably be of more use to you before you travel than when you are traveling, but it's so cool that I'll take any excuse to talk about it. World Atlas HD is produced by The National Geographic Society, so you know it has quality maps and information about countries around the world. It comes with a global map that you can pinch and zoom around to look at whatever part of the planet you care to check out. It features an Executive map, a Political Map, and a Satellite map. The first two are really just different styles for displaying countries, while the satellite map shows pictures of the areas as they appear from satellites orbiting the globe. With these maps, you can tap and hold a country to get some information about that country. You can tap the + button to bookmark that country, and that also places a pin on the map, which is handy for seeing which countries you have and haven't read about. All of these maps are available for online browsing, but you can also download them for offline (and faster) viewing, which I recommend.

WiFi Get HD

by WiTagg, Inc.

$2.99

 If you're traveling with an iPad, you should probably know where you can get a Wi-Fi hotspot. WiFi Get HD can tell you. It comes with 150,000 known free hotspots preinstalled, which means you can browse them even when you don't have a connection. If you have a connection but need to find a different hotspot, or you're planning ahead, you can access the company's online database of more than 200,000 free or paid hotspots. The app allows users to add hotspots they find (hopefully it's not the poor schmuck living near the coffee shop who didn't protect his network), or update known hotspots if their status changed. Wi-Fi is becoming more and more common, but it isn't yet ubiquitous. If you're traveling to a place you don't know well and plan to use your iPad, you should probably take this app with you.

Chapter 3: Social Web Apps

In This Chapter

*A*pps for social interaction online range from clients for gathering all your Facebook or Twitter-type postings in one environment to collections of pictures you can use when instant messaging and online content readers to follow your favorite blogs.

In this chapter, I give you an idea of some social-type apps you might want to explore. The good news: just about every one of them is free.

Friendly for Facebook

by Oecoway, Inc.

Free

What you can do with it: Do everything you usually do on Facebook with a simpler, friendlier interface.

Are you spending way more than the daily recommended allowance of time on Facebook? If so, you'll appreciate Friendly for Facebook. This app was specifically designed for iPad, which makes your Facebook experience — well — friendlier. One of its strengths is filtering your content in logical ways, so you can view things by updates, photos, videos, links, friends, or notes.

Other features are more subtle, enhancing the original Facebook experience in small but useful ways. For example, there's a full-screen photo viewer that lets you see more of your Facebook photos on the iPad screen.

When you're viewing the dizzying amount of constant social content coming at you, speed is also a factor. With Friendly for Facebook, your photos upload faster, you log in faster, and your chats move along with noticeable speed. Of course, the touchscreen experience on iPad adds an interesting dimension as you swipe your way through feeds and photos, truly getting in touch with your friends. There are also some customizing features in Friendly for Facebook that are appealing, including the ability to set colors and fonts up the way you want them.

If you have more than one Facebook account (and who doesn't?) you can switch among them on the fly. And if you want your friends to constantly know where you are, use the Share Where You Are with Your Friends feature that takes advantage of iPad's location technology.

Do be a bit cautious about using any location feature. If you've befriended friends of friends, who are essentially strangers, letting them know your every move might not be in your best interest. Want people to know when you're away from home so they can rip you off? Want your boss to see you're at the mall when you're supposed to be at a client's office? I'm just saying . . .

So how do Facebook and Friendly for Facebook really differ? Let's compare Home pages. On Facebook, you see categories like News Feed, Messages, Events, and Friends along the left side like a sort of navigation bar. On the right are suggestions of friends and sponsored links (ads). In Friendly for Facebook, whose Home page is shown in Figure 3-1, tabs replace the navigation bar in many cases. If you tap the Friends button at the top of the screen, you get another tabbed interface with Friends, Phonebook, and Pages (web pages) dividing information into simple sets.

iPad provides some interesting new functionality in this environment. For example, if you go to the Phonebook tab on the Friends page, you can just tap a phone number to place a call (assuming you're within range of Wi-Fi or have a 3G model). The Friendly menu gives you quick access for sharing Friendly for Facebook with friends, uploading photos, editing your profile, customizing Friendly, switching to another Facebook account, and more.

Bottom line, Friendly for Facebook provides a simple-to-use interface for Facebook customized for the iPad user. Some perks may be subtle, but collectively they make for a smooth iPad Facebook environment.

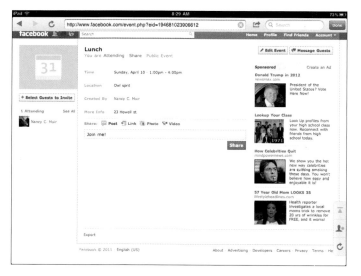

Figure 3-1: Friendly for Facebook's home screen.

Blogshelf

by gdiplus

99 cents

What you can do with it: Subscribe to and read blogs and news feeds. E-mail, Tweet, or post content to Facebook. Save images to an album in Photos.

Blogshelf is touted as "the iPad reader for the rest of us." It makes it possible to view lots of blogs (which is why I've put it in the social web category) and news feeds in one place, avoiding the native environment of these sites until or unless you want to visit them. The plus here is that you get to the content without weeding through the other stuff. If you want to jump to the originating site, you can, and then you can read or post comments to your heart's content.

Pick the blogs and news feeds (up to 90) that appeal to you most, and Blogshelf goes out and gathers content for you. One strength of this app is how easy it is to read blogs with it. It has an attractive magazine-like layout that's easy to navigate. (See Figure 3-2.) The layout gets rid of all the surrounding web page banners and ads you see on the original blog or news page, which is a very nice feature. And swiping through blog content or moving from one blog to the next with iPad's touchscreen feels effortless.

If you are intrigued by exploring blogs from other lands, you'll appreciate the feature for translating foreign languages into your own.

You can browse the blogs and feeds that come set up in Blogshelf or look for more content to subscribe to. Tap the Subscribe button to see a lot of featured blogs and news sites. If you prefer to view a blog in Safari, use the View in Safari or View Original Article links to go to the blog page online. At that point, you can leave replies to express your own ideas on the topic.

Figure 3-2: You can find a variety of blogs on special interests to subscribe to.

If you find something you like, you can e-mail it, tweet it, or publish it to Facebook. You can even save images from a blog or news story to an album in Photos. Don't like one of the presubscribed blogs? Tap the Edit button to delete it.

Another nice feature of this app is the ability to modify the screen brightness, font size, font color, and font style you use to read text. Your blogs are arranged neatly on a bookcase very reminiscent of the iBooks reader library bookshelf.

If you want an e-reader that focuses on blogs and news feeds, this might be one for you to check out.

Twitterific for Twitter

by NPR

Free

What you can do with it: Follow tweets from a variety of sources. Track Favorites and messages. Create customized searches.

Okay, so I admit, Twitter itself has a pretty simple interface, but Twitter clients can add some nice bells and whistles to the mix.

If you live to tweet, you should check out Twitterific for Twitter, which runs on both iPad and iPhone. This client is very popular with Mac users. It's easy to see why: It's very simple to use and sports a clean, intuitive interface. (See Figure 3-3.)

Each tweet offers access to a set of tools you can use to reply to the tweet, retweet, or retweet with comment. There are tools that let you translate a tweet or e-mail it. You can also display tweets in conversations to help you follow along with the crowd.

Figure 3-3: Twitterific shows tweets and conversations in a clean interface.

Don't have time to read all your favorite tweets in real time? If you want to keep track of tweets even when you're offline, you'll like the easy interaction Twitterific has with Instapaper, a $4.99 app you can use to save pages of content to read at your leisure later on.

Use the Trends feature (like the Top Trending Topics you see on Twitter's own site) to view some of the hottest Twitter topics, such as conversations about the latest developments on your favorite TV show or sports team.

Flipboard

by Flipboard, Inc.

Free — Hybrid

What you can do with it: Access Facebook and Twitter postings from a centralized location, as well as news content on topics such as Tech and Style. Add your own sections of news categories to follow.

One of the challenges in today's world is to keep up with all the information that's coming at you through a variety of sites and sources. Flipboard provides a visual way to organize and view all that content.

Now I have to admit, I'm a sucker for good design, and Flipboard is quite simply a nicely designed, graphical, magazine-style interface for accessing blogs, postings, and news in one place. Each item you're following is displayed in a section on the Flipboard home page (as shown in Figure 3-4).

Figure 3-4: Flipboard's interface is neat, clean, and graphical.

Sign into your Facebook or Twitter account and add a Flipboard section on a person to follow in the news as well as view their online postings. For example, you'd be amazed how active the Dalai Lama is online (see Figure 3-5);

there are pictures of his latest activities in the news as well as his comments. ("As human beings, we are all the same, there is no need to build some kind of artificial barrier between us," he posted at 2:36 a.m. one fine morning in April.)

Figure 3-5: The Dalai Lama in words and pictures.

You can add sections from the home page by tapping a blank block sporting the words *Add a Section.* You can also tap the Featured tab, tap some featured content to open that page, and then tap the Add to Contents button to add it as a section in Flipboard Contents.

In adding sections for Flipboard (you're limited to nine items on a page, but you can use your finger to flip to the next page to add more sections), you can choose a persona, list, or blog from Twitter for easy access to that content. There are also categories of news and blogs provided by Flipboard such as News, Business & Finance, and Tech & Science.

I'm particularly fond of the Cool Curators category, where you can follow folks like film critic Roger Ebert, New Yorker Writers, or Big Think, a very interesting blog on current events and politics. If you just can't decide what to view, tap the Featured tab on the Flipboard home page and choose a recommendation from there to view.

To delete a section that doesn't interest you anymore, tap the Edit button and use the Delete buttons that appear on each section to delete one or more.

In short, if you want a very clean graphical way to get to news, blogs, and postings, Flipboard is highly recommended.

Quick Hits

Here are several more apps you should check out.

SocialSeek

by Sensidea

Free

This app is like a police-channel scanner for social content. Scan through blogs, tweets, videos, and events by topic. You can look through categories of topics focused on entertainment, sports, and more to get the hottest news and opinions. One cool feature of this app is the ability to make your own SocialSeek site. Imagine all the videos, photos, tweets, and other content that interests you most all in one place and you get what SocialSeek is all about.

TextPics+

by Mangoo

Free — Hybrid

If using the shorthand language of texting is limiting for you, consider adding some visual zing to your messages. These pictures are made up of text and font images, but they take these to an art form. The Happy Birthday message is formed of little i's representing a row of candles and layers of asterisks forming a birthday cake. Snoopy at a typewriter is drawn with hyphens and punctuation symbols.

There are many categories of images here, from Animals and Celebrations to Scenery and Vehicles. Find an image you like and tap it to display a menu that gives you several options. You can make an image a Favorite so you can access it quickly, copy it and paste it into a text message, or e-mail it to yourself or others, for example.

Try using an IM client such as IM+, covered next, to access popular IM services such as AIM and MSN.

IM+

by SHAPE Services

Free — Hybrid

This instant messaging app works with Google Talk, Yahoo! Messenger, MSN/Windows Live Messenger, AIM/iChat, ICQ, MySpace, Twitter, Facebook, and Jabber. You can share text, photos, voice, and video and organize your various IM messages easily. There are several really attractive backgrounds to choose from to customize your IM environment, making chats an appealing visual experience. You can also see at a glance which of your contacts is online at any moment.

IM+ is free, but you get advertisements. If you want the advertisement-free version, fork over $9.99 for IM+ Pro, which also adds a handy conversation history feature and Skype chat.

Chapter 4: News and Weather Apps

In This Chapter

From what I've been hearing from readers at The Mac Observer — not to mention all the anecdotal evidence I see at my local coffee shops — reading on the iPad is one of the most popular activities for iPad users, especially when it comes to catching up on the news. There are a lot of different newspapers, magazines, and RSS news readers in the App Store, however, and in this chapter, I show you some of the best of them. To keep you out of the rain, I also throw in some cool weather apps, just for good measure.

Many of the apps I talk about in this chapter are apps that were written for the iPad. Some apps, however, have been written by the developer to run as native apps on both the iPad and iPhone (or iPod touch). These are called *hybrid* apps, and you'll find a + sign next to the price for those apps. Hybrid apps have the advantage of allowing you to buy once and use on whatever iOS device you have.

Pulse News Reader

by Alphonso Labs, Inc.

Free

What you can do with it: Follow up to 20 RSS feeds, or create your own Pulses for others to follow. Because each article in a feed is displayed along with any images in the feed, it offers a more graphically intense way of viewing your news.

Alphonso Labs' Pulse News Reader is one of the most interesting apps to come out of the iPad ecosystem yet. Pulse is an *RSS news reader,* but rather than presenting those feeds as straightforward lists, Pulse presents them as graphically rich blocks that look almost like a filmstrip, as you can see in Figure 4-1. If the RSS feeds you are following include images with them, those images are displayed by the text, making it a lot easier to get the gist of each article, and it certainly makes scrolling through your feeds more interesting.

RSS stands for *Really Simple Syndication,* and it's another way for a website to serve up new articles, stories, or other forms of content, usually with a headline link to the full article, a teaser, and sometimes an image. An *RSS news reader* is an app that displays RSS feeds from one or more sites. It's just another way to read a website.

Figure 4-1: Pulse News Reader's home screen.

If you follow a lot of RSS feeds (more than 20), Pulse may not be the best news reader for you. As of this writing, it's limited to 20 RSS feeds and 5 custom feeds called Pulses that you or your friends create (for 25 total feeds). If you're a news junkie with more than that, you'll want to look at NetNewsWire, Reeder (which I tell you about later in this chapter), or some other RSS news reader.

Each of your feeds is featured as a horizontal strip, with the newest article to the left. You can swipe up and down to see more of your feeds, and you can swipe from side to side to scroll the articles in a given feed. It's pretty simple. When you see an article you want to read, just tap its box (articles you haven't read yet are brighter than articles you have already read), and it gets pulled up in its own pane. If your feed offers entire articles, you'll get the whole thing right there. Most RSS feeds (in my experience) offer teasers, though, and for those you'll get the title, the teaser, and any images included. Tap the title, and you're taken to the full web page via the in-app browser.

You can also tap the web button in the upper-right corner of the screen and automatically open the full article every time you tap a block! To go back to reading just the RSS feed, tap the Text button.

One of my favorite things about this app is a real help to a lot of users. RSS readers allow you to add feeds by adding in the direct URL of that feed. That's great on a computer where you have a mouse, cut and paste, and can have two apps open side by side. On iPad, however, it's a little harder. You can copy a URL to your clipboard in one app and then go back to Pulse and paste it, or you can memorize it and type it by hand. Or — and this is that cool feature I mentioned — you can enter a search term, say *The Mac Observer*, and Pulse will give you a list of links it believes contain an RSS feed for that term. Choose the one you want, and boom! It's added! It's a great feature, and I won't be surprised if it makes its way to other news readers sooner rather than later.

Lastly, there's a social networking component in Pulse. When you see an article you like, you can tap the Heart icon and add it to your own Pulse. This is basically an RSS feed that you create that has only those articles you pick. You can have up to five Pulses, as mentioned in the Tip earlier in this section, and your friends can follow them. I'd personally trade these Pulses for more standard feeds, but that's just me.

Pulse is a really cool news reader for casual RSS users, and it offers a much more aesthetically pleasing way of viewing your feeds than any other reader out there.

Instapaper

by Marco Arment

$4.99

What you can do with it: Browse RSS feeds, get articles and other web pages from within other apps, save favorite articles, share articles with others through your Starred list, and view articles offline.

 Instapaper has been . . . dare I say it? An insta-hit! This app taps into one of the fundamental side effects of the information blitz that makes up a big part of our digital lives today, and that's managing all the cool things we see but don't ever get around to actually reading. Instapaper allows us to tag articles, websites, Flickr pics, and just about everything else on the web for viewing later when you have a moment to spare. You can even view your tagged content offline, when you're not connected to the web. You can do it from within the Instapaper app, but there are currently several dozen iOS apps that have added support for Instapaper, too!

To help you understand how cool this is, let me paint a scenario for you. You're catching up on tweets from your friends and some of the cool guys over at The Mac Observer (TMO). One friend links to a hilarious picture of her kitten that can't figure out how to get out of a box, and then another friend has a link to an article with tips on how to get the most out of your iPad. And then there's an editorial over at TMO about how Apple's strategy in the tablet market has thrown the netbook market into disarray. And then . . . well, you probably know just what I mean. We see all these things when we're reading tweets, looking at RSS feeds, or sometimes just reading our e-mail, and we usually don't get around to reading very much of it.

But back up a little bit and look at the app itself. As you can see in Figure 4-2, the app allows you to browse RSS feeds, each with its own folder. When browsing your feeds, you can either read the articles right then and there or save them to your Read Later folder.

 You can also Star articles as favorites. Tapping the star saves the article, but Instapaper also allows users to follow the Starred folders of their friends. (You have to do this on the service's website.)

If you're in one of those other apps that supports Instapaper — say Twitter for iOS — when you're finding all those cool things that I mentioned previously, you can add items to your Read Later folder from within those apps. This is handy for offline viewing, but it's especially great if you're going through a lot of tweets and want to be able to gather everything together at one time, and then read it later.

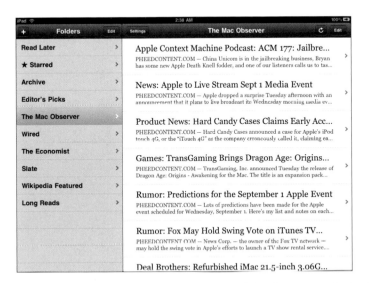

Figure 4-2: On the left are the RSS feeds I've added to Instapaper. On the right are the articles found in The Mac Observer's RSS feed.

Check out the Editor's Picks folder for some interesting articles you might not have otherwise found!

Each article in Instapaper has a link to the original posting on the web, allowing users to view the article with its original formatting and layout, including any ads that paid for it.

Instapaper is a capable RSS news reader, but most users like it for its offline capabilities and the ability to gather lots of material from browsers and other apps for reading all at one time.

I don't want to leave out mention of The Daily, a much-touted news aggregation app. This service touts itself as having a mission to "provide the best news experience by combining world-class storytelling with the unique interactive capabilities of the iPad." You can only get this app for your iPad and it comes with a free two-week subscription — after that it will cost you $0.99 for a weekly subscription or $39.99 for a yearly subscription.

NPR for iPad

by NPR

Free

What you can do with it: Read articles and listen to news reports from NPR's news arm, find and stream public radio stations, and listen to many of the organization's entertainment radio programs.

 NPR (that stands for *National Public Radio)* for iPad is one of those best-in-class iPad apps in terms of its user interface. More importantly, it offers you access to just about everything NPR produces, including written stories, radio news stories, and a broad selection of the entertainment and informational radio shows.

You can browse NPR's content in several ways. The home screen features three scrollable timelines, one each for News, Arts & Life, and Music, as you can see in Figure 4-3. These three streams are all stories and articles produced by the NPR news organization — the different radio programs are offered separately. You can swipe through these three streams from left to right, and once you tap a story that interests you, it takes over the screen, with the category stream at the bottom.

Figure 4-3: The main screen for NPR for iPad.

Some of these articles are offered in text only, but most of them have an accompanying radio report embedded right there. You can listen to the audio report from the home screen by tapping the speaker button in the teaser, or by tapping the Listen Now button in the full article. Better yet, you can queue up stories in a Playlist for later listening. It's a great way to make sure you're hearing all the articles you want to listen to.

Most of these articles have pictures in them. (Tap a pic for a full-screen version.)

NPR for iPad also offers up about 20 of its radio programs, from *All Things Considered,* to *Fresh Air,* to *Science Friday,* to *On the Media.* If you tap the Programs button at the bottom of the screen, you get a pop-up window with each program listed. Tap a show and you get a list of current and recent episodes you can play or add to a playlist. If it has a podcast version on iTunes, you'll find a button for getting it there, too!

Any show currently being aired somewhere in the world has an On Air label. You can tap into these shows live.

Lastly, the app lets you find local public radio stations that offer NPR content, and you can stream that station's broadcast directly to your iPad! This is a great way to listen to your local station, or to listen to what used to be your local station before you had to move. If you're in one of those few places without a public radio station, this makes it easier than ever before to find and listen to a station.

NPR for iPad is a must-have app for any fan of NPR's awesome news and entertainment shows. It looks great, and it's so easy to use that you may find yourself using it more than your radio.

BBC News

by BBC Worldwide, Ltd

Free — Hybrid

What you can do with it: The BBC News app offers you news content from all over the world, as well as one-tap access to BBC Radio.

The BBC is one of the most respected news organizations in the world, and it's also one of the largest. The BBC News app for iPad brings that news to you, including written news reports and BBC radio, too. Some articles even have video additions that include background interviews for added color, broadcast TV reports, and more.

One of the coolest things about the BBC News app is that it is highly customizable. The home screen of the app shows several rows of news articles, with each row representing a different category of news. You can swipe up and down to scroll through these categories, or right to left to scroll through the individual stories in a category.

The app defaults to featuring Americas, Technology, Features & Analysis, and Business, as you can see in Figure 4-4, but there are many more categories available, including Science & Environment, Europe, UK, and several other global regions. The featured categories are expanded to show individual stories, and while you can tap any other category to expand it, you can also define which categories are featured by tapping the Edit button at the top of the screen. This is great for expats who want to start off with news from home, or anyone who is interested in a particular category of news. In addition to being able to decide what is featured, you can also reorder the categories as you see fit.

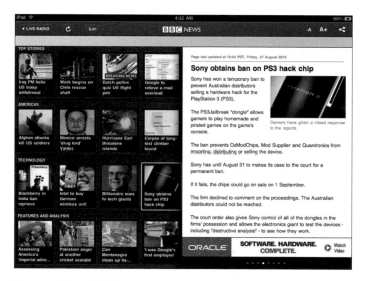

Figure 4-4: The BBC News app.

BBC News even offers news in several languages other than English, including Mundo, Brasil, Chinese (Traditional), Chinese (Simple), Russian, Arabic, Persian, and Urdu. You can find the stories offered in those languages at the bottom of the category list.

The other great thing about this app is that it offers one-tap access to the BBC's great radio news coverage. Just tap the Live Radio button at the top of the screen (make sure to wait a moment while the app buffers the stream), and you'll have whatever is being streamed by BBC Radio delivered straight to your iPad. Now that multitasking is functional on your iPad, you can stream BBC Radio in the background while using other apps.

Just below the red title bar with the navigation buttons is a Latest News ticker. This lets you quickly see whatever has come in recently from BBC News. I wish you could tap the ticker to go straight to the article currently being shown, but this is still a great way to see if there's anything new that you want to read.

Just about every single story has an accompanying photograph or other image, but some stories come with a video component instead, as I mentioned previously. You'll know which is which because the videos have a big label that reads Tap to Play. Follow those directions, and a video player takes over your screen. I've found those videos to be of high quality — they aren't full HD quality, but they look good on your iPad. Note that because they are high quality, you'll want a good connection to the Internet to watch them without interruption. If your connection is slow, you'll want to let them load before playing.

There's one more cool feature of this app I want to mention: Once you're in a story, you can swipe from left to right to navigate to other stories in the same category.

The biggest advantage this app has over some of the other news apps is the BBC's focus on global news. It's well designed, and the developers made great use of the iPad's screen real estate in creating this app. If you have an interest in what's happening outside the borders of the United States, you should try out BBC News on your iPad.

The Weather Channel Max for iPad

by The Weather Channel Interactive

Free

What you can do with it: View several weather maps, get local conditions and forecasts, watch TWC video content, read severe weather alerts, and follow TWC-related Twitter accounts.

I'm a bit of an information junkie, and I regularly check the weather forecast with Apple's Weather app on my iPhone. There is no default weather app on the iPad, for some mysterious reason unknown to me, but (or maybe because of this) there are some great options for you to choose from in the App Store. Now, I'll point out right up front that weather apps are one of those things that people take pretty seriously, and what works for me may not work for you. But for my money (okay, it's a free app), The Weather Channel Max for iPad is one of the best of the bunch.

The Weather Channel Max for iPad is basically like having a big slice of The Weather Channel itself. It has forecasts, weather maps, warnings, and even some of the TV station's video reports. It also has ads . . . a lot of them. This turns some people off, but you're getting a lot of content that is otherwise free. And it's those ads that pay for all that content.

That out of the way, let's look at the app! When you first launch it, it asks if it can use your current location (assuming you have your iPad set to ask for that permission). If you tap OK, you'll see a Google Maps display of your local area and six buttons for you to choose different features of the apps: Maps, Local, Video, Severe, Social, and On TV.

I think the way The Weather Channel — let's call it TWC from here on, okay? — offers up maps is very cool. Some of the other weather apps give you different views (radar, satellite, temperature, and so on), but TWC's app gives you an overlay with all eight types of maps it offers, including Radar, Clouds, Radar & Clouds, Temperature, Feels Like, UV Index, 24 Hr Rain, and 24 Hr Snow. This overlay has example map slices, as you can see in Figure 4-5, which helps you quickly understand what you're picking and what it's going to show you. I like this feature.

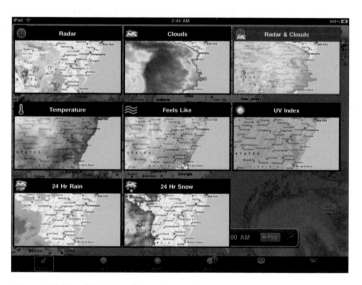

Figure 4-5: The Weather Channel Max for iPad app.

Some of the map views have the ability to play through the observed weather for the last two hours or the forecast for the next four hours. I'm enough of an information junkie to think that's super cool.

The Local pane is what most people use the most, I think. In one view, it offers current weather conditions and the forecast for the next ten days. (Swipe sideways to scroll through all ten days.) With a tap, you can also get an hourly forecast through the next 24 hours, along with four-hour forecasts for the 12 hours after that, and then daily forecasts for the next eight days. There are also mini panes for the other major features (swipe to scroll through them), as well as a pane for ads. Other apps do a better job of displaying just current conditions or a forecast, but there's enough here to satisfy most weather junkies.

The Video pane offers local weatherperson forecasts, regional forecasts, national forecasts, travel forecasts, storm watch videos, weather-related news stories, and other content from TWC's TV network. And you can display these videos full screen, though it's not HD quality. There's a lot here to watch, and I'd call it a premier feature of the app.

Now let's scoot over to the Severe pane, where you can get local and national severe weather warnings. If you live in a place where severe weather can occur, you'll find this a great resource for keeping abreast of these warnings.

The Social pane offers you direct access to TWC-related Twitter feeds, for what that's worth, and the On TV pane is just a one-touch way to get to the video feature stories I mentioned previously.

There's a lot here for the weather junkie, including lots of video content, great map views, and a passable local weather display. If you want a simple display of current conditions and the forecast, look to one of the apps I highlight in the next sections, but if you want to dig around in detailed weather information, try this free app.

Quick Hits

Here are several more apps you should check out.

Newsy for iPad: Multisource Video News Analysis
by Media Convergence

Free

 TechCrunch called this a "must download" app, and it's not surprising. If you like to be updated on world events in small video snippets, choose from categories such as World, U.S., Politics, Business, Entertainment, and Technology to download the video stories that interest you to watch offline.

You can download in either standard quality or HD, read a transcript of each video, look up the source of the story, comment on it, or share it via e-mail, Facebook, or Twitter. You can also create playlists of stories and watch them online.

And yes, for you sports fans out there, you can use the Sports category to look for video coverage of all the big games and accompanying blow-by-blow analyses.

Newsy requires you have iOS 4.3 with AirPlay.

Zinio Magazine Newsstand & Reader

by Zinio, LLC

Free

If magazines are your favorite reading matter, check out this free app from Zinio. You can subscribe to online magazines or buy one issue at a time. If you're the visual type, read full color articles, or if you want to get right to the words, use the enhanced text mode where you can also enlarge the text. You can access your magazine library from your iPhone, iPad, Mac, or PC and even get iPad-only editions of some magazines. Of course, when you find an article you like, you can share it. What I love about this app is the great digital format for a true magazine experience and the wide assortment of magazines available.

Star Walk for iPad

by Vito Technology, Inc.

$4.99

The moon and sun control our weather, right? So in the category of weather (loosely), I include Star Walk for iPad. This is an interactive astronomy guide with fantastic color graphics. But what's truly awesome is the ability to point your iPad toward the heavens and let Star Walk tell you what stars and planets are overhead, in real time. There's even a satellite tracking device that tells you when a satellite is zooming over your head. Want to get all nostalgic and see what the night sky was like on the day your spouse proposed? You can view historical images of the sky's configuration with Star Walk as well. How cool is that?

If you like Star Walk, you might want to check out Geo Walk HD and Solar Walk 3D as well.

LIFE for iPad

by TI Media Solutions, Inc.

Free

 LIFE Magazine has always cornered the market on outstanding photos of world events, places, and people. Download this free app to put LIFE's amazing photo collection at your fingertips. A cool feature figures out where you are and presents relevant photos to you. Follow the You May Also Like link to see other photos that are likely to engage you, and definitely use the Skip This Ad button to breeze past the sales pitches.

The photos in this collection are high definition and look great on the iPad screen. You can use the Email, Facebook, and Twitter buttons to spread the word about your favorite photos. Whether you're interested in current events or historical events, this huge collection has it all. And, it's free!

Wall Street Journal

by Wall Street Journal

Free (subscription required)

 News Corp. has brought *The Wall Street Journal* to the iPad, and in a big way. CEO Rupert Murdoch has talked about the future of newspapers being on devices like the iPad, and the company was among the first to invest major resources in developing a dedicated app for the new device before it was even released. What you get is a sort of print newspaper look on your iPad display. Swipe and scroll, tap, pinch, and zoom, and you can navigate through individual stories and different sections of this business publication. It's not the best iPad app out there, but it's really good. And I personally think *The Journal*'s business coverage is top-notch. One thing about pricing: News Corp. has been experimenting with how to monetize this property online. As of this writing, the iPad app is free with an online subscription, which is where I imagine it will stay, but you should check before you download it.

Chapter 5: Financial Apps

In This Chapter

- ✓ **StockWatch – iPad Edition**
- ✓ **Bloomberg for iPad**
- ✓ **SplashMoney for iPad**
- ✓ **PowerOne Financial Calculator**
- ✓ **Daily Stocks**
- ✓ **QIF Entry**
- ✓ **QuickTimer**
- ✓ **Quick Sale for iPad**
- ✓ **Pageonce – Money & Bills**
- ✓ **E*TRADE Mobile Pro for iPad**

*E*ach of us is likely to think of something different when we hear "financial app." There are apps to balance your checkbook or home budget, apps to buy stocks, banking apps, invoicing and billing apps, apps to read up on financial news, and even a few combinations of all those features. In this chapter, I show you some of the best of them so that you don't waste your finances having to try them all!

Many of the apps I talk about in this chapter are apps that were written for the iPad. Some apps, however, have been written by the developer to run as native apps on both the iPad and iPhone (or iPod touch). These are called *hybrid* apps, and you'll find a + sign next to the price for those apps. Hybrid apps have the advantage of allowing you to buy once and use on whatever iOS device you have.

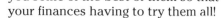

StockWatch – iPad Edition

by Todd Barnes

$5.99

What you can do with it: Monitor one or more stock portfolios, set up stock watchlists, and access financial news relating to specific stocks or the broader markets. You can also sync your portfolios and watchlists with other devices running StockWatch.

 Let's start our look at financial apps with an all-around stock app called StockWatch – iPad Edition. This is a great app for people who want to monitor one or more stock portfolios and follow news pertaining to those stocks or the broader markets. It can be particularly handy for those with investments across multiple brokerage firms.

One of the things I like most about this app is something I'm a little persnickety about, the fact that it's a good-looking app with a good interface. Okay, fine — I'm a lot persnickety about those kinds of things; it's true. It has a color scheme that's muted and easy on the eye; navigation is intuitive; and the app works in both portrait and landscape modes, though I prefer landscape mode for this app. It also has all of the features you'll need to monitor your portfolios, making it a one-stop shop for most users.

There are two main tabs in this app, Watchlist and Portfolios. As the name suggests, Watchlist is for setting up a list of individual stocks you want to watch. This is useful for individual companies you want to monitor from your portfolio, or for watching a company you're considering adding to your portfolio. This tab offers a snapshot of the current status for each of the stocks you're watching, and it includes the name of the company (or index), its ticker symbol, the last trade, and the change that trade represents (green for up and red for down). The middle pane offers you details about the stock in the list you have selected, as well as a chart for the stock. The third pane offers you a list of recent news articles pertaining to the stock or index you have selected in your list.

 Tap the chart to get a larger version, along with different viewing options from which to choose. These include the type of chart (line, bar, candlestick), the time frame (from one day to five years to max), and the different values you want to see in the chart.

The other main tab is the one labeled Portfolios. In this tab, you can set up one or more portfolios and monitor both their individual and collective performance. This is useful if you have a broad portfolio and want to be able to monitor it by sector (or whatever other breakdown you fancy) or if you have your investments spread out among multiple brokerages. In Figure 5-1, you can see that the view for this tab includes a pane that shows the value of all your portfolios, another pane for the portfolio you have selected, and a third pane for the individual stocks in that portfolio. The middle of the screen shows detailed information on the day's trade and a chart, just like the Watchlist tab has. The third pane is for news relating to the individual stock you have selected.

Figure 5-1: Viewing a sample portfolio.

There are a lot of preference options in StockWatch, and they're useful options. There are three date formats to choose from, the ability to set your default tab, preferences for setting your default chart range, and more. Poke around in the Settings tab to see everything you can tweak.

You can set an app-specific passcode if you wish to prevent other users of your iPad from accessing the information in this app. You can find this in the Settings tab.

You'll see another tab in Figure 5-1, called Sync Data, that allows you to sync your data between your iPad and iPhone. Set up your Portfolios and Watchlist once and then manage them on whatever device is convenient at the moment.

E*TRADE customers should use that company's iPad app (and I tell you about it later in this chapter), as I think it is even better than StockWatch, but StockWatch is a must-have app for anyone else looking to monitor her portfolios or set up stock watchlists. Its great design, awesome features, and intuitive interface make it a pleasure to use.

Bloomberg for iPad

by Bloomberg, LP

Free

What you can do with it: Monitor your stocks, as well as all of the world's major equity indices, global currency markets, commodities, futures, and bonds. You also get all of Bloomberg's extensive financial news and several of the company's financial podcasts.

I'm a big fan of Bloomberg's financial news coverage, and I'm a bigger fan of this app. For one thing, it offers instant access to all of that great news coverage, and it provides stock and index data like you'd expect. It also provides currency, commodities, and bond data — one of the few iPad apps I've seen that does so. For some icing on this cake of financial goodness, it offers direct access to a number of Bloomberg-produced podcasts that will be invaluable to traders and investors wanting to learn more about the markets.

Let's start with the home screen (accessed by a button simply labeled Bloomberg when you're in another tab). In Figure 5-2, you'll see that it offers you all the top financial news of the day and snapshots of the major global indices (DOW JONES, S&P 500, FTSE 100, and NIKKEI 225), two of the stocks in a watchlist you set up, current data on the U.S. dollar, and tappable links to the different tabs in the app.

Figure 5-2: Top News in the app, along with snapshots of the major indices.

Like many other iPad apps I talk about, Bloomberg works in both landscape and portrait mode, but I think it looks best in landscape mode. For instance, in the figure, the buttons at the bottom of the screen are laid out nicely in landscape mode, but in portrait mode they take up one-third of the screen because they're stacked three deep.

The best thing about this app to me is all the Bloomberg news articles. In the News tab, you get all of Bloomberg's news coverage divided into many categories over seven swipeable pages. The first page has panes for Worldwide news, the Most Read stories of the day, Bonds, Commodities, and the company's Exclusive content. Swipe to the left, and you get a new page of Currency news, Economy, Emerging Markets, Energy, and Funds. Another swipe, and you get five more categories, and so on. You can edit the order of all these categories, making this a convenient place to catch up on the news that's important to you.

The Equity Indices, Currencies, Commodities, Equity Index Futures, and Bonds tabs all contain simple, scrollable lists of those markets. You can't customize them; but these are finite lists to begin with, so that's not a big deal to me. Having quick and easy access to them is what I think is important.

The other big feature of this app is all the Bloomberg podcasts you listen to on your iPad. Yeah, you can get these podcasts from iTunes, but Bloomberg for iPad gives you easy access to the lot of them without you having to monitor and manage podcast subscriptions. There are podcasts for News, Economics, Politics, and the Markets. You can also listen to them as you are messing around in other parts of the app.

Lastly, I'd be remiss in my duties if I didn't point out that some people are put off by the black background with orange or white text theme of this app, but I personally like it. It makes for easy reading, in my opinion.

There are better apps (like StockWatch, covered earlier in the chapter) if you just want to monitor your stocks, but Bloomberg is the app for people who want to monitor the markets as a whole. The company's financial news coverage is among the best, and access to all of the markets outside of the usual stock markets is convenient.

Book VI
Chapter 5

Financial Apps

SplashMoney for iPad

by SplashData, Inc.

$4.99

What you can do with it: Manage your household budget, download your banking transactions, track your spending, and get charts and reports showing you where your money goes.

Most of us need help when it comes to managing budgets, and the reality is that different things work for different people. I know people who know how much they have in their checking account to the penny but have never recorded a check in the ledger or balanced their checkbook, not even once. On the other end of the spectrum, I know people who spend lots of time and effort in planning their budget, balancing their checkbook, and trying hard to be on top of their spending, yet nothing seems to work for them despite their best efforts. Most of us fall between those two extremes and just need a little extra help in watching what we spend and seeing where our money goes. If that's you, SplashMoney for iPad might be the app for you.

SplashMoncy HD is a money-management app for the iPad that allows you to monitor credit cards and online banking accounts (checking, savings, and so on), create budgets, and track your actual spending. You can sync data between the iPad app and the Mac or Windows version of the company's software, too, which is very handy. You can also directly download online banking information from a list of a couple of hundred banks and online banking services, including most of the major banks. The app is designed well, is colorful, and provides attractive and informative graphs to help you visualize what you are doing with your money. It also includes an app-specific password option for additional security.

Setting up this app takes some work, but once you perform that initial setup, it's pretty easy to work with on a day-to-day basis. The key is to simply make sure you keep up with it. It comes with a few default accounts, including Checking, Savings, and three credit card accounts. In Figure 5-3, I added a couple of other accounts and then added a bunch of (fake) transactions under my (fictional) checking account. When I set up each account, I named it, picked an icon, and established a beginning balance. Then when I make payments, write checks, buy things with my debit card, or make deposits, I just enter each one as I go. I can assign categories, the payee, enter the date, and assign it as either a personal transaction or a business transaction.

Figure 5-3: Viewing a sample checking account with recent checking activity on the right.

Once you've entered a transaction assigned to a particular payee, the next time you select that payee for a new transaction, the category, payment type, and other things you selected are autofilled from the previous transaction. This is a handy timesaver, especially for those transactions you conduct frequently, like buying gas or groceries. You can also set up recurring transactions with reminders, and who doesn't need that kind of help!?

If you're like me, I wouldn't worry about trying to backdate a bunch of transactions when you first start using the app. Instead, just set your starting balances properly and focus on entering new transactions going forward!

Once you've set up all the proper accounts and have some transactions under your belt, you get reports that show you where your money is going. You can view these reports in list form or as a pie chart, and doing both might really change the way you think about how you spend your money. For instance, it turns out that I spend a lot of money on books and games like World of Warcraft. Who knew?

If you're really ambitious, you can even establish budgets for each and every category you want to track. Need to cut back on how much you spend on movies, or maybe coffee? Establish a budget and monitor it throughout the month. SplashMoney will show you what your budget is, what you've actually spent, and the difference. I think a lot of people will appreciate that feature, and most of us should probably use it!

There's a lot to this app, and it's up to you how much you take advantage of all these features. I think that people who are comfortable with (or need to be more comfortable with) maintaining detailed financial records to manage their budgets are going to like this app. It's not what I would call a perfect app, but it's very good, and it's getting better with each update.

One more note: PocketMoney from Cantamount Software ($4.99) is another great entry in this category of personal finance apps.

PowerOne Financial Calculator

by Infinity Softworks, Inc.

$4.99 — Hybrid

What you can do with it: You can perform a variety of complex calculations with it, and it includes many easy-to-use templates for commonly used equations in the world(s) of finance.

Do you remember the days when the math and engineer guys proudly walked around with their calculators from TI and HP? Uhhh . . . yeah, me neither . . . Okay, I'll admit it; I had one back in the '70s, but I had no idea how to use it, which might help explain why I like PowerOne Financial Calculator so much. This app does super complex finance-related calculations for you, but with the included templates, you don't have to really know what you're doing to get the right answers for a lot of things — I call that a score.

For instance, when you're shopping for a car it's sometimes hard to get a straight answer out of the salesperson regarding how much your car is going to cost. Many dealerships like to try to sell you a car based on the car payment, and that can make it hard to understand how much you're really paying! At the same time, if you're price-shopping for a car and know the total price, you do still need to know what your monthly payment is going to be. PowerOne has a template called Auto Loan that will get you the information you need. As shown in Figure 5-4, you enter the price, sales tax, any fees you might need to pay, the interest rate on your loan, down payment, and the number of months you intend to carry the loan, and you can get your monthly payment with a simple tap.

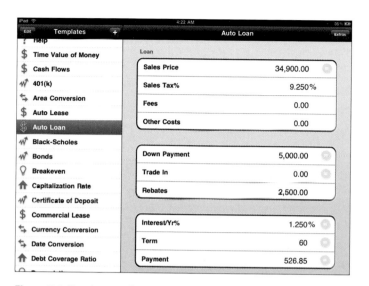

Figure 5-4: Figuring out the specifics of a car loan with the Auto Loan template.

You can work backward, too: Say you want to change what you want your payment to be. If you enter that, you can tap the equal sign next to any of the other categories and get that figure. For instance, if you want to pay a certain amount per month, you can see how many months you'd need to carry the loan to hit that target. Or if you know how much you can pay per month and how long your bank will carry your note, you can quickly get the figure for how much of a down payment you'd need to make, or how much you can spend on your car. If you're working on your taxes (or someone else's taxes), the same template will also give you amortization figures.

Don't worry. There is, of course, a standard calculator in this app. Just choose the Calculator template to get a calculator with both math and trig functions, as well as a history. You can tap away on this like you would any ol' calculator.

But this app isn't just about car loans. There are more than 50 templates included in this app, some for traders, some for accountants, some for super math people, and some that are for us mere mortals. I like the Area Conversion that allows me to fill in one of 11 units of measure and, with a single tap, get that converted to the other ten units of measure. There's also a currency converter that uses the most recent exchange rates (if you have a connection to the Internet when you use it). There's a depreciation template, an inflation calculator, several loan-related calculations, mortgage tools, a sales-tax template, and much more. There's even a tip calculator that will divide your bill among multiple people!

For sure, a lot of what this app offers is pretty specialized, but I'd hazard that many of us will be glad we have this app on our iPad if we need it just once. If you do financial transactions for a living, however, this might be a must-have app for you. Real estate agents, accountants, investors, bankers, and anyone on the other side of those transactions will find it useful.

Daily Stocks

by 13apps

$19.99

What you can do with it: Get a variety of daily technical reports and scans for the markets.

 Let me show you another specialty app for investors, called Daily Stocks. This app provides the user with technical scans of the market (up to 91 such technical scans as of this writing) and is designed to highlight trends in the marketplace based on some highly technical analytical techniques. Those trends, in turn, can help investors identify both opportunities and risks in the markets. This kind of information is mainly the domain of fairly serious traders, so if your eyes start to glaze over as I talk about it, I understand! I think it's important to talk about it here, however, as it is an example of an iPad app for serious investors.

Daily Stocks works just fine in landscape and portrait mode, but landscape mode shows you a little more information. As you can see in Figure 5-5, the left side of the screen offers charts for the three major U.S. indices and five global indices.

Figure 5-5: Looking at the Japanese Candlesticks tab.

It's the right two-thirds of the screen, however, that is dedicated to the real purpose of this app. At the top of the screen in the green bar are three tabs, labeled JC (Japanese Candlesticks), OS (Overextended Stocks), and SS (Stock Scans). These are three different styles of reports, and each offers very different information.

A *candlestick* in the trading world is a kind of bar graph. It shows the opening price of a stock and its closing price, with the color telling you if it was a winning day (opening on the bottom, closing on the top) or a losing day (opening at the top, closing at the bottom).

In Daily Stocks, a red candlestick represents a losing day, and a green candlestick represents a winning day. Simple, eh? And more informative to traders than other graphs.

The JC tab offers ten Bullish trends, ten Bearish trends, and three Indecision trends. These are all attempts to understand where the market is headed based on patterns that have been identified in the past. In other words, they are far from perfect (but their adherents tend to feel strongly about them). Those names you see, like Falling Three Method or Engulfing, are all English approximations of the original Japanese names the patterns were given.

In any event, the trends with more information are shaded darker grey, and a tap gives you a new screen with a definition of what the trend is supposed to identify and a list of the stocks that matched the pattern to begin with.

Overextended Stocks (OS) are stocks that have broken above their resistance levels (Overbought) or below their support levels (Oversold) or that have traveled beyond their Simple Moving Average (SMA). The OS tab gives you a list of the ten most oversold or overbought stocks compared to their SMA over the last nine to 200 days. You can tap through one of those ten stocks in any of the SMA views to get several graphs and charts.

Lastly, the Stock Scans (SS) tab gives you more than 56 reports of stocks that have met some specific criteria (such as new 52-week highs or lows, various volume levels, crossover reports, and many more).

These are all very technical reports and scans, and if you're not an active — and, frankly, a serious — trader, you probably don't need this app. Most of this stuff is over my head, and I've been covering (Apple-related) stock news for more than 13 years. If you are a serious trader, however, you should check out Daily Stocks.

Quick Hits

In addition to the apps provided previously in this chapter, here are several more apps in this category that you should check out.

QIF Entry

by Edwin Hou

$2.99

Intuit has a pretty bad track record of supporting Apple's platforms, especially iOS. Why don't we have Quicken for iPad and iPhone? Who knows, but fortunately, there is still an app for that (managing personal finance). First, Quicken is Intuit's personal finance solution for Mac and Windows. QIF Entry allows you to enter transactions on your iPad that you can then send to your Mac or PC and import into Quicken. That might sound kind of kludgy, but as of this writing, there's no other way that I could find for doing much of anything with Quicken on your iPad. Even then, there are some limitations, most notably that it works only with Quicken 2002 for Windows and Quicken 2007 for Mac and Windows. On the other hand, it has built-in support for Dropbox, making getting your files on and off your iPad a breeze. (I tell you about Dropbox in Book VI, Chapter 1.)

QuickTimer

by William Modesitt

$8.99

While I'm ragging on Intuit, it would seem a propitious time to point out that there's no QuickBooks for iOS, either, unless you want to use QuickBooks Online, which isn't accessible if you don't have a connection to the Internet. QuickTimer is a third-party app that allows QuickBooks users to enter time-tracking data into their iPads in a format that they can then import into QuickBooks. This is crucial for anyone using QuickBooks who wants to be able to use the iPad as an on-the-go solution, and the developer of this app has done a very good job with it. Users can export the data in other formats, too, including comma and tab delimited, and even HTML. That means you can also import data from this app into Excel and other applications that read those formats.

Quick Sale for iPad

by IntelliXense

$9.99

Quick Sale for iPad is a handy app for anyone who needs to do invoicing on the go (at street fairs, at a client's location, on a business trip, at a trade show, and so on) or, for that matter, anyone who wants to interface with customers with an iPad in his hands instead of a computer. It is the future, after all. In any event, Quick Sale for iPad is a fairly complete invoicing solution for your iPad. It offers unlimited inventory items and services (including photos for each one, if you want) that you can organize by category. It also offers reports, the ability to e-mail reports and invoices, and integrates with Credit Card Terminal from Inner Fence for conducting credit card transactions!

Book VI
Chapter 5

Financial Apps

Apple added print services to iPad in November 2010 with the release of iOS 4.2, so you can print invoices directly from your iPad to an AirPrint-compatible wireless printer.

Pageonce – Money & Bills

by Pageonce, Inc.

Free — Hybrid

Pageonce Personal Finance is a personal finance service for the mobile market. This is a free, ad-supported, hybrid app that will work on both iPhone and iPad. It allows you to track your bills and expenses, monitor your credit cards, check your bank account status, check in on your stocks, and even track your frequent-flyer mileage programs. The company also offers the ability to remotely destroy your data through the service's website if you ever lose your iPhone or iPad. There's a Premium version of the app ($12.99) that is ad-free and offers additional features. If you like the free version, you'll probably be willing to pay for the paid version.

E*TRADE Mobile Pro for iPad

by E*TRADE FINANCIAL

Free

 E*TRADE Mobile Pro for iPad is that company's conduit to all of its online brokerage services. The thing I love most about this app is that it's in the top tier of well-designed iPad apps in App Store. The developers made great use of the iPad's screen real estate, and they put a lot of thought into arranging the app's information panes to match the way people will actually use them. That's a touch I really appreciate. When it comes to using the app, you can buy and sell stocks and options, get financial news, watch the indices, and monitor your portfolio. The only thing that's wrong with this app is that most of its services are accessible only by E*TRADE customers. If you're not an E*TRADE customer, check out the StockWatch app I talk about earlier in the chapter.

Chapter 6: Entertainment Apps

In This Chapter

- ✔ **Emoti HD for Facebook**
- ✔ **Netflix**
- ✔ **TabToolkit**
- ✔ **Pandora Radio**
- ✔ **ArtRage**
- ✔ **Seline HD – Music Instrument**
- ✔ **Acrobots**
- ✔ **IMDb Movies & TV**
- ✔ **Marvel Superheroes**
- ✔ **Gravilux and Uzu**
- ✔ **OverDrive Media Console**

Finally! Finally, we're going to get some entertainment on the iPad! I've shown you some great iPad apps, but I saved the best, or at least some of the most fun apps, for last. Entertainment is another one of those broad topics that means a lot of different things to different people, and so in this chapter, I picked several different kinds of apps that I think are entertaining. I've got a social networking helper, music apps, a way to watch movies and TV on your iPad, and a couple of super cool apps that might even entertain your inner nerd!

Many of the apps I talk about in this chapter are apps that were written for the iPad. Some apps, however, have been written by the developer to run as native apps on both the iPad and iPhone (or iPod touch). These are called *hybrid* apps, and you'll find a + symbol next to the price for those apps. Hybrid apps have the advantage of allowing you to buy once and use on whatever iOS device you have.

Emoti HD for Facebook

by nodconcept, LLC

$2.99

What you can do with it: Make posts to Facebook with bright, colorful emoticon images to illustrate your mood or some other aspect of your posts.

Facebook is probably one of the most popular forms of entertainment on the planet today. The company has more than half a billion members these days, and a lot of us waste — I mean spend — countless hours every day posting updates about ourselves and reading up on what our friends and family are doing. I thought it would be a good idea to kick off this chapter with an app that can make this form of entertainment even more entertaining. Emoti HD is an app that allows you to post great-looking emoticons in your Facebook posts, images that can be informative for those reading your posts, but images that can also simply draw more attention to your posts.

In case you've been hiding in a cave for the last 10–15 years before you popped out to pick up an iPad and this book, an *emoticon* is one of those little sideways faces you can make out of text characters, like :) for a smiley face or :(for a sad face. Emoji, on the other hand, started in Japan as a system for including actual images for smiley (and other) faces through SMS text messages. Emoti (for iPhone) and Emoti HD's name is a juxtaposition of the two concepts.

As of this writing, Emoti HD has 186 emoticons. These high-quality images were custom-made by nodconcept, the app's developer, and they look absolutely great. They're colorful, and they just pop off the screen on both your iPad and Facebook in your browser. The app includes all the basic emoticons for happy, angry, sad, ecstatic, crying, proud, goofy, surprised, in love, and even sleeping. But there's much more, too. There are sports and thank-you emoticons, and emoticons to denote that it's raining, snowing, hot, or cold. There are military emoticons, food, music, gambling, and religious emoticons. There are gay-pride, graduation, and baby emoticons (It's a boy! It's a girl!), and even emoticons for the major holidays. That's a lot of emoticons, but the developer says that more are coming!

You can also use Emoti HD to post to Facebook without using an emoticon, too, making this app a one-stop shop for posting. On the first page of emoticons, you'll find a dotted box with the text *no emoti* in it. Tap that, make your post, and your post will have no image and look like a normal Facebook post.

On the left side of Figure 6-1, I'm making a post to my Facebook account about my current favorite band, The Spyrals, out of San Francisco. I could have used one of the music-themed images, but I chose one of the thumbs-up emoticons instead. It's kind of like having my own personal Like and Dislike tool.

 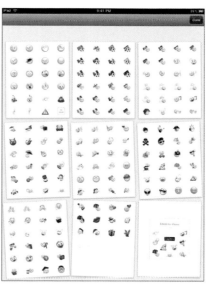

Figure 6-1: Making a post to Facebook with Emoti HD (left) and rearranging the sheets of emoticons by tapping and holding one of the sheets (right).

To make a post, tap an emoticon and you get a keyboard and a spot to write your post. Write the post, tap the Share button, and you're done! On your first post, you'll have a Facebook Connect button you tap to log into Facebook from Emoti HD. If you need to change accounts, you can log out of the current account by tapping the From field in a new post. You can pick your destination (your own Wall, a friend's Wall, a Group, a Page, or a Fan Page) by tapping the second field (Wall in Figure 6-1). It's very easy to use, and it may even be the most direct way to make a Facebook post on your iPad.

There's one more cool feature in Emoti HD that I want to show you. In the upper-right corner of the display is an icon with nine little squares. Tap that and you get all nine pages of emoticons so you can quickly jump to the one you want. This is a cool navigation feature that I wish was in more apps, but nodconcept upped it a notch by adding the ability to rearrange the pages so that you can put them in the order you want. If you tap and hold one of the pages in this view, like I did on the right in Figure 6-1, they start shaking just like apps do when you want to rearrange their order on your iPad or iPhone. Just tap, hold, and drag a page to the position you want it! For instance, I'm not a big soccer fan (and the World Cup is over), so I moved that page of emoticons to the end. That's pretty slick!

All in all, this is a cool app with great-looking emoticons. If you post on Facebook and want a way to make your posts stand out, or if you just want to be able to better illustrate your point, Emoti HD is for you.

Netflix

by James Odell

Free (subscription required) — Hybrid

What you can do with it: You can stream TV shows and movies for instant viewing on your iPad, and you can also manage your Netflix account and Instant queue. But note that you'll need an Internet connection for both features.

Wooohoooo! TV and movies on your iPad! You can watch video content of all sorts on your iPad. You can buy and rent TV shows and movies through Apple's iTunes Store, too. There's also YouTube content, videos you get from your friends and family, and movies that you might have bought on DVD and transferred to your computer and iPad. Some websites offer video content, as well, though much of that is currently Flash-based and therefore unwatchable on your iPad. Netflix, however, is another great choice, but I guess I should begin with a basic look at what exactly Netflix is.

Netflix started life as a mail-based DVD rental service. For a monthly subscription, you can get DVDs of TV shows and movies delivered to your house. Once you've watched them, you can return them, and Netflix sends you the next DVD in your queue. Since you're paying a flat fee, the faster you watch and then return your Netflix DVDs in the mail, the more video entertainment you get for your dollar.

Netflix is a great way to catch up on TV shows you either got behind on or were late watching in the first place. Go back to the beginning of *Breaking Bad*, for instance, or *Mad Men*, or even whole TV shows that went off the air years ago, like *Buffy the Vampire Slayer!*

From there, Netflix started adding other services, including streaming movies and TV shows across the Internet. You can watch TV shows and movies on your Mac or PC, and with the Netflix app on your iPad, you can even watch them on your iOS device, so long as you have an Internet connection. In Figure 6-2, I've got the Bruce Willis flick, *Surrogates*, pulled up. I can add it to my Instant Queue (a queue for those shows I want to stream), or I can just play it right now. I can also read up on the show, get cast information, and more.

Figure 6-2: On a movie or TV show's entry, you can watch it instantly or add it to your Instant Queue (where available).

Another very cool tool for using Netflix is the ability to rate movies. The company uses proprietary algorithms to suggest movies and TV shows you might like based on the shows that you've rated. The system works, more often than not, and gets better as you give it more information.

The video quality looks great on the iPad's display, and I think it's a great way to rent movies and TV shows. It's a hybrid app, too, and it works just as well on your iPhone.

Another option for watching TV shows and movies on your iPad is Hulu Plus. It's a free download, but it requires a $9.99 monthly subscription. Anyone can download the Hulu app. It's just not as useful without a Hulu Plus account. Yet another good TV solution for Mac users is EyeTV ($4.99) from Elgato Systems, which allows you to stream TV from your Mac to your iPad, though it requires additional hardware on your Mac.

TabToolkit

by Agile Partners

$9.99 — Hybrid

What you can do with it: Manage and display guitar and bass tab files. You can download tabs from the Internet directly in the app, or you can transfer them from your Mac or PC through a special file-transfer system the app offers. If you have Power Tab or Guitar Pro file formats, you can play them back, control which instruments you hear, and adjust the tempo.

I play guitar. Not all that well, but I play. Fortunately, the Internet has a ton of guitar tabs out there that make it a lot easier to learn a new song. TabToolkit for iPad makes that process even easier, especially if you need to learn a song on the go.

Tablature (usually called *tab* or *tabs* for short) is a musical notation system popular with guitarists and bassists. Rather than writing notes on a staff, you note which string on which fret is being played. A lot of us don't read sheet music, and tabs have become the most common way to write solos and chords in songs.

TabToolkit's most basic function is to organize and display your tabs. The app doesn't come with any tabs as of this writing, but it's easy enough to find billions of tabs on the Internet. You can get them into this app in three ways, too, which is very cool. The first is to simply browse for them in the in-app browser. Search for a song's name with *tab* at the end, and you'll likely find the right song right away. If TabToolkit detects a tab when you visit the page, it will tell you so — and with one tap, you can import it into the app! Pretty easy! There's also a very cool file transfer system the company developed. If you have tabs on your computer you want to transfer, and both your iPad and computer are on the same network, you can tap the Upload & Download button, shown on the left side of Figure 6-3, to get a URL. Open that URL on your computer, click the Add Files button to navigate to where you have them, select them, and they're added to your app! The third way is to use this same special web page to simply copy and paste text-based tabs into the app.

Power Tab is software for Windows for creating and editing tabs, while Guitar Pro is a Mac and Windows application that you can use to write, edit, and even play back tab files on your computer.

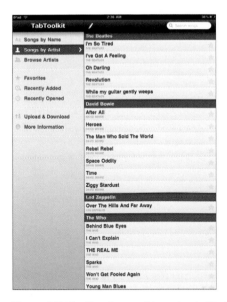
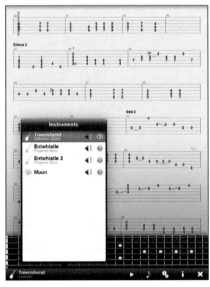

Figure 6-3: The list of songs I have loaded in TabToolkit (left) and playback of a song, including the pop-up window for choosing which instruments you want to hear (right).

If you can, though, find tabs that are in Guitar Pro and/or Power Tab formats, because then you'll see the real power of TabToolkit. With these files, which often also include MIDI information for other instruments, TabToolkit will play them so that you can play along. You can select which instruments you hear, and you can control the speed of playback. (That can be crucial for learning a hard-to-play passage!) You can use a metronome, and you can display a fretboard that lights up the strings and frets that are being played, a great visual learning tool!

Lefties aren't left out of this fretboard feature. When you're in a song, tap the gears icon and you can toggle a preference for displaying the left-handed or right-handed fretboard.

On the right in Figure 6-3, I have "I Can't Explain," one of my favorite tunes from The Who. It's a simple song, but even in his early recordings, Pete Townshend had some interesting ways to play chords. You'll see that I have his part selected (I could have standard notations displayed, too, but I turned that off), and in this tab file, there are two parts for the bass and one for drums that I could also switch to. The red bar denotes where I am, and the fretboard at the bottom of the screen lights up as the notes are played.

If you play guitar or bass and like to learn cover songs, you'll think this app is the bee's knees! It's great for learning solos from the greats (and not-so-greats), and its playback features and tempo controls make learning even the hardest parts easier than you can imagine.

Pandora Radio

by Pandora Media, Inc.

Free — Hybrid

What you can do with it: Pandora offers live streaming radio through stations you set up around bands, songs, or composers.

Pandora Radio is the self-titled app that brings the Pandora streaming radio service from your browser to your iPad (and iPhone). If you like music but don't know what Pandora is, I want you to stop reading, put this book down, and go download it from the App Store right now! Go on; I'll wait.

So I'm guessing that if you're still reading, you either already had it or have installed it now, so we can all be on the same page, right? Excellent! There are a lot of streaming radio stations on the Internet, but Pandora came up with an approach of offering a wide variety of music to people in a way that they actually wanted to listen to it. Imagine that!

Here's how it works, in the online service as well as the iPad app: When you first launch Pandora, you're prompted to sign in with an existing account or create a new one. Once you're signed in, you can create a new station by simply searching for a band (or song or artist). When you do, Pandora starts playing a song by that band, a song that you can then give a thumbs up or down to. Pandora then looks at the songs you like (and don't like) and plays other songs it thinks you will like based on what people with similar tastes have said they like. This allows you to train your stations to play music you're probably going to really enjoy!

You should rate as many songs as you can. The more data Pandora has, the more you'll like your stations!

You can create as many stations as you want, each one starting with an artist, song, or composer. If a station gets out of control for you, delete it and start a new one. In Figure 6-4, I've got stations for The Brian Jonestown Massacre, The Who, The Beatles, Led Zeppelin, Black Rebel Motorcycle Club, The Church, and a band called Jucifer. (A band I was in opened for Jucifer a couple of years ago, and I wanted to hear if their studio stuff was as chaotic as their live sound — it wasn't.)

Figure 6-4: Several radio stations set up (the list on the left) with information on the current song playing on the right.

In that figure, you'll see that I'm listening to "This Is The First Of Your Last Warning" from The Brian Jonestown Massacre. The album cover of that song is highlighted, and you can see the album covers of the songs that played before, allowing you to tap any of them to find out more. You'll see that I gave this song a thumbs up, from the icon next to the name of the band. If I tap the Menu button directly below it, I can bookmark the song or artist, and I can also get taken straight to the song or artist in iTunes!

Which brings me to why I think Pandora is so cool. The stations and song ratings allow me to train those stations to play only songs I'm likely to like, but I'm still going to hear songs and bands I've never heard before! It's like having a personal DJ! I've found lots of new bands this way.

When you give a song a thumbs down, Pandora immediately skips to the next song.

Another feature I really like is the band histories you get with each song — I just love learning more about bands.

Pandora is free, but the free service limits you to 40 hours of listening per month, a limit relating to a royalty agreement between the station and rights holders. For most users, 40 hours per month will probably be enough, but for $36 per year you can have unlimited listening time, no ads, and a desktop app for listening to Pandora without a browser on your Mac or PC. The only real advantage to iPad users is the lack of ads and the unlimited listening;

plus you're supporting a cool service (and the rights holders of all those songs).

As I said previously, if you like music, you should have Pandora on your iPad. It offers you a great way to hear favorite and new music alike, and you can build stations around all your favorite bands.

ArtRage

by Ambient Design, Ltd

$6.99

What you can do with it: ArtRage lets you use your fingers to manipulate various artist's tools, photos, and backgrounds to create digital works of art.

I dabble in mixed media artwork, so it was great fun to find ArtRage, an app that makes creating art on the iPad a lot of fun. Just pick your weapon (that is, your brush, crayon, paint roller, pastel chalk, or whatever) and use your finger to draw, paint, airbrush and otherwise do the digital equivalent of finger painting.

The color wheel lets you choose any color you can imagine by tapping it; then you can use the different tools to create your art using those colors. Once you're satisfied with your masterpiece, you can save it in your ArtRage gallery, and then save it to a photo album, print it, or send it via e-mail.

There are settings for how hard you have to press the screen to make your mark, how blending works, and even the texture of your canvas from smooth to crumpled or even foil.

You can change orientation of the piece as well, and even set the texture of paint you're laying down (a thick gloss to thin and dry on the brush, for example).

One very cool feature is the ability to grab items from your iPad 2 Photos Camera Roll and insert the pictures in your artwork. Imagine the possibilities using other apps both preinstalled on iPad or purchased from the App Store. For example, by using Photo Booth to take a picture of myself with an odd effect applied, and then inserting it on a tinfoil canvas and brushing on a bit of color, I create the weird and wonderful piece of art you see in Figure 6-5.

Figure 6-5: The foil background preset adds sparkle!

Quick Hits

Here are several more apps you should check out, which give you some alternatives to the apps I covered in more detail throughout this chapter.

Seline HD – Music Instrument

by Ilya Plavunov

$9.99 — Hybrid

I picked Seline HD – Music Instrument to show you because it's one of the first musical instrument apps that takes a totally new approach to turning your iPad into an instrument. Rather than trying to bring an analog instrument to your digital iPad, Seline HD is played on an interface designed from the ground up for the iPad, called ioGrid. It allows you to play melodies with your hands while automatically generated backing tracks drone underneath what you are playing. The app has two effects, 20 main instrument voices (plus nine drone voices), and you can record what you play! It's fun, it's cool, and I recommend it.

Acrobots

by Vectorpark, Inc.

99 cents — Hybrid

Come on! Acrobatic robots? What's not to like? I'll tell you; there's nothing not to like about this app, and plenty to just absolutely adore! Acrobots are three-legged things that have suction cups for feet. Those suction cups are attracted to other Acrobots and to the walls, and only momentum and what seems to be a desire to move keep them from huddling in a corner of your iPad's screen in a giant clump. Actually, you tweak their size, gravity, balance, stickiness, speed, and even the amount of air drag they are subjected to, so it's possible to make them clump together. You can tap and drag to toss individuals around your screen, or tilt your iPad to make gravity do your dirty work. But either way, they're just super fun to watch. There's a preset called Spazz that I particularly enjoy because it keeps them moving on their own without any intervention from me. This is a fun, entertaining app, and you should check it out.

IMDb Movies & TV

by IMDb

Free — Hybrid

I use IMDb all the time. The abbreviation stands for Internet Movie Database, but the site includes information about movies and TV shows, and the actors, directors, and even crew who make those shows for us to watch. I watch a lot of TV while I work, which means I watch on my computer. I often see someone and wonder where I saw the actor, or struggle at coming up with the actor's name, and I can look on IMDb to find out. I've also settled any number of bets (or at least debates) with friends and family by looking someone or something up on the service.

With IMDb for Movies & TV on your iPad, you get an enormous amount of data about TV and movies, plus you get what I think is a huge bonus: an interface that's far superior to the service's browser-based home. While the IMDb app will take you to the website if you ask it to, the reality is that it's easier to use the context-oriented menus and buttons on the iPad than it is to click around in a browser on your computer. It's a free hybrid app, too, so you can't really go wrong with it.

Marvel Superheroes

by Deep Powder Software

$1.99 — Hybrid

If you are a big fan of comic books, this app provides you with all the data you could ever want: an alphabetical listing of every Marvel Comics character, equipment, vehicles, and even terms (*zap* and *shazaam!*).

You can learn all about your favorite comic book characters' quirks, from their powers, enemies, and weaknesses, to their weight and hair color. Want to know where Iron Man was born (Long Island)? And though this character weighs in at 225 pounds in street clothes, in armor he tips the scale at 425 pounds.

Okay, so you won't do anything practical, like improve your vocabulary (unless *zap* counts) or get practice playing a musical instrument, but you'll be very popular at those comic book conventions. Finally, if you're a big comics collector, you should know that both Bookman and ComicBookLover are superb ways to enjoy your collection on the iPad.

Gravilux and Uzu

by Scott Snibbe and Jason K. Smith (respectively)

$1.99 each — Hybrid

Gravilux and Uzu are two particle visualizers for the iPad (Gravilux is a hybrid app for iPhone, too), but they both work in different ways, and they're both too cool for words. With Gravilux, you "draw with stars" as your finger becomes the very embodiment of gravity itself. Where you touch your iPad's screen, the stars must react to your immense gravitational pull.

With Uzu, particles career around on your screen, but they obey rules and patterns according to how many fingers are touching it. (There are ten sets of parameters for up to ten fingers, not all of which have to be your own!)

On the other hand, Gravilux has more settings for you to toggle on and off. (Double-tap a corner of your screen to pull up the settings bar.)

Both apps look great on your iPad, and both are frightfully fun. If you download them, just be sure not to forget to feed your pets and/or kids, and you should be fine!

OverDrive Media Console

by OverDrive

Free

 If you are head over heels in love with e-books, you just have to get OverDrive Media Console. This is a very useful app for both researchers and readers of popular fiction alike. OverDrive is a leading publisher of e-content, and this handy app helps you find e-books from retail stores. But the real bonus here is access to libraries — thousands of them.

OverDrive Media Console supports popular e-book, Adobe, and audio book formats. If you're requesting content from a library, you'll need your library card number and PIN, which, of course, may limit your access to remote sources. If you're an international type, you'll be happy to know that the app offers access to libraries in dozens of countries, so if you happen to have a library card in, say Ankara, Turkey, you've got access.

Index

D

F

H

I

Q